Trials of Transition

Trials of Transition

Economic Reform in the Former Communist Bloc

EDITED BY
Michael Keren
and Gur Ofer

Westview Press
BOULDER • SAN FRANCISCO • OXFORD

Published in 1992 in the United States of America by Westview Press, Inc., 5500 Central Avenue, Boulder, Colorado 80301-2877, and in the United Kingdom by Westview Press, 36 Lonsdale Road, Summertown, Oxford OX2 7EW

Library of Congress Cataloging-in-Publication Data
Trials of transition : economic reform in the former Communist bloc /
edited by Michael Keren and Gur Ofer.
p. cm.
Includes bibliographical references and index.
ISBN 0-8133-1564-6. — ISBN 0-8133-1565-4 (pbk.)
1. Europe, Eastern—Economic policy—1989- —Congresses.
2. Former Soviet republics—Economic policy—Congresses. 3. Post-communism—Europe, Eastern—Congresses. 4. Post-communism—Former Soviet republics—Congresses. I. Keren, Michael. II. Ofer, Gur.
HC244.T73 1992
338.947—dc20 92-26065
CIP

Printed in the United States of America

The paper used in this publication meets the requirements of the American National Standard for Permanence of Paper for Printed Library Materials Z39.48-1984.

10 9 8 7 6 5 4 3 2 1

Contents

The editors and all other participants in this project dedicate this volume to

Professor Joseph S. Berliner

on his 70th birthday

Professor Berliner is a founding father of the theory of the firm and of the microeconomics of Soviet socialism. Some of the concepts he coined have influenced the discipline of economics far beyond the confines of comparative economics: the 'ratchet' metaphor, conceived to explain the behavior of planners over time, has been taken over by theoreticians of the dynamics of hierarchies and bureaucracies. His two classical works—*Factory and Manager in the USSR* (1957) and *The Innovation Decision in Soviet Industry* (1976)—and his many articles on this topic have become a fundamental part of our knowledge of the Soviet system. His studies have unlocked the mysteries of the Soviet enterprise and have made the system comprehensible to Western, perhaps also to Eastern, economists. His paper on privatization in this volume is the most recent link in this chain. All these accomplishments, however, describe only a small part of his work on many other aspects of the socialist system.

Joseph Berliner is a teacher and a dear friend. Borrowing from the title of his opening chapter in this book—we are looking forward to benefiting from his scholarship well into the 21st century.

Acknowledgments

This volume grew out of the Carl Melchior conference on "Whither Socialist Society? Economic and Social Transformation in the Soviet Union and Eastern Europe." The conference, held in Jerusalem (April 8–10, 1991), was organized jointly by the Department of Economics and the Marjorie Mayrock Center for Soviet and Eastern European Research at the Hebrew University of Jerusalem. It dealt with the problems of transition from a communist society, often plagued with or threatened by rampant inflation, to a democratic society and a market economy.

The participating scholars—from Eastern Europe, the West and Israel—have followed developments in the region since before the new turn of events and therefore hope that they have a contribution to make to our understanding of the metamorphoses that are taking place. Most of the chapters in this volume are revised versions of conference papers, updated in the beginning of 1992.

We gratefully acknowledge the financial assistance provided by the Research Authority of the Hebrew University; and the Aron and Michael Chilewich Chair of International Trade, the Carl Melchior Chair of International Economics, the Harvey M. and Lyn P. Meyerhoff Chair of Soviet Economics and the Sir Isaac Wolfson Chair of Public Finance, all at the Department of Economics of the Hebrew University of Jerusalem.

We are deeply indebted to all those who contributed to the conference, in particular to Dr. Stephanie Hoffman and Ms. Sharron Elkins of the Mayrock Center. We are also very grateful to Ms. Hyla Berkowitz, who did a great job retyping all the manuscripts, and to Ms. Etka Leibowitz, who prepared the index.

And to Maggie.

Michael Keren
Gur Ofer
Jerusalem

Introduction

Michael Keren and Gur Ofer

Students of the Eastern bloc have long since been aware of the growing economic difficulties encountered by the countries in that area. The weakening economies found it progressively harder to continue to allocate resources for growth and for some improvement in the consumers' lot while at the same time coping with a heavy defense budget. The lure of the West was becoming more threatening and destabilizing as time passed. It was clear that in the long run the bureaucratic communist economic organization could not survive side by side with the successful market economies of the West. Something would have to change.

Change, however, requires political resolve, and the political structure of the Eastern bloc gave every appearance of stability. Observers were too busy with current events to contend with hypothetical problems such as what might happen if communism suddenly were to disappear. When Mikhail Gorbachev rose to power, many expected him to rock the boat, but no one thought that the old *apparatchik* would actually scuttle it. However, soon after coming to power that was exactly what Gorbachev started to do. First he relaxed Moscow's iron grip on the empire and allowed the East Europeans to make their own decisions; he also shook up the political structures while at the same time upsetting the economy's micro- and macroeconomic balance. The result was that the whole seemingly unshakable edifice started to cave in. We social scientists were caught unawares; we had no blueprints for this eventuality, no precedents to follow, no contingency plans. It is with the results of this disintegration that our volume is concerned. Has the break-up of the Soviet bloc expunged socialism from our agenda? Berliner's visionary opening chapter addresses this question, inquiring whether socialism will survive into the 21st century. Berliner believes there will always be a socialist vision of a just and better future, but one that will differ from the vision of socialism we have known in the past, because it will have learned the lessons of the socialist experiments of the 20th century. His vision of future socialism peels away most of the term's fundamental Soviet characteristics.

The remaining sixteen chapters deal with four main topics: political transformation, stabilization, privatization and foreign economic relations. As we view the East European scene some seven years after the early tremors that ultimately shattered the old order, we observe that events have proceeded at a different pace in its various countries: political change preceded social change and the old economic order was the last to give way. Clearly, the economic events are so closely intertwined with social and political factors that a socio-political foundation for this volume was indispensable. We therefore open with a political *mise en scène* to explain the more economically oriented chapters.

Chapters 2, 3 and 5 describe the political foundations of the economic transition. Avineri (Chapter 2) places the events in Eastern Europe in a broader historical perspective. The collapse of communism and the disintegration of the Soviet Union and its empire, while putting an end to the major global ideological conflict of the 20th century, do not signal the 'end of history', as claimed by Francis Fukuyama (though in a different sense) but rather a return to history. The demise of communism rekindled ethnic, national, cultural and religious frictions that had been the bane of the region before the communist takeover. These tensions had been largely repressed in the past 45–75 years, but they always lurked in the background as an inseparable part of the protagonists' human consciousness. It is this human consciousness that shapes the agenda for the future, and the past cannot be erased from it. Most of the countries involved inherited a very meager pre-communist legacy of and experience in democracy (the only real exception is Czechoslovakia) and are only marginally more experienced in the operation of a modern market economy. The juxtaposition of the plethora of ethnic conflicts and the difficulties of the political and economic transition makes for a rocky passage to liberal democracy and a market economy. We are all painfully aware of these difficulties at the present juncture, as spectres of the past hover over the menace of political disintegration and civil war in many parts of the region. The ethnic make-up of the region dictates a political solution to the dual problem of multi-ethnic states and the existence of large national minorities. All this, while the developed world is moving toward unprecedented economic and political transnational integration. The challenge of Eastern Europe may be in developing new ways of fulfilling these diverse national aspirations.

Is there a preferred sequencing of the political and economic changes, one that can make the transition more feasible? This is the subject Brucan addresses in Chapter 3. Brucan draws a very strong conclusion: *Perestroika*, implemented by a strong government, must precede *glasnost* and democracy. His study criticizes the "prevailing assumption that transition to democracy . . . would go hand in hand with the establishment of a market economy. . . [The] initiation of a market economy is an extremely painful social process," and is therefore also politically dangerous. The transition process has turned out to be far costlier than anticipated and has been accompanied by extremely high rates of unemployment and a collapse of the social-insurance safety net. Persons who were hardest hit by the transition process were reluctant to accept the adversity it entailed; the responsibilities and limitations of democracy were usually not adequately understood, which often led to populist demands. This is why, in both the West and the Far East, capitalism and its institutions were established under authoritarian regimes. Even the possibility of establishing a strong (but democratic) government, as proposed by Kornai, is rejected by Brucan as unrealistic. Different views on this theme are found in other chapters.

The next four chapters focus on the ex–Soviet Union. The Soviet Union, cradle of the socialist economic and political system and the imperial power that imposed this system on what was once the Soviet bloc, underwent radical political changes during the *perestroika* period, but was a latecomer to economic change. In addition to the disintegration of the external empire, by the end of 1991 the Soviet Union itself was disbanded and transformed into the Commonwealth of Independent States (CIS), a loose union that is still in its formative stage and whose final shape remains unknown. On the economic front, a series of unsuccessful partial changes helped topple the old system without a proper substitute being available, destabilized the macroeconomic balance, sent production plummeting, and provoked a severe economic crisis. At one and the same time the ongoing political struggle was fanned by the economic crisis and contributed to it.

The new government of the Russian Federation, headed by Boris Yeltsin and Yegor Gaidar, embarked on a radical program of economic reform early in 1992. This was a 'big bang' that included the wholesale liberalization of most prices (including that of foreign exchange) and partial current-account convertibility; a rigorous macroeconomic stabilization effort; freeing internal markets; and promoting rapid privatization in services, industry and even agriculture. At the time of writing the program is still in its infancy, and the results so far have been mixed. On the one hand, open inflation has virtually eliminated the monetary overhang, the operation of markets and the supply situation has improved somewhat, and the fiscal and monetary efforts of the government have been quite successful. On the other hand, a high-inflation spiral seems to be developing, fueled by cost-push factors, by the monopolistic structure of production and markets, by the development of inflationary expectations and by the rapid expansion of unofficial, inter-enterprise credits. The higher-than-expected initial price shock and the inflationary spiral have resulted in a continuing decline in production and in the build-up of inventories.

Perhaps in no other country examined in this volume is the mutual dependency between political and economic developments as strong as in the former Soviet Union. And nowhere else is the problem of the appropriate coordination and sequencing of the major elements of economic change so complex. The four chapters on the former Soviet Union in this volume represent these levels of interaction and complexity.

Bogomolov's contribution (Chapter 4) covers a wide vista, ranging from the political background, through details of economic transition, to some of their international consequences. The political disintegration of the former Soviet Union, a process which is in no way complete at the time of writing, underlies this chapter. Bogomolov lays much of the blame for the economic collapse on Gorbachev's unquestioning faith in the viability of the old, strictly socialist system, his innate conservatism and his attempt to maintain a rigorously centralized Soviet Union. Gorbachev's basic beliefs are to blame, says Bogomolov, not the grave technical error of failing to maintain a macroeconomic balance. With regard to the future, Bogomolov stresses the importance of reintegrating a more closely knit CIS in the world economy, particularly in Europe. In many ways this chapter can be seen as a counterpoint to the view represented by Brucan.

Chapter 5, by Friedgut, also ties in with Brucan, but advances the obverse view: *perestroika* must be built up from below by reconstructing a civil society in place of the one destroyed by the prolonged power monopoly of the communist party and the totalitarian regime. While changes from above are necessary, they cannot take hold without the development of social organizations at the grass-roots level. The chapter describes the early stages of development of just such a civil society in the Ukrainian town of Donetsk in the Donbass coal-mining region, where a series of strikes erupted in the summer of 1990. Two simultaneous processes are taking place here: first, a takeover and radical transformation of existing institutions (trade unions, local communist party newspapers, the city government) and second, the creation of a variety of new social organizations and economic enterprises that improve the population's quality of life, materially, politically and socially, and with little expenditure of additional resources. Viewed from a purely macroeconomic angle, many of these local initiatives and forms of organization may be thought of as exemplifying 'populist', profligate or 'spontaneous' privatization, all of which disrupt the orderly process of stabilization. The new unions described by Friedgut may well be of this ilk, but the chapter underlines the other side of the coin: The new order urgently needs new, smoothly functioning institutions, and when these appear, they may improve the well-being of society much earlier than manna dispensed from the center.

Chapter 6, by Cottarelli and Blejer, is a thorough attempt to estimate the notorious 'monetary overhang', one of the greatest culprits responsible for macroeconomic instability in the former Soviet Union. The main building block of the model is a savings function adapted to conditions of a 'shortage economy' by introducing constraints on consumption. Using an ordinary savings function to estimate the monetary overhang is justified on the grounds that, under the old system, monetary assets were virtually the only form of capital (other than human capital) that people could accumulate. The most interesting finding is that the main part of the overhang came into being *after* 1985 and therefore could not have been the cumulative outcome of decades of 'shortage economy' as is so often claimed. Rather, it is the combined result of an expansion of the budgetary deficit, the relaxation of controls over the expansion of credit and the 'monetization' of the production sector's 'non-money' balances that fueled (repressed) inflationary pressures in the Gorbachev era. By the end of 1990 undesired asset holdings (forced savings) are estimated at about one-third of all financial holdings. Of these, only one-third was inherited from the old (pre-1985) regime.

In the last chapter in this group, Chapter 7, Ofer discusses the problems of sequencing the major economic reforms, especially in relation to the choice between a 'big-bang' and a more gradual approach, both under the last Soviet government and under the first Russian regime. The first part of the chapter discusses alternative modes and sequences of price reform that could not only achieve the major goal of creating competitive markets, but would also stabilize the economy, foster the secure and calm environment needed for privatization and further structural change, and prevent the development of a cost-push inflationary spiral. Ofer proposes a sequence that starts with an administrative price revision followed by a temporary price freeze, after which the time is ripe for price liberalization. The stabilization program implemented by the government in 1991 proceeded along these lines but failed, mostly owing to the political struggle that took place at the time. The present inflationary spiral and continuing decline in production may be the result of the abrupt price liberalization by the first Russian government.

The second part of this chapter discusses policy choices regarding privatization. The major issue is what should be done with large government enterprises. Here, too, Ofer favors a gradual approach. In the first stage, infrastructure for large-scale privatization should be prepared by small-scale privatization and the expansion of a private service sector. At the same time a major management reform should be undertaken to transform the state sector into something more compatible with a market economy. As is evident from other chapters on privatization in this volume, the issue is far from settled.

Finally, Ofer's contribution considers the topic raised by Brucan and suggests that a conservative government may not have enough political power, public trust and credibility to implement a gradual reform. A strong government, with a clear radical stance on reform, would have such power and thus could and should use it to move ahead more gradually if this is warranted by economic considerations. At least in the present case, the stronger of the two governments turned out to be the one that was more democratically elected.

The East European countries represented in our volume—Poland,

Czechoslovakia, the ex-GDR, and Hungary—are those that have traveled farthest down the road of transition. The questions that appear on their agenda are therefore of a more 'advanced' type. The remaining chapters therefore deal less with the 'whys' of the present situation or with the general direction of movement than with various 'hows'. Two subjects take pride of place: the first is the problem of parallel versus serial advance toward the new system; the second is one of the nuts and bolts of forming a private business sector. Although none of the chapters in this volume proposes a clear sequence of steps of transition (cf. Nuti, 1991)—a 'turnpike', so to say—such a sequence does lie in the background of several contributions that criticize the policy followed in some of these countries (Kolodko and Hrnčíř, in Chapters 9 and 10, respectively). This view is opposed by others, who recommend the 'big-bang' (or 'cold-turkey') treatment approach to transition (Gomulka, Chapter 8). Privatization is another topic addressed in several chapters; some deal with single countries (Hungary—Chapters 12 and 13), and the second chapter by Berliner (Chapter 14) takes a broader view of the subject. Keren's Chapter 15 is also germane to this topic.

Poland was the trailblazer in economic policy: It was the first to introduce a harsh anti-inflationary policy and the first to effect a big-bang transition to capitalism. The two chapters on Poland (Gomulka and Kolodko) provide alternative perspectives on these twin policy lines. They are significant in that the two authors represent polar positions in the gamut of Polish economic opinion (though one of the authors does not, at present, reside in Poland), and in a way one can gauge the size of the divide by the distance between their views.

As one of the team of reformers, Gomulka indicates the choices available to the policy makers in the first stages of the post-communist rule in Poland. The challenge facing the new government was to change the economic system and create, before the next millennium, "a full-fledged market economy of the Western type" while simultaneously having to cope with accelerating inflation. The twin tasks were inseparable: stabilization and the introduction of the new system had to go hand in hand. Even though the new economic system was to be introduced in a single 'big bang', the combined goals imposed a certain sequence of policies, which involved freeing prices, a strict incomes policy, and structural reform. Inflation itself eroded the monetary overhang; real wages fell, and the slashing of subsidies and income policy also helped shrink the budget deficit. During the period of exchange-rate stability the fight against inflation received first priority, while the under-valued zloty helped maintain the balance on foreign payments. Gomulka's paper includes an important section on the economic ideas underlying the policy arguments of the Polish reformers.

Gomulka goes on to describe the unpleasant surprises encountered by the Polish reformers in the execution of the reform program. Although they were aware of the time it would take to effect structural changes, they were not prepared for the steep dip in GDP, the depth of unemployment, and the long time it is still taking to make any progress in privatization. This is a topic that many of our contributions take up.

The opposition's view on Poland appears in Kolodko's chapter, built largely on a model developed by the author and Walter McMahon. Parallel to the Phillips curve, which displays the rate of price rise associated with any level of unemployment in a market economy, Kolodko and McMahon posit a 'shortageflation' function—a relation between shortage and inflation in centrally planned economies (CPEs). Like the Phillips curve, which shifts over time in response to past levels of inflation, the shortageflation function grows steeper as time lengthens under a shortage regime. The problem of transition is to get from one phase (shortageflation) to the next (the Phillips—or stagflation—phase) in the cheapest way possible. Kolodko judges the success or failure of the transition policy by this criterion, i.e., according to the degree of minimization of both inflation and unemployment on the path from a Soviet-type economy to a market economy. It is this change of phase that introduces a difference in kind between stabilization programs in East and West.

The aim of stabilization policy is to achieve a low rate of inflation, a moderate decline in GDP, low unemployment, and (roughly) balanced trade. It is against these aims that Kolodko judges the success of the stabilization program. In all these respects, the Polish program misfired: the inflation rate, the decline in GNP and industrial output, and unemployment increased much more than had been anticipated, and the costs of stabilization were much higher than planned. The trade balance also improved more than was planned. The error of the policy makers, says Kolodko, was in failing to realize that the supply response of the state sector was so weak in comparison to that of a market sector. This led to strong asymmetries in behavior—to a reduction in output (but not in employment) rather than in prices when demand fell, and in prices rather than in production when demand increased.

Kolodko does not claim that the transition from severe shortageflation to stagflation was avoidable, or that there was an alternative to the 'cold-turkey' stabilization policy. He does maintain, however, that the costs of transition could have been reduced if the sequencing had been smoother.

Our Czechoslovak contribution (Hrnčíř, Chapter 10) is also concerned with the problem of gradualism versus a 'big bang': could there not have been a smoother and less costly path from the centralized economy to the market? Unlike Poland and Hungary, Czechoslovakia pursued a fairly stable and conservative macroeconomic policy and had barely any monetary overhang. It also had no experience with decentralization after the unhappy events of 1968. Should the confluence of these two factors have led to a faster or slower Czechoslovak passage to the market? Hrnčíř shows that in many respects the path of Czechoslovakia was uncomfortably similar to that of Poland, with output declining much more than expected and employment declining less than output. Even sharp price changes and the consequent reduction in real income were not avoided, in spite of the absence of serious macroeconomic imbalances, suggesting that macroeconomic policy in Czechoslovakia might have been too restrictive.

The chapter on the demise of the GDR and its incorporation into the Federal Republic (Chapter 11) is a joint venture by two Germans (Haendcke-Hoppe-Arndt of West Berlin and Nötzold of the former GDR) and one Israeli (Keren). The East German case is of interest in spite of its being *sui generis*—the only case of a country that has ceased to exist, and the only case of an economy that was integrated into the European Common Market. What can be learned from this case is that money—nearly limitless infusions of hard DM—cannot overcome the difficulties of transition capitalism. It can, perhaps, cushion some of the blows, but it cannot eliminate them. Furthermore, money is no substitute for proper policies.

The chapter opens with an historical background that identifies the economic roots of the collapse of the Berlin Wall in the policy errors of the 1970s. These errors led to a drain of resources that forced drastic cuts in investment and stagnating consumption in the 1980s. It is against this backdrop that the Wall collapsed in November 1989, an event that sparked a chain reaction in all countries of the region. The first attempts at reform à la the 1960s were made under the last SED government, which also set up the *Treuhandanstalt*, the organization which was later to be entrusted with the privatization of the state sector. But that came too late; the elections held in spring 1990 led to the currency union of July and to the political reunion of October 1990. The currency union fused the two countries, but it failed to fulfill the hopes pinned on it by both Easterners and Westerners. The reasons for this failure are discussed in the middle part of the chapter.

The criticism of the currency union arrangements proceeds along two lines: macroeconomic and microeconomic. The former is the choice of the conversion rate, a strategic element of the currency union criticized by many observers outside Germany. On the microeconomic level, the *Treuhand* is criticized for not giving higher priority to the establishment of a new private sector and to the avoidance of new monopolistic structures in the ex-GDR. The final section describes the results of these policy errors and finds their cause in the deep ignorance of Eastern and Western architects of unity regarding the economic problems of what used to be the GDR.

Problems of privatization are naturally high on the agenda of those at the helm of the transformation process in Eastern Europe. Our two Hungarian contributions deal with privatization in a country that has the longest history of economic decentralization in the former Soviet bloc. The chapters by Nuti (12) and Tardos (13) are in many ways complementary. Nuti deals mainly with the history of the privatization process, while Tardos is more programmatic. Has the passage of over 20 years since the New Economic Mechanism (NEM) was launched in 1968 made the transition to a private market economy easier? It is with this question in mind that Nuti's contribution should be read. The initial—perhaps unavoidable—spate of 'spontaneous' privatization in Hungary was nipped in the bud, and a more orderly process is now underway. The foundations of a legal system and the financial institutions were laid under the NEM, and some budding entrepreneurs may have learned their craft under the more liberal economic regime. The authorities felt it was possible to institute a privatization agency akin to the German *Treuhandanstalt*. They felt they could forge ahead with sales of the former state sector. And, unlike the Polish and Czechoslovak leadership, they did not try any giveaway method of issuing shares or vouchers to the public. The process is described by Nuti, and today, early in 1992, we can only ask whether it will really be successful.

In view of the failure of communism to achieve its announced aim, ". . . the complete and planned satisfaction of people's needs," there is no alternative but to return to ". . . a system of production resting on the institutions of private property, which were almost completely eliminated. . . ." It is this opening passage by Tardos that provides the setting for his chapter. Privatization is a necessary means to achieving given ends, and it is in this context that it has to be organized. The aims are to provide for the reconstruction of the economy: raising efficiency, investing so as to increase GNP, reducing state indebtedness and competing in the world market. All these aims could not be achieved under communist rule, as evidenced by the various attempts at reform (and here we once again join the argument on the theme raised by Brucan in Chapter 3). The practical problems of privatization are many, and maintaining public support is not the least of them. This imposes the need for overt social justice, i.e., a process that will ensure that property is sold for a fair price with as little corruption as possible. Tardos examines two widely proposed methods of privatization (and Berliner takes up this topic in the following chapter): a voucher plan that privatizes all state enterprises in a single sweep, and a more cautious approach, recommended by Kornai, that would limit sales to the stock of local savings and refrain from selling enterprises to foreign investors until they are first put on a profitable basis. The former approach would enrich some and impoverish others; the latter would take too long. Tardos favors an eclectic process, combining outright sales with some share sales to workers on favorable terms, restitution of nationalized property, and transfers to various holding companies. He also criticizes the reliance on a single privatizing agency, *Treuhand*-style, and suggests that the privatization task itself should be competitively privatized.

Berliner's second contribution in this volume (Chapter 14) juxtaposes two privatization plans: the incorporation strategy, i.e., the plan to transform all state enterprises into joint stock companies run by holding companies until they are sold to the public, versus the so-called 'evolutionary' strategy of keeping the state sector under tight central control, gradually selling off as many enterprises as possible, both at home and abroad. Berliner proposes five criteria by which to compare the two alternatives: equity, efficiency, technical and institutional feasibility ('macro-privatization'), valuation, and the ability to cope with unemployment. The evolutionists' prescription comes out on top on four points: it promises to be more efficient and feasible, it permits safer evaluation (hence a fairer and less risky path of sales) and it allows for the unavoidable subsidization of enterprises to avoid unemployment without at the same time destroying the fledgling private economy. It is also no less equitable than the other plan. To assuage popular prejudices against a give-away of the people's property, Berliner suggests the establishment of a National Property Bank, which would be the conduit through which all current income from state property, as well as the proceeds from their sale, are transferred to the population at large. This would also make it possible to distinguish between popular ownership and popular control.

Chapter 15 (Keren) is the most pessimistic of those that deal with privatization. It takes the evolutionist argument to its logical conclusion and maintains that most enterprises in Eastern Europe cannot be run profitably because they were never designed to do so. Their transformation into efficient and profitable enterprises is impossible as long as they are in the hands of the state. Privatization is a prolonged process, which raises two dangers: that the building of a new private sector will be held up, and that the unhealthy state sector will continue to bleed the resources of the state by continuing to waste them on useless new projects. In other words, Keren believes that one of the main problems facing the economic leaders will be how to pry from existing enterprises those assets needed by the new private sector and how to starve the hungry, as yet-unprivatized, state enterprises of new resources.

The last two chapters deal with the legacy of the now defunct COMECON. Richter (Chapter 16) is concerned with the collapse of trade among the former member countries of that organization and examines institutional arrangements for its resuscitation. Although this trade was in the past one of the fetters that hindered innovation and that helped perpetuate technological backwardness, high costs and poor quality in Eastern Europe, its collapse as a result of the switch to trade in hard currency led to severe unemployment in the reforming countries of the East. Before any new arrangements can be established, the institutional 'leftovers' from COMECON days have to be swept away: the former regime has left behind a tangle of outstanding obligations—TR debts, accumulated surpluses and even payments to Soviet military installations—all of which have yet to be unraveled. Richter outlines several institutional alternatives to revive trade among the reforming countries, among them an East European Free Trade Area and a Central European Payments Union, but is not too sanguine about their prospects. Enthusiasm for these arrangements in the affected countries seems quite limited; their priority seems to be trade with the West. The route to trade among the countries of Eastern Europe may eventually pass through Western Europe, i.e., Eastern goods can establish markets for themselves in the region once they have proven their quality through success in the West.

Hillman, in the final chapter, uses the tools of the new political economy to analyze the transition policies pursued in the post-CMEA (or COMECON) era. The new political economy rejects the old view of the government as a benevolent exogenous arbitrator; rather, government agencies are seen as political actors, with interests of their own and subject to the pressures of other actors, e.g., the economic units. As such, they are committed (in the present context) to maintain full employment or to an extreme aversion to unemployment. It is this that has led to absolute protection under the CMEA regime, protection that assured the continued survival of any enterprise, regardless of its economic contribution. Such protection is a hindrance to structural adjustment. The failure of Edward Gierek's investment policies in the 1970s is a case in point: the borrowing spree that financed them was to be repaid by exports to the West by the new facilities. But the enterprises were protected by CMEA institutions and their exports were directed to the East. The necessary structural adjustments cannot be undertaken without privatization. But while privatization may be necessary, it is not sufficient: the 'big bang' did not make enterprises adjust either, and private firms are just as likely to press for protection as are publicly owned ones. Hillman also asks whether protection should be swept away instantly or whether there was a case for a transitional period of protection. But can any government credibly commit itself to ending protection at some preannounced future date?

The dilemma between an abrupt shift to a new order versus a more gradual approach exists in the sphere of foreign economic relations as well. Should the old COMECON style of trade (and, for that matter, the mode of trade among the former Soviet republics) be discarded before a viable alternative is created? Should protection be cut off in one stroke or be lifted gradually? Here, too, the 'big bang' approach may guarantee that the change takes place, but not without exacting a toll in terms of trade disruption, declining production and higher unemployment.

We are now in the midst of a process that will last well into the third millennium. When this process got underway, seven years ago, it raised hopes for a better world, a peaceful and harmonious new order. Today, two years or so after the final collapse of the social order that no one believed would ever change, the region is in alarming disarray. Breaking down old regimes, national units, social institutions and centralized control proved far easier than building a new regional and national social, political and economic order. The city of Sarajevo, where a fateful shot was fired in 1914, is once again the center of a new conflagration. This time, however, there seems to be no immediate threat to world peace. For all the anguish suffered by the people involved, this could be a sign that the world has entered a saner era.

*

The seventeen chapters in this volume attempt to shed light on some of the problems encountered and to spell out some of the riddles that will remain with us for years to come.

1

Socialism in the Twenty-First Century

Joseph S. Berliner

The idea of socialism is as old as the philosopher's quest for the good society. Whether one dates its origins in antiquity or in the mere two centuries since the Industrial Revolution, the idea has been with us for a long time. The 19th century gave the movement its name and laid the groundwork of modern socialist thought and of revolutionary organization. But throughout that long history socialism remained only an idea; a dream for some, a nightmare for others. It remained for our century to convert the idea to a reality by bringing into being the first group of societies dedicated to the implementation of the socialist idea.

Now, as the century draws to a close, the world watches in unbelieving fascination as country after country abandons its tryst with socialism. Rarely do historical experiments end with such decisive results. The populations that have lived under socialism have overwhelmingly rejected it and are now embarked on the transition to a new form of economic society. While there is no agreement on the form that the new society should take, the mass of opinion is that it should decidedly not be based on the same institutions that formed the socialist societies of the past.

This century has laid up a store of treasures of historical experience for the instruction of future centuries. We have much to teach them, but it would be naive to think that they will learn what we seek to teach. And it is only right that this should be so. For one thing, we are so close to the events that the passions and commitments of our time must inevitably give a certain cast to our assessments. As the present recedes into the past, our passions will appear archaic to the historians who follow us, and their assessment of our times will differ from ours. Moreover, we have witnessed only the first chapter of mass defection from socialism, while they will have the advantage of the later chapters.

It therefore behooves us to be modest about what we think we have to teach the 21st century. But while modesty has its place in personal affairs, it can make for a very dull opening of a book such as this. I shall therefore throw caution to the winds and try to see the past and present with the eyes of the future. My question is, what will the 21st century learn from the 20th century's experience with socialism?

Transfixed as we are by the events of the past few years, it may appear to us now that the only lesson to be learned is that socialism failed. The passage of time, however, will telescope the whole socialist experience of our century into an historical episode. In the longer time perspective, the assessment of 20th century socialism will take account of the world out of which it emerged, predating the Russian Revolution.

Looking back to the 19th century's concerns, socialists confronted an extensive array of political, economic and moral arguments against their programs. Among the major challenges was the widespread conviction that an economy without private property and without the capitalist profit motive was contrary to human nature and simply could not work. The critics foresaw an economy in which people would lose all motivation to work, to save or to improve their lot. Production and employment would therefore simply collapse and the population would become destitute. H. G. Wells expressed the frustration of socialists having to confront that viewpoint when he wrote, "I will confess I find it hard to write with any patience and civility over this argument that humanity will not work except for greed or need of money and only in proportion to the getting."[1] Only in that context can one appreciate the sense of triumph embodied in Lincoln Steffens' celebrated phrase, "I have seen the future, and it works."[2]

From that long historical perspective, when the dust has settled and the next century looks back at ours, the first lesson they will learn is that in the 20th century a socialist economy was finally tried, and it worked. This will sound perverse to us who are living in the midst of a wholesale rejection of socialism. But the reason for the rejection, as I shall argue shortly, is that it did not work very well, a proposition that is not at all inconsistent with the assertion that it did work.

Now there are contexts in which there is little merit in merely having worked, but there are others in which the fact of having worked at all is of crucial importance. I have in mind not simply the parable of the Talking Horse—the fact that it talked at all was indeed remarkable, even if one could not understand what it had to say. More generally, in the history of innovation, whether it be James Watt's first steam engine or the first human organ transplant, the proof that something worked is far more significant than the fact that it did not work very well. The demonstration that something has worked is the crucial step; it silences the nay-sayers and launches the continuous effort thereafter to make it work better.

So well did the Soviet experience defeat the nonviability argument that in the course of time the very question simply vanished from the agenda of discourse. By the middle of our century, indeed, the focus of serious debate was whether the Soviet economy would actually overtake the capitalist economies, and how long it might be before that would occur. It has been downhill ever since, but no one seriously questions any longer whether socialism can work at all. Our century has simply ceased to ask the question that most concerned the last century. The next century will not ask whether socialism can work at all, but whether it could have worked better than it did. The proof that it can work is the gift of the 20th century to 21st century socialism.

To be sure, the current economic situation in the CIS does raise the possibility of nonviability, but the cause in this case is to be found in the political and economic complexities of the transition. The patient may have been ill, but what he is now suffering from is not the illness but the cure. It is also true that at various times other socialist countries skidded very close to collapse, but that was usually the consequence of inept government policy. No economy—socialist, capitalist or hermaphrodite—can survive all the ineptitudes of which governments are capable.

It is certainly arguable that by 1985 the system was working so badly that it was bound to collapse, which is the very reason that the leadership turned to *perestroika*. I do not believe that to be the case, and I cannot explore the matter here, but I propose that we can test the proposition by imagining that there were no capitalist countries in the world in 1985. There would then have been no external standard of comparison for judging the performance of their socialist economy. I would guess that the economy would have continued functioning indefinitely. There might have been a sense of malaise, but not of impending disaster, and there would therefore have been no Gorbachev, no *perestroika*, and no books exploring its demise. The system was rejected not because of the imminence of economic collapse but because of its unsatisfactory performance relative to Western Europe, the United States and Japan—which introduces my second lesson.

Twentieth-century socialism failed to deliver on one of its major promises—to surpass the productivity of capitalism. I will not dwell on the evidence, for anyone could write his or her version of that lecture. Suffice it to say that none of the socialist economies has come near to matching the economic performance of the best of the non-socialist economies.[3]

That lesson will no doubt have a sobering effect on future socialists, but it is unlikely to deter them from new efforts to build a socialist society, nor perhaps should it; at least not for the reason that has so mesmerized our generation—the relatively poor economic performance of our century's particular forms of socialism. The experience of our century is unlikely to put an end to a dream that has survived so long.

There will always be a small reserve army of believers for whom socialism is a creed that no conceivable empirical evidence could shake. Like true Christianity, it will never have been really tried. There will be a larger class of socialists, however, who will acknowledge that the Soviet system, although a member of the socialist family, was a rather disreputable distant cousin who gave the family a bad name; and for that view of the matter there is something to be said. Twentieth-century socialism followed only one of the many paths that might have been selected at various branchings of the tree of history. It followed the Marxian branch, instead of the many non-Marxist and anti-Marxist socialisms of the 19th century. It followed the Leninist branch of Marxism instead of the many non-Russian and non-Bolshevik varieties of Marxism. And it followed the Stalinist version of Leninism instead of that of other old Bolsheviks who perished in the prisons of the secret police. Almost all the socialisms that followed the Second World War were tainted by the poison, either having been forcefully imposed by Stalin or imitative of Stalinism, as in Asia.[4]

The next century need not, therefore, conclude that the comparatively poor performance of this century's socialism portends an equally poor performance next time around. For many, the lesson will be that future socialisms must learn from the mistakes of the 20th century if they are not to perform as badly again in the future.

The major mistake made is the subject of the third lesson. No socialism of the future is likely ever again to organize its economy on the basis of central economic planning.[5] One can understand why the early Soviet leadership opted for central planning. To Marxists like Lenin, the great advantage of socialism was that the society would be spared the fluctuations, depressions and inefficiencies of capitalist markets, and the natural alternative to markets was central planning. Even non-Marxists like Enrico Barone, who wrote the pioneering paper on socialist economics in 1908, took it for granted that socialism meant central planning.[6] It was not until 1936 that Oskar Lange published his famous essay demonstrating for the first time that socialist economies did not have to use central planning but could use markets instead. Moreover, he argued, a market-based socialism would be more efficient than both capitalism and centrally planned socialism.[7]

It is tempting to speculate that had the Russian Revolution been postponed, from 1917 to, say, 1937, 20th century socialism might have been based on markets rather than on planning. But the first socialism did occur in 1917, and it did occur in a country with a long history of centralized government, which conspired to hitch socialism inevitably and unfortunately to the cart of central planning.

Much emotional energy has been expended in our century wrestling with the question of whether planning is the only ideologically acceptable economic mechanism for a socialist society and whether the acceptance of markets means the end of socialism. The next century, I believe, will have no doubts on that score. They will accept the viewpoint of Deng Xiao-ping that, on an issue of this sort, "it doesn't matter whether the cat is red or white as long as it catches mice." Nor will there be any doubt that markets catch more mice than planning. Twenty-first century socialism, if any exists, will be based on markets rather than on the old-fashioned mechanism of central planning, and therefore, in my view, it will surpass the economic performance of our century's Soviet-type socialism.

How it will perform relative to the capitalism of the next century we cannot know. It is easy to see some clouds on the capitalist horizon, and socialism may find the competition in the next century not quite as overpowering as it has been in this one. The economic environment of the next century is likely to be so different from ours, however, that neither the socialism nor the capitalism of the future may bear a close resemblance to their 20th-century forbears.

The fourth lesson is that the next century's socialism will accept the personal autonomy of citizens as inviolable. Socialists decisively rejected the Hobbesian view that man was like one's Uncle Willie: he's no good, he never was any good, and he never will be any good. They appealed to the workers in more benign Rousseauian-Marxian terms that said, in effect: It is true that you are no good and you never were any good, but it's not your fault; you are the product of a class society. With the abolition of property-based classes, however, the egocentric citizen bred by capitalist society would be transformed into the good, socially motivated New Socialist Man.

The lesson of this century's socialism, in this respect, is that socialism did not succeed in transforming its workers and managers into essentially different beings from those who live under capitalism. Take the case of economic managers, for example. In the analysis of capitalist corporations, Western economics has focused on the problem generated by the fact that owners (stockholders) have to hire professional managers to run the company for them; the managers, however, tend to pursue their own personal interests rather than those of the owners. The owners therefore confront the so-called 'principal-agent problem'; that is, to design an incentive scheme so that managerial agents will not find it in their interest to feather their own nests at the expense of the owner-principals.

Now, it happens that this principal-agent theory, invented for the purpose of explaining managerial behavior under capitalism, has proven to be an exceedingly fruitful approach to the explanation of managerial behavior under socialism as well. That is to say, if you want to understand how socialist managers run the enterprises entrusted to them, you would do best to assume that will take care of their own interests first, in the same way as managers of capitalist enterprises. The same may be said about workers deciding what job to accept and how much effort to put into their jobs, and about consumers deciding how much meat to buy if the price of meat goes up or down.

Twentieth-century socialism was the battlefield on which this issue was fought out. The Soviet leadership started off determined that the motivation for labor should be not 'greed or need of money', but rather dedication to the building of socialism. Equality of pay was the expression of that determination and moral incentives replaced the material incentives of capitalism.

Stalin first breached that orthodoxy with his biting attack on 'equality-mongering', followed by the introduction of differentiated wage and salary scales, over the intense opposition of many trade-union and Party members. That reversal of policy was the socialist society's first concession to the autonomy of the individual. Instead of designing social policy to transform the people, social policy accommodated to people as they are. The leadership continued to strive to mold the character of the people in proper socialist ways, but the effort atrophied in the course of time.

Mao Zedong and Che Guevara later mounted a massive challenge to Soviet-type socialism on the same issue. They shared the primeval conviction that an appeal to self-interest, in the form of a few extra rubles, could never arouse the energies of the masses as powerfully as the call to the building of socialism. In the end, however, their revolutionary challenge also failed, and their socialist societies returned to a policy of paying the workers in money instead of in dreams.

A quiet challenge was also issued in Israel, in the socialist kibbutz. As I read that history, the lesson is that, under certain conditions, people will subordinate their self-interest out of a concern for the group interest, and that a successful socialist society can be built on that basis. The kibbutz is perhaps the only significant example of that possibility that the 20th century has to offer, and is therefore an important part of our century's legacy to the next. But the conditions of its success are so specific that few societies will be able to duplicate them. Among other things, the kibbutz reflects the potential of small-community social organization, not that of a full society; and even on that limited scale, its promise is not as bright as its past.

Twenty-first-century socialism will therefore fully accept the self-interest of its people without the embarrassment that many of our century's socialists felt about it. They will regard their task as one of designing socialist institutions that will harness self-interest in the service of the public good, rather than hoping that self-interest will one day go away. They will seek to redesign institutions to fit the people, rather than redesign people to fit the institutions. They will not *celebrate* self-interest in the manner of laissez-faire neo-liberals, but neither will they apologize for recognizing it as a fact of socialist life.

The fifth lesson is that a socialism that accepts the legitimacy of markets and the inevitability of self-interest will most certainly permit a certain extent of private enterprise. The activities in which private enterprise could make the largest contribution are services and farming. The 21st century will look back upon the nationalization of all small-scale private enterprise and on the forced collectivization of all agriculture in the Soviet Union not as imperatives of socialism, but as the products of the special politics and dogma of the first socialist society. The consuming public fared far better in those socialist countries that maintained small private shops and restaurants as in Hungary, and small family farms as in post-Mao China.

The extent of private enterprise will no doubt differ from country to country, depending on its historical traditions. The major source of difference, however, will be the policy regarding the ownership of the large state-owned enterprises that so dominated the economic life of 20th-century socialism.

The question of ownership should be the subject of the last lesson. Unfortunately we do not yet have enough experience to warrant a guess about what the lesson will be. None of the socialist countries has yet concluded the process of transition to the new society, and until they do, we cannot say which form of ownership of the former state enterprises will have the greatest appeal to the next century.

A broad spectrum of proposals is presently under consideration. At one extreme, the enterprises would continue to be owned by the government, but they would be given a wide range of autonomy so that they could operate in a market environment. At the other extreme, the enterprises would all be sold off to strictly private owners, so that in the end the society would be virtually undistinguishable from capitalism. In the middle is the form of a public corporation whose shares would be owned by various public and quasi-public organizations, and perhaps also by workers, managers and other private persons.

The decision regarding ownership will determine whether the 21st-century socialism I have sketched out could rightly be called socialism at all. If the state enterprises continue to be state owned, or if they are transformed into public corporations, the economy could still lay claim to the name of socialism, for it would still be characterized by 'public ownership of the means of production'. That those enterprises conduct their business in markets, pay the market wage for workers and managers, and operate side-by-side with private enterprises, ought not disqualify them from membership in the socialist family, except for those to whom the very expression 'market socialism' is a contradiction in terms. Future socialists will have little sentimental attachment to those institutions of 20th century socialism like central planning that contributed to its poor economic performance relative to the capitalist world of the time.

They may decide, however, that public ownership also contributed to the poor economic performance, which also happens to be my own view of the matter. Central planning, in my opinion, explains the greater part of the lag in socialist economic performance behind that of the capitalist world, but part of the lag is due to the non-private ownership of the capital stock. The reason, in a nutshell, is that private ownership produces a more powerful drive for technological innovation than that which a public-ownership economy can offer to its entrepreneurs.

What will count, however, is what future socialists believe in this matter. They may reject my opinion and choose public ownership; or they may share my opinion but nevertheless opt for public ownership, fully prepared to accept the somewhat poorer economic performance for the sake of the benefits of that form of socialism. On the other hand, they may share my opinion and decide that the cost of public ownership is too high a price to pay for that last anchor of socialism. In that case they should resign from the socialist family.

However, they need not abandon all of the socialist vision. That vision has always consisted of two compartments: one containing values, and the other containing institutions. Among the values are concern for the disadvantaged, an aversion to excessive social and economic inequality, and, for most socialists, individual freedom under law. Among the institutions are public ownership and central economic planning. One can reject the institutions without abandoning the values. My own view is that, paradoxically, liberal democratic capitalism offers a greater opportunity for the attainment of most socialist values than any socialism we have yet known. For many socialists, therefore, liberal capitalism may turn out to be the socialism of the 21st century.

The question of ownership is now at the very center of political controversy and intellectual debate in the former socialist countries. By the end of this decade all will have made their choices on the role of private ownership and of the former state enterprises, and there may be sufficient experience for the 21st century to make its assessment of which worked best. I must therefore defer announcing the results of the sixth lesson until the century ends.

Notes

1. Wells (1919), p. 96.

2. It now appears that the phrase originated as a wish, rather than as an observation of fact. William Bullitt, in whose company Steffens made his first trip to Russia in 1919, reported that it was on the way to Stockholm, to make contact with the Bolshevik agents who conducted them to Russia, that Steffens "had begun to rehearse his celebrated mantra. In its perfected form—'I have seen the future and it works'—it would ring in Western ears for the next two decades" (Kaplan, 1974, p. 250.

3. The criteria of economic performance I have in mind are rate of growth, technological progress, living standards, and so forth. There are some criteria, such as job security and, perhaps, income distribution, in which the socialist countries might be said to have performed better than the capitalist world. I take the rejection of socialism to have revealed, however, that the populations themselves regard the first group of criteria as more important.

4. Cf. the following from a letter to the editor of the *New York Times* (January 8, 1992): "Genuine democratic socialism in the Soviet Union hasn't been tried since Stalin's rise. Mikhail S. Gorbachev and Boris N. Yeltsin follow in Stalin's, not Lenin's or Trotsky's footsteps." I recently also came across a graffiti in Florence, Italy, proclaiming, "Gorbachev, No! Trotsky, Si!"

5. This is not to say that there will be no advocates of central planning in the future. Very recently I encountered the spirited argument that the trouble with the Soviet economy was not central planning itself but the undemocratic bureaucratization of planning. The next time around, in this view, planning will be carried out by the workers, and not imposed on them by the bureaucrats. These views, set forth by young American socialists, were heatedly attacked by some citizens of (then) socialist countries.

6. Barone (1935).

7. Lippincott (1952).

References

Barone, E. 1908. "The Ministry of Production in the Collectivist State." Reprinted in F. A. von Hayek, *Collectivist Economic Planning*. London: Routledge and Kegan Paul, pp. 247–290.

Lippincott, B. E. (ed.). 1952. *On the Economic Theory of Socialism*. Minneapolis: University of Minnesota Press.

Kaplan, Justin. 1974. *Lincoln Steffens: A Biography*. New York: Simon and Schuster.

Wells, H. G. 1919. *New Worlds for Old*. New York: Macmillan.

2

The End of the Soviet Union and the Return to History

Shlomo Avineri

Since 1989, the dramatic events in Central and Eastern Europe have given rise to a number of questions—and false hopes—about the alternatives to communism in countries that were ruled by Marxist-Leninist governments for many decades. The dissolution of communist regimes in the former Warsaw Pact countries, the inner travails of the former Soviet Union and the continuous disintegration of its political structures make the question of the alternatives a central issue of current international politics. They also pose some tough challenges for political analysts about the limits of their own professional expertise.

It is obvious that the defeat of communism is seen in the West primarily through an ideological prism; it is equally obvious that such a prism may sometimes impose triumphalist distortions on the interpretive faculties of the observer. Thus, in the rush of initial enthusiasm over the demise of communism, even the End of History has been messianically announced by some Western analysts. Finally—so it was argued—liberal democracy, with the free market as its mainstay, has now unequivocally won the ultimate victory. Western liberalism, after triumphing over fascism and Nazism in World War II, has finally triumphed over the other alternative ideology challenging it, communism. Thus the court of history—to use Hegelian language—has convincingly and irretrievably pronounced its ultimate judgment: liberal capitalism is the ultimate form of human society, no alternative system or ideology can ever successfully challenge it. The Sons of Light have finally triumphed over the Sons of Darkness. Hallelujah.

A more sober observation of developments in Eastern Europe and of the currently unfolding drama in the former Soviet Union itself, should, however, advise caution. While there is no doubt that the communist system as such—a one-party dictatorship coupled with a planned command economy—is clearly dead and buried in Central and Eastern Europe (the PRC,

Vietnam and North Korea may be a different story), it is becoming less and less clear whether the emerging alternative is an unequivocal victory of democracy and a free market society. Even in the short period that has elapsed since the drama of the autumn of 1989, clear differences in the developments in several post-communist societies suggest that not all of them are travelling on the same tracks or moving in the same direction: Czechoslovakia and Romania, for example, show completely different patterns of development. If one looks more carefully at these differences and at the vastly different course taken by the various former Soviet republics, it becomes abundantly clear that the single most pronounced determinant in these different developments are historical factors. Far from seeing an end of history, Eastern Europe now goes through a massive return of history and to history. Past structures and ideologies become a more reliable guide to the general contour of things to come than any other indicator, and pre-1914 atlases give a better picture of the tangled conflicts emerging in post-communist societies (e.g., in Yugoslavia) than more recent atlases; paradoxically, they are simply more up to date precisely because they are older. Anyone who has studied the Balkan wars of the 1910s is better equipped to understand the current developments in Yugoslavia than one who studied recent GNP or other indicators of these societies.

But before one can adequately assess the meaning of this return to history, it would be helpful to try fitting the developments of the last few years in the former Soviet orbit into a broader historical perspective; otherwise only a fragmented picture appears. These fragments do not make much sense, nor are they helpful in trying to formulate policies for the future. What we are witnessing is, in historical terms, far more encompassing—and complex—than the mere disintegration of communism.

In the wake of World War I, three centuries-old continental empires collapsed in 1917–18: the Ottoman, the Austro-Hungarian and the Russian. While the collapse of the first two empires was final, the reverberations of this collapse are still very much with us. Many of the regional conflicts in the Middle East and Central and Eastern Europe can be traced to the aftermath of this collapse. Thus in the Middle East, the Israeli-Palestinian conflict, the civil war in Lebanon, the Greek-Turkish conflict in and over Cyprus, even some aspects of the Iraqi-Kuwaiti dispute, can be traced to the fact that the borders as delineated after 1918 in the Middle East have been far from stable, and the conflicts mentioned are, in essence, disputes between successor states of the Ottoman Empire over the heritage left by it. Similarly, in Central and South-East Europe, tension between Hungary and Romania over questions connected with Transylvania, the current war in former Yugoslavia, even the possibility of the break-up of the Czechoslovak federation—all stem from the unfinished business of carving up the defunct Austro-Hungarian Empire.

When continental empires collapse, the reverberations continue to haunt the successor states for decades—in the two cases mentioned, for more than 70 years now, and the end is not yet in sight. This should sound a cautionary note for anyone expecting a 'quick fix' to the aftermath of the collapse of the Soviet Union and its orbit.

The story of the collapse of the old Russian Empire in 1917 was more complex than that of the end of the Ottoman or Austro-Hungarian systems. On coming to power in November 1917, Lenin and the Bolsheviks recognized and announced the right of the non-Russian nations within the old Russian czarist empire to secede and form their own states. This was in tune with the socialist (and, incidentally, at that time the current Wilsonian) notion of self-determination. As a consequence of this initial Soviet policy, Finland and the Baltic states attained their independence with Soviet blessing; the Russian part of Poland aligned itself with the Polish areas under German and Austrian rule to establish the independent Polish republic; Ukraine declared its independence, as did the Transcaucasian nations of Georgia and Armenia and other regions in the Central Asian parts of the old czarist empire.

This policy was, however, short-lived and was reversed during the ensuing civil war and Western anti-communist interventions, when some of the seceding republics became involved in the war against communist rule in Russia. Eventually, central authority—this time under the communist, not the czarist banner—was re-established by force in some of the seceding areas, mainly in Ukraine and Transcaucasia. Up to a point, the old Russian empire was re-established, this time with a revolutionary, internationalist ideology. During and after World War II this old-new Russian/Soviet empire was able to re-annex the Baltic republics and some additional areas in Eastern Poland and Northern Romania. Moreover, due to the Soviet victory over Nazi Germany, the Soviet army was instrumental in imposing in 1945–48 communist rule over Poland, Czechoslovakia, Hungary, Romania, Bulgaria and East Germany (Yugoslavia was a different story)—thus adding an unprecedented outer periphery to Russian/Soviet domination.

It would, however, be a mistake to attribute the existence of this extended empire to force alone: it was held together by a powerful combination of force and ideology, of terror and messianic conviction. While force and terror characterized the system throughout its existence, this was always accompanied by a vision held before the people's eyes, which hailed communism as the harbinger of a New World Order of equality, social justice and solidarity. Flawed as communist society was, one can never understand its staying power only in terms of its coercive instruments of repression; there was always the vision, and it was this vision which made it possible for people in Moscow and Kiev, Riga and Tashkent, Yerevan and Tbilisi to believe that despite their differences—in language and customs, religious background and national origin, culture and race—they were still united in an unprecedented effort to create a new world and a new man.

Thus *homo Sovieticus* was seen to arise out of this debris of the old world, transcending ethnicity, nationality and differences in culture and history. Similarly, communist leaders—and followers—in Warsaw Pact countries were not merely stooges hoisted into power on Soviet bayonets; among them were some of the best and brightest of East European intelligentsia, who believed that given the history of the region's economic backwardness, social conservatism and ethnic strife and fascist or near-fascist past history, only the promise of communism could deliver these societies and lead them to a new, bright and peaceful future. This dream might have been naïve, but it was born out of the noblest sentiments—and the nobility of this vision makes the abyss of Stalinist horrors even more tragic, as so poignantly shown in Arthur Koestler's *Darkness at Noon*. Only those who understand the attraction of communism for East European intellectuals can understand the depth of the catastrophe brought upon that dream by Stalinism and its aftermath.

Today, these two pillars of communism—force and ideology—are both dead. The repressive system has disintegrated, but so has the dream: no one believes any longer in the redemptive potential of communism. The void is almost fathomless, and frightening.

What will replace this dream and its political structures? After the first shock waves of 1989, pious Western conventional thinking, sometimes conditioned by facile cold-war slogans about 'captive nations', naïvely believed that communism would invariably and automatically be replaced by democracy and a market economy. First in the Warsaw Pact countries, and then in the Soviet Union itself, there was no dearth of leaders—some extremely appealing, some less so—whose anti-communism was immediately seen as signifying a commitment to democracy.

But what was lacking in many of those countries was a viable civil society, that network of voluntary associations, modes of thinking, traditions and institutions—cultural, economic and religious—which make democracy, and the market, possible. Political reality turned out to be much more complex—and disappointing—than the rhetoric surrounding the fall of the Berlin Wall. The fact of the matter is, that before the advent of communism only one country in Eastern Europe (Czechoslovakia) had a viable democratic system coupled with a thriving market economy, and even that was encumbered by grave problems of ethnic minorities (Sudeten Germans, Slovaks, Ruthenians and Hungarians).

Poland did try to achieve a democratic structure between the two world wars, but the nobility of this intention was not matched by the reality of its politics and economics: parliamentary fragmentation, and the fact that almost a third of its population consisted of non-Polish minorities (Ukrainians, Germans, Jews) undercut its fledgling democratic structures. Between 1918 and 1939 Hungary, Romania, Bulgaria, Yugoslavia and the Baltic states developed a variety of authoritarian regimes, with varying degrees of xenophobic repression and semi-fascist tendencies. Last, but not least, Russia itself, despite the historical yearnings of many of its poets and scholars, never had a viable democratic tradition of self-government, pluralism, civil society, tolerance and individualism. With all the best intentions in the world, post-communist societies find themselves, in most cases, lacking the building blocks of democracy which made the West European and North American experience of freedom possible.

1989 and ensuing developments suggest that the best predictive indicator of a country's post-communist future is its past. Not that the past is about to be repeated: Heraclitus maintained that you cannot step into the same river twice. But the past does, to a large degree, circumscribe the contours of the future political discourse—and its potentialities.

Thus Czechoslovakia, with its liberal, secular, Western-oriented traditions, is the most successful attempt at developing along democratic lines. Even so, this is more of a success story in the Czech lands than in Slovakia, whose historical tradition is much more lacking in these ingredients and which did go through an autochthonous fascist phase (the Slovak fascist independent state between 1938 and 1945). Poland and Hungary are able to draw with some success on historical resources and traditions to which representative government was not wholly foreign, although Polish parliamentary fragmentation and some lingering ethnocentric traditions in Hungary may make further developments problematic.

But countries like Romania and Bulgaria, let alone Albania, with hardly any democratic or civil society tradition, show how difficult the transition is. And in Yugoslavia, two parallel throw-backs to history are discernable: the historical enmities, mainly between Serbs and Croats, are coming back in all their ferocity, and in the vortex of this ethnic conflict, both independent Croatia and the Serb-dominated rump-Yugoslavia show clear signs of developing along the historical authoritarian lines of their past traditions. Only Slovenia, with a history of relative tolerance and decency (mainly under benevolent Habsburg rule) may yet escape this slide into ethnocentric authoritarianism of various stripes now engulfing the former communist attempt at bridging those centuries-old conflicts.

This return to historical patterns is also exemplified by the unification of Germany. Few thought this would happen, and happen so quickly, when the Wall came down on November 9, 1989. But once the Wall did come down, and the communist system in East Germany was being transformed, there was no *raison d'être* for the separate existence of a German Democratic Republic, and the forces of national unity and historical memory very quickly turned the battle-cry of East German dissenters, *Wir sind das Volk* (We are The People) to *Wir sind ein Volk* (We are One People).

Once the communist carpet is pulled away, it appears that under this Soviet permafrost nothing was lost: all the grass, and all the dirt comes back. Forty-five or 75 years of communism appear to have been a hiatus in time, and post-communist societies go back to the political discourse of pre-1917 or pre-1945, respectively. This has become even more clear in the former Soviet Union. With the disappearance of communism as an ideology and a system of power, the disintegration of the once second-strongest Superpower into its national components appears complete—and even Russia itself is being challenged by some of the smaller nations incorporated into it by czars and commissars alike (Tatars, Chenens, and the list will grow). Erstwhile communist leaders have become champions of nationalism overnight—thus Leonid Kravchuk in Ukraine and Nursultan Nazarbayev in Kazakhstan. Georgia and Armenia emerge as separate nation-states, with at least the former showing some rather repressive features.

Russia itself, while possessing a leadership extolling democracy and the market, lamentably lacks the infrastructure for both, and the dangers of an authoritarian, populist regime are manifest. That 25 million ethnic Russians live outside the borders of the Russian Republic (11 million of them in Ukraine) suggests enormous potentialities for Yugoslav-like problems. The break-up of the old Russian empire—which did collapse in 1917, but was then put together again by Soviet power—now appears to be final.

This return to history is nowhere more evident than in the return to the old names of streets, squares, and cities: Leningrad is once again St. Petersburg; Kalinin—Tver; Sverdlovsk—Yekaterinburg; Ordzhonikidze—Vladikavkaz (the last, a nice czarist triumphalist name: 'Conqueror of the Caucasus'), etc.

And with the return to history and historical memory comes a return to religion, which in Eastern Europe is closely intertwined with ethnicity and national consciousness. The void left in the belief system of East European societies by the demise of communism is being replaced by a revival—sometime uncritical—of religiosity and religious symbolism. During the days of Solidarity's struggle against communism in Poland, the Church was a symbol, a system of beliefs, and a helpful alternative organizational structure all in one; but the phenomenon is much wider. Not only Czestochowa, but also Zagorsk and many other shrines in Eastern Europe now enjoy a degree of popularity that few comparable religious sites can claim in the West. Out of the communist experience many post-communist societies may emerge as being more religiously devout than most contemporary Western societies—but also more devout than these societies themselves were before the advent of communism.

In Soviet Central Asia, fundamentalist Islam may become the strongest political force in the process of replacing communist structures. Similarly, many Jews in Russia, who viewed communism (for all its repressive, anti-Jewish policies) as a passport to general society, are now discovering that with the demise of Soviet Man and the re-assertion of Russian, Ukrainian (or Uzbek) nationalism, often coupled with religious connotations, they have to redefine the problems of their own identity; no longer can they claim to be Soviet citizens 'of Jewish origin'. It is this, as much as economic hardships and the ravings of some marginal antisemites, that drives so many (former) Soviet Jews to choose emigration and seek a new homeland in Israel.

This return to history, with all its attendant dangers, also poses a question to social scientists. After all, social science was not very successful in grasping, let alone predicting, the dramatic processes that brought about the disintegration of communism. One only has to read learned tracts written only two or three years ago by some leading Sovietologists to feel embarrassed for their sake.

There is a lesson in this for social scientists, and it can be touched upon only briefly here. It is a need for more humility with regard to the usefulness of quantitative data, for reverence for historical contexts—i.e., for the role of human consciousness in human affairs. History is not an ontological entity, existing outside human consciousness. Ultimately, it is the totality of choices human beings make about what they decide to remember and transmit to their descendants. As Hegel once remarked, all revolutions are preceded by a quiet and lengthy revolution in human consciousness, "a revolution not visible to every eye, especially imperceptible to contemporaries, and as hard to discern as to describe in words."

It is these revolutions in consciousness that should be studied, because, as Hegel goes on to suggest, "it is the lack of acquaintance with this spiritual revolution which makes the resulting changes astonishing." These changes in the core of human thinking have to be studied concretely—in the way human beings express themselves and behave; their study requires knowledge of the language used by the societies under discussion, their literature, their concrete human discourse.

This cannot be done through diagrams, nor can it be quantified or observed from a distance through digests of official statements and press cuttings (usually in translation). This can be glimpsed when one is confronted by thousands of young female pilgrims on Assumption Day in Zagorsk in 1974 and when one realizes that none of them had even been born when the communist revolution broke out; or when one is told in 1986 that the prime topic of discussion among Moscow intellectuals is whether local street names should be changed to their pre-revolutionary names, because otherwise 19th century Russian literature, with its *genius loci*, loses so much of its meaning.

It is fair to guess that these two instances—and hundreds of similar ones—were never documented in the voluminous files kept by Western observers, or Western intelligence services who were trying to gather every piece of what they considered relevant information about the Soviet Union.

It is this humility before the obdurate nature of human consciousness that should, hopefully, guide our understanding in the future of these momentous events connected with the decline and fall of communism and the Soviet empire.

3

Democracy at Odds with the Market in Post-Communist Societies

Silviu Brucan

Initially, after the successive revolutions in Eastern Europe took political analysts in both East and West by surprise, the prevailing assumption was that the transition to democracy in that part of the world would go hand in hand with the establishment of a market economy. Since both tasks were considered a must, idyllic programs were drawn up in all Eastern European countries promising a quick advance of both reforms in perfect harmony. It did not take long to discover, to our deep chagrin, that there actually is a striking contradiction between the two basic tasks facing us.

The initiation of a market economy is an extremely difficult and painful social process. The old Stalinist economic model was a politico-ideological construct, in which social (dictatorship of the proletariat) and political (party monopoly of power) considerations overshadowed economic ones. Economic data were tailored to fit ideological claims; the whole economic picture was a big hoax, but the painting was so well done that even Western economists were sometimes taken in. East Germany is probably the most glaring illustration of that make-believe, and was praised as the 'Communist showcase' by quite a few Western analysts. Therefore, the demolition of that monumental hoax is not only a daunting economic and social undertaking but also a psychological trauma for the people involved. And since there is no previous historical experience for such a U-turn, and therefore no theory to guide the new 'revolution from above', we are all groping in the dark. The old methods of the command economy no longer work, while the new forms and institutions of the market are not yet in place. We thus go through a period of confusion and chaos, trying to make an intelligent guess each time we encounter a new problem.

The situation is propitious for social explosions. The price reform designed to make prices reflect economic reality—absolutely essential for the market—triggers rampant inflation and deep dissatisfaction among blue-collar workers, white-collar workers and pensioners. Mikhail Gorbachev was reluctant to face the social effects of price reform, particularly in basic food staples. The other facet of the change, the privatization of industrial plants that were over-staffed under communist rule, generates massive unemployment, which also makes workers who were accustomed to job security angry, if not desperate.

The difficulties encountered by the initiation of a market economy are best illustrated by the case of the former German Democratic Republic. Here, indeed, the most favorable preconditions for a market economy did exist: plenty of West German capital for investment, the best possible advice and expertise for rapid modernization of the industry, a huge potential market for every product of the European Economic Community and, above all, the most hardworking and efficient workforce in Europe—the Germans. The East Germans, irresistibly attracted by Chancellor Kohl's promises to bring them overnight into the fold of Germany Incorporated, voted enthusiastically in favor of unification. Two years later, the East Germans are confronted with the grim reality of an economy in utter collapse. Nearly 3 million are jobless or on terminal leave; industrial production has dropped by half, even the once-successful giant state airline—Interflug—and the famous optical company—Zeiss—are teetering on the edge of bankruptcy and awaiting a bailout from Bonn. The political folklore in the West has it: "The whole of East Germany is a Trabant"—the small car made of pressed cardboard and moved by a two-stroke engine emitting foul exhaust gases. Official economists who once figured unification would cost DM 4.5 billion a year, now speak of DM 200 billion. The economic crisis is compounded by social discontent and psychological trauma. Crime, alcoholism, drug abuse and mental illness are all increasing against the background of what the Germans call *Existenzangst*, which is nothing less than fear of life itself, and that feeling is epidemic.

Let us now turn to *democracy*. People in Eastern Europe have embraced the new rights and freedoms brought about by the transition to democracy and have started exercising them in full measure—but without the discipline and feeling of responsibility ingrained in the citizenry over many decades by the democratic regimes in the West. In Romania, for example, almost a hundred political parties have been founded, free unions are cropping up every month, and the number of newspapers and weeklies has jumped from less than one hundred to over two thousand.

The point is that people in Eastern Europe are using their new rights and freedoms, especially the right to strike and to demonstrate, to protest against the privations brought about by the initial phase of the transition to a market economy. At a time when production and productivity go down (in Rumania 25–30 percent, in Poland 30 percent, in Hungary 15 percent, in Bulgaria 30 percent, and in East Germany 50 percent), the unions are demanding higher wages and the governments, operating under populist pressures, are forced to meet such grievances. Leaders in the East are 'soft on democracy'. Thus, a legitimate question arises: how can one overcome the recession if prices and wages are going up while production and productivity are going down?

The first political casualty of that contradiction between market and democracy was the Polish Prime Minister, Mazowiecki, the serious man of reform, praised throughout the West for his brave shock therapy. His adversary in the presidential elections, Wałesa, came to power on a platform of authoritarianism blended with Polish nationalism, hardly the ideal model of the triumph of democracy in Eastern Europe.

In an historical perspective, the advent of the modern market economy in its capitalist stage has always gone through a classical authoritarian phase: Cromwell in England, Napoleon in France, Bismarck in Germany. It took Western capitalism about two centuries to reach the present balance between democracy and market. The shock therapy in Poland could be viewed as a daring attempt to achieve in a couple of years what Western capitalism achieved in a couple of centuries. Galbraith, in his article, "Which Capitalism for Eastern Europe?" examines precisely this issue:

> Never mind that we are urging on Eastern Europe a kind of capitalism that we in the West would not dare to risk. In the last century, when Marx wrote, and continuing on into this century and in the years of the Great Depression the survival of capitalism in its original and ideologically exact form was very much in doubt. . . . The system did survive, however, because the Welfare State mitigated the hardships and the cruelties of pristine capitalism. Also, trade unions were legitimized and soon began to exercise countervailing power. (*Harper's Magazine*, April 1990)

Two remarks are in order here: (a) In the West, society became sufficiently productive and wealthy (partly thanks to colonial exploitation and later on through unequal exchange between the industrial nations and the underdeveloped continents). Such sources of wealth do not exist in Eastern Europe. (b) Experience shows that blue- and white-collar workers do not view a capitalist system in its classical form as an alternative to a bankrupt communism. They, too, have enjoyed a sort of Welfare State, however poor its communist version, and therefore they are not prepared to go back to the free market of Adam Smith. Galbraith is right in concluding: "The alternative [to communism] they see is the modern state with a large, indispensable mellowing and stabilizing role for government." I suggest that even some features of the present capitalist system would not be acceptable in post-communist societies. Suppose, for example, that Romania were to introduce the kind of tuition costs and on-campus living expenses that American students are required to pay these days. Riots would break out, and I am afraid that college presidents and deans would be in great physical danger!

The fact is that under present conditions, the transition to a market economy in Eastern Europe will be a period of social confusion and turmoil.

The question is whether democracy can cope with the present situation. Probably the most appropriate model of contemporary societies that have overcome such a situation through capitalist methods are the 'Four Tigers' of the Pacific rim: South Korea, Taiwan, Singapore and Hong Kong. They made it, however, under authoritarian regimes, some of them extremely brutal. It is only lately that the information revolution—changing the underlying efficiency and productivity, and shifting the emphasis from the state to the individual, whose creative power becomes the engine of progress—is compelling the tigers to gradually adapt their political systems to the imperatives of democracy set forth by the information society.

There is a sad comment to be added here, but in science facts must prevail over principles of political morality. The only society in the whole East that has turned into a market economy but nevertheless enjoys a high rate of economic growth is China, the regime that committed the odious massacre of Tiananmen and continues to proclaim the 'People's Democratic Dictatorship' (why not 'popular tyranny'?). *The New York Times* (April 18, 1991) tells us that:

> China is booming again. Production, consumption, wages and bonuses are all sharply higher, but inflation, brought under control last year, is rising again. . . . While last year output of state-owned industries grew only 2.9 percent, in the first two months of 1991 production by large and medium-size enterprises grew 14.3 percent.

Such an upswing in the economy is inconceivable in Eastern Europe these days; here, all economic indicators are in decline with the Soviet Union once again leading the way.

In my recent book (Brucan, 1990), I make two basic points with regard to the Chinese exception: (a) China lags one social stage behind Eastern Europe—almost 80 percent of the population still lives in the countryside, and here one must recall that modern democracy is originally linked with urbanization. (b) The need to assimilate the computer and information revolution, that plays such an important role in Eastern Europe's drive for democracy and openness, does not have the same urgency in China.

Janos Kornai has recently published a new book dealing with the transition to a market economy in Hungary in particular, and in Eastern Europe in general. His conclusion is that "only a strong government can implement the economic policy outlined in this study." Of course, he qualifies this statement, opposing a government whose strength lies in repressive measures, advocating instead "a government whose strength lies in the support of the people, one to which free elections have given a real popular mandate to set the economy right with a firm hand" (Kornai, 1990). This sounds like the opinion of an economist rather than that of a political scientist. Most of the governments in Eastern Europe have the required popular mandate through free elections but can nevertheless hardly "set the economy right with a firm hand."

In Romania, the market-democracy contradiction is striking the nation with a vengeance. The government's decision last October to liberalize prices, hailed in the West as a crucial test of political will to go for the market, has been met by some unions with a wave of strikes. The recent strike of railway workers pushed the national economy close to the brink of collapse. The union leaders acted according to the classic French adage: Après moi le déluge. They did not care at all that the disruption of the economy may undermine the very basis of the new and yet fragile democratic regime. And although they talk all the time about their model, that is Western trade-unions, they choose to ignore a very relevant principle of behavior established by those unions: never go on strike during a recession, because employers will be quite happy to shut down the enterprise and all workers will be jobless.

One of the great achievements of modern postwar liberalism is the decision to review its initial creed and join forces with social-democracy to disprove the claim of the *Communist Manifesto*—"the workers have no fatherland," by persuading the workers that their welfare is actually tied to the state of the national economy. The moment the workers in Eastern Europe reach that level of consciousness, social conditions for overcoming the pains of the market will improve considerably. This is perhaps the critical point where the learning process of democracy could meet the hard demands of market formation. However, recent developments in Eastern Europe have confirmed the 'gap' between the establishment of democracy and the initiation of a market economy.

In Poland, last November, in the first fully free parliamentary elections since World War II, only 43.2 percent of the electorate even bothered to vote. Most analysts concluded that both public apathy and the choice of voters were motivated by a general dissatisfaction with the economic conditions created by the shock therapy. "We listened to the West and we made too big a leap" noted Poland's President Wałesa, and his behavior became increasingly authoritarian. He even suggested that he himself should also take up the job of prime minister and eventually settled for a "government endowed with full powers to enforce economic policies," warning that failure to do so could lead to the dissolution of the new parliament. Boris Yeltsin soon followed suit, asking the Russian parliament to give him 'emergency powers', and as soon as he got them he issued a batch of decrees lifting most controls over imports, exports and currency transactions in Russian territory, and last but not least, liberalizing prices of consumer goods, from food to computers. To forestall the protest of those with fixed incomes, he raised the minimum monthly wage to 200 rubles, and for certain categories of state employees by 90 percent. But 200 rubles in Russia today is peanuts, and Yeltsin is faced with tremendous protests and demonstrations. The leader of Ukraine, Kravchuk, is also the type of a strong-man on a white horse. And, of course, all leaders of the Asian independent states have an inclination toward authoritarianism.

The West, when confronted with the stark choice between market and democracy, seems to favor the former, being ready to forgive the poor showing of the latter. Yeltsin and Kravchuk enjoy the support of the Western governments and the IMF so long as they go for the market and service their foreign debt. Chinese Premier Li Peng was equally welcome in Western capitals lately—for the same reason.

In Romania, enraged by skyrocketing food prices stirred up by the Petre Roman government's shift to shock therapy, thousands of rampaging miners converged on Bucharest in September 1990, hurling rocks and firebombs at official buildings, eventually toppling the prime minister. Of course, the first priority of the new Stolojan government was to conclude a sort of social contract with the unions, promising indexation of wages to rising prices and measures of social protection.

Even the popular president of Czechoslovakia, Vaclav Havel was booed in Bratislava by Slovak nationalists, and had to accept a referendum over the independence of Slovakia.

An authoritative voice, the architect of Singapore's economic miracle, ex-Premier Lee Kuan Yew, had this to say about the choice between democracy and economic reform in Eastern Europe:

> The more dissension, the more contention and less consensus, the less you get on with the job. In the early stages you need to achieve clear-cut goals like universal education, high savings, high productivity, low consumption. Those are simple truths that everybody has to accept, in order to accumulate the surplus to build up the infrastructure. You need the capital to get going. And you can't have contention over these simple truths indefinitely (*Time*, November 4, 1991).

In the Soviet case, he argued that *perestroika* should have come first, and only afterwards, *glasnost*.

The final conclusion is obvious: the transition to a market economy under present domestic and international conditions requires an authoritarian political regime. What kind, bearing in mind the hostility of the population against dictatorship accumulated over decades of harsh communist rule, remains to be seen. Equally true, Western Europe would veto any attempt to establish a dictatorial regime over here, and no post-communist society can afford to ignore the viewpoint of the Council of Europe. What then?

Theoretically, one could conceive of a popularly elected government with a mandate to enforce economic change, whose authority is based on the right mix between respect for basic freedoms and harsh enforcement of law and order. *Dura lex sed lex,* as the Romans used to say. Democracy, precisely because it lacks repressive ways and means, must be more, not less demanding with regard to observance of laws by all citizens—from top to bottom. A state of *lex* (*Rechtstaat*) in which the judiciary becomes a major source of authority, is essentially what we are talking about.

Could such a political system work with nations that have not known democracy for half a century? That remains an open question.

References

Brucan, Silviu. 1990. *Pluralism and Social Conflict*. New York: Praeger.

Kornai, Janos. 1990. *The Road to a Free Economy: Shifting from a Socialist System: The Case of Hungary.* New York: Norton.

4

The Collapse of the Communist Empire: An Avenue to European Civilization

Oleg T. Bogomolov

The transition of the former Soviet Union from totalitarianism to Western-style democracy, from a command to a free-market economy, is evolving painfully and inconsistently. Resistance on the part of obsolete structures, psychological inertia, lack of credibility of the central authorities and a low level of political culture and morals—all render the final outcome of the ongoing changes indefinite and give rise to the appearance of distorted forms of democracy and market relations.

Profound Historical Changes

The changes that occurred until August 1991 were only partial and the fundamental principles remain essentially unchanged: the party still plays a leading role, state-ownership is still predominant, Marxism-Leninism is still the official ideology, fear is still the major instrument of power. While Gorbachev's first attempt at *perestroika* failed to satisfy social needs and did not extricate the country from its crisis (rather, the opposite is true), it did promote the development of free thought and considerably lessened the danger of military confrontation between the two superpowers.

The unfolding events in Eastern Europe provide clear proof that the existing system cannot be improved by applying piecemeal *perestroika*, which has by now fallen into complete disrepute. It is now obvious that what is needed is a completely new social organization that will ensure true social and economic progress. This calls for the total elimination of the existing command, monolithic system and the formation of a new society and a new community of republics—a society that eschews dogmatism and utopianism and upholds the rule of law, guarantees human rights and freedoms, and fosters integration in the world economy.

Gorbachev's error, before the take-over bid, was in failing to recognize the non-viability of the existing system. He took every opportunity to affirm his commitment to the socialist ideal and communist credo; he accused both radicals and democrats of extremism and of conspiring to undermine the Union. The abortive coup has accelerated the dissolution of the centrist Union and many of its pillars (the Communist Party, the KGB, the military-industrial establishment) are crumbling. Gorbachev was forced to acknowledge the evils of the Soviet socialist model, while holding on to his faith in the socialist idea. Several major cities such as Moscow, St. Petersburg, and provinces (Kirgizstan) underwent pro-democratic, anti-communist revolutions. The entire empire collapsed in a matter of days; the republics of the Soviet Union shook off central rule, proclaimed independence and asserted their desire to establish an entirely new framework of relationships.

In what used to be the USSR there emerged a mosaic of states with different political regimes: anti-communist, neo-communist, communist-feudal. The Baltic States, Georgia and Moldavia want full separation. Other former republics are warily debating the possibility of forming a confederation-style union with joint armed forces and coordinating agencies for the promotion of common endeavors in the field of economics, technology, environment protection and the prevention of crime.

The decisive role in suppressing the coup was played by democratic forces in Russia, led by Yeltsin, who was the primary object of the reactionary drive in the first place. The successful stand against the plotters gave an enormous boost to the prestige and influence of the outspokenly anti-communist Russian leader, severely shaking communist elites in other republics (especially in view of the weakened position of the Center). One consequence of these events was the revival of a nationalist-inspired desire for independence in Ukraine, Kazakhstan, Belaru, Uzbekistan and other republics. These developments are occurring against the background of a true economic upheaval. GNP dropped 5 percent in 1990 and dropped another 15–20 percent in 1991. Harvests (not all in at the time of writing) are low, and will be further eroded by familiar factors such as losses in transportation and storage; the situation is aggravated by farmers' reluctance to enter the less-than-profitable transaction of shipping their produce to the cities. The threat of widespread hunger is a genuine one.

The former Center has proved completely bankrupt financially. Both Union and Republic budgets are running huge deficits—estimated at 20 percent of the GNP. The Pavlov government tried to halt the downward slide by doubling and tripling prices of basic consumer goods (and raising the prices of fuels, raw materials, many types of chemicals and machinery) leading to mounting inflation, which may run out of control. Standards of living have fallen by at least one-third since these measures were taken in April 1991 and half the population found itself beneath the poverty line. While the purchasing power of the population has been severely curtailed, shop shelves remain bare. Stocks of foodstuffs hoarded in anticipation of price hikes will eventually run out, money reserves will trickle away, and the general discontent may well bubble over and out into the streets. No less ominous is the growth of speculative activity, corruption, and crime, all of which are closely related to the destruction of the consumer market and the distribution apparatus. Reduced petroleum and coal output is causing great concern. Wear and tear of industrial and transport equipment leads to breakdowns and costly accidents. Foreign trade has diminished considerably, down to half in the case of Eastern Europe. The external debt now exceeds $60 billion.

The collapse of the economy is most frequently explained in official circles as being the result of the disintegration of the administrative system before a viable market-economy alternative could take root. Other causes cited are ethnic conflicts and the separatist mood in various republics. The truth is that although the administrative system was, indeed, shaken and weakened, it was by no means demolished. What *was* utterly destroyed was the fledgling consumer market, which had played an important role even while the command economy was in power by maintaining some sort of material incentive for labor. The demise of the consumer market therefore resulted in lower productivity and loss of labor discipline.

Of course, many of today's economic difficulties are merely the heritage of decades of neglect and mismanagement: chronic lags in the production of agricultural produce and consumer goods, and the preference accorded to the enormous military-industrial complex over the civilian sector. But the major cause of the present plight lies in the unsound economic policy pursued by the Center during *perestroika*, first and foremost in the money-credit and budget spheres, and in agriculture. Producers will not sell their wares for worthless money; they would rather barter. The result is disruption in contractual relations between enterprises to the detriment of overall production. The scarcity of hard currency with which to finance even the most vital imports (of both raw materials and manufactured components) means that the production of numerous goods has ground to a halt.

Despite the impressive victory of democratic forces in Russia, the resistance of conservative forces, of the party apparatus and of the military-industrial complex has not yet been fully overcome. One cannot dismiss the possibility that some elements, be they in the Center or in the periphery, might attempt a comeback. Nor should one underestimate the discontent of the masses. Their indifference (or, perhaps, their tacit approval) during the abortive putsch could turn into violence directed at the democratic authorities for failing to immediately improve their lot. It is difficult to foresee the negative consequences of growing nationalism. Nationalism, and its attendant leaning toward authoritarianism (if not totalitarianism), is gaining ground in both communist and anti-communist regimes in different republics. In short, the political and economic situation is still extremely unstable, and it is far too early to speak of any sort of turn for the better.

Prospects for Rebirth

The Soviet Union has ceased to exist as a unitarian state. It is now going through a process in which its obsolete centralized power structure is falling apart and new, independent states are emerging, shaping a new economic and political entity that is not likely to incorporate all the republics of the erstwhile Soviet Union. It is difficult to estimate the duration of this period of transition; it will probably last longer than a year. Some optimism was generated by the President of the USSR and leaders of republics who seemed to understand the necessity of preventing the spontaneous disintegration of the Union and of a smooth, coordinated transfer of power.

The Congress of Peoples' Deputies, meeting in September 1991, established a provisional mechanism of central power during the transition period and until the signing of a new Union Treaty. But in December the Congress itself was abolished as a result of the establishment of the Commonwealth of Independent States, which rendered the existence of the all-Union structures meaningless.

These are the new starting positions of the geopolitical entity once known as the Soviet Union. With respect to its future political and economic stability, a great deal depends on the ground-rules of the economic and political alliance. The Commonwealth should be based on principles of independence and territorial integrity, respect for human and national rights, social justice, and democracy. Its members are going to have common strategic armed forces, but they prefer to have other military forces under national command. All international agreements and obligations of the USSR are to be strictly observed, including those on arms limitation and control, the protection of human rights, and economic affairs.

The Community will clearly be flexible enough for candidates to join it under various terms of association, though in many other respects the basic concept of the community remains obscure. If Russia is to be the core around which the community crystallizes, its character will be determined predominantly by Russia. Nor is it quite clear just how the republics themselves envisage the new entity; will it share a common currency? will there be a customs union removing barriers between republics? will the Union pursue a common budget and reserves policy and a common external economic policy within the framework of a single economic and legal space? The answers to all these questions are probably affirmative, but in the short run, at least, many republics will probably prefer to have their own currencies. The ruble cannot be stabilized as the all-Union currency as long as such great differences exist between republics as regards their economic situation, their fiscal, monetary and credit policies, the degree of faith in (or reliance on) the Union center. One could, of course, do away with all price controls (thereby releasing the brakes on hyperinflation). Alternatively, one could restructure the market to include such 'new' assets as land, housing, and company shares—assets that the republics naturally claim as their own—but this would require prior agreement on the center's share with a view to safeguarding the purchasing power of money. It is not clear whether such an agreement is feasible.

The institution of a sound (and eventually also convertible) currency unit will also require reaching and abiding by other important accords on permissible deficit and internal debt levels in each republic and the unification of banking procedures, taxation, customs, prices and social policies. This combines with the inevitable question of the country's foreign debt service burden and each member-republic's share in it. It will be difficult to reach accord on all these matters, and a single dissention may severely hamper inter-republic trade for all the rest.

In my opinion, it would be expedient to try and establish a banking and payment union, using a common currency with joint regulation of money and credit emission. Several republics are likely to consent to such an arrangement. If it proves impossible to settle on a stable currency unit and to coordinate policy on vital cross-republic issues, there remains the hope that Russia may rehabilitate its monetary system and turn its national currency (the ruble or the chervonetz) into the mode to be used in inter-republican transactions.

A departure from the former practices employed in setting up the Union budget and regulating inter-republican trade based on arbitrary prices is inevitable. This is what the separate republics desire, namely, a restoration of their right to trade with a view to their own advantage and to exploit their own GNPs. One likely consequence of such a move will be an increase in Russia's trade balance with other republics, at the expense of Ukraine, Belarus, the Baltic states and the Central Asian republics. To weaken the shock, it will be necessary to reach an agreement on a gradual transition from the former arrangements to a new system, including a deliberate effort to slow down the dissolution of the single monetary system.

By now the republics are determined to take their destinies in their own hands, to solve their economic difficulties without relying on the 'wisdom' (and interference) of the supra-national center. Russia, for example, is prepared to take vigorous, radical steps to achieve economic stabilization and to set up a free market economy, either as part of of a new economic community or—if such a community does not emerge—independently.

Recovery can commence based on a change in people's attitude to their own labor, resulting in growing output and increased labor productivity. To accomplish this calls for the introduction of real material incentives, and the instillation of motivation by real money and a change in the relations of ownership, all of which could be introduced first of all in agriculture.

The first, indispensable step in this direction is to heal the monetary system and create a stable, sound, and eventually convertible currency. A large (and growing) money overhang is the result of unrestrained money and credit emission, designed primarily for the purpose of covering the budget deficit. Price controls ruined the market because of the unmet demand for goods and services. Normal trade was replaced by barter deals; material incentives lost all value; labor discipline suffered seriously; and the economy found itself in what might be called a state of 'free fall'. It can start off on the road to recovery by changing peoples' attitudes to labor, leading to greater output and productivity. To accomplish this task, real material incentives must be reinstituted, motivation must be ensured by offering real money rewards and a new system of ownership (agriculture is obviously the prime candidate for such a change).

How can the ruble be turned into a truly hard (and ultimately convertible) currency? Can this be accomplished in a reasonably short run? I believe it can—at least in Russia. It is by now abundantly clear that the reformation of the money system can be delayed no longer. But the steps taken so far by the central authorities (doubling and tripling prices by administrative means, purportedly in order to achieve gradual price liberalization) proved futile, merely resulting in soaring prices, heightened inflation, declining production, and increasing social tensions. The liberalization of one-quarter of all prices in January 1992, has exacerbated these negative trends. Reducing the population's real income must be combined with other measures; the most important of these is to increase the supply of goods in the market and to cut the budget deficit by reducing expenditures. The state can sell some of its property (land, structures, shares in firms) at market prices assessed by Western experts. These assets could be turned into an anchor of stability for the monetary and credit systems, provided, of course, that a considerable portion of the property is made freely tradable.

The strategy proposed above is, of course, fraught with difficulties. The people, whose incomes have been deliberately curtailed by the government in order to prevent the accumulation of large sums of money, are in no position to buy even an insignificant portion of the state's property. They are also confused by the very notion, having been under the impression that as citizens they were co-owners in the state property to begin with. One possible solution offered in Russia and in some other republics, which is gaining increasing support, is to grant every adult a voucher whose value will equal about 30–40 percent of his or her share in the common property. This voucher is to serve as payment for land, housing, company shares, or savings (for 2–3 years). A sizable portion of state property could be privatized by this method; the remainder would remain at the disposal of the authorities for sale on the market as required. This method of privatization can, theoretically at least, bolster the market and the monetary system by increasing the supply of goods and providing a broad segment of the population with property—i.e., by creating an active middle class bent on the accumulation of more wealth. Part of the income from such sales of property should be withdrawn from circulation or frozen for a period of 3–4 years.

Other measures will also have to be implemented: strict rules regulating banking operations; anti-monopoly legislation to foster competition; liberalization of prices and imports; and the introduction of market rates of exchange on foreign currency. It will quite possibly be necessary to exchange old for new currency notes and coins in order to limit the demand for goods.

However, the main prerequisite is, of course, the liquidation of the enormous budget deficit and the alignment of state expenditures with state income. Hence the urgent need for demilitarization of the economy and for slashing military spending. But the military-industrial complex is firmly entrenched and strongly resists such moves. The country simply cannot bear the already excessively heavy burden of military expenditures and large-scale investment programs financed by extra-budgetary means. After the abortive coup, cuts in military spending have become quite feasible. It is also clearly impossible to further postpone strict budget restrictions on subsidies to losing enterprises.

Improvements can be achieved fairly rapidly in agriculture by instituting a radical reform in the virtually feudal system of obligatory deliveries of produce. It is high time we enabled private ownership of and trade in land (even for nonagricultural uses such as country homes and so forth) and permit farmers to sell their surplus produce freely (after payment of taxes, possibly in kind). The land allocated free of charge and in perpetuity to collective state farms must return to state ownership and then sold or leased to the farmers. Artificial barriers to the development of private farms should be abolished; rather, state support should be given to such farms, including machinery, fertilizer, seed, and other necessities.

These are, in my opinion, the primary measures that, if implemented, will act as catalysts in the upturn of the economy, inspiring the people to hope for a possible rebirth. But it will take many years to create a normally functioning market economy.

Breaking Out of Isolation—Western Support

The revolutionary changes in Russia, which have spread to other republics as well, make it possible to end the country's isolation from the rest of the world and opens up new prospects for international trade. This is evident from the removal of the state monopoly on foreign trade, new laws promulgated to boost foreign investment, the creation of joint ventures, etc. But many obstacles to cooperation with the West still remain: export and import licensing regulations, customs duties, regulations for obtaining raw materials and components by joint ventures, taxes, and banking practices. The main point, however, is that both in Russia and in other republics the required market environment—with convertible currency—is lacking. This is still the most serious obstacle to integration into the world economy.

Once market mechanisms are available it will be possible to increase exports and thus finance growing imports. The necessary small businesses already exist, as do municipal authorities; what needs to be done is in the realm of large-scale industries, which have to be restructured in order to set up a powerful and competitive export sector. Converting the country's defense industries to civilian purposes would be one way in which to make the high technology accessible to the economy at large, thereby permitting exports of new goods. This is one of the most promising areas for joint ventures with the West.

The West is not likely to sell machinery and equipment on a credit basis—the high price of credit also precludes this possibility. Given the inefficiency with which imported equipment is utilized, it is clear that the economy will have to bear an increasingly onerous foreign debt. Consequently, the emphasis will probably be put on alternative forms of collaboration with the West, such as industrial cooperation, joint enterprises, direct foreign investments, and free-trade zones. Nonetheless, the search for new sources of credit will have to be maintained, in view of the poor state of the economy as a whole.

In the present context one should bear in mind the role of multinational corporations in the ongoing process of world-wide economic integration. Despite the nature of these corporations' activities, which serves anything but the national interests of the countries in which they operate, they do contribute to the acceleration of technological progress and to interdependence between countries, exerting more and more influence on the dynamism and geographical flow of world trade. Of all the developed countries in the world, only the Soviet Union does not have large multinational corporations of its own, with subsidiaries spread all over the world. Nor are there—as yet—any subsidiaries of Western multi-nationals in the Soviet Union. It is patently clear that Russia, Ukraine, and other republics will have to create a favorable economic environment for such foreign companies. In time, it is not unreasonable to expect that these republics will eventually have investments of their own in the West.

The means of achieving economic recovery need not be sought abroad; they exist *within* the country. The decisive factors are the democratization of society, the emancipation of public consciousness, the awakening of talents and a moral and cultural upsurge in the population at large. The major obstacles are the immaturity of the civil society and the lack of experience and professionalism in the new corridors of power. The West can speed up the reawakening of ex-Soviet society by offering to compromise on such issues as arms reduction (both conventional and nuclear), by continuing the political dialogue with the CIS and republic leaders, and by widening contacts and cooperation in all spheres. The difficult process of dissolution of totalitarianism and the shift in the direction of democracy and a market economy requires not only the moral and diplomatic support of major industrialized countries, but also their technological assistance, capital and managerial expertise. Removal of restrictions on transfers of technology would be of enormous help; likewise granting most-favored-nation status in trade agreements and the admission of the newly emerged Independent States to international economic organizations.

Humanitarian aid from the West will also be vital, in view of the food shortages experienced in urban concentrations and the pauperization of a sizable portion of the country's population. Any help will, of course, be gratefully accepted, regardless of the indignity involved. The mess in which our people find themselves was caused by the ills of the social system inflicted upon them by the leaders. Food supplies and other assistance will, to some extent at least, alleviate dangerous pressures and facilitate the transition to a market economy. However, the aid will not reach those in greatest need without some help in setting up the proper distribution apparatus as well; otherwise, most of it is liable to find its way into the hands of speculators and bureaucrats.

The greatest contribution to our economy's recovery would made by direct investment in enterprises that improve the quality of life, namely, the improvement of product quality, the reduction of losses, the liquidation of acute shortages and the dissemination of high technology. Such investments will not be forthcoming unless backed by safeguards and guarantees, either by governments or by banking institutions. Western governments could be of great help by extending such guarantees and setting up the necessary banking mechanisms.

Of course, until the questions of political instability and inter-republican relations are resolved, potential business partners in the West will, understandably, be constrained. Nonetheless, the West can already provide a tremendous push to the process of Soviet democratization simply by adopting a broad-minded approach. Whatever the form of aid offered (including unilateral grants), it will be solicited not only by entrepreneurs, farmers, infant industries, and democratically elected governing bodies, but also by representatives of reactionary forces whose aim is to preserve old structures and *prevent* the transfer of power from the now defunct Soviet Union to the new democracies. The West must therefore move cautiously.

New Realities in European Policy

The transformation of what used to be the USSR 'empire' into an entirely new entity is bound to bring in its wake critical changes in the political map of Europe and to have serious consequences on a global level. The effects are, of course, impossible to predict, but clearly the victory of democratic forces in Russia, the overthrow of the communist party, and the market-oriented reforms will clear the way for newly independent republics to join forces with the 'family of nations' and enhance global cooperation. But the changes and reforms that have already occurred have not yet acquired the necessary all-embracing impetus. They are inconsistent and sporadic.

The political instability accompanying the decomposition of the Soviet Union is a threat to international security and poses several new problems for the West. How can the West best grasp the historic opportunity presented by the radical changes taking place in the Soviet Union and Eastern Europe? How can it prevent the destabilization of the global situation (especially in Europe)? Only very broad suggestions can be made at this point. The Soviet Union's enormous military might is now less of a threat than before. The republics on whose territory the nuclear arsenal is deployed —Ukraine, Belarus, Kazakhstan—intend to declare themselves nuclear-free zones and to restore their nuclear armaments to Russia. This will lead the Russian leadership to strive for a reduction of strategic nuclear and conventional arms and the liquidation of tactical nuclear weapons. The fact that a major part of the most dangerous arsenal is located within Russian territory and is apparently under the control of the democratic, anti-communist president there, minimizes the risk of any incidents flaring up. Russia is in a position to ensure the strict observance of all the Soviet Union's obligations under international agreements, such as the CSCE framework for control and reduction of arms, safeguarding human rights, and so forth.

The country's international relations are no longer fueled and distorted by an ideological bias with its attendant 'class approach' which so noticeably hindered the achievement of accommodation and compromise in the past and kept the cold war going. It is quite certain that the foreign policy of Russia, Ukraine and other newly independent states will wish to join European civilization and integrate into European and global political and economic structures. This, no doubt, is in full accord with the interests of the West. The integrity and security of Europe is more evident today than ever before; prosperous Western Europe cannot hope to advance any further while cut off from Eastern Europe or from the newly emerging states in former Soviet territory, including the latter's problems and tragedies. If Europe is divided into rich and poor parts, this may create even more problems than its former division into ideologically opposed camps. These pitfalls can be avoided by rendering the necessary assistance.

Whether or not Eastern Europe can be stabilized depends largely on the manner in which ethnic and territorial problems—highlighted by the collapse of the totalitarian system—are settled. Given the weaknesses, inexperience and immaturity of the emerging democracies, these problems can easily escalate into armed conflict, as, for example, in Transcaucasia and in Yugoslavia. The European community faces an extremely difficult task in contributing to the resolution of these conflicts by exercising its powers of mediation.

Obviously, peace in Europe must rest not only on the recognition of nations' right to self-determination within existing borders. It also requires that all states should uphold human rights, including the rights of minorities, and eschew the use of force in settling domestic ethnic problems.

The dissolution of the Warsaw Pact and COMECON has left a vacuum in the European political scene. The Soviet Union has lost its interest in Eastern Europe, while the West is in no hurry to fill the vacancy. But there are signs indicating that the vacuum will soon be filled by new forms of political and economic interaction: Russia is apparently interested in renewing its relations with Czechoslovakia, Poland, and Hungary; the latter countries, for their part, seek a mutual tri-partite alliance in the military-political sphere. They do, indeed, have a great deal in common: They have progressed farther toward market reforms than other former communist states and the relations between them are not clouded by political or territorial disputes. They are therefore capable of setting up a form of regional integration that could eventually be joined by other states such as Lithuania, Latvia and Estonia. Similar tendencies towards alliances on a regional basis can play a positive role in the process of European consolidation.

The situation in other parts of Eastern Europe, however, gives little cause for optimism with respect to such a process of consolidation. A new international system is coming into being, but has not yet stabilized: Germany is reunited, the Baltic states have declared independence, the Soviet empire is falling to pieces, and the federation in Yugoslavia is breaking apart. All of this will eventually lead to an entirely new geopolitical alignment that will require novel approaches to problems of security and economic cooperation.

The bipolar global alignment of powers after World War II placed the two super powers in juxtaposition to one another, and the presence of the United States in Europe was designed to foil the designs of the USSR in that arena. Now that the Soviet threat no longer exists, the role of the United States in Europe (and, for that matter, of NATO) is debatable. Several former Soviet republics, including the Baltic states, are considering joining the EC and NATO (although it is no longer clear whether the threat is from a disintegrating Soviet empire or from Germany). Clearly, the future of our continent, its peace, prosperity and aspiration to evolve into a Common European Home, depend crucially on the process initiated by the Helsinki Accord.

5

Popular Efforts Toward Self-Government: Political, Social and Economic Initiatives in Donetsk

Theodore H. Friedgut

Two interlinked hypotheses underlie the present chapter. The first is that a democratic political system can survive only on the foundation of a developed civil society in which the citizen has numerous roles and numerous interactions with his or her peers, thus reinforcing the social fabric and encouraging stability. The civil society must have a plethora of varied and autonomous institutions within which the individual can find protection from the state. At least some of these institutions must include property rights, giving civil society an economic base independent of state control.[1]

The second hypothesis is that within the political, cultural and historical context of the Soviet Union, only a movement of '*perestroika* from below' can provide such an institutional foundation and expedite the difficult process of developing a civil society. For some time now, I have been pointing out the process of institutional demolition that took place under Stalin, in which nearly all the central political and social institutions of the Soviet Union were either totally destroyed or stripped of their functions, leaving a useless, empty husk. In the words of Franz Neumann, the state became 'peculiarly shapeless'. Whether we speak of elections, the soviets, religious bodies, village and neighborhood meetings, cultural and scientific bodies, or the Communist Party itself—their personnel, agenda, and procedures were controlled from the center, and used to further the purposes of the center, whether that center was Stalin alone, or a consensual Politburo. This does not mean that the state was rendered ineffective; on the contrary, centralized control was highly effective for enforcing the mobilizational priorities of the regime. But the efficiency gained from the functional specialization of institutions was lacking, and the shifting mix of assignments, dominated from the center, almost totally prevented any aggregation of alternative interests, any articulation of alternative viewpoints, and most of all, any truly political contention for public support. Over the years in which such a system was operative, the public at large was effectively denied legitimate experience in autonomous political activity—the defining, articulation and advancement of particular interests. Khrushchev began the repair of some of this damage, restoring the form of many destroyed institutions, and the content of some party bodies. Nevertheless, beyond the limits of the CPSU, society as a whole was still denied any such autonomy of institutions. Under Brezhnev, even the incipient springtime with which Khrushchev had experimented was nipped in the bud, and there was a reversion to the slogan that had ruled even in czarist times, "*Bez kontrolia nel'zia*" [there must be supervision].

It remained for Gorbachev to restore the full functions of political institutions, and the political revolution of *perestroika* finds expression in the effort to transform the Communist Party back into a political party, instead of a controlling administrative elite. In Gorbachev's vision, the Communist Party was to persuade the public of its ideas, rather than impose them by *fiat*. He thought to turn the Supreme Soviet into a full-fledged legislature where party proposals would be subject to open and frank debate; and last but not least, through these two moves, to create a 'political space' in which the Soviet citizen can apply his or her energies to the needs of the society in which he or she lives, organizing, whenever he or she feels the need, into autonomous groupings. It is unlikely that Gorbachev understood from the outset the high costs and risks entailed in this. Almost surely the results have been largely both unintended and unexpected. Nevertheless, I would contend that analysis based on the premise that it was Gorbachev's intention to reform and transform the party and to inspire the citizenry to supportive autonomous participation, provides a coherent and economical explanation of his domestic political policies.

But even without the entrenched resistance of the party apparatus, there would have been a narrow limit to the efficacy of such reform from above. Seventy years of a jealously guarded totalist, often totalitarian, power monopoly have largely destroyed any memory and experience of pluralist politics. Neither the Communist Party nor its newly formed rivals, nor for that matter most of the public, are psychologically or experientially prepared for pluralist politics. Under the influence of the example and the pressures of resentment engendered by the Bolshevik political culture, politics remains a matter of 'winner take all', rather than a process of negotiation and compromise based on the prospect of a repeated circulation of power holders, in which the loser in any particular round retains a legitimate place in politics.

The learning of democratic politics is of necessity lengthy, even unending. Attempting this at a time of acute social frustration, economic deprivation, and overall instability and insecurity is almost certainly doomed to failure. The most promising level at which it can be begun is the grassroots level of face-to-face relations between persons who are interdependent and relate in many different roles; as work-mates, as neighbors, as fellow enthusiasts of sport or culture, in short, in numerous and differing facets of society, and not only as ruler and citizen. This is not to say that reforms at the top are irrelevant. Gorbachev's re-institution of free elections, and his success in having the CPSU renounce its political monopoly and in having the Congress of People's Deputies amend Article 6 of the Soviet constitution, create a legitimate framework for pluralist politics. This is the meaning of the 'political space' of which I spoke earlier. These are necessary steps, but in and of themselves, they are not sufficient.

The Workers' Movement and *Perestroika*

When, in 1987, Gorbachev initiated his support of 'informal organizations' as foci of aggregation for social opinion, the workers of the USSR were not to be left behind. A recent investigation of workers' organizations in the USSR lists close to fifty local, regional and national organizations, ranging from workers' committees in individual enterprises to organizations purporting to be nation-wide in extent.[2] Many of these were short-lived, others, for instance the Workers' Trust group, or the Workers' United Front (*Obedinennyi front trudiashchikhsia*), spread from local origins to a number of cities. Nearly all of them, however, were marked by the fact that they were the creatures of non-workers, intelligentsia or engineers, with workers joining the established groups as individuals and making up a minority of the members. The number of workers actively involved in founding groups was said to be a few dozen in the whole country, while the overall proportion of workers among the members of such groups as Workers' Trust, *Perestroika*, and Democratization of Trade Unions, was put at one third.[3]

Although we deal here only with those groups whose names indicate an orientation to the problems of the working class, not all were in fact so oriented. Some of them arose in the context of particular national groups, and their activities centered around national, rather than class problems. Such, for instance, are the various 'Interfront' groups in the Baltics, in Moldova, and even in the Donbass.[4] This element is of considerable importance since, to date, with the exception of the two great coal strikes of 1989 and 1991, the vast majority of industrial unrest has been linked to ethnic conflict. Indeed, in the first half of 1990 no less than 80 percent of man-days lost were associated with the conflict over Nagorno Karabakh.[5]

Yet these groupings are so disparate and amorphous that their thorough analysis would go far beyond the framework of the present research. More rewarding—from the point of view of evaluating the efficacy of '*Perestroika* from Below'—is the analysis of grass-roots organization in a single community. Here we may trace the development and efficacy of institutions, more easily understanding their influence on society as a whole.

As an object for analysis I have chosen the city of Donetsk, one of the centers of the historic July 1989 coal miners' strike. Here, a purely workers' movement originated and branched out into society over a period of two years.

Donetsk, capital of the Donbass, epitomizes the history, achievements and problems of industrial society in the USSR.[6] In the summer of 1989, its miners joined those of Vorkuta and of the Kuzbass in a two-week strike.[7] Beginning with individual mines forming strike committees, the strikers rapidly created an elected city-wide strike committee that remains in existence to this day. Yet the institutional effects of the strike and its aftermath go far beyond this. They have had a profound effect on the institutions of work at the mines, and within the general framework of *perestroika*, the Donetsk miners, through their new institutions, have been the catalyst of both social and political change in the city of Donetsk, in the Donbass region, and in the Soviet coal-mining profession as a whole.

The first effect of the strike was to establish a new framework of relations of labor and of society in the mines. This was achieved through the revitalization of the Workers' Councils (*Sovet trudovogo kollektiva*) at each mine. These groups, established by legislation in the early 1980s, had been docile havens for conformist supporters of management, the Communist Party and the trade unions. The newly militant workers held new elections, easily ousted the incumbents, and began exercising the STK's rights to elect management and determine many aspects of workers' welfare. In the Kuibishev mine, the STK set up a number of sub-committees to deal with welfare problems of housing, youth and women workers, as well as the standard subjects of working conditions within the mines. While such activities provided an institutional framework for broader participation, they did not, of themselves, guarantee the solution of the pressing problems facing the miners and their families. Faced by a mass of such unresolved questions, the miners sought to learn how to go beyond 'meeting democracy', how to set priorities and how to solve problems. Here, at the initiative of Gennadyi Kush, their chairman and one of the leaders of the mine during the strike, they reached out to intelligentsia, concluding a contract with one of the institutes of higher education in Donetsk, to obtain training and counselling for their active members.[8] In this way, the efficacy, and consequently the stability of the STK and its sub-committees, was enhanced. While not every STK has been as actively innovative, the general atmosphere after the strike has been one of transformation of a formerly empty institution into an active forum of grass-roots democracy and self-government.

More conspicuous in its activities, and better-known, is the independent trade-union activity of the coal miners. Beginning from the mine strike committees and city committees formed during the July 1989 strike, the Donbass miners progressed in August to a regional organization that eventually included representatives of neighboring mining districts. This movement coincided with a similar development in the Siberian Kuzbass and in Vorkuta. The main activity of this group was to supervise the adherence to the agreement with the miners that had ended their strike (government decree 608). At the same time it provided for the testing and emergence of an authoritative local leadership, and the practicing of 'rules of the game' in a local setting. When, in November 1989, the regional committee was split 14–14 on a one-day warning strike protesting non-fulfillment of the strike settlement, no general strike took place, although the Donetsk City Strike Committee took a more militant stand and voted for a two-hour strike of the city's 21 mines, with 800 representatives of the mines demonstrating on the square in front of the Communist Party headquarters. This test of the leadership's skill in negotiation and compromise stood it in good stead when a meeting of representatives of all the regional strike committees fended off an attempt by the *apparat* to co-opt the committees by calling a national Congress of Coal Miners in Moscow, under the auspices of the Ministry of Coal Production and with an organizing committee hand-picked by the minister. Instead, the First All-Union Congress of Miners was held in Donetsk in June 1990.

This meeting was a tough test for the miners. The three main groups of representatives were very differently disposed. The Vorkuta group, representing a small (26,000) but militant constituency, had, from the beginning, raised political demands. The Kuzbass miners (178,000) stood on the middle ground, concerned, because of their difficult living conditions, with civic issues of ecology, food supply and housing, and becoming rapidly more politicized as the local officials of the Communist Party opposed their organizing and reform efforts. The Donbass miners—many of them second and third generation in the mines, living in *relatively* better housing and surroundings, and enjoying a comfortable southern climate—were almost non-political in July 1989, and many of their activists remained Communist Party members until after the 28th Party Congress, supporting the Democratic Platform.[9] The focus of the demands presented by the Donbass miners was a restructuring of the coal industry to give them additional professional and economic security.

Despite these differences, the personality conflicts between the leaders of various groups and the parliamentary inexperience of the delegates that more than once threatened to break up the conference, agreement was reached regarding a framework of continuing activities and an executive committee was elected to prepare a second All-Union Congress at which an independent trade union of coal miners was to be formed. This congress was held from the 24th to the 27th of October, 1990, and set up the independent mine union with an agreed charter, by-laws and a 20-member *buro*.[10] It is this union that coordinated the two-month-long strike that broke out on March 1, 1991. The strike illustrates both the achievements and the limitations of this fledgling union. It achieved coordinated and prolonged action.

While it has not grown into a general coal strike, the union's strike call has commanded the loyalty of close to half the coal workers in the USSR. At the same time, the rawness of the union as an institution, and the lack of specialization of the new and as yet uncrystallized political institutions that are arising under *perestroika* is evident from its demand for the government's resignation and for the resignation of Mikhail Gorbachev, demands that are intertwined with economic and professional grievances. It would appear that what we have here is a case of radicalism driving out realism, which is certainly a characteristic of uninstitutionalized politics. One of the proponents of this extremist stand, a deputy of the USSR Supreme Soviet, urged this political role on the union at its birth, basing his argument on the monopoly of political power and information enjoyed by the CPSU.[11]

Yet in Donetsk neither monopoly remains in the hands of the party. The dispute over the local newspaper, *Vechernii Donetsk* was relatively brief, though often bitter. As in most Soviet localities, the newspaper appeared jointly in the names of the city committee of the CPSU and the Donetsk Municipal Soviet. In the beginning of 1990, under pressure of demands to limit the party's activities and transfer full political power to the city soviet, the Donetsk City Communist Party Committee—the Gorkom—resolved to hand over the paper to the soviet. This was overturned by a party conference after the March 1990 elections resulted in a reform-dominated soviet. Continued pressure by the public and the soviet caused the party to hand the newspaper over to its staff, who now run it as an independent cooperative.[12] One of the reasons for the protracted and bitter resistance of the Communist Party to relinquishing the newspaper is the fact that it is an income-producing enterprise with 138,000 subscribers in addition to newsstand sales and a rapidly growing income from advertising, and its loss deprives the local party group of valuable resources.[13] It may be stated that the party's inability to retain control of the paper is a measure of its declining power in the city.[14] Meanwhile the pluralism of information has been enhanced by the founding of a privately published city newspaper, *Donetskie Novosti* (a clearly commercial newspaper preferring popular content to political and social commentary), and one district committee of the city's Communist Party organization has begun publishing its own newspaper, *Pervaia liniia* (Main Street).[15] It should also be noted that many of the city's 21 coal mines, as well as the steel plant, publish in-house newspapers which are largely in the hands of the STK, featuring discussions on the administration and production of each enterprise as well as frequently reprinting articles on topics such as economic and political reform from major journals and newspapers.

The Communist Party monopoly on information has been shattered in Donetsk. The significance of this is evident if we remember that in the electoral campaign at the beginning of 1990, a 'democratic bloc' of fifteen candidates could not get its program published either in *Vechernii Donetsk* or in *Sotsialisticheskii Donbass*. In addition, the platform and recommendations of the independent Union of Donetsk Voters went unpublished until late February 1990, when a divided session of the Donetsk Regional Party Committee—the *Obkom*—heard bitter complaints of the persistence of 'old thinking'.[16]

Was Obolenskii's urging of direct political roles on the union justified (see fn. 11)? Certainly this is not so if we simply examine the presence or absence of political movements or parties. Donetsk, like the entire USSR, is taking full advantage of the legitimizing of political activity, and enjoys a broad spectrum of groupings. A Social Democratic party was established in Donetsk in June 1990. There exists a 'Popular Movement for the Rule of the Soviets'. In a more serious vein, the city strike committee, and in particular one of its leaders, Iurii Alexandrovich Boldyrev, encouraged the formation of the Union of Donbass Workers (*Soiuz trudiashchikh Donbassa*)—the STD—that has subsequently given its support to the Democratic Platform of the Ukraine. Here the movement that started with the coal miners has found an institutionalized political framework, embracing a broad, interprofessional public. In addition, the Popular Movement of the Ukraine for *Perestroika* (*Rukh*), and its radical offshoot, Democratic *Rukh*, both have active branches in Donetsk. But all these are fledgling institutions, with untested leaders and uncrystallized programs, and as a consequence, are unstable. While they may play an important role in local and republic politics in the future, they had no organizational influence in the election campaign for the local soviets of the region and the Supreme Soviet of the Ukraine held in the early spring of 1990. Even the reform-inclined city soviet has no organized ruling faction, but rather is based on the common desire of the majority to prevent a comeback of the communist apparatus. This is facilitated by the refusal of the majority of deputies who are Communist Party members to have an organized Party faction in the soviet. Once again we may bring evidence of the newness of these institutions, pointing in particular at Democratic *Rukh*, which carries on most of its activities in the streets, and refuses, as a matter of principle, to apply for demonstration permits. In 1990, the group staged 27 such street demonstrations in Donetsk, several of them ending in the arrest of some participants.[17] In addition, the content of their activity reflects a strong particularism, focusing on the Ukraine, and largely ignoring issues concerning the Soviet Union or Donetsk as an economic and social unit.

In the absence of established party identities and loyalties, citizen participation in elections is likely to fluctuate sharply, giving rise to an emotional disillusionment with the new politics. With pressing problems and an entirely new institutional framework, the inexperienced citizen looks for a panacea. Politics is regarded as an event, rather than an ongoing process. While two thirds of the eligible voters turned out for the early rounds of the elections to the local soviets, later run-offs often had difficulty attracting the statutory quorum of 50 percent. In a central district of the city, only 5,514 of 14,445 voters turned out for the third round, blaming empty promises, empty store shelves, and general political fatigue for their fellow citizens' indifference.[18]

Social pluralism has done rather better than has political pluralism. Donetsk is a city of many ethnic groups, and such minorities as Greeks, Germans, Jews, Armenians and Assyrians have all established cultural centers serving their communities. The Jews, the Greeks and the Germans have taken advantage of the policy allowing Soviet minorities to contact co-nationals abroad to establish working relations with their respective peoples. But these groups have also contributed to the city's society and its stability. Each minority, anchored in its own group, is able to relate to others, and together they are able, when there is common need, to submit their needs to the city authorities.

What of the new soviet elected in the beginning of 1990? We will not go into all its trials and tribulations, noting only some of its initiatives toward creating a stable framework of activities and broadening its institutional contacts. Donetsk, a city of over one million, is divided into nine urban districts, each with its district soviet. The relations between them, once sternly hierarchical, are now unclear. The budget process is, of course at the heart of the matter. There have been recurrent meetings between the city manager (chairman of the executive committee in today's local soviets) and executives of the district soviet. "All agree. If life is to be normal, budgets must be built up from below."[19] But social tension in the city is largely a matter of unmet demand for services; for educational, health and recreational institutions, for consumer services and housing, the bulk of which is in the hands of the city and district soviets. The needs are great, and Kuibishev District wants its budget doubled from 13 to 26 million rubles next year. But everyone here who was once a student of public administration remembers that budgets are built on the dual principles of 'fair share and precedent', and by neither of these criteria can such a demand be justified.

An additional problem arises in these conferences. The districts, as the basic links of government, demand taxation rights to meet their needs, with surpluses passed on to the city government for general need. This view is strongly supported by Kuibishev District, which has two large coal mines and a number of ancillary coke and chemical plants within its jurisdiction. But Proletarskii District is a 'bedroom suburb' without the productive enterprises that produce tax revenue, yet as the home of many of the city's workers it needs services. How should tax income be redistributed? The city and district executives are learning together to wrestle with these problems, but both the problems and the executives are largely new, time runs short, the needs are pressing, and the people, as masters, are becoming increasingly impatient. The City Soviet drafted a bill to regulate city-district relations and tabled it with the Supreme Soviet of the Ukraine. The legislation on local government adopted in December 1990 did not, however, reflect the Donetsk Soviet's approach.

But the Donetsk City Soviet is not alone in wrestling with these problems. In June 1990 the soviet initiated a conference of city soviets to work out a common solution for such problems. Twenty cities from three republics attended. At the second conference, held in Volgograd, forty cities attended, representing more republics, and a third conference was scheduled to be held in Sverdlovsk. A common platform of administrative and economic principles was adopted, and an inter-municipal information bank established. This means, for instance, that the experience of Lvov, which is said to have worked out a practicable and economical program for transferring city housing assets to the hands of the citizens, can be easily acquired and examined by other municipalities.[20] The frequency of meetings and their growing attendance attests to the efficacy as perceived thus far, and to a growing stabilization of the institution.

The economic sphere cannot be neglected here. While the general economy of Donetsk is suffering the same shortages and tensions prevalent in the USSR, there are clear signs that the program of de-nationalization, privatization and de-monopolization enunciated by the conference of city soviets is beginning to take form. Here again, *perestroika* from below appears to be the most promising beginning toward guaranteeing a successful transition of Soviet society to a new basis. As in the political sphere, new relations and institutions at the grass roots level are no substitute for macroeconomic policy, and as the economists so forcefully demonstrate, macro reforms are necessary as a foundation for further development. Nevertheless, it may be suggested that they are not only insufficient, particularly at this stage of the Soviet economic crisis, but may well be ineffective without initiative from below. The advantage of initiative from below lies in its small scale and hence in the speed with which it can take effect; its direct contact with the market, making it sensitive to changes in demand, in prices or in supply conditions; and the small amount of capital risked. The limited effect of the small enterprise can be offset by multiplying the units by as many branches and localities as there are entrepreneurs and customers.

What happened in Donetsk? Myriad new businesses appeared; insurance, information, manufacturing and auto repair as cooperatives and as individual private enterprises in a broad range of fields. Half a dozen joint ventures in computer sales, software and applications, and in specialized industrial production have been launched in conjunction with foreign firms. But the key phrase is 'the small enterprise'. Naturally, these are, despite their generally small scale, risky enterprises, given the instability of economic conditions, the social framework that embodies bureaucracy, cultural antipathies and a lack of supportive institutions. But this, too, offers opportunity, so a 'Business League' was formed, providing its customers with up-to-date documentation regarding Soviet laws on business; forms for the registration of small businesses with the authorities; guidance and assistance in the registration process; and seminars on management, marketing and allied skills. In addition, 'Business League' will provide financing, arrange joint ventures and assist in setting up commercial exhibitions.[21]

Do these small businesses make a difference? As with the political parties, it is to soon to tell. Nevertheless, they serve as stimuli and as training grounds, blazing a trail, and proving that such things are possible. Some are mentioned in admiring articles on efficiency, courtesy, and productivity. My personal experience was in noticing the improved quality of women's fashions between 1987 and 1989, and discovering that it was largely due to newly formed clothing cooperatives. In addition, the courtesy, efficiency, and initiative of 'Intertour', a Donetsk travel cooperative that serves local tourism as well as foreigners, far surpasses anything that 'Intourist' ever offered. These suggest that even in the currently limited scale, a significant beginning can be made toward improving the economic environment, particularly as regards provision of everyday goods and services.

But the path to the market is anything but smooth. One aspect is the 'burden of history' mentioned elsewhere in this volume. Immediately after the July 1989 strike, when the Communist Party was seeking a field of demonstrative action to prove its devotion to popular welfare, the prejudice against commercial initiative and self-betterment surfaced in the form of decrees closing down the trading cooperatives that had been formed in the city, on charges that they were speculating and profiteering without producing. Nor does ingrained bureaucratic habit change easily, particularly in the midst of crisis. The city soviet, together with its plans for de-nationalizing and de-monopolizing the city's economy, still maintains its deep involvement in and essential control over the supply and sale of foodstuffs and other consumer goods, passing regulating decrees to prevent out-of-towners from buying in Donetsk and other similar measures. The director of the steel plant still envisages deep involvement in housing, allotment of telephones for his workers, provision of services from the factory budget, etc.[22] The tradition of paternalistic control persists. Perhaps most important of all is the fact that there is no way to privatize the Donetsk coal and metallurgy economy. It is too large and too costly to survive privatization without inflicting a major shock on the entire social fabric of the city. Nonetheless, the market economy is making inroads, and as party conservatives are winkled out of one position after another, the difficulties of innovation ebb, and the prospect of more and more citizens having a personal stake in the future of the city brightens.

The point of this discussion has been to emphasize that change at the bottom of Soviet society appears to have taken place somewhat more than at the top, and to expose for our consideration the prospects and limitations of such change. The Soviet citizen was never instructed to be passive. He had it drummed into him ceaselessly that he was sovereign, that he had unprecedented rights, and that everything done by the state was done for his welfare. He was mobilized into carefully supervised frameworks of activity which he soon learned to regard with apathy as the narrowly constrained institutions that they were. He was well aware that theory and reality were poles apart, yet he retained a sense that this propaganda idyll of citizen competence was, in fact, the way things ought to be.

When Gorbachev removed the limitations and let the Soviet citizen express his desires and grievances, anarchy threatened, for authoritative institutions were lacking. Remember the words of Adam Michnik: "We are free! We can do anything we wish! But we do not know how to rule ourselves." Social frustration generates a high level of political participation, and if this is not contained and channeled within stable, authoritative institutions it becomes a flood of revolution, sweeping away everything in its path. Institutions are not created overnight, particularly when they have been consistently repressed for decades. They must grow from roots of confidence and they need time to mature and develop. It is in this sense that *perestroika* from below is the most promising road to both political and economic recovery in the USSR.

Notes

1. For a Soviet expression of this latter point see Shatalin *et al.* (1990), p. 5. "Property in the hands of each [citizen]—this is the guarantee of the stability of society...."

2. See the listing and analysis in Berezovskii *et al.* (1990), pp. 53–58.

3. Sergei Voronitsyn (1989), p. 9, notes 9, 12.

4. The Donbass 'Interfront' was formed in December 1990.

5. *Pravda vostoka*, August 30, 1990.

6. For the history of the founding and development of Donetsk see Friedgut (1989), and *Iuzovka and Revolution*, vol. 2: Politics and Revolution in Russia's Donbass, 1869–1924 (forthcoming).

7. For an analysis of the strike see Friedgut and Siegelbaum (1990).

8. *Vechernii Donetsk*, April 14, 1990.

9. For examples of this group's beliefs see the stenogram of the enlarged Donetsk *Obkom* plenary session, *Vechernii Donetsk*, February 12 and 13, 1990.

10. *Vechernii Donetsk*, October 27, 1990.

11. Speech of USSR People's Deputy A. Obolenskii at the Second All-Union Congress of Miners, *Vechernii Donetsk*, October 24, 1990. At the same time, the suggestion to create the union was based on the perception that in conditions of a free market economy, the protection of workers' rights and living standards made necessary a trade union independent of management and the state.

12. See the report of the early negotiations in the report of V. M. Krasnov, chairman of the Donetsk City Soviet Standing Committee on Human Rights, *Glasnost'*, Activities of Social and Political Organizations, and Religious Affairs, in

Vechernii Donetsk, June 6, 1990. The announcement of registration of the paper as an independent social and political organ is in *Vechernii Donetsk*, October 19, 1990.

13. For circulation figures see *Sotsialisticheskii Donbass*, November 6, 1990, and *Vechernii Donbass*, June 6, 1990, for reference to the newspaper's profitability.

14. Additional indications of this are the growing number of members resigning from the party, a widespread phenomenon in the USSR today, and the drop in the numbers of letters addressed to the *Gorkom*, 43% less in 1989 than in the previous year. See *Vechernii Donetsk*, March 19, 1990.

15. *Ibid.*, October 31, 1990 and November 2, 1990.

16. See the transcript of the *Obkom* plenary session, *Vechernii Donetsk*, February 12, 1990, speech by Charodeev.

17. *Vechernii Donetsk*, November 12, 1990.

18. *Vechernii Donetsk*, November 2, 1990.

19. *Vechernii Donetsk*, November 2, 1990.

20. *Moskovskie novosti*, No. 39, 1990, p. 2.

21. *Vechernii Donetsk*, November 2, 1990.

22. *Vechernii Donetsk*, October 23, 1990.

References

Berezovskii, Vladimir, Nikolai Krotov and Vladimir Cherviakov. 1990. "From a Workers' Movement to a Working Class Movement," *Dialog*, No. 14, (September): 53–58.

Friedgut, Theodore H. 1989. *Iuzovka and Revolution: Vol. 1. Life and Work in Russia's Donbass, 1869–1924*, Princeton, NJ: Princeton University Press.

—— (forthcoming). *Iuzovka and Revolution, Vol. 2, Politics and Revolution in Russia's Donbass, 1869–1924.*

—— and Lewis H. Siegelbaum. 1990. "The Soviet Miners' Strike, July 1989: *Prestroika* from Below," Carl Beck Papers, University of Pittsbugh Center for Russian and East European Studies, paper No. 804.

Pravda vostoka, August 30, 1990.

Moskovskie novosti, No. 39, 1990, p.2

Shatalin, S. *et al.* 1990. *Perekhod k rinku: konseptsiia i programma* [Transition to the Market: Concept and Program]. Moscow: Arkhangelskoe, p.5.

Sotsialisticheskii Donbass, Nov. 6, 1990

Vechernii Donetsk, April 14, 1990, Feb.12, 13, 1990, October 27, 1990 October 24, 1990, June 6, 1990, October 19, 1990, March 19, 1990, October 31, 1990, Nov. 2, 1990, and Nov. 12, 1990

Voronitsyn, Sergei. 1989. "The Soviet Working Class—the Silent Majority?" *Report on the USSR*, Munich, Vol. 1, No. 28, July 14, p. 9, notes 9, 12.

6

Forced Savings and the Monetary Overhang in the Soviet Union

Carlo Cottarelli and Mario I. Blejer

Introduction

The recorded rate of inflation in the Soviet Union, as measured by official price indices, has traditionally been extremely low. In the period 1960–1980, the retail price index (which reflects largely the prices prevailing in official markets) remained basically unchanged, while it increased by slightly more than 1 percent a year in the past decade. This, of course, reflects the pervasiveness of price controls, which, in all likelihood, prevented markets from reaching their equilibrium levels. This resulted, particularly in recent years, in repressed inflation and scarcities of consumption goods in the official market.[1]

Excess demand in official markets could cause price increases in the parallel markets that would tend to equalize demand and supply for each consumer good. However, if parallel markets are too narrow, incomplete or inaccessible to the large majority of consumers, actual consumption would remain below its desired level, resulting in the emergence of involuntary savings with the consequent accumulation, over time, of a higher-than-desired level of wealth. If a wide menu of financial and real assets is available, this 'wealth overhang' could be allocated across saving instruments of different maturities and terms, and may, in this way, be partly frozen. However, if asset markets are underdeveloped and the variety of financial assets is limited, as in the case of the Soviet Union, forced saving is likely to be accumulated largely in the form of liquid assets (cash and saving deposits). This gives rise to a 'monetary overhang,' which, in the event of price liberalization, would most likely lead to substantial price increases.

In this chapter we first attempt to clarify the concepts of involuntary savings, monetary overhang and repressed inflation, as well as to disentangle the issues involved in defining and identifying them within the Soviet context. Next, we calculate a quantitative measure of the monetary overhang accumulated until the end of 1990, based on an econometric study of consumption behavior and of forced saving. A short discussion of the implications of the findings follows together with an update of developments in 1991.[2]

Analytical Considerations

The concept of repressed inflation, as defined by (among others) Barro and Grossman (1977) and Portes (1989), refers to a situation in which aggregate demand exceeds supply and, therefore, the elimination of price controls and rationing leads to an increase in the average price level. If all excess demand is for consumer goods, rationing implies *forced savings* and an increase in nominal wealth above the desired level. The difference between the nominal stock of wealth actually held and the amount desired in the absence of rationing can be defined as *wealth overhang*. When households' portfolio choice is limited to very liquid assets, as has been the case in the Soviet Union and in most centrally planned economies it is likely that practically all the involuntary increases in the stock of wealth will take the form of higher holdings of monetary balances, which are defined as excess liquidity or *monetary overhang*.

Although the concepts of wealth and monetary overhang have frequently been equated, they only coincide under certain circumstances, mainly when money is the only available store of wealth or when other assets are fixed in price and quantity. This may be the case when regulations and intervention in financial and asset markets severely limit the financial alternatives to monetary assets and restrict the flexibility of their returns.[3]

While in countries with an underdeveloped financial structure such as the Soviet Union wealth and monetary overhangs tend to coincide, their conceptual difference is important and its implications for an appropriate measurement of the overhang are not always fully appreciated. If we admit that the monetary overhang in the Soviet Union is primarily a wealth overhang arising from forced savings, then its measurement will have to be based on the analysis of desired against actual wealth accumulation, i.e., looking at household consumption behavior (Pickersgill, 1980a). It also follows that indicators of monetary disequilibrium that are useful for countries with a developed financial system, such as the deviation of the money-to-income ratio from its 'normal' level, may be misleading in the Soviet Union. In countries where money is held primarily for transaction purposes, a continuous and rapid increase in the money-to-income ratio (i.e., a decline in velocity) is likely to signal the emergence of a monetary overhang, unless it can be explained by changes in payment technology, interest rates, etc., and the measurement of the overhang could be based on the behavior of that ratio (as suggested, for example, in Dornbusch and Wolf, 1990). However, if money is by far the main store of wealth, as in the Soviet Union, the money-to-income ratio could, and should, be interpreted as a wealth-to-income ratio. The extent to which an increase in this ratio signals a disequilibrium will therefore have to be assessed against the factors influencing the desired wealth to income ratio (see pp. 55–56).

There are two further conceptual issues that require attention when analyzing the validity of disequilibrium notions such as wealth and monetary overhang: (a) the role played by unofficial (or parallel) markets in eliminating imbalances, and (b) the observed coexistence, in the presence of price controls, of shortages and slacks in different markets.

The Role of Unofficial Markets

The presence of well-functioning parallel markets, where prices are unregulated, could be inconsistent with the concepts of involuntary savings and monetary overhang if these markets, which could be legal (such as the *kolkhoz* market in the Soviet Union) or illegal, are very widespread and large. If they are accessible to everybody and supply most goods, they will tend to absorb most, if not all, of the excess demand spilling over from the official markets. Prices in these markets will be higher than in official markets, reflecting relative scarcities, transaction costs, risks of operation and expectations about the future evolution of price controls. The relevant price level for the economy would be a weighted average of official and parallel market prices and total expenditure would be equal to desired expenditure, involuntary accumulation of wealth would be zero, and no monetary overhang would be present since the supply and demand for money in real terms would be equal when deflated by the relevant, weighted price level. Indeed, a fully flexible and clearing commodity market contradicts the notion of involuntary savings and undesired monetary holdings.[4]

Such a scenario, however, may not be realistic in many instances, including the Soviet Union. Parallel markets may not be wide enough to supply most of the relevant goods and they may tend to be largely concentrated geographically. Access to these markets and the variety of goods available may be highly discouraged by penal sanctions and by non-competitive practices typical of illegal markets where intimidation and preferential treatment are common. The goods exchanged in the parallel markets would, therefore, be seen only as imperfect substitutes of those exchanged in official markets. In these circumstances, it has been shown by Gardner and Strauss (1981) that the presence of clearing (if limited) markets does not prevent the emergence of involuntary savings.[5] Moreover, if price liberalization is expected in the near future, parallel markets, even if extended enough, may not absorb all of the excess demand from official markets. Households may restrict their buying in parallel markets because the expected relaxation of official price controls would usually lead to a fall in parallel prices. Therefore, when a price reform is expected, parallel markets could easily coexist with the continuous buildup of a monetary overhang.[6] Similarly, one would observe people eschewing parallel markets (and an ensuing buildup of monetary balances) when the supply of goods in the official market is expected to increase significantly in the near future and when the probability of buying these goods at lower prices in the official market increases with queuing.[7]

Although secondary markets in the Soviet Union are fairly large and important,[8] it is unlikely that they could have prevented the emergence of significant monetary imbalances, particularly in recent years. Given the high uncertainty about the quality and timing of goods available in official markets, purchases at much higher parallel prices have been contained, and money is accumulated for 'lucky' purchases in official outlets. Ultimately, however, the clearing function of secondary markets is an empirical question that cannot be easily be answered with the available information. From a policy point of view, however, price liberalization would presumably trigger increases in official prices not likely to be compensated for by a commensurate reduction in parallel prices so as to keep the relevant 'weighted' index unchanged.[9]

Shortages and Slacks

The second issue of analytical interest is the effect of multiple markets on the conceptual validity of macroeconomic rationing. It has been argued that the simultaneous presence of slack and scarcities does not pose any conceptual problem.[10] If, at the prevailing vector of official prices, aggregate demand across all markets exceeds aggregate supply, the economy suffers from repressed inflation in the sense that the absolute level of prices is too low to clear the overall market. At the same time, if excess supply in some markets coexists with excess demand in others, and if the sum of excess supply is equal to the sum of excess demand, this requires an adjustment in relative prices, not in the absolute price level. Note, however, that the simultaneous existence of shortages and slacks creates some problems for the measurement of forced saving.

The observation of an 'abnormally high' level of saving based, for example, on econometric estimates does not necessarily imply the existence of aggregate excess demand, as it can be offset by increased accumulation of stocks of unsold products. Again, the problem might simply be one of relative prices, not of absolute prices. This implies that the potential effect on absolute and relative prices of the undesired accumulation of wealth will have to be evaluated against possible increases in stocks. These comparisons raise complicated empirical issues (the most serious one being that the value of stocks has to be evaluated at the equilibrium price vector, which is not known). Despite the difficulties, it is reasonable to accept the hypothesis that, in principle, the existence of many markets, some of which are possibly characterized by excess supply, does not prevent the measurement of an aggregate disequilibrium.[11] In addition, the overhang estimates reported in the following sections are compared with some available data on the accumulation of unsold consumer goods in the Soviet Union.

Consumption Behavior and Monetary Developments in the USSR

It is a widely accepted notion that households' consumption in the Soviet Union was below the desired level in the second half of the 1980s and that, therefore, savings were being involuntarily accumulated, mostly in the form of monetary balances. There is much less agreement on the nature of consumer behavior and the extent of suppressed inflation before the mid-1980s. In this section, a number of issues related to the debate about repressed consumption in the Soviet Union are reviewed and a summary account of the recent monetary and credit developments underlying the growth of households' disposable income is presented.

How Long Has Consumption Been Repressed?

There is a large body of literature that sustains the view that forced savings and repressed inflation have been a permanent characteristic of all CPEs, including the Soviet economy.[12] According to this view, the existence of some (possibly mild, but chronic) degree of macroeconomic rationing is an essential component of macroeconomic management in CPEs. In the first place, due to the 'soft' budget constraint of enterprises, the wage bill always tends to exceed targeted figures (Winiecki, 1985; Kemme, 1989). Moreover, the wage targets themselves tend to allow some degree of excess demand, because the distribution of purchasing power in excess of what is required to absorb the supply of consumer goods (at desired saving rates) allows policy planners to avoid the risk of insufficient demand for consumer goods (Ofer, 1991). In the second place, the persistence of shortages enhances social discipline: social tensions, for example, could be eased by allowing temporary increases in the supply of consumer goods at the most appropriate moment. Due to this deliberate policy of the authorities, saving therefore tends to exceed its desired level giving rise to a wealth overhang.[13]

It is also often argued that in an economy characterized by chronic shortages, not only are forced savings present but *voluntary* savings also tend to be higher because buyers maintain very high reserves of purchasing power in order to be able to acquire goods that appear in the market sporadically (Kornai, 1980, pp. 457, 458; Schroeder and Severin, 1976; Grossman, 1990). Such a precautionary increase in purchasing power tends to inflate the observed saving rate. This point is important as it implies that the desired level of wealth is not independent of both current and expected shortages in the system. If the shortages were relieved due, for example, to a price liberalization policy, the share of wealth voluntarily maintained for precautionary purposes would become part of the overhang. Therefore, even if empirical evidence shows an absence of forced savings in a shortage economy, it may still be possible that a credible elimination of price controls could raise equilibrium consumption demand, putting pressure on the price level.[14]

Given its nature, chronic excess saving would be difficult to detect even by sophisticated analysis of macroeconomic consumption behavior because it would result in a permanent increase in the average observed saving rate.[15] In order to prove the existence of chronic shortages in the Soviet Union, some authors (e.g., Birman, 1980; Birman and Clarke, 1985; Pindak, 1983; Winiecki, 1985; Nove, 1986) rely mainly on an indicator of stock disequilibrium, namely on the ratio between household monetary holdings and consumption or disposable income.[16] These ratios have indeed exhibited very rapid growth throughout the past 30 years (Figure 6.1) which has been interpreted as indicating an increasing undesired accumulation of monetary balances.[17]

Many authors have challenged this evidence as well as the view that repressed inflation and involuntary savings have always been characteristics of the Soviet economy. The main critique is that, in countries with limited capital markets, money-to-income ratios (such as those reported in Figure 6.1) have a different meaning than in economies with well-developed financial markets. As mentioned on p. 52, in the Soviet Union, money is primarily a store of wealth and therefore its behavior in relation to GDP should be interpreted as a wealth-to-income ratio. Viewed in this way, several factors could explain a voluntary increase in the aggregate wealth-to-income ratio. Ofer (1991) has explained the increase in the wealth-to-income ratio as arising from (a) the expansion of expenditure in durable goods, given the virtual absence of consumer credit, and (b) the deterioration in the quality and availability of public services and social security payments. Moreover, as the level of households' wealth in relation to income or consumption was extremely low at the beginning of the 1960s (compared, for example, with wealth-to-consumption ratios in Western countries), it should not be surprising to observe a steady rise in the desired wealth-to-income ratio (Asselain, 1981; Portes 1989). Finally, a well-known implication of the life-cycle approach to consumption behavior is that, due to aggregation, the equilibrium aggregate wealth-to-income ratio is a negative function of the growth rate of income (see e.g., Modigliani, 1986). Thus, the increase in the wealth-to-income ratio in the Soviet Union may be explained by the deceleration of disposable income growth between the 1960s and the 1980s (Figure 6.2, top panel).[18]

These arguments are quite persuasive and it could be asserted that, before the second half of the 1980s, there seems to be no reason to assume *a priori* the existence of wealth and monetary overhangs; this 'agnostic' view is reflected in the empirical analysis results reported in the next section.[19]

Figure 6.1. USSR: Household Wealth, 1955–1990

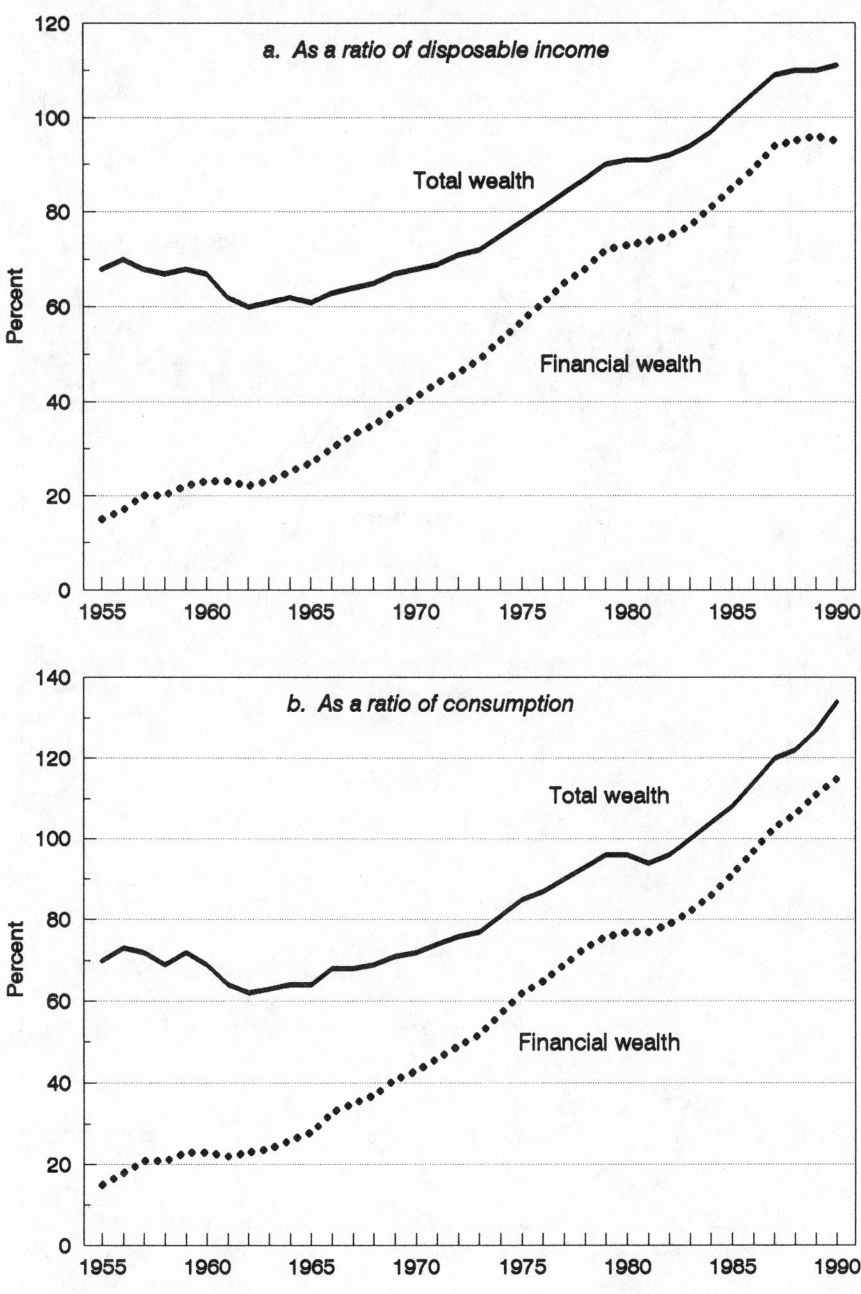

Source: See Appendix.

Figure 6.2. USSR: Disposable Income and Household Savings, 1955–1990

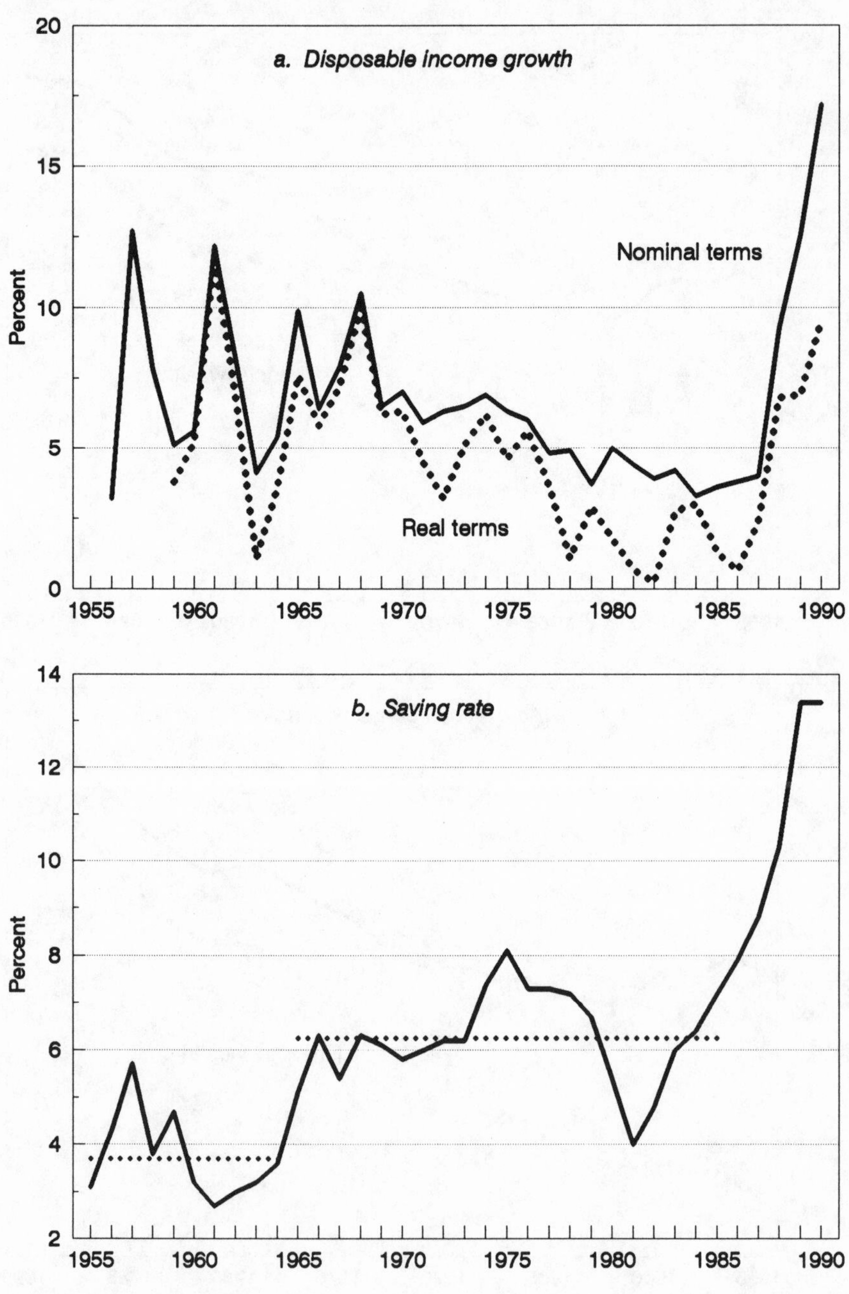

Source: See Appendix.

Monetary and Credit Developments in the 1980s[20]

Two important monetary developments characterized the 1980s. In the first place, the increasing deficits that emerged in the 1980s led to a progressive acceleration in the expansion of bank credit to the government and, in the second half of the decade, to a sharp crowding out of enterprise credit. Second, the last part of the decade saw a strong increase in both household disposable income and savings rates (Figure 6.2), the latter reflecting, as is claimed here, increasingly strong constraints on consumption expenditure. As the decade drew to an end, these two elements, together with the growing freedom granted to enterprises to keep a higher share of their internal resources, combined to produce a picture of overextended monetary credit conditions, which continued to deteriorate in 1990.

The monetary developments over the decade can be broadly separated into three main phases (see Table 6.1).

1. **1981–1985.** The behavior of money and credit in this period reflects the traditional behavior of these variables in pre-*perestroika* Soviet Union: bank credit, both to the government and to enterprises, increased at a relatively fast rate as a consequence of the preeminence given in the plan to investment over consumption. However, by restraining the expansion of nominal (and real) wages, the increase in households' monetary holdings was contained and the counterpart to credit growth was primarily represented by higher balances in enterprises' accounts, that could only be used for specific authorized expenditures. Given the limited liquidity and fungibility of these funds, credit expansion did not have strong expansionary consequences because its monetary impact was effectively blocked.

Table 6.1. Main Monetary and Credit Aggregates in the USSR (average annual growth rates)

	1981–85	1986–87	1988–89	1990	1990[a]
Total bank credit	8.7	5.2	11.2	10.5	902.9
Government credit	8.6	30.4	39.4	16.6	378.0
Credit to the economy	8.7	−2.3	−4.7	4.3	524.9
Money (M2)	7.5	11.6	14.4	15.3	708.8
Households	7.2	9.6	13.1	13.5	555.3
Enterprises	...	18.3	18.4	20.0	153.5

[a] End-of-year stocks, in billions of rubles.

Source: IMF *et al.* (1991).

2. **1986–1987.** This is a short transitory phase that separates the pre-reform period from the full-blown monetary expansion of the late 1980s. The period is characterized by an attempt by the authorities to offset, by curtailing enterprise credit, the rapid acceleration in the bank financing of larger budget deficits (at an annual rate of over 30 percent). As a result, total credit expansion decelerated, as the decline in enterprise credit largely offset the rise in government credit. However, already in this period the rate of growth of broad money (M2) of both households and enterprises accelerated.

3. **1988–1989.** As government deficits started rising rapidly, the squeeze of enterprise credit became insufficient to prevent an overall acceleration of total credit and monetary creation. Credit to the government rose about 40 percent per year, while credit to the economy (enterprises and households) declined only 5 percent. The result was that the growth rate of total bank credit more than doubled with respect to the previous period, averaging over 11 percent a year.

Moreover, despite a tightening in their ability to borrow, enterprises became increasingly liquid since the reforms significantly raised the volume of profits that could be retained and used without major restrictions. This, together with the relaxation of wage constraints, led to an unprecedented growth in wages and a major acceleration in households' income growth, fueling (in the absence of adequate increases in consumer goods) the growth of households' monetary holdings at increasing rates. It is in this last period that the monetary overhang appears to have assumed sizable proportions. This rapid buildup of monetary balances is the culmination of a process of progressive acceleration in the rate of growth of households' financial holdings, which rose from an average of 7 percent in 1981–1985 to 9 percent in the following year, to 13 percent during 1988–1989 (Table 6.1).[21]

Actual and Desired Consumption in the Soviet Union

In view of the discussion above, our measurement of the overhang will be based on the analysis of the behavior of actual and desired consumption. Consumption behavior is analyzed in terms of standard consumption theory.

The Analytical Framework

Standard consumption theory based on the Life-Cycle Hypothesis stresses the proportionality between (desired) households' consumption and households' human and nonhuman wealth (see, e.g., Blanchard, 1985):

$$C^d = A(W + H) , \tag{1}$$

where C^d is household consumption,[22] W is nonhuman wealth,[23] H is human wealth,[24] and A is the equilibrium ratio between consumption and wealth, which will depend on a set of variables affecting the intertemporal distribution of present resources. We assume that A can be expressed as

$$A = b_0 \exp(X\mathbf{b}), \tag{2}$$

where **b** is a vector of coefficients and X stands for a set of variables that affect consumption behavior and that will be detailed below. Equation (1) assumes a unitary wealth elasticity of consumption; moreover, it is based on the hypothesis of an equal effect of human and nonhuman wealth on consumption (i.e., that the composition of total wealth is irrelevant and only the total matters[25]).

In order to allow for more flexibility in the empirical specification of consumption behavior we assume, instead, that

$$C^d = A(W + H)^{a_1} W^{a_2}, \tag{3}$$

where a_1 and a_2 are parameters. Of course, if $a_1 = 1$ and $a_2 = 0$, equation (2) collapses to equation (1). In addition, in order to reduce the collinearity between regressors, it is convenient to write (3) as

$$C^d = A(1 + H/W)^{a_1} W^{a_1 + a_2}. \tag{4}$$

Consider now the possibility that even in the absence of a limited supply of consumer goods and of sticky prices, observed consumption differs from desired consumption. Without loss of generality, the relation between actual and desired consumption can be written as

$$C = C^d R \qquad 0 < R < 1, \tag{5}$$

where C is actual consumption and R is the ratio of unrequited consumption. Note that R is, of course, equal to one in the absence of disequilibrium and, as long as C is measured exactly, it reflects all possible forms of forced substitution, including purchases in the black market.[26] For the sake of generality, we express R in the following way:

$$R = c_0 \exp(c_1 IR), \tag{6}$$

where c_0 and c_1 are positive and negative constants respectively, and IR is an observable variable which is an increasing function of the degree of rationing. Equation (6) thus allows for the presence of macroeconomic rationing embodied in an unobservable component (i.e., $c_0 \neq 1$) that remains approximately constant in relation to consumption.[27] We assume that c_0 incorporates possible *voluntary* shifts of consumption due to the existence of rationing at the micro level (due, for example, to increasing precautionary saving as argued by the 'chronic rationing' school). IR (the rationing indicator) is, in our case, the ratio between the price level in the nonofficial market (specifically in the *kolkhoz* market) and in the official market (weighted or unweighted for the size of the *kolkhoz* market with respect to official markets), which is assumed to increase with the level of rationing. It is, therefore, implicitly assumed that the *kolkhoz* market is extended enough to provide a reliable indicator of excess demand, but is not sufficient (especially because of the limited number of products supplied) to eliminate excess demand at the macro level.

By substitution of (2), (4) and (6) into (5) we finally obtain (in log form):

$$\log C = (\log b_0 + \log c_0) + a_1 \log(1 + H/W) + (a_1+a_2)\log W + X\mathbf{b} + c_1 IR \,. \tag{7}$$

It remains to specify the variables, included in X, assumed to affect consumption behavior. The following four variables were considered:

a. The real interest rate on deposits;[28] given the low level of private wealth in the Soviet Union, the expected sign of this variable is negative as the substitution effect prevails over the income effect.
b. The 'dependency ratio', defined as the ratio between the nonworking population (children below 16 years of age and pensioners) and the remaining population. This is expected to have a positive sign, as a large number of children and old people imply a high share of people with relatively low saving rates.
c. The 'benefit ratio' defined as the ratio between Social Consumption Fund benefits (mainly pensions and other grants) received by each nonworking member of the population and the wage rate. This has an expected positive sign, as high nonlabor incomes reduce the need to accumulate savings.
d. The inflation rate, with an expected negative sign, as high inflation reduces the real value of accumulated wealth, which has to be restored by increased saving.[29]

A dynamic specification was postulated, assuming a slow adjustment of consumption to changes in wealth; in particular, the following 'quasi-error-correction mechanism' was adopted:

$$\begin{aligned} \mathrm{Dlog}(C) = d_0 + d_1 \log(W/C)_{-1} + d_2 \log(1 + H/W)_{-1} \\ + Xd + d_3 IR + d_4 \mathrm{Dlog}(Y) \,, \end{aligned} \tag{8}$$

where Y is disposable income and D is the first difference operator.

In the above framework the difference $C^d - C = S - S^d$ represents forced saving, which, when excluding the unobservable chronic component of rationing, c_0, can be measured from the estimates of (8). To move from the definition of flow disequilibrium (forced saving) to that of stock disequilibrium (the wealth overhang), note, first, that the choice of desired consumption involves a choice of (end-of-period) desired wealth; calling W^d desired end-of-period wealth, and in the absence of capital gains, we obtain:

$$W^d = W_{-1} + S^d(W^d_{-1}, H, \ldots) \tag{9}$$

where $S^d = Y - C^d$.[30] Thus, if desired saving is smaller than actual saving, actual wealth will be higher than desired wealth, i.e., there will be a wealth overhang at the end of the period.[31] We now define the overhang at time t as the difference between actual wealth holdings and the amount of wealth that would have been held in the absence of current and past forced saving. This is given by

$$OV_t = W_t - W_t{}^d = W_t - W_0 - \sum_{j=1}^{t} S_j{}^d = \sum_{j=1}^{t} S_j - S_j - S_j{}^d \,, \tag{10}$$

where W_0 is the initial value of wealth (i.e., the value of wealth before the first period of rationing). Note that if in any of the periods between time 0 and t actual saving is lower than S^d,[32] the overhang will be reduced.

Assume now that we have an estimate of all parameters of equations (7) and (8), including a judgmental estimate of the breakdown of the constant allowing for the identification of c_0 (the 'chronic overhang'). Desired saving could be obtained through a dynamic simulation of the equation over the complete period, starting at a point in which the overhang is considered to be zero or small,[33] and the parameters reflecting the amount of rationing c_0 and c_1 are set to zero. The cumulative sum of desired saving (*plus* the initial value of wealth) represents the desired level of wealth. Comparing this level with actual wealth, as in equation (10), it is possible to evaluate the stock of the wealth overhang at any given date.

In order to evaluate the monetary overhang, the first step is, therefore, to estimate equation (8). As that equation takes the possibility of rationing explicitly into account, *in principle*, there is no need to exclude from the estimation period years in which rationing was considered to be strong (such as in the late 1980s). It was found, however, that estimating equation (8) over the entire range of available data, including the second half of the 1980s, yielded poor results. More specifically, it was clear that the parameter reflecting the degree of observable rationing (d_3) was not stable. This indicated the existence of a structural break, probably due to an increasing degree of rationing.[34] The above procedure for the measurement of the overhang was therefore modified as follows: first, equation (8) was estimated in a period in which behavioral parameters appeared to be stable. The sample period included 1964–1985, and the estimated equation was then used to simulate over the entire data sample (including the late 1980s) the behavior of desired consumption (after setting the rationing coefficients, if significant, to zero in the estimates); forced saving was finally measured as the difference between actual and desired saving.

Estimates of Households' Consumption Function, Wealth and Monetary Overhang[35]

As discussed above, the wealth overhang can be derived by cumulating excess saving which, in turn, can be obtained as the difference between desired and actual consumption. The first step therefore involves the estimation of a consumption function along the lines of equation (8). After performing substantial specification searches and estimating a large number of variations of potential consumption behaviors, including and excluding different variables, it was concluded that consumption behavior between 1964 and 1985 could be adequately represented, on the basis of both fit and diagnostic tests, by a relatively simple representation of the following form: (t values in parentheses):

$$\begin{aligned} D\mathit{log}C &= \underset{(2.83)}{-1.39} + \underset{(2.84)}{0.41}\mathit{log}(W/C)_{-1} \\ &+ \underset{(2.84)}{0.41}\mathit{log}(1 - H/W)_{-1} + \underset{(11.50)}{0.85}D\mathit{log}Y \end{aligned} \tag{11}$$

Adjusted R^2	0.90	Heteroskedasticity 2	46.9%
Standard error	0.0075	Chow test	92.2%
Normality	67.7%	Variance ratio test	26.6%
DW	1.56	Generalized Chow test	94.1%
MLM	46.7%	Harvey's PS1 (forward)	−1.22
Ljung-Box	44.6%	Harvey's PS1 (backward)	0.99
Heteroskedasticity 1	58.4%	F test on $d_1 = d_2$ (eq. 8)	48.2%

Some of the properties of this equation deserve further comment.

a) The specification implies a stable long-run relation between consumption behavior and the total (i.e., human and nonhuman) wealth of the household sector. As the elasticity of consumption with respect to wealth is one, the long-run marginal and average propensities to consume are equal. Moreover, it has been shown that (as $d_1 = d_2$) changes in human and nonhuman wealth have the same effect on consumption. As to the dynamic properties of the equation, the fact that the coefficient of the change in disposable income is 0.85 implies that the short-run effect of income changes, possibly because they are not perceived as permanent, is lower than the long-run effect; this can explain why, in years of strong decline in real disposable income (such as 1981–1982), the saving propensity tended to be low (Figure 6.2). Moreover, as the nonhuman wealth variables enter only in lagged form, changes in human wealth tend to affect consumption faster than changes in nonhuman wealth.

b) While for empirical purposes the behavior of consumption can be considered as dominated by disposable labor income movements,[36] the specifications in which consumption is related to human and nonhuman wealth appear to dominate those in which only disposable income is included.

c) The selected specification (reported above) is relatively parsimonious as it explains the movements in consumption simply in terms of wealth and disposable income movements, without making use of additional variables. The failure to identify additional effects, including the impact of rationing, may, of course, be due to the absence of sufficient variability of some of the other regressors included in the specification search, or to measurement problems. However, the fact that the estimated model produces a remarkable fit and generates small i.i.d. residuals indicates that *within the sample period* the main movements of consumption expenditure in the Soviet Union can be explained without the use of additional variables.

d) The possible existence of some 'chronic' rationing will have to be taken into account judgmentally in the measurement of the overhang.

As the selected equation reported above does not include any rationing proxy, it can be concluded that desired and actual consumption were equal during the sample period, i.e., that there was no overhang (save, possibly, for a chronic overhang component). It can also be shown that the estimated consumption function presents a high degree of parameter stability during the sample period. However, as we move toward the second half of the 1980s, it becomes clear that the relation between *observed* consumption and the regressors included in the preferred equation progressively breaks down.

In this respect, Figure 6.3 reports the one-step-ahead prediction errors of equation (11):[37] these errors are consistently negative, implying that actual consumption is lower than projected consumption outside the sample period (and exceeds the two standard errors band as of 1987). To test formally for the existence of instability, the equation was re-estimated over

Figure 6.3. USSR: One-Step-Ahead Prediction Errors[a]

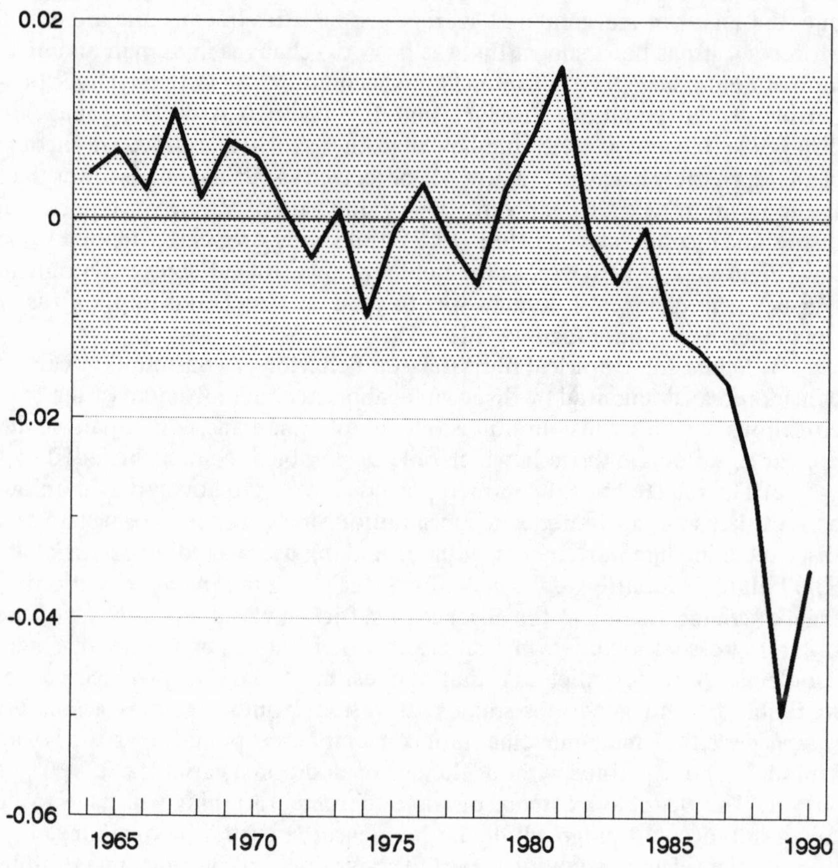

[a] Shaded area marks the two-sided standard error band.

1964–1990 and the hypothesis of parameter stability (against that of a structural break in 1985) was evaluated by a Chow test. The value of the test statistics (7.64) falls beyond the critical value even at the 0.5 percent level.

This instability may be due to three reasons. First, the structural relation determining desired saving may have changed; more specifically, Soviet households substantially increased their propensity to save. Second, as unrecorded consumption transactions in parallel markets increased, measurement errors may account for the apparent increase in saving rates.[38] Finally, actual consumption differed from desired consumption because of rationing. Clearly, there is no statistical basis to attribute the behavior of projection errors in the second half of the 1980s to one of the above specific reasons. However, we find the third reason more plausible. Consumption behavior remained particularly stable in the Soviet Union over two decades, and it is hard to explain why, in the absence of rationing, it should have changed in such a drastic manner. As to the second reason, the expansion of consumption on secondary markets may have been relevant, but it is at least partly taken into consideration by the use of adjusted figures for income (see Appendix). In conclusion, the strengthening of rationing appears the most likely reason for the 'oversaving' that characterized the late 1980s. It is therefore assumed that all the projection errors observed outside the sample period are due to forced saving.[39]

Assuming now that there was indeed a break in the consumption function around 1985, the cumulated value of forced saving at the end of 1990 could be derived as the sum of the differences between the consumption projected by equation (11) and actual consumption. Following this procedure, the cumulative sum of forced saving at end 1990 reached Rbl 115 billion. This, however, does not include the possible presence of a 'chronic overhang', i.e., undesired savings that were present in the system before 1985. Consideration of a possible overhang has to be entirely judgmental; the only indication of its possible existence is derived from surveys of household saving and wealth conducted by the Soviet authorities: according to these surveys, the stock of involuntary monetary savings at the end of 1985 was Rbl 59 billion. By adding these estimates to the accumulated volume of undesired savings after 1985 we could estimate the total wealth overhang at the end of 1990 at about Rbl 174 billion.[40]

The above estimate would be equivalent to about 31 percent of the actual stock of financial wealth of households at the end of 1990, and to 45 percent of the desired stock. Note that it is convenient to compare the wealth overhang with the financial component of wealth (rather than with total wealth), because this is the component subject to erosion in case of price liberalization. In particular, the ratio between the overhang and *desired* financial wealth represents the increase in the price level necessary to wipe out the monetary overhang (under the hypothesis that the desired amount of wealth in real terms is independent from the price level[41]).

Three observations must be made with reference to these results. First, lack of consideration of the effect of past inflation on the value of real wealth may imply that the above figures overestimate the size of the overhang. On the other hand, the overhang may be underestimated if expectations of future price increases actually led to an increase in the current propensity to consume, an effect not measured by the estimated equation. Next, as noted in Section 2, the size of the overhang should be compared to the stock of unsold consumer goods. Data on this amount show a very rapid decline in the past twenty years; the estimated stock was Rbl 62 billion in 1970, Rbl 31 billion in 1985, and Rbl 15 billion at the end of 1989, a very modest proportion of the overhang.

This finding confirms that, in the presence of price liberalization, the overhang would not lead simply to a change in relative prices (e.g., to a decline in the price of the unsold inventories of consumer goods and to an increase in the price of the goods for which shortages are observed) but it would bring about an increase in the average price level. Finally, it must be recalled that the reported estimate of the overhang refers to the cumulative sum of involuntary saving incurred in the past.

Under normal circumstances (i.e., assuming stability of past behavior, as summarized by the estimated equations), Soviet households are unlikely to try and spend all the undesired accumulation of wealth in a single period (say, one year). According to the life-cycle behavioral hypothesis they should allocate the expenditure of the undesired stock of wealth over time. Of course, a quantitative estimate of 'how rapidly' the overhang would be released in the presence of price liberalization is extremely difficult to make; it would depend on the type of consumption forsaken in the past, on price expectations and on the extent to which price liberalization is seen as a temporary or permanent situation.

Having defined and measured the *wealth* overhang of households, let us consider the issue of evaluating their *monetary* overhang. This is equivalent to asking whether the composition of wealth (specifically its distribution between monetary and nonmonetary assets) resulted mainly in the accumulation of money or of other stores of value. Indications of this appear in Table 6.2, describing the evolution in the composition of households' wealth and savings.

The table shows the trend increase in the financial component of total wealth, almost entirely matched by a decline in the share of housing. While this decline may be influenced to some extent by miscalculations in the valuation of houses at current prices,[42] the increased role played by financial wealth is confirmed by the data on the allocation of saving flows. Whereas between the mid-1950s and the mid-1960s investment in real assets represented around one third of total saving, in the following period this percentage fell below 10 percent, mainly as a consequence of the decline in the share of private housing investment.

Table 6.2. USSR Composition of Household Wealth and Savings (percent)

	1955–1959	1960–1964	1965–1969	1970–1974	1975–1979	1980–1984	1985–1989
Wealth[a]							
Net financial wealth	32.7	40.4	57.1	70.7	79.9	83.3	87.2
Houses	62.4	53.5	34.3	22.9	15.1	11.7	9.0
Other real assets	4.9	6.1	8.6	6.5	5.0	5.0	3.9
Total	*100.0*	*100.0*	*100.0*	*100.0*	*100.0*	*100.0*	*100.0*
Saving[b]							
Net financial wealth	66.7	65.8	84.9	89.8	93.0	90.4	91.9
Houses	28.8	29.8	9.4	5.9	3.7	4.9	6.1
Other real assets	4.5	4.4	5.7	4.3	3.3	4.7	2.0
Total	*100.0*	*100.0*	*100.0*	*100.0*	*100.0*	*100.0*	*100.0*

[a] Composition of wealth at the end of the period.
[b] Average composition of saving during the period.
Sources: See Appendix.

In the beginning of the 1990s, the composition of households' wealth is clearly biased towards financial assets, accounting for around 90 percent of both total wealth and savings.[43] In addition, financial wealth is almost entirely represented by monetary assets; throughout the period under review, M1 components (cash and demand deposits) always represented around two-thirds of total financial assets; and M2 components (including M1, time deposits and lottery bonds[44]) stood at slightly above 90 percent.

The main conclusion from these data is that given the limited share of the real component of saving in the past 20–25 years, the involuntary accumulation of saving has almost certainly been in the form of financial (specifically monetary) assets. In addition, in light of the size of the imbalance between monetary and nonmonetary wealth, it is likely that even in the absence of involuntary saving (wealth overhang), the monetary overhang would be substantial: the amount of monetary assets held by the Soviet population appears to exceed the amount likely to be demanded if other assets (both real and financial) were freely available. This has two implications: the demand for nonmonetary components of wealth may be high in the Soviet Union and may be exploited to bring about a non-inflationary, voluntary reduction in monetary holdings; and the absence of adequate forms of investment may have discouraged households' savings in the past. Thus, the availability of new forms of investment may stabilize the saving rate and transform an involuntary accumulation of wealth into voluntary holdings.

Conclusion and Update

Approximately in the middle of the 1980s the stable relation between consumption and wealth in the Soviet Union broke down as actual consumption consistently fell short of projected consumption. This development is attributed primarily to macroeconomic rationing in the consumers' goods market. The amount of undesired wealth holdings at the end of 1990 was estimated by cumulating the difference between desired and actual consumption. It was concluded that the undesired holdings of monetary balances in the Soviet Union (including an estimate of the 'chronic' overhang accumulated before the mid-1980s) amounted to around Rbl 175 billion at the end of 1990, close to 20 percent of GDP and about one-third of existing financial assets.

In assessing the macroeconomic consequences of these estimates it is important to bear in mind that they refer exclusively to households' involuntary savings. Estimates of excess liquidity in the hands of increasingly decentralized enterprises ranged between 80 and 90 billion rubles by the end of 1990.[45] The combined magnitude of this imbalance represents a volume of pent-up demand that is certainly an element of concern in the design of any stabilization package. Even if flow balance could be reached, i.e., if the expansion of monetary income is kept in line with the developments in production and fiscal policies are adjusted accordingly, the problem of the current overhang stock remains to be dealt with.

The most meaningful interpretation of the overhang, in a policy sense, is its translation into price increases once price liberalization takes place. The above estimates indicate that if prices had been liberalized by the end of 1990 the very first round price effects could have been in the range of 45–50 percent.[46] Liberalization did not take place, of course, and developments in 1991 have changed both the magnitude of the problem and its expected consequences when prices are finally decontrolled. Given the current radical changes in the former Soviet Union it is highly likely that further disruptions are taking place in the behavioral functions and, therefore, even if the necessary data were available, estimates using the same methodology may be neither appropriate nor quantitatively precise. Some observations could be made, however, in view of the developments in 1991.

The most relevant developments for the assessment of the magnitude of the problem include the following:

a. At the beginning of 1991 the Soviet government retired large-denomination bills from circulation. After significant pressure, many exceptions were allowed and the net result is estimated by Gosbank to have been a reduction of liquidity of no more than Rbl 4 billion, or slightly more than 2 percent of the initially estimated overhang.
b. Over the first 10 months of 1991, cash in circulation increased more than 60 percent, from 136 billion to 219 billion rubles.[47]
c. Household saving deposits increased 58 percent in the first 9 month of the year, from 387 billion to 612 billion rubles. This includes Rbl 31 billion in compensation for the April price rises.[48]
d. As a whole, total household financial assets increased by about 68 percent over the first ten months of the year.
e. Following the price increases in April 1991 and the de-facto liberalization of many prices (e.g., through the generalization of contract prices), it is estimated that by the end of September 1991 the General Retail Price Index (which is the official index reflecting state store prices and collective-farm markets, but excludes cooperative stores and free market transactions) increased about 70 percent. Wholesale price index (producer prices, including contract prices) increased 120 percent.
f. The volume of transactions (in physical terms) in the free market seems to have remained constant. But given the sharp reduction in production (estimated at about 10 percent), this implies more leakages from official markets and, therefore, a lower share of the latter in the total volume of transactions. This is not reflected in the above-mentioned indices.
g. There has been an expansion in the use of dollar bills for internal transactions. Although there are no precise figures, it is thought that about US$ 2 billion are held by households at this time.
h. Enterprise deposits also increased sharply. This reflects an aggregate increase in enterprise profits of about 80 percent (reflecting, among other things, the spread of transactions at contract prices). Enterprise deposits also became more liquid, in the sense that they could be more freely used, but the generalized shortage of cash in the country has led to the emergence of a 'cash market' for enterprises where deposits are sold, for cash, at a discount (currently about 25–30 percent).

The meaningful conceptual interpretation of the overhang is its potential impact on *official* prices once they are deregulated. In this sense, it is apparent that, in terms of official retail prices,[49] the real amount of highly liquid financial assets has not changed significantly. This would imply, *ceteris paribus*, a current overhang of a similar *real* magnitude as at the end of 1990 (roughly Rbl 400 billion). It is highly likely, however, that in view of the facts described above, the monetary overhang, defined in these terms, is now larger than at the end of 1990. This assertion could be sustained on the base of the probable evolution of both actual and desired velocity.[50] In order to assess these developments it should be considered, first, that there has been a forced decline in velocity, implied by the acceleration in liquidity expansion in the face of declining output.[51] At the same time it is reasonable to assume that, in view of growing uncertainty about inflationary developments, currency reforms, and the monetary status of the various republics, desired velocity may have increased considerably. These two opposite trends could widen the gap between desired and actual liquidity holdings, compounded by the apparent spreading of currency substitution (dollarization) that further reduces the value of the ruble as a transaction mechanism. In addition, the increase in volume and liquidity of enterprise deposits may, through a number of indirect channels, be increasing the pressure in consumer markets. Probably offsetting some of these effects is the increased share of consumer transactions performed through the free and cooperative markets. It is possible that desired wealth and the demand for financial assets is increasingly being evaluated by households in terms of a price index that combines official and free market prices rather than in terms of prices and goods availability in state shops. This implies a lower perceived real value of households' wealth and therefore a lower level of repressed consumption.

All things considered, it is highly improbable that the current overhang could be more than 50 percent of total household financial assets even if desired velocity has indeed already increased, and this would imply that the initial rise in the price level needed to restore *stock* balance to the money market should not exceed 70–75 percent. Under the current circumstances, however, it is reasonable to assume that price increases would not be limited to the initial adjustment and that the process could rapidly degenerate into an inflationary spiral fed by further increases in velocity arising from self-fulfilled expectations. This outcome is likely to take place if price liberalization is accompanied by widespread implicit and explicit indexation, lax credit policies and the monetary validation of fiscal imbalances. Such imbalances, in turn, could be further exacerbated by the inflationary process itself if the budget has to bear the cost of incomplete price reforms (e.g., in the form of continued increases in consumer subsidies) and when budgetary resources do not increase in line with the burden of social-protection programs.

Notes

1. In addition, it is likely that official price indices underestimate the actual price increases in official markets. 'Hidden' inflation may occur because official price lists lag behind actual prices or changes in the quality and characteristics of goods sold in official markets. See Nuti (1989).

2. An econometric approach similar to the one reported here, as well as a discussion on the monetary overhang of Soviet enterprises is presented in IMF *et al.* (1991).

3. Of course, a monetary overhang can also exist in the absence of a wealth overhang, as when total wealth is equal to desired wealth but the composition of wealth is sub-optimal (and biased toward money).

4. It has been claimed that this is the case in many CPEs where parallel markets are common. See Nuti (1989) and Grossman (1977).

5. Relative to the level of savings that is expected to prevail in the absence of price controls in the official markets.

6. Such overhang is, however, 'voluntary' in the sense that it arises from speculative reasons and not only from current commodity scarcities.

7. If official allocations are not implemented through coupons but rather by queuing, and the probability to obtain the desired good is, for each individual, larger than zero, households may prefer to delay their purchases and queue longer (at the same time accumulating more undesired balances) rather than pay the higher parallel market prices.

8. The kolkhoz market and the private supply of housing services (particularly housing construction) are the most important legal parallel markets in the Soviet Union (Grossman, 1977). Official data on expenditure and consumption partly take into account economic activity outside the state sector, but exclude incomes from illegal activities entirely.

9. In the empirical estimations, partial consideration of parallel markets is given by using adjusted (instead of official) data on consumption and prices. To the extent that this is not sufficient to take into account the role of parallel markets, indications on the effect of unreported transactions on the estimate of the overhang are also provided.

10. See, for example, Portes and Winter (1980).

11. It has been argued, instead, that the concept of aggregate disequilibrium is not well defined in economies where chronic shortages are pervasive (Kornai, 1980, 1982). According to this view, in an economy in which shortages are chronic, forced substitution is widespread: households that cannot obtain the commodities that they seek will buy substitutes and will not, generally, involuntarily increase their savings. If this is, indeed, the case, it would be correct to say that there is *no overhang* because income is always spent anyway. There would of course, be an involuntary component in consumption behavior since household utility is clearly affected by the distortions in the desired expenditure basket, but there would be no accumulation of undesired balances.

12. For an extensive discussion of the debate about the existence and extent of repressed inflation in the CPEs see the surveys by Davies and Charemza (1989a), Portes (1989), and Van Brabant (1990).

13. Note that according to this view, households cannot react to excess saving by reducing their labor supply, given the structural rigidities characterizing labor markets in CPEs.

14. It could be argued, however, that precautionary savings may actually rise in the wake of systemic reforms if these imply increasing uncertainty regarding employment, social services, etc.

15. This point is similar to that raised by Kornai (1982), p. 35.

16. Other indicators, not available for the Soviet Union, have been used for other CPEs. Kornai (1982), for example, suggests considering the number of people queuing for officially allocated housing, the time invested in search for goods and the physical length of queues.

17. A second indicator of repressed inflation, sometimes used for the Soviet Union, is the ratio between secondary (*kolkhoz*) market and state prices; this ratio shows a continuous increase in the last 30 years, accelerating at the end of the 1980s (Figure 6.2, top panel) which has been taken as indicator of chronic excess demand (Nove, 1986, p. 255, for example). However, as indicated by Holzman (1960), repressed inflation should be measured by the secondary/official price ratio weighted by the share of *kolkhoz* market expenditure in total consumer expenditure. When this is done, there is no visible trend in the ratio over the period discussed here (Figure 6.2, bottom panel).

18. Note also that if we took the money-to-income ratio as an indicator of a monetary overhang we would have to conclude not only that the overhang accumulated throughout the past 30 years, but also that its rate of growth did not accelerate in the second half of the 1980s, which is hardly credible in light of well-reported phenomena of increased rationing characterizing the most recent years.

19. Previous econometric analysis of consumption behavior in the Soviet Union also reached ambiguous conclusions on the state of the consumption-goods market before the 1980s. Pickersgill (1976) finds that consumption behavior between 1955 and 1971 can be explained mainly by movements of disposable income without the use of proxies for rationing effects. However, Pickersgill (1980b and 1983) identifies the existence of a structural break in consumption which occurred in the middle of the 1960s (reflected in the increase of the saving rate; see Figure 6.2); she suggests that this break is due to rationing effects.

20. For complete details of recent developments and a discussion of the evolution of monetary institutions in the Soviet Union see IMF *et al.* (1991), Vol. I, Chapter III.2 (pp. 359–377) and Vol. II, Chapter IV.5 (pp. 107–137).

21. In addition, in the later period there was a marked shortening of maturities, as the most liquid components, namely demand deposit and currency, rose more rapidly than saving deposits and bonds. This represents a change in the trend observed during the previous two decades, since until 1987 the composition of households' financial assets had shifted decisively towards longer maturities. This 'flight to liquidity' may be a symptom of increasing uncertainty (including the fear of administrative measures against bank deposits), or it may reflect a precautionary demand for cash in the context of an increasingly scarce and unpredictable supply of goods.

22. In our definition, consumption includes consumer durables. This is an approximation. In theory, one would like to include in consumption only the value of the 'services' obtained from the current stock of consumer durables; in this case,

wealth could be defined as including consumer durables. Lack of adequate data on consumer durables, difficulties in estimating the value of their services and uncertainty as to the inclusion, especially in a country like the Soviet Union, of consumer durables as components of wealth, led to the specification reported in the text.

23. As detailed in the Appendix, wealth is defined as the sum of financial wealth (currency, bank deposits, government bonds and insurance policies net of households' borrowing), plus houses and other real wealth (mainly livestock and other property held by rural households). The value of wealth at the beginning of the period is considered for each time period.

24. Human wealth is defined as the present discounted value of disposable labor income; this has been computed by adding to a three-period centered moving average of current disposable labor income the discounted expected stream of income in the next 27 years; in this respect, it is assumed, for simplicity, that per capita real income was projected to grow at a constant annual rate of 2.5 percent (close to the average for the sample period 1965–1985, considered in the estimates); the average interest rate on bank deposits was used as discount factor. The 27-year interval was been selected in the following way: the average expected life *at birth* of the population in the Soviet Union has been close to 69 years throughout the sample period (see Kingkade, 1987, p. 11). Assuming an average expected life-time of 72 years for the population age 18 (taken as average starting year of working life), 27 (= (72−18)/2) is the average number of years for which a middle-aged worker expects to receive labor income (including pension payments) for the rest of his/her life.

25. The most obvious reason why this may not be the case is that, in the absence of (efficient) capital markets, households cannot borrow against future labor income and that, as a consequence, an increase in human wealth has a more contained effect on consumption than an increase in nonhuman wealth. It must be recalled, however, that this aspect becomes relevant only in the presence of liquidity constraints, i.e., when desired consumption (based on human and nonhuman wealth) exceeds the amount of resources available in the current period. Therefore, we cannot *a priori* rule out the possibility that even in the absence of efficient capital markets (such as in the Soviet Union), desired consumption is equally influenced by both wealth components. It can also be argued that uncertainty about future incomes implies that the discounted income flow may have a lower 'weight' than nonhuman wealth; this aspect may, however, not be very relevant in the Soviet Union, given the high degree of 'certainty' attached to future labor incomes (see, on this point, Ofer and Pickersgill, 1980).

26. Thus, if forced substitution (between different goods on the official market or between goods on the government and on the black market) is large, so that actual expenditure (albeit not its composition) approaches desired expenditure, R is close to 1.

27. This corresponds to the existence of a 'normal' degree of rationing, as suggested by the 'chronic rationing' school.

28. The real interest rate was computed by deflating the nominal interest rate on bank deposits with an estimate of actual (as opposed to official) inflation (see Appendix).

29. Lack of adequate information on the stock of consumer durables prevented its use as an additional explanatory variable, despite its potential relevance in

explaining saving movements in the Soviet Union (as argued in pp. 55–56). Note that the variables indicated in (b), (c) and (d) are included only because of the imperfect way in which the current real value of human and nonhuman wealth is computed. If wealth were computed by aggregating all individual discounted income streams of the population (plus the current real value of nonhuman wealth) it would be necessary to include only the real interest rate.

30. Note that for all periods desired saving has to be evaluated along the equilibrium path, i.e., it has to be derived by using in the consumption function desired wealth and not actual wealth.

31. Note that even if households desire to spend this 'wealth overhang', they may not necessarily want to spend it entirely in one period. The share of the overhang that households want to spend in the current period will depend on several factors, including the type of consumer goods and services that was rationed in the past and all factors affecting the intertemporal distribution of households' resources. In the extreme case in which forsaken consumption has not created an overhang of 'unsatisfied needs', the overhang has the same effect on expenditure of a 'windfall gain' which, in a life-cycle perspective, will be spent only gradually.

32. This can occur because, after a period of rationing, supply may again increase allowing for a gradual absorption of the initial overhang.

33. As we are considering a growing economy, it is always possible to start the simulation in a period (e.g., the early 1960s) in which the overhang was 'small' with respect to the value of the overhang at the end of the period.

34. In theory, if the included proxy for rationing were very good, an increased degree of rationing would not necessarily induce instability in the equation. But, in practice, it is possible that the proxies used are inadequate to describe fully the extent of the increase in rationing occurred during the late 1980s.

35. This section summarizes the detailed results reported in Cottarelli and Blejer (1991).

36. This is because human wealth in the Soviet Union, which is derived from (permanent) disposable labor income, is in the Soviet Union much larger than nonhuman wealth. Even in the United States human wealth is estimated at around 12 times nonhuman wealth (Jorgenson and Fraumeni, 1989); it is not surprising that in the Soviet Union this ratio is around twice as high.

37. Until 1985, these errors are equal to the residuals of the equation estimates.

38. I is also possible that actual inflation (i.e., inflation taking into account price behavior on parallel markets) exceeded measured inflation. While, possibly due to insufficient inflation variability before 1985, inflation did not appear to have influences on consumption in the Soviet Union, it stands to reason that in the presence of strong inflationary pressures desired saving may have increased in the late 1980s to restore the value of financial wealth eroded by the higher-price level.

39. This is, of course, a simplification as we are implicitly assuming that the error term of the equation is always close to zero outside the sample period.

40. Cottarelli and Blejer (1991) provide a more precise and elaborate estimate of the evolution of the 'chronic overhang'. If the 'chronic overhang' is considered to increase after 1985, the total wealth overhang at the end of 1990 could vary between 173 and Rbl 197 billion.

41. This assumption is appropriate as long as households perceive that the price increase will not permanently erode their real labor income (i.e., as long as wages

moved in line with prices). Note, however, that while an equal increase of prices and nominal incomes can eliminate the initial stock of the overhang, it would not eliminate the source of the overhang accumulation, i.e., the 'excessive' real income of the population. Thus, equilibrium of both stock and flows may require some decline in real distributed income (albeit not a decline in consumption standards).

42. The value of houses included in the definition of wealth reflects an evaluation at current prices; however, the series provided by *Goskomstat* reflects official house prices which may underestimate, in both level and growth rate, the actual value of houses.

43. As reference, financial wealth in G7 countries ranges from 30 to 50 percent of households' total wealth.

44. Lottery bonds are government bonds whose 3-percent interest rate is paid in the form of lottery winnings; although their maturity is formally rather long, their can be cashed in at the State Saving Bank.

45. See, for example, IMF *et al.* (1991).

46. This does not consider possible expectations—induced acceleration in velocity that would take place if it is widely believed by the public that any initial price increase would be fully validated by further monetary expansion arising from widespread indexation, widening of budgetary imbalances, etc.

47. This figure includes the Rbl 4b. taken out of circulation by the measures described under (a) since Gosbank statistics have not yet been adjusted to account for this measure.

48. In July 1991 it was decided to increase by 40 percent the nominal value of all saving deposits up to a maximum of Rbl 500. This compensation amounted to Rbl 31 billion. Deposits in excess of Rbl 500 were also increased 40 percent but the compensation (amounting to a total of Rbl 120 billion) was frozen for up to 3 years.

49. Since the estimates of the overhang were conducted for the household sector, the relevant index for this purpose is, indeed, the retail price index.

50. Given the predominant share of financial assets in total household wealth, short-run velocity considerations could be used as reasonable proxies for the analysis of changes in households desired wealth.

51. The analytical counterpart of a forced reduction in velocity in terms of the framework used to estimate the end-1990 overhang, is that forced savings have increased in real terms given that real wealth has not been eroded (in terms of the retail price index) while the availability of goods has declined.

References

Asselain, Jean-Charles. 1981. "Mythe ou Realité de l'Epargne Forcée dans les Pays Socialistes." In: M. Lavigne (ed.), *Travail et Monnaie en Système Socialiste*, Paris: Economica.

Barro, Robert and Herschel Grossman. 1974. "Suppressed Inflation and the Supply Multiplier," *American Economic Review*, 61: 62–83.

Birman, Igor. 1980. "The Financial Crisis in the USSR," *Soviet Studies*, January.

—— and Roger A. Clarke. 1985. "Inflation and the Money Supply in the Soviet Economy," *Soviet Studies*, October.

Blanchard, Olivier. 1985. "Debt, Deficits, and Finite Horizons," *Journal of Political Economy*, April.

CIA. Various years. *Handbook of Economic Statistics*. Washington, D.C.: CIA.

Cottarelli, Carlo and Mario I. Blejer. 1991. "Forced Savings and Repressed Inflation in the Soviet Union: Some Empirical Results," IMF Working Paper, Washington, D.C., June.

Davies Christopher and Wojciech Charemza. 1989. "Introduction to Models of Disequilibrium and Shortage in Centrally Planned Economies." In: C. Davies and W. Charemza (eds.), *Models of Disequilibrium and Shortage in Centrally Planned Economies*. London and New York: Chapman and Hall.

Dornbusch Rudiger and Holger Wolf. 1990. *Monetary Overhang and Reforms in the 1940s*. NBER Working Paper Series No. 3456, October.

Gardner, Roy and Jonathan Strauss. 1981. "Repressed Inflation in the Soviet Union," *European Economic Review*, pp. 387–404.

Grossman, Gregory. 1977. "The Second Economy in the USSR." *Problems of Communism*, September–October.

——. 1990. "Monetary and Financial Aspects of Gorbachev's Reform." In: Christine Kessides *et al.* (eds), *Financial Reform in Socialist Economies*. EDI Seminar Series, The World Bank, Washington, DC.

Holzman, Franklyn D. 1960. "Soviet Inflationary Pressures, 1928–1957: Causes and Cures," *The Quarterly Journal of Economics*, May.

Howard, David H. 1976. "A Note on Hidden Inflation in the Soviet Union," *Soviet Studies*, 28 (No. 4, October): 599–608.

Hutchins, Raymond. 1983. *The Soviet Budget*. London: Macmillan.

IMF, The World Bank, OECD and EBRD. 1991. *A Study of the Soviet Economy*. Paris.

Jorgenson, Dale W. and Barbara M. Fraumeni. 1989. "The Accumulation of Human and Nonhuman Capital, 1948–84." In: Robert E. Lipsey and Helen Stone Tice (eds.), *The Measurement of Saving, Investment and Wealth*. Chicago: University of Chicago Press.

Kemme, David M. 1989. "The Chronic Excess Demand Hypothesis." In: C. Davies and W. Charemza (eds.), *Models of Disequilibrium and Shortage in Centrally Planned Economies*. London and New York: Chapman and Hall.

Kingkade, W. W. 1987. *Estimates and Projections of the Population of the USSR: 1979 to 2025*. CIR Staff Paper No. 33, U.S. Bureau of Census, December.

Kornai, Janos. 1980. *Economics of Shortage*. Amsterdam: North-Holland.

——. 1982. *Growth, Shortage and Efficiency*. Amsterdam: North-Holland.

Modigliani, Franco. 1986. "Life Cycle, Individual Thrift, and the Wealth of Nations," *American Economic Review*, June.

Nove, Alec. 1986. *The Soviet Economic System*. Boston: Allen & Unwin.

Nuti, Mario D. 1989. "Hidden and Repressed Inflation in Soviet-type Economies: Definitions, Measurements and Stabilization." In: C. Davies and W. Charemza (eds.), *Models of Disequilibrium and Shortage in Centrally Planned Economies*. London and New York: Chapman and Hall.

Ofer, Gur. 1991. "Macroeconomic Issues of Soviet Reforms," *Macroeconomic Annual 1991*, NBER, pp. 297–334.

—— and Joyce Pickersgill. 1980. "Soviet Household Saving: A Cross-section Study of Soviet Emigrant Families," *Quarterly Journal of Economics*, August.

Pickersgill, Joyce. 1976. "Soviet Household Saving Behavior," *Review of Economics and Statistics*, May.

——. 1980a. "The Financial Crisis in the USSR: A Comment," *Soviet Studies*, October.

——. 1983. "Household Saving in the USSR." In: F. Modigliani and R. H. Hemmings (eds.), *The Determinants of National Savings and Wealth*. New York: St. Martin's Press.

——. 1989b. "Recent Evidence on Soviet Households Saving Behavior," *Review of Economics and Statistics*, November.

Pindak, Frantisek. 1983. "Inflation under Central Planning," *Jahrbuch für Wirtschaft Osteuropas*, 10/2, reprinted in SUERF Reprint Series, No. 29, Tilburg.

Portes, Richard. 1989. "The Theory and Measurement of Macroeconomic Disequilibrium in Centrally Planned Economies." In: C. Davies and W. Charemza, *Models of Disequilibrium and Shortage in Centrally Planned Economies*. London: Chapman and Hall.

—— and David Winter. 1980. "Disequilibrium Estimates for Consumption Goods Markets in Centrally Planned Economies," *Review of Economic Studies*, 137–149.

Schroeder, Gertrude E. and Barbara S. Severin. 1976. "Soviet Consumption and Income Policies in Perspective." In: *Soviet Economy in a New Perspective*, Joint Economic Committee, Congress of the United States. October.

The USSR in Figures. Various years. Moscow: Finansy i Statistika Publishers.

Van Brabant, Jozef M. 1990. "Socialist Economics: The Disequilibrium School and the Shortage Economy," *Journal of Economic Perspectives*, Spring.

Winiecki, Jan. 1985. "Portes ante Portas: A Critique of the Revisionist Interpretation of Inflation under Central Planning," *Comparative Economic Studies*, Summer.

APPENDIX
Statistical Sources

a. Financial Assets and Saving

All data on financial assets between 1964 and 1989 have been provided by the Gosbank; data on bank deposits for the previous period can be found in Hutchins (1983), who collected them from official Soviet publications. Data on currency and other financial assets of households were estimated by imposing a constant ratio with respect to bank deposits (at the 1964 level); this may underestimate the actual amount of cash before 1964 if the declining trend in the ratio between cash and deposits, observable after 1964, started before that year. In the absence of capital gains on financial assets, net financial saving has been equated to the change in the nominal stock of financial assets net of the change in households' credit, also available from the above sources.

b. Households' Disposable Income

Data on disposable income for the 1980s were provided by Goskomstat; these data, however, were adjusted by adding to the official series the income from private sales of agricultural produce as estimated by the CIA (1990). The value of these sales after 1987 (not available from the above source) was computed by using the growth rate of the sale of agricultural produce to the socialized sector incremented by 3 percent in 1988, 6 percent in 1989 and 9 percent in 1990. The growth rates of the CIA series was also used to compute disposable income between 1965 and 1979. Information on the previous period was derived from Pickersgill (1983).

c. Real Household Investment

This item included two components: houses and other real investment (both considered net of amortization). As to the first component, Goskomstat provided data from 1970 to 1989; data for the previous period were derived from Smith (1973). The second component (comprising mainly livestock and other property of the rural population) was also provided by Goskomstat from 1970 to 1989; for the previous period this series, which is rather small, was kept constant with respect to financial saving.

d. Households' Wealth

Total wealth was derived as the sum of three components: (a) net financial wealth, (b) houses and (c) other real wealth. For financial wealth see Section a. above; the value of houses owned by the population, net of depreciation and at current (official) prices, was provided by Goskomstat from 1965 to 1989; the housing investment series was used to derive the stock of houses for the previous period. The value of the third component was also provided by Goskomstat, but only for 1970–1989, and not at current prices but as a cumulative sum of previous investments. For the pre-1970 period the corresponding investment series was also used to derive the stock of this component of wealth. A 'discrepancy' (or 'capital gain') series was also derived by subtracting total (real and financial) investment from the change in wealth. Given the procedure followed above, this residual series represents entirely net capital gains on houses (it was fairly small).

e. Household Saving and Consumption

Household saving was derived as the sum of the three saving components (net financial saving, investment in houses and investment in other real assets). Consumption was derived residually as the difference between disposable income and net saving.

f. Other Series

The inflation series was derived from CIA (1990) and from Pickersgill (1983); inflation in 1988, 1989 and 1990 was assumed to be 2.4, 5.4 and 6 percent, respectively. Data on population were derived from the *Statistical Yearbook* published in the Soviet Union (*Narkhoz*). Most recent estimates of the composition of the population by age were published by Kingkade (1987); data from Howard (1976) were used for the previous period. Nominal interest rates were provided by the Gosbank; real interest rates were derived by using the above-mentioned inflation series. Data on monthly wages and the expenditure of the Social Consumption Fund are published regularly by *The USSR in Figures*.

Note

All data for 1990 are estimates based on preliminary information on 1990 developments.

7

Stabilizing and Restructuring the Former Soviet Economy: Big-Bang or Gradual Sequencing?

Gur Ofer

Introduction

By the end of 1991 the final target of the states of the former Soviet economy became very clear: to become an open market economy with a dominant private sector, within the range of the Western variety of a market system. There is relatively little talk of 'third' type solutions of intermediate models, somewhere between socialism and capitalism, especially as regards the structure of ownership of productive assets. It is now also much clearer than before that the road leading to this goal is strewn with pitfalls, which makes the journey riskier, costlier and longer than initially assumed.

The two pivotal clusters of steps in the creation of a market economy, the so-called 'structural' reforms, are price liberalization and the establishment of competitive markets and the creation of a profit-maximizing production sector by nurturing new enterprises and transforming existing state enterprises (which we will refer to as 'privatization'). In addition, the early period of reforms in the Soviet Union, especially between 1987 and 1990, seriously destabilized the macroeconomic balance of the economy and raised an urgent need for 'stabilization'.

Two major schools of thought have addressed this three-pronged task: the 'big-bang' school, which advocates the application of sweeping simultaneous radical measures, and the more gradualist school, which prefers a more carefully prepared sequence of steps, each preparing the ground for a smoother introduction of the next one. The main arguments of the big-bang school are that only a consistent set of steps across the entire economic panorama can produce positive results, and that any gradual reform is self-contradictory due to incompatibilities between the new and the old elements of the system during the transition. The gradualist school emphasizes the need to clear the way for radical steps through intermediate ones, so as to minimize the economic and social costs of the transition. This chapter attempts to assess the arguments of these two schools in the context of the economic reform efforts of the former Soviet Union and Russia. The emphasis is on conceptual considerations; the empirical evidence is used mainly for illustration.[1]

Both major clusters of structural reform, as well as the need for stabilization, can be implemented step-wise or all at once, and in a variety of sequences: price liberalization can proceed in stages, starting from a price *adjustment*, followed by price *reform*, either gradually or all at once. 'Privatization' has a far richer set of optional modalities and sequences (as surveyed by Berliner in Chapter 14 of this volume). Then there is the question of the interaction between the two main types of structural change: what kind and sequence of price liberalization should accompany a certain form of privatization and to what extent is progress on one front a necessary condition for proceeding on the other. In each case, in addition to the internal economic logic of each sequence, account must also be taken of its likely effects on production and unemployment, on economic pressures exerted on the population, and on the political endurance under such pressures. From the political point of view, the stronger the government and the more generous external technical and financial aid, a big-bang approach may be more feasible (as in the former East Germany) than otherwise (as in the former Soviet Union). But a strong government and generous aid can also support a more gradual change if such an approach is deemed preferable. The former Soviet Union is also characterized by the fact that the old system was much more deeply entrenched than in most other East European countries and the infrastructure for change there was less prepared. A big-bang approach, therefore, may be more needed but at the same time much more difficult to implement, whereas a gradual approach may become entangled in a web of inconsistencies and low-level bureaucratic opposition.

Another issue is how to address the question of macroeconomic stabilization that emerged in the former Soviet Union and several other East European countries as a consequence of initial reform measures. One aim of price liberalization was to turn the systemic 'shortage economy' under central planning into an economy with balanced markets. Under central planning, some degree of repressed inflation in both producer and consumer markets was a major tool of control, management and planning; at the same time it was the outcome of past errors in planning and implementation. Thus, the goal of macroeconomic 'stabilization' was a major element in the 'structural' reform from the very start. Stabilization became a much more pressing target of the reforms in the Soviet Union and other East European countries owing to economic (and political) developments during the early phase of the reforms—especially a number of partial, unsuccessful changes in the fiscal and monetary spheres.

While the changes that occurred in the Soviet Union since 1985 failed to generate a meaningful production response, they did destabilize both consumer and producer markets because a large monetary expansion emerged as a result of several events: since 1985 the consolidated state budget deficit grew from a few points to around 10 percent of GDP by 1988–1990 and to between one-quarter and one-third of GNP by 1991. At the same time, there was a significant expansion of the credit system and of credits, and the hitherto 'non-money' balances of enterprises were gradually 'monetized'. Both wages and government transfer payments grew much more rapidly than did the production of consumer goods. As a result, money income accruing to the population (as well as to enterprises) increased much more rapidly than the available bill of goods, while prices, fixed by the government, remained virtually unchanged until the end of 1990. By the end of 1990 an accumulated monetary overhang, consisting of cash and savings-account balances of households, accounted for between one-third and one-half of the annual consumption bill (Cottarelli and Blejer, Chapter 6 in this volume).

The consequences of the repressed inflation were very serious: the disintegration of the supply and distribution system caused shortages; long lines and empty stores; hoarding; corruption; and alternative, parallel and black markets. Until the end of 1990 there was only a very small decline in production and no decline at all in personal consumption. But in 1991, the last year of the Soviet Union (and, so far, in the beginning of 1992) the decline of production has been accelerating to an annual rate of about 15 percent (*Economic Situation*, 1992). All these events had serious effects on the political stability of the Soviet government and no doubt contributed to its fall. They continue to constitute a threat to any government, at present or in the future. The problem of 'stabilization' thus grew into a much larger issue than previously envisaged, an independent problem that, as perceived by many observers, certainly by the then Soviet government, had to be solved before any serious approach to structural reform could be attempted.

Faced with worsening macroeconomic imbalances and increased shortages, the Soviet government, starting in the fall of 1989, presented a succession of 'reform' packages whose main goal was to restore equilibrium, mostly through an assortment of fiscal and monetary measures. The cornerstone of these packages was a radical price *adjustment* aimed at eliminating part of the monetary overhang and at the same time reducing budget subsidies to food products, transportation and other services (and thus narrowing the fiscal deficit), and at correcting, at least in part, the gross distortion in the structure of relative prices. Each successive plan included larger doses of price *liberalization* of certain groups of goods as well as more daring 'privatization' schemes. The government justified the priority accorded to stabilization as a necessary precondition for structural reform, but was charged by opponents with conservatism, even revisionism. Possibly the most vigorous opposition was to the planned price revisions. The accepted view among many economists, politicians and most policy makers had been that under the unsatisfactory and deteriorating circumstances in the consumer markets and the resultant deep dissatisfaction of the population, the government was in no position to initiate a 'classical' stabilization scheme that necessarily imposed initial (though temporary) hardships on the population. For this reason all government proposals for price revisions until the end of 1990 were sent back 'for further consideration'. It was only for 1991 that the Supreme Soviet approved a reform program including a major price revision and a corresponding cut in subsidies, but not before it was substantially watered down by increasing income compensation to the population. The first major price revision *plus* some price liberalization of wholesale prices (January 1991) and retail prices (April 1991) was thus finally implemented. Owing to the political strife in 1991, which culminated in the abortive coup within the government itself, the program was cut short in August 1991, and cannot yet be adequately evaluated on its economic merits.

The Soviet government's program was replaced in October 1991 by one proposed by the new Russian government headed by Yeltsin and Gaidar (*Memorandum*, 1992). In the first phase it replaced the old price adjustment scheme with a sweeping price liberalization, including prices of foreign exchange and wages, but retained a few exceptions (for basic foods, energy prices and some services), where prices were only revised upward but remained under government control. Macroeconomic stabilization remains one of the main goals of the first phase, which includes radical fiscal and monetary restraining measures. Nevertheless, price liberalization is a more integral part of structural reform than is price revision.

The new government, whose radical stance was outspoken and highly credible, also plans to move ahead with privatization and other market-oriented changes. Its current stabilization and reform program is the granddaughter of the August 1990 'Five Hundred Days Program' and the daughter of the May 1991 'Grand Bargain', the two radical reform programs offered to Gorbachev as substitutes for the government's program, both with Gregory Yavlinski as the main driving force (Shatalin, 1990; Allison, 1991).

Being more radical, the Five Hundred Days Program also included an important chapter on privatization, which, in addition to its natural structural role, was presented as an important means of stabilization. Instead of the controversial price revision, part of the monetary overhang could be absorbed by the government through the sale of property to the people, and part of the proceeds used, at least temporarily, to help balance the budget. The sale of government assets and enterprises, is, of course, an integral part of most stabilization programs in the West and in the Third World. The Soviet advantage in this respect was (and still is) the huge size of the stock of the government-owned assets and the extremely skewed (in favor of financial assets) portfolio held by the public, which is the result of the dogma that all productive assets should be in the hands of the state. The possibility of killing two birds (stabilization and reform) with one stone also lies at the basis of many privatization schemes such as that proposed by Feige (1990). This possibility was expressed by the Shatalin group in an article in *Izvestiya*:

> The program's task is to take everything possible from the state and give it over to the people. There are good reasons to believe that giving the people back a considerable part of property and resources on various terms will ensure its more effective use *and will avert many negative effects in the process of transition to market*. . . . And only when resources devoured by the giant state machine will be channeled to serve the people, and when the people perceive that, only then will the leadership of the country will be in a position to appeal to the people to be patient, to bear another heavy load . . . in the name of their future. . . . (September 4 1990, italics mine; G.O.)

This issue—whether privatization can precede stabilization and thereby become one of its main instruments, or whether it should wait until after stabilization is achieved by different policies (and there are, of course, intermediate variants)—is not only very challenging theoretically, it is also crucial from the point of view of policy. Can some degree of privatization ameliorate the short-run hardships inherent in any classical stabilization program?

Russia's overhang problem was virtually eliminated by the sharp price increases in the first months following price liberalization. Stabilization has not yet been achieved because, at least to date (April 1992), the repressed inflation and shortages of the previous phase were replaced by rapid inflation and a continuing decline in production. Inflation in March 1992 is estimated at anywhere between 15 and 30 percent, and production continued to decline at an annual rate of 12–15 percent (*Economic Situation*, 1992). These can be explained, in addition to citing usual demand-side reasons, mainly by the absence of even partly competitive markets, existing monopolistic structures and the inertia of the old modes of supply, together with strong self-fulfilling expectations for continued high rates of inflation. All these help to create the well-known inflationary cost-push spiral accompanied by a decline in production and enterprise hoarding. The debate about privatization thus shifted from its role as a potential absorber of excess monetary resources to its function as a necessary condition for the creation of competition.

The big-bang approach, previously defined as an all-out price liberalization *plus* current-account convertibility and the abolition of government controls, is now being expanded to include wide-scale privatization as quickly as possible (Lipton and Sachs, 1990b). This raises a chain of subsequent queries: can significant privatization be achieved in the short run as part of a big bang? If not, is there a reasonable substitute? Can privatization be achieved while in the throes of a rapid inflationary process? If it proves difficult, could an alternative scheme of price liberalization be devised? Finally, if a big-bang is deemed non-viable, might not some second thoughts be necessary about the virtues of a more gradual approach to reforms?

This chapter discusses a number of key reform sequencing problems, mostly in a context of a big-bang versus gradual reform. First, I discuss sequencing alternatives of price reforms, with special emphasis on the possible role of an initial stage of price revision prior to price liberalization, and the interrelation between the different schemes for prices and stabilization combined with structural reform (especially privatization). I then discuss alternative sequencing variants of privatization and conclude by placing price policies and privatization within the context of existing political constraints and feasibilities.

The chapter is deliberately expositional and non-quantitative, as it seeks to concentrate on the arguments. A more detailed exposition of developments in the last years of the Soviet Union appears in Ofer (1991), CEC (1990), IMF *et al.* (1991), and Aslund (1991a). Recent economic development in Russia can be found in *Economic Situation*, 1992; "The Economy of the CIS in 1991" (1992).

Price Reform, Stabilization and the Creation of Markets

Under the old regime and until very recently almost all prices were determined by the State Price Commission, based on a peculiarly Soviet theory of value and accounting practices, but with considerable discretion depending on the industry, region, type of good and many other factors. Most prices remained fixed for very long periods, sometimes for several decades, despite changes in costs.

The 'functional autarky' of the Soviet economy and of its foreign-trade sector almost completely divorces internal prices from world market prices, and a system of subsidies and sales taxes divorced many retail prices from their Soviet-style producer prices. As a result, there were extreme distortions in *relative prices* vis-à-vis true scarcities. In addition, the *absolute* price level was in any case too low, much more so in recent years, as shown by the country's extreme macroeconomic disequilibrium. A price reform that corrects both these distortions and that frees price determination from administrative intervention must therefore be a first step in any reform package.

A realistic system of relative prices with flexible responses to changing market conditions is the first step toward the creation of genuine markets. False relative prices under central planning are somewhat less distortive, since the plan overrules demand and supply based on such prices, but if prices are to become the main allocative tool they must be correctly set in order to avoid inefficiencies, eliminate waste and emit the right signals. The creation of markets with *totally wrong* and inflexible relative prices is clearly dysfunctional and irrational. Next, correct relative prices are also a prerequisite for the very first steps toward any kind of de-statization, privatization or leasing processes: they serve as the base for the initial evaluation of the value of firms and assets, they allow the germination of a capital market to provide a sound foundation for true accounting of profitability and of loss making, and therefore a rational criterion for closure and bankruptcy; they are needed in order to encourage foreign investments, to determine the worthiness of exports, etc.

Following that, the establishment of correct prices will free many enterprises from the need for subsidies, extricating them from the environment of soft budget constraints and dependency on the government. As a result many enterprises will begin to suffer losses and some temporary public support may be needed in order to mitigate the shock of unemployment. The key word here is 'temporary' and the support will have to be tightly connected to a schedule for the reconstruction or liquidation of non-viable enterprises. Finally, just as a sound system of relative prices was needed in the past in order to alleviate the disputes between republics over fair mutual exchange prices, it is still needed in order to facilitate trade between their successors.

The macroeconomic stabilization effect of the change in the absolute price level is no less important. The fiscal effects of reducing subsidies and the monetary impact of slashing the overhang of both households and enterprises, *plus* the support of stabilization, a restraining fiscal stance (partial income compensation) and tight monetary and credit policies, can restore macroeconomic equilibrium. In addition to the obvious benefits, a shift towards a buyers' market and the elimination of shortages will reinvigorate the distribution system and create the conditions necessary for the development of a market-oriented infrastructure and its related institutions, and the right marketing mentality to replace the inefficient atmosphere of the sellers' market. Even with no immediate supply response, goods will re-appear in the stores, lines will shorten, and the need to hoard goods will be reduced. Even if the 'technical' real purchasing power of households declines—as indeed it must—the level of overall consumer welfare will be much higher than under present conditions (Lipton and Sachs, 1990a; Kornai, 1990). But such a program can succeed only if the level of income and asset compensation to the population is partial, concentrated mostly among lower-income groups.

In addition to the benefits derived from setting the appropriate price level, the actual implementation of the reform immediately reduces the high levels of uncertainty prevalent while waiting for the axe to fall. The past (and even present) shortages are due in part to the refusal of producers (farmers and others) to sell, in anticipation of price increases.

While the centrality of an early price reform is obvious, the sequence of its implementation is not. We have mentioned the internal debate in the Soviet Union between the more gradual approach, starting with a major price revision, as implemented by the last Soviet government, and the big-bang approach implemented by the first Russian government. While both programs actually adopted a more mixed approach (both contained some price revisions and some price liberalization), their respective impacts correspond very closely to the more extreme models. In what follows we compare the major advantages and drawbacks of two distant variants, a mostly one-time price liberalization versus a gradual approach with a major price revision in the initial stage.

The advantages of the radical approach are obvious. Under the present Soviet conditions a big-bang has several additional advantages: first, releasing prices signals the end of the old regime of government intervention and the move toward the market in a credible way. The alternative option of an initial administrative price revision signals the opposite, namely, continuation of administrative controls and the preservation of the central bureaucracies. Paradoxically, even a 'normal' degree of government intervention in price determination, as practiced in many market economies, may be suspect in Russia. Secondly, price rises resulting from a market process are likely to be perceived as a 'natural' process rather than as the direct outcome of government policy; as a result, both political opposition and demands for compensation may be less severe.[2]

A related third advantage of price liberalization is in freeing the government from the very difficult political task of periodically updating previously set prices as inflation (or other changes) moves away from par with liberalized prices. Fourth, following such a long period of absence of markets and of isolation from world markets, it is claimed that only the operation of free markets, and no bureaucrat, can guide prices to their new correct relative levels.

The major advantage of an administrative price revision followed by a short period of a price freeze prior to full price liberalization is that it stands a better chance of achieving tenable stabilization and reducing the danger of open inflation. If prices are freed before stabilization is achieved—indeed, if price liberalization is used as a major means of achieving stabilization—the odds are that (a) the initial price shock itself will be much larger than necessary and (b) that an open inflationary process will then ensue with all the familiar attributes of an inflationary spiral fueled by expectations and by rising wages and costs. Both the price shock and the cost-push *plus* expectations of an inflationary spiral cause production to decline more steeply than otherwise (Bruno, 1992).

Unlike many countries in need of stabilization, the Soviet Union had not developed such an open inflation until the end of 1991. Avoiding it was an important factor in entering the first phase of market economy. Given the paucity of experience among the Russian people in the operation of markets, market stability tilted toward a buyers' market is much more important than in many Western countries undergoing periods of rapid inflation.

The danger of a cost-push inflationary spiral emerging under Soviet or Russian conditions is much greater owing to the highly monopolized structure of Soviet production and distribution; to the lack of market institutions, infrastructure and tradition; and to the lack of enough profit-maximizing enterprises prior to privatization. In the production sector, the old ministerial structure defined the allocated product to each ministry, each department and in many cases individual enterprises; but beyond this there were also exclusive areas of sale both for enterprises and wholesale organizations. This rigid structure was somewhat relaxed in the past few years, but the main problem still exists. Part of this monopolistic structure is artificial, created by decree, and can be eliminated simply by issuing an official announcement that anyone may produce whatever he chooses and sell for the best price. Indeed, this was what the new Russian government did, but implementation will be more difficult, as tradition and inertia may prevail for some time. Another part of the old monopolistic structure will be weakened as part of the 'conversion' program of encouraging producers of military goods to shift to the production of civilian and consumer goods. Further encroachment on the monopolistic structure will be provided by the growing private sector, especially in services and small-scale production.

Even so, inertia in distribution links and in supply and marketing routes, and the remaining main core of production according to ministerial fiat may preserve monopolistic power and produce monopolistic prices. This further underlines the importance of shifting the market equilibrium as rapidly as possible to a buyers' market, but it also requires, in addition to a regulation regarding freedom of production and distribution, an effort to break up some key production associations, both horizontal and vertical. Before all this happens and under conditions of an open inflationary spiral, there may be much more opportunity for the monopolists to push prices up and contribute further to inflation. In the meantime, a one-time price revision that will by itself stabilize the economy might mitigate the effects of such a dynamic process.

Another factor contributing to market rigidities and cost-push effects is the lack of properly operating market institutions, services and traditions. Missing are proper institutions such as goods exchanges, a legal infrastructure, financial services and proper banks, basic competence in operating all the above and also markets, mutual trust and credibility, basic respect for the middleman, and many more. Under more stable conditions it may have made sense to set aside a period of preparation to establish some of these services before shifting to market transactions. Such a sequence may have been reasonable three or four years ago, before the disintegration of the old distribution system. There now seems to be no way back; it is impossible to reimpose the old discipline and control and, under the present macroeconomic conditions it is doubtful whether the old system could have performed even under strict discipline.

Finally, the most glaring lack is private (or at least independent) enterprises, in both the production and the distribution sectors, that act as normal profit-maximizers in a market environment. These will slowly evolve as the so-called 'privatization' process proceeds, but until this happens more rigidities will generate more inflation under price liberalization. Intermediate steps to encourage existing state enterprises to behave in accordance with market principles should be considered to alleviate these problems (see the next section).

The danger of a cost-inflation spiral developing out of a big-bang price liberalization exists whether or not the act of price liberalization is accompanied by a proper restraining fiscal and monetary policies. If such a policy is effectively pursued, the cost-inflationary pressure will cause production to fall and unemployment to develop—through the standard stagflation syndrome (a shift upward and to the left in the ordinary AS–AD model). If, in addition, there is also accommodating fiscal and monetary expansion under pressures from the production sector and the parliament, the rate of inflation will be higher and production (or at least marketing) may decline owing to the combination of inflationary expectations and the availability of enough credit to finance increased inventories. Such behavior may be even more common among monopolistic enterprises. A combination of such phenomena has been observed in several East European countries, and may also be developing in Russia in the spring of 1992. Thus, inflationary expectations may assume the role previously played by too low prices in encouraging hoarding and shortages.

All of the above, including the possible negative effect of the excessive initial price shock and the ensuing inflationary spiral on the decline in production, raise doubts about the optimality of the big-bang approach under the initial conditions prevailing in the centrally planned countries (see Bruno, 1992). Any discussion of the nature of such a major price change must deal with the policies on wages and the rate of exchange, both in their own right and in their relation to other prices. The partial liberalization of wage determination over the past few years has been a major source of destabilization and of monetary expansion. Under any kind of price reform and stabilization, wage determination cannot be left to the new market forces. This is a well established principle of *market economies* both in unsettled periods of stabilization and in more tranquil times. Under such conditions wage hikes make a major contribution to the inflationary spiral from both the cost and the demand sides.

Paradoxically, the need for control over wages may be more difficult to explain, and to enforce, in a country that is moving toward a market system, but it is nonetheless very risky to relinquish control over wages. A further difficulty under present conditions is the increasing power and control of labor over the enterprises. If at all possible there is a clear advantage to a one-time increase in wage levels on 'day one' of the program, an increase that provides partial compensation for the expected rise in prices, but that will not constitute indexation. The various stabilization efforts of 1991 introduced indexation legislation but attempts were made to keep it partial. Heavy taxes were imposed on excessive wage increases. Under the new Russian big-bang, wages were liberalized together with most other prices; they were not set aside as an anchor as was done in many Western stabilization efforts. Therefore wage increases apparently make an important contribution to the inflationary cost-push. The stiff marginal tax rates on 'above norm' wage hikes are very difficult to define, let alone to enforce.

The second key price to be considered is the rate of exchange. In the choice between a one-time price liberalization or a preliminary price revision followed by more gradual price liberalization, considerations relating to the rate of exchange have two sides: one is the immediate institution of a convertible exchange rate (current account convertibility only, of course), which may contribute to the cost-push inflationary spiral (as indeed happened in many countries).

In centrally planned economies immediate convertibility may also cause a further decline of production in sectors that were effectively protected by the internal distorted price structure. Immediate current account convertibility may, however, be highly desirable as a credible signal of the shift toward an open market economy and of the normalization of the relative price structure. On the other hand, an initially fixed exchange rate, following a one-time real devaluation, can serve as a stabilizing monetary anchor and, at the same time, temporarily shield vulnerable industries from a drastic initial shock. Such a policy has been used in many countries, even as part of stabilization programs that included internal price liberalization. The drawback is that an overvalued fixed rate of exchange could foster destabilizing expectations.

The initial situation in the Soviet foreign currency 'market' was one in which the ruble was extremely overvalued, the state monopolized all external transactions, and a very narrow and illegal black market for foreign currency existed, with extremely high prices. Over the past few years a gradual process of liberalization has taken place, including decentralization of the monopoly, devaluation of the official exchange rate and increasing legitimization of the 'free' market for currency. As part of the January 1992 liberalization program the exchange rate was liberalized, as was the market for currency, and the foreign-trade monopoly was abolished. While imports were completely liberalized (tariffs are very low), exports are still restricted by licenses and export taxes have been imposed on most exports in a variety of forms, including the surrender of part of the hard currency earned at a favorable exchange rates to the government. The restrictions on exports are to be gradually removed (*Memorandum*, 1992).

The remaining restrictions on exports keep the present rate of exchange significantly above its (current account) equilibrium level, thereby protecting vulnerable industries and enabling the authorities to keep the domestic price of energy (Russia's main export good) at artificially low levels. A gradual upward adjustment of the domestic real price of energy, and whatever foreign exchange that may be made available to Russia through external assistance programs, will allow a reduction (through liberalization of exports) in the real exchange rate and prevent it from further contributing to the inflationary spiral. Taxes may have to be imposed on some imports in order to prevent too drastic a shock to weak industries. There is, however, a danger that the present inflationary spiral will soon catch up with the rate of exchange and bring back the dilemma of whether to stay with a free rate or to fix it as part of some future new stabilization efforts.

Most of the above discussion on alternative sequences of price reform centered on questions related to macroeconomic stabilization and inflation, that is, the price level. But if the functioning of markets under price liberalization is, indeed, as described above, beset by any number of major imperfections, and if there is a real danger of an inflationary spiral emerging, then it is far from certain that price liberalization—especially if there is no true current-account convertibility—will produce a vector of correct *relative* prices. Different levels of monopolization, market segmentation, varied modes of operation across marketing networks and uneven inflation rates in different sectors all may distort relative prices to a significant degree for extended periods of time, thus compromising one of the most important advantages of free prices. Against such a standard, an administrative determination of the right relative price structure of major groups of goods and services may be considered less absurd.

To these one should add the fact that even under radical schemes of price liberalization, some prices, notably those of mass consumption goods, of housing, and (in Russia) all energy and energy-related prices, may be administratively fixed or managed, thus creating the problems of lagged adjustments mentioned above. Exactly such a situation developed recently with respect to the price of energy, where the initially adjusted price (five times the original), rapidly moved back to its initial relative position, relative to all other prices, and where its subsequent adjustment became the focal point of a major political struggle (the price of energy was raised again by a factor of six on April 20, 1992, but it is still much too low).

My conclusion on sequencing is therefore that an initial, administrative, major one-time price revision to approximately correct the structure of both relative prices and the price level is a necessary condition for full price liberalization and for meaningful privatization. This step must include other stabilizing measures in wages, credit, the budget, etc., and should be followed by a relatively short price freeze. Only then can most prices be liberalized and privatization commence. While the initial one-time price revision is basically adopted from the series of programs implemented by the last Soviet government, the next step, early price liberalization, is closer to the present program of the new Russian government. Indeed, one policy option possible in the not-too-distant future is that a standard scheme of heterogeneous stabilization program, including a price freeze, will have to be enacted in order to stop the present inflationary process.

The role of 'privatization' or, as it is sometimes termed, 'structural reform', appeared twice in the debate on the sequencing of the price reform: once as a potential absorber of the monetary overhang, thus helping the stabilization effort, and again when the absence of a critical mass of private or any kind of profit-maximizing enterprises was presented as a major obstacle to the emergence of competitive markets in response to price liberalization. The sweeping move to price liberalization in Russia in the beginning of 1992 eliminated the overhang (for the time being) and with it the need for privatization as a remedy for this particular problem. The second role, however, is now at the forefront of discussion.

Long-term Economic Reform: Privatization, De-statization and Structural Change

Under the old regime the Soviet economy's version of socialism with respect to ownership of the means of production was very extreme. With the exception of small private agricultural plots, almost all other productive capital was in government hands. Not even private small producers in services, distribution and small-scale production in urban areas were tolerated, as they were, to some degree, in a number of East European socialist countries.

Since 1985 some laws departing from that doctrine were enacted, accepting the concept of 'multiple property relations' under which the activities of cooperatives, and even of small private enterprises, were permitted in agriculture and in cities, including the leasing and purchasing of government enterprises. The main real activity during the Soviet period was the establishment of nearly 100,000 small cooperatives and private enterprises, including a few thousand farms, several hundred joint ventures with various degrees of foreign control, and a multitude of various leasing arrangements of farms and parts of government-owned enterprises. By the end of 1991 the entirely new private (or semi-private) sector employed about 10 percent of the labor force in the Russian Federation (*Economic Situation*, 1992, p. 51). The new Russian government is seriously committed to an extensive privatization effort, although so far the only definite program that was executed is one for small-scale and service enterprises; the fate of large-scale enterprises remains unclear (Memorandum, 1992). To date, however, this process is only just getting underway and it is difficult to determine its real pace.

The mutual interdependence of privatization and the development of stable and competitive markets raises a very serious quandary for the big-bang approach in its broad definition. A more feasible approach may opt for first privatizing those sectors that are most likely to survive even without a full-fledged infrastructure, and that can help create markets and such an infrastructure, and then to gradually turn to the large-scale production sector. The discussion that follows traces this logical sequence.

The Private Sector

The private sector (small- and medium-size enterprises, private or co-operative) has been developing from two different origins: first are small state-owned and run enterprises that can be sold or leased to private operators with relative ease. Even when such small plants belong to much larger state organizations, such as retail trade or service networks, they can be separated and set up as independent small producers. Under the old system, due to perennial difficulties of supply and of acquiring outside services, the typical Soviet enterprise developed as an autarkic self-sufficient unit by incorporating in-house secondary and subsidiary functions. Now such functions can be separated out and be performed much more efficiently. The main criterion of such an encroachment on the public sector is the economic separability and viability of the branch, department or store from its parent organization.

The second origin of private firms is the establishment of *new* enterprises in most areas, in which activity is far lower than in market economies with similar levels of development (Ofer, 1990). To the extent that the size of the service and related activities in a market economy can serve as a norm, the Soviet service sector can and should just about double its present size; most of this growth should take the form of private firms. If we add small- and medium-scale production of consumer goods, and small construction and transportation companies, this new private sector will also represent the main direction of the likely and desirable structural change of the Soviet economy—away from large-scale, heavy and military industry toward light industry and services. This means that the sector's potential for growth is large and that a private sector of this type can potentially attain a significant size and impact in fairly rapid order.

An early emphasis on the development of such a private sector has several distinct advantages: The first is the *relative* ease with which an individual firm within the service can be established. The funds needed to purchase or establish such a company are relatively modest and most of the resources required could be financed from private sources. The infrastructure of business and credit services, even legal services and know-how, can be acquired relatively easily and on the job and, at least in principle, there should be less social resentment to the transfer of ownership of these outfits to persons who are often their present operators. The persistent outcry against 'speculators' is partly a protest against widespread shortages, partly a reflection on the relatively scarcity of such operators, and partly the result of obstacles still raised by local bureaucracies and supply constraints. A rapid increase in the number of private enterprises will help solve many of these problems.

The second advantage is that small private operators in services and other branches are much more efficient and customer-friendly than their government-run predecessors. This is the sector where the advantage of a private operator over central planning is most pronounced. There is therefore a large potential for a rapid rise in consumer welfare, urgently needed in the sequence of the reforms, in the form of more and better consumer goods and services and of shorter lines. In particular, private operators in distribution and transportation can help relieve the chronic bottleneck in supply that exacerbated the shortages created by the production sector and the planning system.

The rapid development of the private sector in distribution and services will also help change the population's mental order of priorities. Under the old regime, 'production' came first and the consumer came last, an attitude deeply ingrained in Marxist theory. Consumers were residual claimants, constantly short-changed. The new private sector can help shift priorities toward consumer sovereignty and the chain of command from the producer to the buyer, with trade organizations as leaders who determine the assortment and quality of products.

Early privatization of the distribution sector can help achieve this goal, and a deeper encroachment on the public sector may be necessary, in addition to the privatization of many large wholesale and supply organizations. The lack of domestic experience requires the mobilization of some large Western retail chains in a wide range of aid functions, ranging from training and consulting to the establishment of branches (this theme is developed in great detail in *IMF,* 1991, Vol. 3, Chapter V.2, pp. 31–54).

Finally, the growing private sector will interact favorably with the public sector. It will absorb workers released from loss-making enterprises, thereby making the marketization of the public sector even easier. It will provide improved business services to enterprises in the public sector, and it will *compete* with the public sector, forcing the latter to raise efficiency in order to survive or, alternatively, to privatize. The business and financial services developed by the private sector will form part of the infrastructure needed for enterprise privatization and may produce home-grown entrepreneurs who will invest in larger state enterprises.

One of the reasons for the slow development of the private sector during the Soviet period was the state of shortages and macroeconomic disequilibrium. While some obstacles have been removed by the new Russian government, it must be emphasized that continuing inflation is hardly conducive even to small-scale privatization and entrepreneurship. Economic instability has prevented the development of a viable private sector in the past and may continue to do so if present conditions persist.

Large-Scale State Enterprises

This sector accounts for a major part of Soviet production capacity, not only in heavy and military industry but in all production branches. This sector is therefore the main target of long-term structural reform and 'privatization'. It is now quite clear that the 'long run' goal is to transform this sector into an ordinary corporate and private business sector as in most market economies, possibly with some proportion of publicly owned large corporations. The main dilemma here is a short- and medium-term one, between emphasis on immediate wholesale privatization as against a continuum of intermediate solutions concentrating mostly on reorganizing the rules of operation of managements, on new incentives, and on the nature of firms' relations with the state, all in line with market principles, but without radical change of ownership.

The choice is between two options: either embarking on radical transformation of both management and ownership—indeed, management *through* ownership—or concentrating (for the time being) on management reform, postponing the question of ownership to some future date. The second option is, in essence, the 'evolutionary' approach developed by Murrell and analyzed in great detail by Berliner in Chapter 14 of this volume (Murrell, 1990), which, of course, also allows a gradual, orderly process of purchase of state enterprises by domestic and foreign entrepreneurs and corporations. The first option is that of 'instant incorporation' and transfer of ownership from the state to a variety of public and private bodies; it is advocated mostly by Lipton and Sachs (1990b) and fully analyzed by Berliner (Chapter 14 in this volume). It would be superfluous to repeat the very careful argumentation made by Berliner on the relative merits of the two options. While I fully concur with Berliner's inclination in favor of the more gradual approach, I believe that some form of incorporation, with the state retaining its ownership status, can serve as a novel administrative device that will mark a departure from the past and serve as a base for new managerial norms of behavior.

The main arguments against immediate, across-the-board privatization are the lack of an infrastructure of legal, financial and other services to handle the problems of evaluation and fairness (if not equity), the absence of institutions and operation of capital and corporate markets, and the doubtful nature of many of the proposed surrogate initial owners.

It is not clear whether this version of privatization will be more successful in creating the right incentives for managers than a properly reformed sector. In any case, even this 'immediate' process is bound to take much longer than first envisaged, and the production sector will continue to deteriorate in the meantime.

Under the alternative model the state assumes full ownership rights, possibly through a new administrative system of management and control, along the lines of a holding company or a system of holding companies, and concentrates its efforts on radically changing the rules of the game for enterprises and managements. Incorporation under a new state authority such as the newly established State Committee on Property (GKI) as proposed by the 'incorporation' school, could serve as a break with the past not only in terms of the rules of the game but also institutionally, by breaking away from the old conservative ministerial system. A decisive move in this direction could also mitigate the worst aspects of 'spontaneous privatization'. If all legal property rights are assigned only through a tightly controlled process, it may be less difficult to prevent present contenders (including local authorities and other administrative bodies, labor collectives and unfit managers) from usurping such rights (see also discussion in Shleifer and Vishny, 1992). Under incorporation, the chosen managers should be remunerated according to performance, including the right to own shares. The main effort under this gradual approach will thus be directed at the development of entrepreneuring market-oriented *managements*, regardless of the form of ownership.

While the concept of the separation of management from ownership is well established in the West, where it serves as the cornerstone of the corporate sector, it is based largely on private ownership and on active capital markets. These two are the main guarantors of a smoothly functioning principal–agent relationship and of efficient performance. In the post-Soviet environment, and with state ownership, special efforts will have to be made to approximate Western-style conditions.

The new state authority will have to enforce a credible hard budget constraint by being as independent as possible, completely separated from the central budget and other government institutions. One important precondition for this to happen is to accept bankruptcy as a possible, even likely event; the actual closure of some heavily money-losing enterprises is a critical element of the plan, and is, indeed, included in both major Soviet plans. The possibility of bankruptcy is an important stimulating factor for managements and workers alike. The fact that workers may have to switch jobs, may be sent to look for jobs in the new private sector, or may even be temporarily unemployed should be established as early as possible. Programs for retraining, orderly replacement and unemployment compensation should be established, using some of the money saved from subsidies. All of the above does not advocate putting off privatization entirely for a later stage, but rather emphasizes the advantages of going about it at a slow pace. The privatization option must remain open at all times and should take place whenever a sound offer by private investors is made.

A special effort will have to be made to create a credible hard budget constraint for the new corporations, and strong credibility for the new kinds of managerial incentives. The other new instruments described above should help in achieving that.

Lest the above scheme of gradual privatization be perceived as a prescription for a new or old-new form of market socialism or a 'Third Way' of ownership relations, let us emphasis the temporary nature of this scheme and the fact that even as a temporary device, it should at most be considered a third-best solution, better only than the alternatives. Keeping most large enterprises under a system of transitory government-owned holding companies will serve to underline the temporary nature of the intermediate forms of ownership by a variety of public organizations as suggested under the incorporation school. Assigning a temporary ownership role to labor may be perpetuated and lead to some kind of labor management or 'share economy'—the first a proved failure and the second an untried experiment.

The main problem with the advocated gradual solution is that any transitory or permanent new scheme involving a continuation of any kind of direct government intervention in the ownership or management of enterprises may turn out to be (and will certainly be regarded as) the perpetuation of the old system under a new guise. This is even more the case if the same bureaucrats of the old system are placed on the new boards of management of the new enterprises or the various holding companies. Before the present changes the Soviet system went through several less radical reforms, in which new arrangements repeatedly turned out to be the same old ones with different names. Paradoxically, it seems that any form of government involvement of the sort that might be fully acceptable in market economies will always be highly suspect and therefore counter-productive under new arrangements in Russia today. In a country where private property was anathema for so long, some bending backwards may be needed to build up trustworthiness and credibility. In order to attract new private entrepreneurship people need to be convinced that there is no overt or covert government intervention. This is also why even long-term leases (on land) are often not accepted as virtually private property, as they certainly are in the West.

Here, too, foreign participation can be of great help. There is no need to repeat all the functions that foreign enterprises and foreign investors can perform, from training to outright investment. One of their most important functions is in guaranteeing the free entrepreneurial nature of their activities in the former Soviet Union and independence from government intervention. The active participation of foreign capital and management in new investment banks or funds, joint stock-holding companies or in individual enterprises will help ensure their market-oriented nature. It would seem that deep involvement in a small number of key organizations and enterprises, with substantial backward and forward linkages, will provide foreign investors with the ability to serve as role models and provide the challenge of competition to many domestic companies. As mentioned above, large domestic trade organizations can assume such leading roles. More generally, foreign capital can move into the borderline zone between the private and the government sectors and help develop a sector of new limited liability stockholding corporations. Such a sector can grow gradually as smaller private companies emerge and incorporate, and as government enterprises are sold off.

In considering foreign aid and international cooperation the main emphasis is usually on opening the recipient economies and assisting in the creation of export capabilities. These are also very important goals of foreign aid and investment in the former Soviet Union, especially in sectors with a promising export potential such as energy. But it seems that the *domestic* role of helping establish and develop an *internal market economy* is much more important and urgent, even when the clear overlap of the two is acknowledged. Even if export potential is the final goal, its gestation period may be much longer than in other countries. Thus, if shortcuts are made (e.g., through isolated free trade zones) the prior target of restructuring the domestic economy may be missed. The main difficulty with foreign investment for domestic purposes, other than the absence of a hospitable business infrastructure, is the inability to create foreign-exchange incomes as profits. It follows that one of the main roles of international aid is to bridge this gap by providing—as credit or outright subsidy, for a number of years—the necessary foreign exchange for repatriated profits. This will put investors who fulfill Soviet domestic needs on an equal footing with the developers of Soviet exports.

*

To conclude, early emphasis should be placed on the creation of a private sector of small-scale operators, including the distribution and housing sectors, and on creating the service, legal and financial infrastructure and preconditions for the introduction of competitive goods and capital markets. In large-scale government enterprises a new system of holding companies should run the enterprises according to market principles and under 'incorporation' and concentrate on training and motivating managements to follow suit. Large-scale privatization should proceed slowly, concentrating mostly on legal and infrastructure preparatory work.

Conclusion: Political-Economic Considerations

The above arguments in favor of a more gradual approach to economic transition rely mainly on economic considerations, given the initial conditions prevailing in the former Soviet Union. The main justification for recommending price revision prior to price liberalization was that such a revision may avoid the emergence of a cost-push inflation spiral and a deep decline in production, thereby fostering stabilization, which is a precondition for structural reform. The main arguments cited were the extreme lack of an adequate infrastructure, the danger of privatized enterprises falling into the wrong hands and the belief that concentrating on new forms of management under government incorporation can provide a smoother transition to a market system.

Regardless of whether or not these arguments have any economic merit, radical transitions of the magnitude dealt with here must also take into account the interaction between economic and political considerations. What steps are likely to be accepted by the population and from which government? How will different economic agents respond? What policies implemented by which government will be credible enough to produce the expected positive results? How much should a government be willing to pay, in terms of economic cost, in order to accommodate popular or political demands?

Broadly speaking, I suggest that the last Soviet government had an economically sound stabilization and price reform program; it failed due to the utter mistrust of the population and to the political struggle over the nature of the reform. The present government, which projects absolute credibility as to its radical intentions, can afford to pursue a more gradual approach.

The last Soviet government failed to stabilize the economy for a number of reasons, some of them beyond the realm of economics, even of political economy: the national aspirations of the republics and the personal and group aspects of the political struggle over the control of the country. That political struggle was, of course, also concerned with the debate over the direction and pace of economic and political changes. The last Soviet governments, headed by Nikolay Ryzhkov and Valentin Pavlov, despite their declared commitment to democracy and to a 'regulated market economy', were considered by the radical opposition as conservative guardians of the old system. Gorbachev was indecisive, but since the end of 1990, sided with the government.

I think that it can be demonstrated that if the last Soviet government had enjoyed greater political support it would have had a good chance to stabilize the economy in 1991, thus setting the stage for further structural changes. This is not the place to advance all the supporting evidence, but a three-way comparison of the original fiscal and monetary program presented by the government for 1991, its systematic mutilation by the Supreme Soviet and the republics throughout that year, and the resultant economic events on the eve of the coup, provide some indication. The original plan, centered around narrowing the budget deficit, suffered during implementation from two ills: first, expenditures designed to compensate households for the proposed price revision were continuously increased, while the severity of price hikes was reduced. At the same time, one of the main weapons used against the central government was withholding of tax revenues by the republics and local governments, revenues that soon found local spending targets. Even so, and despite progressive disintegration of central control, by August 1991 there was a significant decline in the monetary overhang (Vavilov and Viugin, 1991; Ofer, 1992; Cottarelli and Blejer, in Chapter 6 of this volume, conclude that there was no decline in the overhang, but this is based on an underestimation of inflation in my view).

The entire endeavor failed because the government was too weak to withstand populist demands and not credible enough as a reliable reformer. The more gradual reform program was believed to be no more than a cover-up for no reform; indeed, it may have been just that for at least one of the government ministers.

The new Russian government started out with much stronger popular support based on the popularity of Yeltsin after his triumph over the coup. Yeltsin was, and still is, the only major political figure elected to office in a national democratic process. The newly established government grasped the opportunity and embarked on a program of radical reform, described above. The reform, including price liberalization, was announced in advance, late in October and officially came into effect on January 2, 1992. Even this strong government bowed to populist pressure and parliamentary demands to keep the prices of more goods, mostly some basic foods and services, under government control, following the one-time hike. The government also succeeded during the first months to sharply restrict the cash budgetary deficit and the expansion of money. Even so, as mentioned above, the initial price shock exceeded expectations and went far beyond what was needed to eliminate the monetary overhang. In fact, most of the monetary overhang was eliminated in the last two months of 1991 as a result of the inflation that developed in anticipation of the price liberalization.

Following a pause in February, the inflationary spiral resumed in March with very high rates that cannot be explained by official monetary expansion. (To make up for shortage of credit there has been a very fast expansion of illegal inter-enterprise credits, reaching, in April, a level equal to the entire outstanding official bank credits.) At the same time pressures are mounting on both the credit system and the budget; some compromises have already been made in both spheres, and production continues to fall, at least according to official accounts. With all the above it has to be emphasized that the program is still in its initial stages and its fate is far from clear.

The question is whether the present government is strong enough, and its credibility as a promoter of radical reform firm enough, to afford a more gradual approach from the outset, without eroding its credibility. Can it now proceed with a more cautious, though no less decisive privatization plan, as advocated by Berliner in this volume, *plus* self-incorporation, especially if the prospects of an extended period with no stabilization cannot be ruled out. These seem to be hypothetical questions, primarily because the present government is a firm believer in the big-bang approach. One can also present a strong argument that once the loss of control immediately after the coup set in, the option of a program of price revision was doomed from the outset. A similar argument may be made with respect to privatization, that is, that 'spontaneous privatization' has already gained so much momentum that the only option left to the government is to join it rather than fight it (see Shleifer and Vishny, 1992). I doubt that this is already the case, at least with respect to large-scale enterprises, the core of the former Soviet production sector. A conservative government may not have enough political power, public trust and credibility to implement a gradual reform; but a strong government, one with a clear radical stance on the reforms, will have such power and should use it to move ahead more gradually if the economic circumstances warrant such a policy.

Notes

1. The first draft of this paper was prepared at the end of 1990 and was updated in the spring of 1991, when the first scheme of price adjustment was introduced in the Soviet Union. The present version was rewritten in April 1992, as the new radical reform of the Russian government entered its second quarter and a critical stage.

2. This argument seems to have influenced the two Soviet reform programs proposed in the fall of 1990: in the May 1990 version of the government's program, presented by Ryzhkov, the total additional costs to the consumers of the planned price hikes was 200 billion rubles (BR) and the promised compensation was BR 135. In the September version administrative price hikes and compensation were put at BR 135, and the other BR 65 of price hikes were left for the free market to take care of. Likewise, the main 'populist' pitch of the Shatalin program is to avoid direct responsibility for increased prices and leave most of it to the market. If the data that accompanied the plan are correct, such free price hikes would have reduced real incomes by about 10 percent by the end of the first 100 days. Note that the Shatalin plan advocated the preservation of the prices of most subsidized goods for a time and thus, too, the subsidies themselves.

References and Selected Bibliography

Allison, Graham, and Gregory Yavlinski. 1991. *Window of Opportunity*. Cambridge, Mass. and Moscow.

Abalkin, Leonid *et al.* 1990. "Program on Regulated Market Economy Structure and Mechanism Formation" (The Government Reform Program; official English Translation). September.

Alexashenko, Sergey and Leonid Grigoriev. 1990. "Privatization and Capital Market." July. Mimeograph.

Aslund, Anders. 1991a. "The Soviet Economic Crisis: Causes and Dimensions,"

Stockholm Institute of Soviet and East European Economics, Working Paper No. 16.

——. 1991b. "The Soviet Economic Crisis: An Abortive Search for a Solution." Stockholm Institute of Soviet and East European Research, Working Paper No. 17.

Berliner, J. S. 1983. "Managing the USSR Economy, Alternative Models," *Problems of Communism* (January–February): 40–56.

Bruno, Michael. 1992 (forthcoming). "Stabilization and Reform in Eastern Europe, a Preliminary Evaluation." IMF Discussion Paper.

CEC. 1990. *European Economy: Stabilization, Liberalization and Devolution, Assessment of the Economic Situation and Reform Process in the Soviet Union.*

Economic Situation, see State Committee of Statistics.

Feige, Edgar. 1990. "Perestroika and Socialist Privatization: 'What Is to Be Done: And How?'" San Francisco: International Center for Economic Growth, Working Paper No. 1. March.

Fischer, Stanley and Alan Gelb. 1991. "The Process of Socialist Economic Transformation," *Journal of Economic Perspectives*, 5 (Fall, No. 4): 91–105.

Gorbachev, Mikhail. 1990. "Basic Directions for Stabilization of the Economy and the Conversion to a Market Economy" (program presented to the Supreme Soviet, October 15).

Hanson, Philip. 1990. "Property Rights in the New Phase of Reforms," *Soviet Economy*, No. 2: 95–124.

Hewett, Ed, A. 1990–1991. "The New Soviet Plan," *Foreign Affairs*, Winter: 146–67.

IMF *et al.* 1991. *A Survey of the Soviet Economy.*

Kornai, Janos. 1990. *The Road to a Free Economy: Shifting from a Socialist System: The Example of Hungary.* New York: Norton.

Lipton, David and Jeffrey Sachs. 1990a. "Creating a Market Economy in Eastern Europe: The Case of Poland." In William Brainard and George Perry (eds.), *Economic Activity*, No. 1. Washington, D.C.: Brookings Institution.

——. 1990b. "Privatization in Eastern Europe: The Case of Poland," *Brookings Economic Papers,* Vol. 2, pp. 293–339.

"Memorandum of Economic Policy" (in Russian) *Nezavisimaya Gazeta*, March 3, 1992 (The economic program of the Russian government for 1992 and beyond).

Ministry of Economics of the Russian Federation. 1992. "Forecast Evaluation of the Basic Socio-Economic Growth of the Russian Federation During the Fourth Quarter of 1992 and During 1992." Mimeograph (in Russian). Moscow.

Murrell, Peter. 1990. "Evolutionary Privatization," *Plan Econ Report*, June 29.

Ofer, Gur. 1990. "The Service Sector in Soviet Economic Reforms: Does Convergence Finally arrive?" Paper presented at the Fourth World Congress for Soviet and East European Studies, Harrowgate, 21–26 July.

——. 1991. "Macroeconomic Issues of Soviet Reforms," *Macroeconomic Annual 1991*, Cambridge, Mass.: NBER, pp. 297–334.

——. Forthcoming 1992. "Fiscal Developments and Economic Reforms in the Soviet Union, 1991: Can a Gradual Reform Work?"

Shatalin, Stanislav *et al.* 1990. *Transition to the Market*. Part I. Moscow: Arkhangelskoe, August. [The Shatalin Plan].

Shleifer, Andrei and Robert W. Vishny. 1992. "Privatization in Russia: First Steps." Mimeograph.

State Committee of Statistics of the Russian Federation. 1992. *The Economic Situation of the Russian Federation in January–February 1992*. Mimeograph (in Russian). Moscow.

"The Economy of the CIS in 1991." 1992. Mimeograph in Russian.

Vavilov, Andrey and Oleg Viugin. 1991. "Inflation in the USSR." Mimeograph.

Weitzman, Martin. 1984. *The Share Economy: Conquering Stagflation*. Cambridge, Mass.: Harvard University Press.

8

Polish Economic Reform: Principles, Policies and Surprises

Stanislaw Gomulka

Reform Principles

Overall Aims of the Reform

It is often emphasized, quite correctly, that unlike the economic reforms of 1960s, 1970s and early 1980s, the long-term purpose of the present wave of reform in Eastern Europe is no longer the marketization of Soviet-style socialism but the embracement of Western (welfare state) capitalism, and that therefore the reforms involve not merely a change within the system, but a change of the system itself. Such a dramatic change requires extensive remodelling of institutions, skills and attitudes, and it must therefore be a process extending over a number of years. In this process, privatization of ownership is the dominant concern. However, in the initial phases of the reform the public sector continues to dominate. Since central planning and management is already limited or no longer exists, the immediate aim of reformers is to put into place a market-based price system. This system would take over the traditional role of planners in guiding economic agents, especially state-owned enterprises, about their allocative choices. The transformation in this first stage may be described as one from a modified (indirectly) centrally regulated economy of the Hungarian type to a market-regulated economy, the latter to be changed, in the course of the 1990s, into a full-fledged market economy of the Western type.

In the autumn of 1989 the new Polish reform government faced another urgent problem: the restoration of internal and external credibility of its macroeconomic policies. Internal credibility was severely eroded in 1988 and especially in 1989, when massive subsidies led to large budget deficits and near hyperinflation. External credibility was low and declining further with the rapid rise of international debts.

A recently drafted policy memorandum defines the aims of the Polish reform in the following way:[1] At the beginning of 1990, the government of

Poland launched a far-reaching program to stabilize the economy and transform it progressively into a market system. The underlying aim is to improve efficiency in an equitable and environmentally compatible manner, to raise living standards on a sustainable basis, and to restore external creditworthiness. During 1990, the principal focus of policy was directed toward stabilization objectives and, in particular, to achieving a sharp drop in the underlying rate of inflation. At the same time, however, important steps were taken toward reducing structural rigidities and developing the legal, institutional and regulatory framework for further systemic reform. The government of Poland is determined to build on this progress and, in particular, to accelerate the implementation of structural and systemic change. This memorandum outlines our objectives and policies for the period 1991–1993. (A summary of these objectives and policies is given in the Appendix to this chapter.)

The Sequencing Problem

It is useful, perhaps even essential, for the reformers to formulate a 'game plan' that sets out the main reform measures to be taken and the sequence in which they are to be implemented. Polish reformers of the Mazowiecki government faced this task in September 1989, and they came up with the Balcerowicz Plan. The crucial principles of this Plan, in my opinion, were (Gomulka, 1990a):

a. Price liberalization, substantial reduction of subsidies and internal convertibility of the domestic currency must come first, before major structural reforms are initiated.
b. To protect internal convertibility, expansion of international reserves must take priority over price stability in the initial period of the reform. A large up-front devaluation and high inertial inflation may therefore be necessary.
c. Stabilization of the liberalized prices must be based on the standard IMF approach, with an important role assigned to a tough incomes policy, in addition to a balanced budget, rather than being based solely on a restrictive monetary policy.
d. Structural reforms must involve both a radical increase in the number of independent enterprises (by breaking up large firms) and an ownership reform, with the dual aim of creating competitive markets and a large—ultimately predominant—private sector.
e. International assistance for the reform program should include the recognition, by both private banks and governments, that radical reforms call for large sacrifices and that, therefore, a substantial part of the debt accumulated in the pre-reform period cannot be repaid or serviced without putting the reform program at risk. Specifically, balance-of-payments considerations must take second place in any stand-by agreement with the IMF.

These principles represented the common ground within the inner 'reform group' of the Mazowiecki government. They also defined what is usually termed the sequencing of the reforms. In that respect, principle (a) is particularly crucial. The urgency to stabilize prices arose from the fact that a near hyperinflation had been raging since the beginning of August 1989. However, it might have been (and was) argued that price liberalization should wait until the big monopolies are dismantled. The problem with this argument was that proper de-monopolization would take a long time. In the meantime, given the poor quality of the price system, it would be impossible to know which enterprises were really profitable and which were not. It was recognized that some price regulation could remain, but that the key price signals should be provided by markets as soon as possible, so that structural changes—involving the closure or restructuring of loss-making and really hopeless enterprises—could proceed already in spring 1990, and be conducted on a sound economic basis. But to reduce the impact of monopolized market structure, convertibility became essential. In this respect, the experience with auctions and a legalized (since March 1989) free dollar market for households became helpful in providing information about the appropriate level of the unified exchange rate. Convertibility was also very important in its own right, as a psychological signal to enterprises and the public that this reform is qualitatively different from past experiments, and as an economic instrument to improve the mobility of resources between net exporters and net importers.

The anti-inflationary program did not involve any new economic theory. Its principles were well known. But it did involve the necessity for (statistical) real wages to drop sharply, something which can be implemented only by a strong government.

Under (d), privatization, unemployment and competition policies are the key reforms. Placing price liberalization before privatization is partly deliberate and partly inevitable. Principle (e) is based on the view that it could eventually be accepted by the Western creditors that the success of reforms in Eastern Europe is in their long-term interest, whether or not the debts are repaid. The debt and the large burden of their servicing have helped to expose the weaknesses of the centralized economic systems, and have consequently helped the reform process. In that respect they have already served an important purpose.

The distinct emphasis of the Plan on regaining and maintaining macroeconomic control had important microeconomic implications (initially not fully anticipated by the reform designers), in the form of a few bankruptcies and a slow pace of structural adjustment in 1990. Macroeconomic concerns dictated a course of action that resulted in a steep drop of real wages. Low wages maintained the high profitability of enterprises despite the recession. This, in turn, ensured high revenue for the government budget and low expenditure on salaries in the budget-funded sector of the economy. High profitability was also helped, in 1990, by a large devaluation of the zloty, designed to promote net exports and maintain stability of the exchange rate. This exchange rate policy sharply improved the external position of the country. The policy was inflationary in two ways—it increased unit costs and contributed to monetary expansion—but it helped the budget and reduced recession. The overall outcome of this macro policy was that inefficient enterprises continued to make a profit, and therefore did not come under pressure to undertake any drastic, cost-cutting measures.

The strategy itself was deliberate, even if it went too far in the first half of 1990. It was motivated by the desire to avoid a catastrophe of the East German type: large-scale bankruptcies and large-scale unemployment at the start of the reform. The implicit choice of sequencing was after all to deal first with macro problems such as the budget deficit, inflation and foreign debt, and only later with the more fundamental, difficult and time-consuming problem of microeconomic inefficiency.

How Fast? Gradualism Versus a Big Bang

A structural adjustment can be slow or fast, but it must always be gradual. (So far the only exception to this rule is East Germany, where plunging into a completely open system with highly competitive markets has destroyed much of the existing economic structure; however, large human and capital resources of West Germany are available there to help create a new system, and, in the meantime, to provide adequate social safety nets.) In contrast to such structural adjustment, stabilization and liberalization measures are easy to devise and implement.

Moreover, a case could be made for introducing the measures all at once (Dornbusch, 1990), especially if initial conditions are those of a crisis, as they were in Poland in the second half of 1989. Strong measures are then needed anyway to avoid a collapse. In a crisis situation the population is also more inclined to accept a large dose of sacrifice in exchange for some prospects, however distant and unclear, of an improvement.

The Polish package of measures was implemented on January 1, 1990. It represented a distinct discontinuity in the process of reform. The package was also a strong psychological signal to the population that the government was taking charge of the crisis situation and that the imminent reform might this time be real.

On January 1, 1990, Poland also unilaterally suspended servicing the debt to commercial banks. Despite this measure, on February 5, 1990, the Executive Board of the IMF approved a stand-by arrangement with Poland for a period of 13 months. This support of the IMF opened the way for a wide range of other forms of Western assistance, among them substantial loans from the World Bank and grants and loans from the European Economic Community.

On April 18, 1991, the IMF approved a three-year Extended Fund Facility

(EFF) arrangement in the amount of SDR 1,224 million. On April 19, 1991, The Paris Club reduced Polish debt of $33.3 billion by 30 percent ($10 billion) promising a further reduction of 20 percent of the present volume of debt in three years' time, conditional upon successful implementation of the EFF arrangement. This and some other debt reduction measures appear to make the servicing of the Polish debt manageable.[2] The consequent gain of external credibility may open the way to closer economic relations between Poland and the Western community and thus provide vital long-term support for the reform process.

Initial Conditions

The inflation rate of some 30 percent monthly in the second half of 1989 served one useful purpose: it drastically slashed real money balances.[3] The monetary overhang was eliminated. Inflationary pressure was still high due to the excess of the flow of income over the flow of consumer supplies. The purchasing power of wages at the beginning of each month was excessive, and prices rose in the course of the month to eliminate that excess. In Figure 8.1 it is assumed that the money wage is spent in equal daily installments of 100 units, and the inflation rate is 1 percent a day. This inflation reduces daily purchasing power from 100 units on day 1 to 70 units on day 30. The inflation would be eliminated instantly by an up-front reduction of money wages by 15 percent, from 100 to 85 units.

The budget deficit dropped sharply in the closing months of 1989, but the government budget was still overburdened with large subsidies. Price distortions were large; for example, the price of coal was about 10 percent of the world price. Interest rates rose sharply in December 1989, but remained strongly negative in real terms. The official exchange rate also was increased sharply in November and December 1989, but remained far below the free market rate, making rationing of foreign exchange necessary.

In 1989 the statistical real wage (with bonuses) was 28 percent higher than in 1987. A sizable fall in wages following liberalization and stabilization was thus necessary. In 1990 the real wage (also with bonuses) was 15 percent lower than in 1987, the fall reflecting lower productivity as output declined more than employment.

The War of Economic Ideas

Modern economies are so complex that, even if uncertainty were not present (which it is in large measure), no one can predict all the economic implications of any policy decision. In addition to this technical difficulty, the same economic outcomes have different welfare and political implications for different policy-makers. Judgments on all these matters have to be made continuously. In making these judgments policy-makers are helped by analytical discussions based on empirical evidence (including the experience of other countries) and on theoretical considerations.

Figure 8.1. The area OABC represents the real wage. The shaded area ABD represents the inflation tax

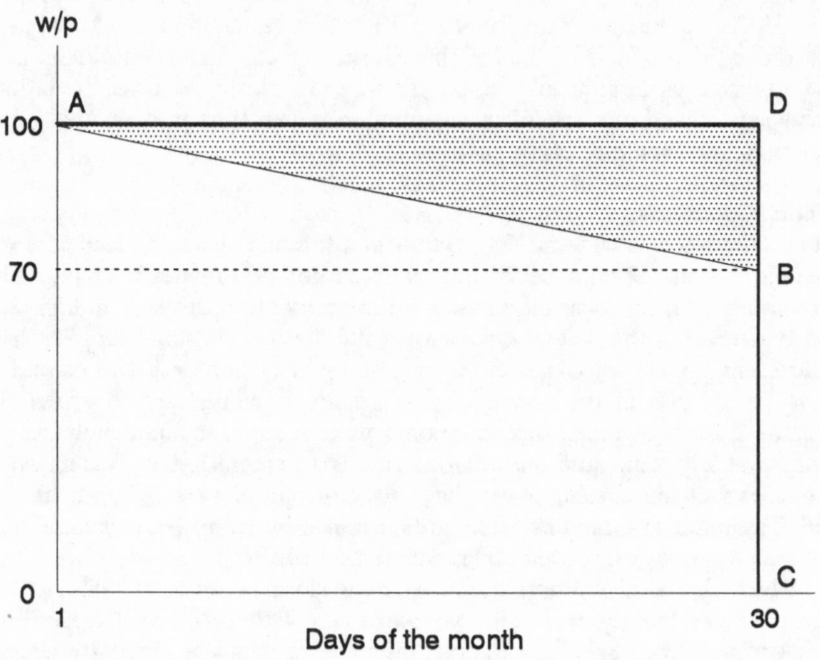

Before discussing specific macroeconomic policies it may be useful to dwell briefly on the major economic ideas that played a part in motivating the choice of these policies between September 1989 and the end of 1990.

1) Keynesian-type versus structural causes of recession. This was perhaps the most fundamental debate, affecting policies on wages, budget deficits and monetary expansion. The structuralists are those who, in the particular circumstances of post-communist countries in transition, regard major changes in the microeconomic environment of enterprises as the primary cause of the recession. Specifically, sharp rises in some input prices have made the production of specific goods unprofitable, and sharply increased output prices have reduced specific demands. The new relative prices required a corresponding change in the entire product composition of the economy's supply side. But owing to the presence of various rigidities, some resources had to remain idle before they could be redeployed to produce what, under new prices, was in demand and profitable.

This micro-adjustment of the supply side was reinforced by the disappearance of shortages and therefore of forced buying of other goods—the so-called forced substitution. The collapse of trade with the former CMEA area was another important factor of the same category. Since all these adjustments are large and necessary, the structuralists, such as this author, expect the East European recession to be deep, long and inevitable. They therefore regard it as a Schumpeterian 'creative destruction' phenomenon, similar in type to (though larger in scale than) the Western recession of the early 1980s, following the oil price shock of 1979.

Pure Keynesians, on the other hand, conduct their analysis in purely aggregate terms and emphasize the potential impact on economic activity of policies that reduce aggregate demand. The implicit assumption of their analysis is that 'full employment output' has remained essentially unchanged, despite the change in the micro-environment. Polish policy makers were divided as to the weight of aggregate versus micro factors. However, the main thrust of the policy assumed that the structuralist analysis was the dominating doctrine.

*2) **Demand-pull versus cost-push causes of inflation.*** This issue relates to the question of assumptions about price formation underlying Polish economic policy: were short-term prices believed to be demand determined or of a 'cost-plus' nature? and if the latter—how did this belief affect macro-financial policy?

The short answer to this question is that, following price liberalization, most prices were assumed to follow the cost-plus principle, with supply adjusting to demand at these prices. The anti-inflationary policy therefore aimed to restrict the growth of unit nominal costs, especially wage costs. Incomes policy was the primary instrument of wage control, especially in the state sector. However, it was believed that this policy instrument would not survive for long unless supported by the full combination of other (monetary, fiscal and exchange rate) policies. The purpose of the support was to harden the budget constraint of enterprises and to increase competition. Profit margins did vary significantly among enterprises and industrial sectors, as well as over time, indicating that demand factors were also important. The view that relaxation of financial policies would increase wages, prices and imports rather than domestic output was tested in the second half of 1990 and the results of this test were interpreted as confirming that view (to be discussed further in the next section).

*3) **Market-driven versus state-driven industrial restructuring.*** Past experience with excessive state intervention has prompted key policy makers to leave the task of reorganizing their activities largely to the enterprises themselves. The idea of formulating an active industrial policy was rejected. In any case, the central authorities did not have the human and material resources required by an 'active' industrial policy. These resources—such as they were—were held by enterprises and banks. Still, selective industrial policy was pursued through direct subsidies[4] and new institutions created for that purpose. Another instrument of restructuring was privatization, and this endeavor was mainly in the hands of central and local authorities. It was also hoped that increased financial discipline, elimination of the central allocation of inputs and increased competition would prompt state enterprises to apply themselves more vigorously to the job of restructuring. While the desire to avoid large-scale bankruptcies was paramount, there was also a desire to allow some closures to emphasize the break with old, paternalistic attitudes.

Macroeconomic Policies

In Figure 8.2, the short-term equilibria of the Polish economy, before and after the January 1, 1990, measures were taken, are represented by point E_0 (before) and point E_1 (after). Point E_0 lies on the vertical segment of the initial supply curve S_0 in order to indicate the presence of excessive demand and inflation. The price liberalization shifted the horizontal part of the supply curve upwards and reduced (maximum) potential output from Y_0 to Y. The difference $(Y_0 - Y)$ represents the impact of the supply shock arising from the sharp change in the composition of demand in response to changes in relative prices (see Gomulka, 1991, for a further discussion of this impact). Ideally, the demand curve should have shifted only from D_0 to D so that, at new prices, aggregate demand would still suffice to buy the new (reduced) maximum output. Suppose, however, that the demand curve was shifted further, from D_0 to D_1. The difference $(Y - Y_1)$ would then be attributed to an excessive contraction of aggregate demand. The problem is that Y is not known, and only the aggregate outcome of the two effects, supply shock and excessive demand contraction, is observed.

Given the switch on January 1, 1990, to a demand-constrained regime, the standard IS/LM analysis may be used to discuss the shift of the aggregate demand function caused by the reform package. The two key equations are:

$$Y = I(r) + C(Y^d, M/p) + G + X(Y, e/p)$$
$$M/p = L(Y, r)\,,$$

where $C(Y^d, M/p)$ is consumption as a function of disposable income Y^d and monetary wealth M/p; X is net export as a function of income Y and the real rate of exchange of the zloty, e/p; and $L(Y, r)$ is the demand for money.

Figure 8.2. Shifts in Aggregate Supply and Demand Functions Following Stabilization and Liberalization Measures

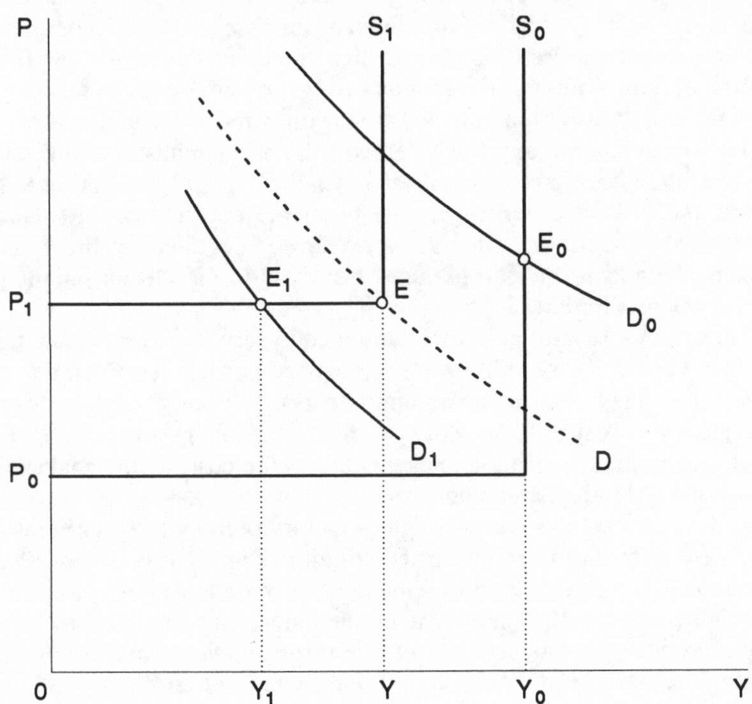

$Y_0 - Y$ — the effect of supply-side shocks.
$Y - Y_1$ — the effect of excessively restrictive policies.

Assuming G is constant, a fall in the real money holdings, M/p, generates or requires a rise in the interest rate, r, and a fall in output, Y. The magnitude of the fall in income depends on the elasticities of the four functions, I, C, X and L, with respect to appropriate variables.

The key policy instruments used in an attempt to stabilize prices and improve external equilibrium were the standard four: interest rate, exchange rate, the budget and a tax on excessive wages. In what follows I briefly discuss the policies and motivations of the policy makers in making their particular choices.

Interest Rates

The structure of interest rates is largely determined by the base rate (called the refinance rate in Poland). The central bank (National Bank of Poland, NBP) is empowered to set that rate. Formally, the NBP is independent of the government; its governor is appointed by Parliament at the recommendation of the country's President. In practice, the dependence of the NBP on government authorities is and remains strong. Policies on interest rates and exchange rates since September 1989 are the outcome of discussions between the Ministry of Finance and the NBP, with the prime minister and the IMF being consulted once a consensus was reached. (The only exception to this rule was the NBP decision to set the base rate for February 1990 at 20 percent, five percentage points above the rate suggested by the Finance Minister. The role of the IMF in that decision, and generally during the first half of 1990, was important.)

Active interest rates policy was designed to serve three main functions: (a) Control demand for credit by enterprises and households. (b) Induce the transfer of savings from dollar accounts to zloty accounts, and in this way support convertibility of the zloty at the set exchange rate. (c) Provide correct information to economic agents about the cost of financial capital. Let us discuss these functions in turn.

a) The ability to mount a tough monetary policy was essential in the government's attempt to reduce price inflation. High interest rates, reserve ratios and informal persuasion of the central bank have been used, quite successfully, to control demand for credit. There was the concern that, if banking credit were too limited, inter-enterprise involuntary credit could escalate. The latter credit did increase sharply in the first half of 1990, and again in the first half of 1991, but credit of this type is not a liquid monetary asset and therefore only a minor threat to the effectiveness of the overall monetary policy.

b) In December 1989, the share of zloty-denominated money in total money was a mere 28 percent (foreign currency deposits valued at the exchange rate of January 2, 1990; if valued at the average December rate of Zł 5,235 per US$, the share was still a modest 41 percent). A substantial increase of this share was essential and, indeed, has been a major policy objective of the stabilization program. In early 1990 the credit squeeze prompted enterprises to sell most of their foreign currency deposits to the central bank. But the household sector—the major holder of these deposits—has continued to keep its foreign exchange, even though its purchasing power would have been much better protected if exchanged into zloty-denominated deposits. The interest rate policy was nevertheless successful in persuading the households to keep all new savings in zloty-denominated form. Consequently, by the end of 1990, the share of zloty-denominated money in total money was 59 percent; it increased to 72 percent by the end of February 1991. The persistence of households in hanging on to their dollars is evidence of the limited credibility of the stabilization program throughout 1990.

c) The interest rate policy was also guided by the idea that real interest rates on long-term deposits should be positive. The money markets are being developed with an aim to provide a more precise guide for policy makers about the right levels of interest rates.

The Exchange Rate

The internal convertibility of the zloty and the relative stability of the exchange rate are two major achievements of the reform so far. The unexpected durability of the initial exchange rate is not yet fully understood. In setting the rate the policy makers were largely guided by the following two considerations: the rate should withstand the expected increase (75 percent) in domestic prices in the first quarter of 1990, and the rate should remain unchanged at least during that first quarter despite low international reserves. The large uncertainty as to what the right choice should be prompted the government negotiators to resist the suggestion to make the stability of the exchange rate a performance criterion under a standby arrangement with the IMF.

The stability of the exchange rate may seem remarkable in view of the fact that the increase in prices in 1990 was about 250 percent rather than 94 percent assumed in the program. The pegging of the zloty to the US dollar was helped by the devaluation of the latter against all major OECD currencies during 1990. The liberalization of exports and the deep recession must also have been important factors behind the stability of the zloty/dollar exchange rate and a large increase in dollar exports in the course of 1990. However, the key factor was a succession of devaluations of the real exchange rate in November and December 1989, and on January 2, 1990.

A good indicator of the (relative) real exchange rate is the ratio of the official exchange rate to the rate implied by the purchasing power parity (PPP). Using the parities provided for Poland by the International Comparison Project, this (relative) real exchange rate is given in Table 8.1.

In the light of these figures and the fact that the exchange rate has remained constant for much longer than planned, the 65 percent devaluation of the zloty on December 26, 1989, and January 2, 1990, may appear to be excessive for the purposes the policy makers wished to achieve. The devaluation resulted from lack of confidence in the official exchange rate, stemming from the estimate that in the past some 20 percent of Polish exports had been unprofitable, and from the fact that the market exchange rate used to be much higher than the official exchange rate. (The state of mind of the Polish reform group may be illustrated by the fact that it expected the average exchange rate in 1990 to be Zł 14,500, despite the expected inflation rate of 94 percent compared with the actual rate of 250 percent.)

Table 8.1. Relative Exchange Rates, 1985–1990

	PPP	Exchange rate (PPP = 1)
1985	71.6	2.05
1986	82.7	2.12
1987	99.9	2.66
1988	153.7	2.80
1989	505.0	2.85
1989, XII	1,269	4.11
1990, I	2,228	4.26
1990, II	2,734	3.46
1990, III	2,872	3.31
1990, IV	3,081	3.08
1990, V	3,217	2.95
1990, VI	3,310	2.86
1990, XII	4,200	2.26

Source: Marczewski (1991).

The Polish experience in 1990 suggests that the PPP should be taken seriously in gauging the proper exchange rate under a regime with internal convertibility. Having said that, I am not proposing to accept that the January devaluation also was 'excessive' in the sense that it contributed to recession and was therefore a mistake.

The link with recession often is made on the grounds that before any devaluation has a chance to stimulate exports, it increases prices and therefore reduces the real money balances in the economy, and is therefore equivalent to a contractionary monetary policy. This argument, however, does not hold in the particular circumstances of Poland where, in December 1989, nearly 60 percent of total money supply was dollar-denominated. The share is much greater than the share of imports in GDP and, therefore, the January 1990, devaluation increased money supply much more than it increased prices.[5] To be more precise, the dollars held by households should be converted into zlotys at the market rather than at the official exchange rate. With this correction, the increase in the nominal money supply caused by the end-December 1989–January 1990 devaluations was about 25 percent, while the direct inflationary impact of the devaluations was about 15 percent.

Any substantial up-front devaluation runs the risk of a large gap opening between international and domestic prices for tradables. When such a gap exists, the convertibility of the currency and the opening up of the economy to the world market cannot serve the purpose of enhancing competition and restraining inflation. On the contrary, domestic producers would then be given the green light to pass on any cost increases in prices.

However, in the Polish case the large dollar deposits of households and the much lower official reserves of the central bank represented an immediate grave threat to the sustainability of the convertibility of the currency, and hence to the reform program itself. The policy of high initial devaluation was designed to promote exports and limit imports, thereby quickly improving the balance of payments position. The high interest rate policy was, in turn, designed to discourage households from using their zloty savings to buy foreign exchange in the open market. The purpose of both policies was to preserve, and preferably increase, the international reserves of the banking sector. In 1990 this policy objective took priority over price stability.

The fixed exchange rate began to act as a nominal anchor by the end of 1990. Evidence in support of this view is provided by the sharp deterioration of the trade balance and some reduction in profit margins, despite an improvement in the level of economic activity. In view of the continuing high inflation, it became necessary to alter the exchange rate policy at some point, from a fixed peg to a crawling peg. The timing of this change became a major policy problem at the end of 1990 and during 1991. Since official reserves had improved substantially, it was now feasible to make the reduction of inflation a primary concern. Accordingly, the exchange rate continued to be fixed for most of 1991.[6] This policy soon came under extreme pressure, since it contributed to the collapse of enterprise profits and to the consequent crisis in the state budget. On the other hand, the collapse of profits helped to relieve the pressure exerted by the trade unions on the government to suspend the incomes policy in the state sector of the economy. The preservation of this incomes policy was seen as crucial to reducing inflation.

Pricing, Subsidies and Fiscal Policy

The respective shares of freely determined agricultural, industrial and consumer prices in early 1991 were 100 percent, 88 percent and 83 percent, respectively (Republic of Poland, 1991). Administered prices apply only to alcohol, electricity, gas, heating and hot water, state-housing rents, postal services and telecommunications, and state rail and road transport.

The price liberalization enabled the government to reduce subsidies: in terms of GDP shares, subsidies dropped from 15 percent in 1989 to 6 percent in 1990. Government finances also improved as a result of the nearly total elimination of tax exemptions granted to enterprises. Another major (and unexpected) factor that bolstered the fiscal position was the high profitability of state-owned enterprises, due to factors which we have already discussed. The purpose of the fiscal policy was simply to have a balanced budget. In fact, the program for 1990 allowed for a budget deficit in the first half of the year, to be followed by a budget surplus in the second half. The actual developments were very much the other way round, largely due to the fact that real wages followed quite a different path from the one assumed in the program (see the next section).

Incomes Policy

The original intention of the policy makers was to use a tax-based incomes policy as an instrument to protect profits (and hence revenues) for the budget and investment finance of the enterprises themselves. The chief reason was uncertainty about how effective monetary policy alone would be as an instrument to control wages. It was feared that under Polish (indeed, under any East European) conditions, in order to be really effective, monetary policy would have to be extremely contractionary. Although corrective inflation in the first quarter of 1990 was much higher than assumed, the authorities decided, for fear of even larger inflation, to stick to the original monetary targets in nominal terms. Consequently, real money balances fell much more sharply than planned and the enterprise sector experienced an unprecedented liquidity squeeze. The result of this, and of the general uncertainty about future sales, was that during the first six months of 1990 wages remained significantly below the ceiling levels specified by the tax-incomes policy.

As already explained, in June 1990, the authorities decided to somewhat relax fiscal and monetary policies for the second half of the year. In practice, the relaxation proved greater than intended. The liquidity position of enterprises and business prospects began to improve significantly, enabling them to increase wages above the ceiling levels specified by the incomes policy for the second half of 1990. The wage increase reserve accumulated in the first half of 1990 was so large, however, that the policy started to be a binding constraint only in the latter part of the year. The continuing application of the policy compelled enterprises to reduce nominal wages in the beginning of 1991, precisely when inflation accelerated due to a new wave of increases in administrative prices. As mentioned earlier, this coincidence caused a near mass revolt against the policy.

The policy's survival in the early part of 1991 was again helped by a substantial deterioration of the liquidity position of state-owned enterprises. The deterioration was caused in part by a new supply-side shock in the form of a massive loss of exports to the former CMEA area and a large increase in the price of imports from this area following the dollarization of trade. The continuing fixed exchange rate has given rise to two additional factors: the lower profitability of exports to Western markets and the much higher competitiveness of Western imports. Finally, the need to rapidly reduce inflation prompted the authorities to conduct a non-accommodating monetary policy. This time the new pro-recessionary developments on both the supply and the demand side are causing grave problems in the budget. But they are also bound to accelerate the structural adjustment, albeit at a cost in the form of bankruptcies and increased unemployment.

Surprises and Policy Disputes

I have already alluded to instances of policy makers making wrong forecasts or wrong assumptions and being surprised by subsequent developments. (Of course, not all policy makers or their advisers were truly surprised.) Some of the forecasts, e.g., of prices and output, were dictated primarily by political expediency and were designed to produce a more optimistic outcome than really possible. Some of the other surprises were both favorable and genuine, e.g., the strong budget stance in 1990, the unusual export boom and the longevity of the fixed exchange rate. But if I had to name some major unpleasant developments that caught not only many policy makers, but also economists and, possibly, the general public by surprise, they would be the following: (i) deeper and longer recession, (ii) higher unemployment and inflation, (iii) a slower pace of restructuring and (iv) less foreign investment.

These surprises have given rise to major policy disputes, centered (among other things) around the following questions. Is having a stabilization policy a precondition for or a hindrance to sustained growth? Was controlled macroeconomic relaxation, such as the one implemented in the second half of 1990, insufficient or an unnecessary blunder? Is an incomes policy a lesser evil or a socially divisive and avoidable hindrance to efficiency and structural adjustment? Given the underdeveloped condition of many markets and the slow pace of privatization, should not the economic policy of the government assume, for some time yet, a more active role in enterprise management and resource allocation?

Let me very briefly discuss three of the surprises.

Deeper and Longer Recession

If official statistics are to be believed, Polish GDP fell nearly 12 percent, domestic expenditure fell 20 percent and private consumption fell 14 percent in 1990. The level of economic activity in 1991 is substantially lower than it was a year ago. Compared to the last four months of 1990, industrial output is down some 15–20 percent. It becomes evident that instead of the anticipated recovery in GDP of some 3–4 percent on a year-to-year basis, there is likely to be a further fall of some 8 percent. This, and the likely spread of bankruptcies, are accelerating the increase in unemployment.

The crucial unknown is the reaction of state-owned enterprises to the harsher financial environment. The prospects of privatization increase uncertainty among managers and workers, providing them with no strong incentive to think long-term. But large-scale and rapid privatization seems to be the quickest way to establish an incentive structure promoting efficiency, which is a precondition for sustainable growth. In the short run, higher efficiency is likely to imply more unemployment and more recession.

Higher Unemployment and Inflation

Much higher unemployment is likely, perhaps reaching 20 percent or more of the non-agricultural labor force in 1992. In enterprises threatened with partial or complete closure, the workers may prefer lower real wages to unemployment; there is already some evidence of this. Lower real wages may slow down restructuring, but they should keep unemployment and inflation in check and thereby allow the reform process to survive. Such a fall in real wages would also apply to the budget-funded sector and therefore help keep the government budget deficit under control.

The reform could be blown off course by any strong resistance to lower real wages, in the face of lower output and productivity. The likelihood of such strong resistance cannot be dismissed. If it happens, and if monetary authorities accommodate, an acceleration of both unemployment and inflation would inevitably ensue.

Slower Pace of Restructuring

A really fast restructuring policy, which is the East German solution, is likely to be socially and politically suicidal in other post-communist countries. Small-scale privatization involves lower transition costs and is therefore promoted, as, indeed, it should be. The privatization of large enterprises begins with their commercialization, a step that has a chance of improving the performance by clarifying the role of managers as industrial leaders. Their subsequent privatization has to be well prepared if it is not to risk large social costs.

Conclusion

The cost of the Polish reform so far, as measured by the fall in GDP in 1990–1991, is 15–18 percent of the pre-reform GDP. The second year of the reform is proving substantially more difficult than the first, critically straining social support for the reform process. However, activity has probably reached its nadir, and macroeconomic equilibrium has been maintained.

International reserves have been increased substantially and a large part of international debt has been canceled. The costly readjustment of foreign trade away from the former CMEA area, mainly to Western Europe, has been completed. The convertibility of the currency at a unified rate has been maintained without much difficulty. Inflation has been brought down (from about 30 percent monthly in the second half of 1989 to about 2 percent monthly in the second half of 1991). The quality of the price system has improved radically and small-scale privatization is nearly complete. Structural changes, including privatization, represent disturbances which, however, are unlikely to cause any major deterioration. If the reforms continue at the present pace, a noticeable improvement should begin in 1993. A return to the pre-reform level of GDP is therefore unlikely before 1995.

Postscript

At the end of 1991 a new (third) post-communist government came to power in Poland. It has the difficult task of counteracting the continuing recessionary trends and promoting the privatization reform while at the same time defending the substantial stabilization gains of the past two years. All this in circumstances of rising concern among the population over the social costs of the transition and with a divided parliament.

In early 1992 the government took stock of the situation and considered policy corrections for 1992. The starting point was to note the adverse developments in 1991, as follows:

1. High price indexation of wages and wage indexation of welfare benefits, and an accommodating monetary policy, led to a persistently high inflation rate despite a sizable appreciation of the real exchange rate and substantial unemployment.
2. Delays in the introduction of personal income tax and VAT and excessive increases in pensions and other benefits led to a crisis in public finances.
3. The mistaken utilization of the exchange rate as a key nominal anchor, while incomes and monetary policy were lax, combined with delays in the introduction of higher import tariffs, led—through the large appreciation in the rate—to a spectacular rise in consumer imports and the disappearance of the trade surplus.
4. This influx of imports was, in turn, a major factor in the excessively rapid increase (from about 10 percent to about 35 percent) in the number of state enterprises that became loss-making and suffered a decline in credit-worthiness. This development has threatened a further dose of recession in 1992 and a financial crisis in the banking sector.
5. Despite a steep drop in GDP, private consumption has increased significantly, especially consumption of imported luxury goods, while investment in fixed capital declined further.
6. The financial support of the IMF for the Polish program was suspended in autumn 1991, after Poland failed to meet the performance criteria on the budget deficit and the expansion of credit for

quarters II and III. This support is crucial for the debt reduction program and the flow of Western credit and direct private investment.

An excessive criticism of the policies in 1990–91, often for populist reasons, was the intellectual starting point of the new parliament and the Olszewski government. It soon became apparent, however, that the necessary policy corrections would be costly in social and political terms, and that the room for safe anti-recessionary policies, both macro and micro, was very limited.

The new government guidelines (CM, 1992) are an attempt to face problems 1–5 above by calling for a tougher incomes policy, a larger turnover tax, a real depreciation of the exchange rate, and a sizable reduction in some welfare benefits.

The broad macroeconomic aims of the new program are: to limit the budget deficit to 5 percent of GDP, to reduce inflation from 60 percent in 1991 to about 45 percent in 1992, and to initiate a modest recovery (or limit a further decline) in GDP through a trade surplus and, possibly, higher investment.

Since the new government inherited a likely budget deficit of 10–12 percent of GDP, the guidelines in effect call for a package of tax hikes and spending cuts equivalent to about 5–7 percent of GDP. The cuts must focus on the outlays on pensions. Meeting the 5 percent limit on the budget deficit is an essential part of the government's anti-inflationary policy. It is assumed that the introduction of VAT in January 1993 will improve the government's revenue position, enabling a reduction of the deficit to about 3 percent in 1993. Such a reduction is required if the rate of inflation is to drop to about 25 percent in that year and to, say, 15 percent in 1994.

Although Poland again came close to losing macroeconomic control, no real harm has been done. The government and Parliament have been made aware of the threat and are apparently prepared to meet the challenge.

Notes

Financial support from the Leverhulme Trust is gratefully acknowledged. The Centre for Economic Performance is financed by the Economic and Social Research Council.

1. Republic of Poland (1991).

2. The 30 percent reduction will permit a reduction in the stock of debt by $4 billion and an 80 percent reduction in interest payments for 3 years.

3. Monthly increases of the consumer price index in the last five months of 1989 were (in percent): 39.5 in August, 34.4 in September, 54.8 in October, 22.4 in November and 17.7 in December. This gives the average monthly rate of 33.1 percent, and the annual rate of 3,000 percent.

4. For example, exports to CMEA in 1990 attracted subsidies of about 1 percent of GDP.

5. Any devaluation also redistributes real income from the consumers of imported goods to net exporters. Excessive devaluation may cause sharp changes in the composition of demand and these may lower activity in the short-run.

6. In May 1991, the zloty was devalued by 17 percent and the peg was changed from the US dollar to a basket of five currencies (45 percent US$, 35 percent DM, 10 percent UK pound, and 5 percent each French and Swiss franc). A pre-announced crawling peg to this basket was introduced on October 14, 1991.

References

Beksiak, J. and J. Winiecki. 1990. "Comparative Analysis of our Program and the Polish Government Program." In: J. Beksiak *et al., The Polish Transformation: Programme and Progress*. The Centre for Research into Communist Economies.

Blanchard, O. and R. Layard. 1990. "Economic Change in Poland." In: J. Beksiak *et al., The Polish Transformation: Programme and Progress*. The Centre for Research into Communist Economies.

Calvo, G. and F. Coricelli. 1990. "Stagflationary Effects of Stabilization Programmes in Reforming Socialist Countries: Supply Side vs. Demand Side Factors." Mimeograph. August.

Council of Ministers (CM). 1992. "Guidelines for the Social and Economic Policy in 1992." Warsaw. February 14. Mimeograph.

Dornbusch, R. 1990. "Priorities of Economic Reform in Eastern Europe and the Soviet Union." Mimeograph. December 29.

Frydman, R., G. W. Kolodko, and S. Wellisz. 1990. "Stabilization in Poland: A Progress Report," Mimeograph. May.

—— and S. Wellisz. 1990. "The Ownership Control Structure and the Behaviour of Polish Enterprises During the 1990 Reforms." Mimeograph. September.

Gomulka, S. 1990a. "Reform and Budgetary Policies in Poland, 1989–1990," *European Economy*, No. 43 (March).

——. 1990b. "Stabilization, Recession and Growth in Poland," LSE Centre for Economic Performance, Working Paper 68, May.

——. 1991. "The Causes of Recession Following Stabilization," *Comparative Economic Studies*, 15.

Jozefiak, C. 1990. "The Quarrel about the Program," *Weekly Survey*, 28 (October).

Marczewski, K. 1991. "Purchasing Power Parity and Exchange Rate Parity in Poland, 1985–90, and in Other Countries in 1985." Mimeograph (in Polish).

Republic of Poland. 1991. "Memorandum of the Government of Poland on Economic Reform and Medium-Term Policies, 1991–93." March 25.

Rosati, D. 1991. "The Polish Road to Capitalism: A Critical Appraisal of the Balcerowicz Plan," *Thames Papers in Political Economy*. London: Thames Polytechnic. Spring.

Wilczynski, W. 1991. "Return of Poland to a Market Economy: the Bequest of 1990 and its Consequences." January. Mimeograph (in Polish).

Winiecki, J. 1991. "Remarks on the [Polish] Economy Important for the New Government and its Policies." January. Mimeograph (in Polish).

Appendix

Poland: Summary of Intended Structural Adjustment Policies, 1991–1993

Policy	1991	1992–1993
1. Privatization, commercialization and enterprise restructuring	Commercialize about 1,000 enterprises; privatize 150 large enterprises; reduce the size of the state enterprise sector by 15 percent; complete major sector restructuring studies.	Reduce the size of the state enterprise sector to 50 percent of its 1990 level through privatization; accelerate restructuring.
2. Competition policy	Activate private wholesale trade; demonopolize grain processing; create new, smaller dairy-processing units.	Increase competition in agricultural inputs supply, road haulage, the power industry and steel industry.
3. Rural policies	Begin privatization of state farms, transformation of agricultural cooperatives; create favorable conditions for land consolidation.	Develop services, trade and small- and medium-sized industry in rural areas; accelerate the restructuring and modernization of agriculture and related activities.
4. Pricing and subsidies	Free coal prices, abolish the coal export duty; reduce state budget subsidies from 6 percent of GDP to 5 percent of GDP.	Begin phasing out housing and transportation subsidies; increase the share of freely-determined industrial producer and consumer prices; reduce state budget subsidies to about 3 percent of GDP.
5. Wages and employment	Introduce more flexible wage controls; introduce instruments to improve the labor market.	Reduce the scope of wage control in line with commercialization and privatization; promote a more efficient and absorptive labor market by liberalizing the housing market, improving information flows, retraining programs and support for new businesses.

Policy	1991	1992–1993
6. Fiscal reform	Improve expenditure monitoring and reporting, cash management and budgetary planning; review public investment program.	Implement value-added tax and personal income tax; develop domestic and external debt management systems.
7. Financial sector reform	Introduce Accounting Plan for banks; establish system of prudential regulation; develop plans for bank restructuring; commercialize state-owned banks; reform the NBP refinance system and introduce flexible, more market-determined interest rates; limit the growth of subsidized credit.	Privatize a substantial part of the state-owned banking sector; strengthen competition in the banking sector, especially in the rural economy; reorganize the activities of the NBP.
8. External policies	Liberalize regulations governing foreign investment in Poland; reduce the number of commodities requiring export licences; modify the foreign exchange surrender system; establish an export credit guarantee agency.	Abolish most remaining export licence requirements; reform the tariff structure.
9. Environmental policies	Launch an investment program in the field of environmental protection; revise the environmental protection laws and regulations; continue the enforcement of the environmental protection laws (including the elimination of environmentally hazardous technologies).	Broaden the size of environmental investment; continue strict enforcement of environmental protection laws; register an initial improvement in the environment in the most polluted areas.

9

Transition from Socialism and Stabilization Policies: The Polish Experience

Grzegorz W. Kolodko

Introduction

The fundamental issues to be considered in this paper are the theoretical and practical problems of stabilization in a post-communist economy, in particular the Polish experience, since stabilizations of this type must, by their very nature, differ from classical stabilization policies (Bruno *et al.*, 1988) in at least two fundamental aspects:

a. In a post-communist economy it is not only stabilization at a low, controllable price inflation level that matters, but also—and even more important—the elimination of shortages. In other words, the goal of stabilization is the formation of a mechanism of prices which, with as low a rate of increase as possible, will help to clear the market.
b. Stabilization should be perceived in a broader context, one of a systemic transformation from a planned and bureaucratically administered economy to a market economy. In light of this perception stabilization is both a prerequisite and a mechanism of the market-oriented transition, while the systemic transformation is of prime importance.

It is from this point of view that the Polish experience of 1989–1990 and the resulting perspectives must be evaluated, since Poland's case is not unique. Both the emergence of very high inflation and the attempts to fight it under conditions of market-oriented systemic transformation, may be the most spectacular, but still only one aspect of certain more general trends in the post-communist world.

The empirical analysis and certain generalizing theoretical conclusions in this chapter will focus on the character and sources of the Polish inflation in the period immediately preceding the 1990 stabilization package. This is of particular importance because the resultant conclusions for economic policies of the post-communist countries are hardly to be overestimated. Many other countries—from the Soviet Union to China, from Estonia to Albania—are facing options similar to the Polish dilemmas of 1989–1990. True, they are in different development stages of inflation and of attempts at controlling it; and they are in different situations as to the pace and direction of the market-oriented transition. But the Polish experience should nevertheless be highly instructive for all these economies.

The second section briefly discusses the development of inflation in the late 1980s, especially the so-called induced inflation of the latter half of 1989. The third section presents the fundamental assumptions of the stabilization package whose implementation was started at the beginning of 1990. The fourth section describes the announced program goals, while the fifth presents its real results after one year of implementation. The sixth section outlines the favorable economic processes and developments connected with the stabilization and systemic transformation policy. It is against this background that the seventh section attempts to deal with the causes that led to such a huge divergence between the targets set and the results achieved. Do the causes lie in the assumptions or rather in the sphere of program implementation? The eighth section poses the question of applicability of the 'cold-turkey' versus the graduated approach to stabilization in post-communist economies in general and the Polish one in particular; the ninth section discusses the transition from a shortageflation-type crisis to stagflation. Finally, the tenth section sums up the discussion and attempts to outline the perspectives of stabilization policy in Poland as well as conclusions for other economies of the post-communist world.[1]

Inflation in the Late 1980s

Several distinct phases can be distinguished in the Polish inflation of the 1980s. After the acceleration of prices in 1980–1982, it slowed down after the 1982 stabilization and fell further until 1985. At the same time, the shortages were also somewhat reduced. Then, from 1986 to mid-1989, a renewed acceleration of price inflation can be observed, from less than 15 percent in 1985 to about 160 percent in the first half of 1989. This time, however, shortages grew more acute. So we have to deal with the shortageflation syndrome (Kolodko and McMahon, 1987). This syndrome is a state in which, under conditions of a socialist economy undergoing reform and still characterized by soft budgetary constraints (Kornai, 1980), a price inflation-versus shortage trade-off appears in the short run. Whereas in the long run—because of the inconsistent and soft fiscal, monetary and income policies—both the so-called price (open) inflation and the repressed inflation with its accompanying permanent shortages grow simultaneously (Kolodko, 1989a). The shortageflation curve shifts ever further upward and to the right. (Figure 9.1).

The essence of the shortageflation syndrome is that when both open and repressed inflations exceed a certain critical level, the syndrome cannot be overcome without recourse to price liberalization, the latter being—as is well known—contrary to the command-type economy management system.

Attempts at partial price liberalization unsupported by other necessary measures that tighten the budget constraints of all economic agents through appropriate fiscal, monetary and income policies, leads in the long run to an acceleration of open inflation, and can by no means eliminate the shortages. Moreover, not only the position of the *shortageflation* curve in relation to the origin, but its slope, too, are changing. With time, it becomes ever steeper (Figure 9.1). This means that the scope for specific substitution between the

Figure 9.1. The Shortageflation Syndrome

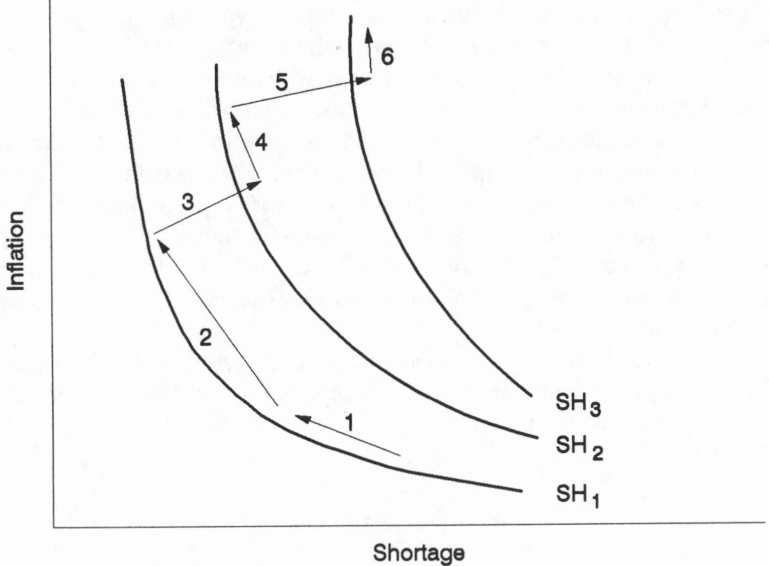

open and repressed inflation is narrowing down. Reducing the shortage scale by one additional point requires ever greater increases in open (price) inflation. This is precisely the path Poland took since 1985 until, in mid-1989, it reached a situation of extreme exhaustion caused by the shortageflation syndrome. In spite of the increasing pace of price rises, the shortages not only did not diminish, they actually grew. This resulted not only from a faster increase in nominal incomes than in prices, but also from the fact that, beginning in May 1989, we already witness an onset of recessionary developments in the real sphere.

It was against this background that the transition from galloping price inflation, with the accompanying shortages, to quasi-hyperinflation took place in Poland beginning in August 1989. Till the initiation of the stabilization package, this hyperinflation was accompanied by shortages, so for half a year we had to do with hyper-shortageflation. This resulted from the liberalization of prices having been only partial (liberalization of food prices in August 1989). The huge inflation acceleration was also a result of the introduction of a general income indexation system imposed by Solidarity. After the takeover by Solidarity in August of that year, indexation rules were somewhat modified, but this change was already unable to stop hyperinflation.

This temporary hyperinflation was of an induced character (Kolodko, 1991). It was, to a certain extent, provoked by the macroeconomic policy carried out in the period of fundamental political transformations in Poland. The hyperinflation was caused, on the one hand, by political struggle and, on the other hand, by the conviction that under hyperinflation conditions it would be substantially easier to lower the level of real wages and to depreciate the value of money balances held by economic agents, notably households. In addition, the induced quasi-hyperinflation, when perceived in this way, resulted from the conviction that hyperinflation would be easier to overcome than the shortageflation syndrome. But above all, the deliberate option for hyperinflation stemmed from the priority given to objectives with a bearing on the transition to a market economy, since the implementation of this task requires, among other things, an almost full liberalization of prices and a deep money devaluation as well as a rise in credit costs up to their real level.

Under conditions of such a considerable monetary destabilization, the achievement of the above objectives was not possible other than by passing through a hyperinflation phase.

The Stabilization Package

The stabilization package was structured so as to induce processes that would achieve several goals: (a) demand and supply equilibrium in the commodity market or, more exactly, formation of a mechanism of market-clearing prices; (b) reduction in the inflation rate to the lowest possible level; and (c) equilibration of the current-account balance.

Putting aside some technical details (Frydman, Wellisz, Kolodko, 1991), the stabilization program included five main planes of action: (a) fiscal adjustment, (b) price liberalization and adjustment, (c) tough monetary policy, (d) wage control, and (e) exchange-rate unification and introduction of internal convertibility of the zloty.

The fiscal adjustment policy was aimed at equilibrating the budget. In the year preceding the stabilization, the budget deficit amounted to 6 percent of the state balance and 7.4 percent of the consolidated general government balance. Subsidies made up about one-third of state budget expenditures. It was assumed that in order to eliminate the budget deficit, their level should be reduced by at least one half and their share in the reduced expenditures had to total about one-fifth. The improvement of the budget situation was also achieved through better fiscal discipline, and possible temporary deficits were to be covered either by limited commercial bank credits or by contracting debt in the newly formed open market. In addition, budget revenues of 2.5 percent were planned from issues of treasury bonds with an option of later conversion into equities of privatized enterprises. As a result of all the above measures the state budget had to show an insignificant deficit of 0.2 percent of expenditures, and the consolidated general government balance—a surplus of about 1.6 percent.

The second main plane of action of the package was liberalization and adjustment of prices. Contrary to widespread opinion—especially in light of the not always justified talk about the so-called Polish Big Bang—the scope of price liberalization performed when the package was launched was very limited, since most prices had already been released in the course of the reforms of the 1980s or—with regard to food prices—in August 1989. Thus, in the period preceding the stabilization, the price system, considered from the point of view of price control, was as in Table 9.1.

In 1990, free prices of consumer goods and services accounted for 82.6 percent of total sales value in this category, intermediate goods prices were liberalized by 89 percent, and purchasing prices of agricultural products by 100 percent. Thus, the sources of the huge price explosion which took place immediately after the program was launched must not be sought in the initial, limited price liberalization, but in the centrally determined price adjustments and especially in the administratively directed energy and coal price rises (in the latter case, as much as sevenfold). These price rises were aimed, on the one hand, at reducing heavy subsidies, and, on the other hand, at changing the price relations through a stepwise relative appreciation of fuels (especially hard coal) that play a key role in the Polish economy.

The third main avenue of stabilization had to include a tough monetary policy manifested in the strict control of money supply and regulation of its

Table 9.1. The Price Structure in Poland, 1989

Category	July	December
Share of contractual (freely negotiated) prices in total sales		
Consumer goods and services	71	86
of which: food	58	93
State purchasing prices of agricultural produce	30	41
Intermediate goods	86	89
Raw materials and components	89	89
Share of prices subject to limited maximum increase and obligation to give notice of intended rises		
a. Maximum price rise indices:		
Consumer goods and services	12.4	6.6
Intermediate goods	24.7	21.0
b. Obligation to inform about intended price rises:		
Consumer goods and services	23.6	21.4
Procurement goods	4.6	5.5
Share of fully free prices in total sales value		
Consumer goods and services	35.0	58.0
Procurement goods	56.7	56.5

Source: Price Department of the Ministry of Finance.

growth rate through the use of positive real interest rates. The negative real interest rates on both credits and deposits, typical of the shortageflation period, were to be replaced by positive interest rates. After a short period of so-called 'corrective' inflation, which aimed at 45 percent in January (in comparison to the average price level in December) and 20 percent in February, the interest rate had to exceed the inflation rate by the third month of program implementation.

The tough monetary policy was to have several effects. First, to radically reduce the demand of economic agents for credit and lead (through limitation of the liquidity of all sectors in the economy) to a reduction in demand and consequently to a decline in the inflation rate. Next, it was intended to force enterprises to reduce their excessive demand for investment, which was one of the chronic sources of inflation in the previous period. Finally, the positive real interest rates were expected to permanently increase the households' propensity to save and overcome their inflationary expectations.

It is only in such an environment, i.e., with tightened budgetary constraints resulting from restrictive fiscal and monetary measures, that price liberalization and adjustment are not doomed to degenerate into hyperinflation. It was also assumed—and this is the fourth program plane—that in spite of the general trend toward liberalization, nominal wage rises would be subject to strict control. In Poland—as distinct from, e.g., the Yugoslav stabilization program carried out at the same time (Coricelli and Rocha, 1990)—wages were not fully frozen; rather, a mechanism of partial indexation was adopted, which provided for linking enterprises' wage-bill increases to the inflation rate through officially fixed coefficients. In the first 6 months of 1990 these were set at 0.3, 0.2, 0.2, 0.2, 0.6, and 0.6, respectively. For July, this coefficient was exceptionally set at 1.0 and, then, for the rest of the year, reduced back to 0.6. Clearly, with this kind of indexation the higher the inflation rate, the greater the erosion of real wages.

The fifth main stabilization program plane was the introduction of internal convertibility of the domestic currency at the same time as an exchange rate unification. Enterprises would be obliged to sell their foreign export receipts to the state at the stabilized exchange rate, while banks would be obliged to sell foreign currency to importers. The foreign-currency turnover in the household sector had already been liberalized (in March, 1989). Liquidity was to be guaranteed by means of a stabilization loan obtained from OECD countries in the amount of US$1 billion. This point of the package also required a devaluation of the Polish zloty. After gradual devaluation (from Zł 1,440 to 6,000 per US$) between September and December 1989, it was decided at the beginning of the package implementation to drastically devaluate the domestic currency by over 50 percent over the black-market level, down to Zł 9,500 per US$1. And a decision was made to adopt just this exchange rate as the nominal anchor supporting the whole stabilization program.

Let me add that very high (around 20 percent) customs duties were imposed on imports to which was added a turnover tax of 20 percent. As a result, the cost of a dollar imported was often 44 percent higher than the value obtained by an enterprise for a dollar earned through export. This was intended to limit the enterprise sector's demand for foreign currency and in this way to contribute to exchange-rate stabilization and to inflation stabilization at a low level.

Program Goals

The stabilization program outlined above was approved by the International Monetary Fund and its basic points were set down in the Letter of Intent. There was also explicit social support for this program in Poland, above all as a result of fundamental political transformations toward democratization.

Both these facts—international as well as public support, or, more exactly, the government's belief in it—led to the formulation of unrealistic program goals and, what was worse, to a general overshooting of the program, since it was assumed inflation would drop in the middle of the year to 1 percent monthly. At the same time it was assumed that after six months the economy would already be on the road to economic growth. But this was to be achieved at the cost of a 20 percent fall in real wages.

As far as trends in the real sphere were concerned, a 1 percent(!) drop in consumption, a 3.1 percent drop in GNP, and a 5 percent drop in industrial production were assumed (compared with 1989). This relatively small—for the project scale—recession, coming after a 0.2 percent GNP increase in the preceding year, was to be accompanied by unemployment amounting to 400,000 persons, or about 2 percent of the total labor force.

Regarding foreign trade it was assumed that implementation of the stabilization program would lead to such export and import development that in the so-called I-payments zone (non-convertible currencies) a small surplus of TR 0.5 billion would ensue, whereas in the II-payments zone (convertible currencies) a deficit of about US$ 0.8 billion would emerge. It was also assumed that in the initial implementation phase the nominal exchange rate of Zł 9,500/US$ would be maintained, which, in view of the expected inflation, was equivalent to a small real appreciation of the złoty.

Implementation

If the achievement of the goals presented above serve as the exclusive measure of the Polish stabilization program's success we would have to pronounce it a failure. This is clearly illustrated by the comparison presented in Table 9.2.

Thus, not only were the announced goals not achieved, but what *was* achieved cost far more than the cost envisaged for better results. Specifically, the decline in the standard of living and in real wages was much steeper than originally announced by the government: real wages dropped by as much as 30 percent,[2] and money balances held by the household sector plunged even lower. The burden would hardly be justifiable—or less socially acceptable—even if one of the basic goals, namely, reducing the monthly inflation rate to 1–1.5 percent (between 13 and 20 percent annually) was achieved. Even more important, the inflation rate in late 1990 and 1991, when it was even higher, cannot be compared with the above-mentioned quasi-hyperinflation, merely because of the induced character of the latter. It is even less admissible to compare the inflation in arbitrarily chosen months with its (entirely induced) record level of January 1990 (79.6 percent monthly). It is worth remembering that in the last quarter of 1989 the inflation rate was already falling, dropping from about 55 percent in October to 23 and 17

Table 9.2. Polish Stabilization Program: Goals and Results

	Assumptions	Results
CPI (percent)	20	90[a]
Industrial output	−5.0	−25[b]
GNP	−3.1	−12
Unemployment	2.0	6.1
Trade balance		
In billions of US$	−0.8	+2.2
In billions of rubles	+0.5	+6.6

[a] In the second Letter of Intent to the IMF (August) the average monthly inflation rates for October, November and December 1990 were already assumed to be at 1.5, 1.0 and 2.0 percent, respectively, i.e., about a 20 percent annual rate. The real annual inflation rate in this period was almost 100 percent (or about 6 percent monthly).

[b] Index for 1990 with respect to the public sector, whose share in the industrial output amounts to almost 90 percent. If the private sector is included, industrial output contracted by 23 percent altogether.

Source: Main Statistical Office and author's computations.

percent in November and December, respectively. Hence, if the argument about the induced character of the Polish hyperinflation holds, the proper reference point for the 100 percent inflation driven by the stabilization package and the accompanying processes (among others things, recent adverse external developments) is the 160 percent inflation of the first half of 1989. It is only in this perspective that one can see how poor the results of the Polish Big Bang have been with respect to inflation stabilization.

No wonder that in the presidential elections of November 1990, when the incumbent prime minister, running for the presidency, got a poor 18 percent of the vote, the Polish people expressed dissatisfaction with the economic situation. It is precisely because its stabilization program failed that Mazowiecki's government was voted out of power, and not vice versa. It is not true that destabilization caused by the elections made the program's implementation impossible; rather this program contributed to the political destabilization accompanying the elections. This is an extremely important statement, and one with special importance for the proper assessment of the Polish experience from the point of view of other post-communist economies that have yet to undergo similar anti-inflationary and stabilizing therapy.

Stabilization versus Transition to a Market Economy

Assessing the results of a stabilization program separately from the broader context of a systemic transformation toward a market economy is one-sided and simplistic. The stabilization package being implemented in Poland must be perceived in a broader perspective of the complex market-oriented transition process.

One might hypothesize that, in reality, stabilization has been subordinated to transition insofar as transition is the primary strategic goal —even at the cost of failure of the stabilization policy. What is more, to a certain extent, transition induces destabilization especially in post-communist countries of Central and Eastern Europe where, before the acceleration of the market-oriented systemic transformation, inflationary processes were relatively moderate (Czechoslovakia, Bulgaria, Romania and the Baltic republics). This results from the simple fact that market-oriented transition requires, among other things, policy measures such as price liberalization, reduction in subsidies, devaluation, significant rises in interest rates, etc. So, in the initial period, orientation toward a market economy brings about an acceleration of inflationary processes.

In Poland's case, when the stabilization program was initiated, serious market-oriented economic reforms were already underway. One must bear in mind that in 1989 the Polish economy was already at the forefront of countries—at that time not yet called post-communist (post-socialist)—that were progressing towards a market economy. In theory, a different stabilization policy from the one actually chosen—and similar to the attempt undertaken in 1982—could have been adopted. At that time, however, the main aim was inflation stabilization with a simultaneous reform of the socialist economy without any infringement of its fundamental principles. After achieving stabilization, the State was to remain the dominating agent in almost all spheres and the scope of economic liberalization, including price liberalization, was limited (Kolodko, 1989b).

The 1990 stabilization effort, on the other hand, is not only a fight for internal and external equilibration of the economy, but also for the creation of a different economic mechanism. It is accompanied by the construction of appropriate institutional surroundings for market operations and by the use, especially in the fiscal and monetary areas, of more and more typically market-economy policy instruments. When looking at the Polish stabilization program in this perspective, the negative assessment of the preceding section must be qualified. It is true that the stabilization policy of the first post-communist government led to the deepest recession ever known in post-war Poland and in contemporary Europe. But it is equally true that the Polish economy is obviously closer to a market economy—as regards institutional transformation and economic policy—than any other post-communist country. Subsidies have been slashed, the budget is balanced and its possible deficit cannot, by law, be monetized, prices are largely liberalized, internal currency convertibility has been introduced, privatization has been set in motion, elements of financial markets are being developed, etc.

The question now is whether the high cost of certain positive results achieved in the transition to a market economy must unavoidably entail destruction of the productive sector and a decline in the population's standard of living. These costs are indeed huge and ungrounded attempts to play them down (Sachs, 1990) do not change the facts; rather they purposely present them in a false light. Detailed analyses show that the enormous costs of market-oriented institutional transformation and stabilization policy were not unavoidable: they could have been much lower—and achieved not worse but perhaps even better results with respect to systemic transformation if the numerous errors of the stabilization package had been avoided and if the package had not overshot the target (Rosati, 1990).

Overshooting

One of the basic erroneous assumptions of the stabilization package was the expectation of a quick positive supply response on the part of the business sector. Enterprises behaved—and some still do—differently than they would in a market economy (Jorgensen, Gelb, Singh, 1990). The supply responsiveness is very slow and the enterprises have generally responded to a shock reduction in internal demand not by improving their efficiency but by raising prices—which, this time, in the phase of radical departure from the shortage economy, is already limited by an effective demand barrier—and by reducing the absolute output level. At the same time, there is a time lag in employment adjustment; the decline in employment is much slower than the decline in production: the former fell by about 10 percent in 1990 while the output of the socialized (state-owned and cooperative) industry fell 25 percent.[3]

Wrong assumptions with respect to the production sector included the naïve belief that output would automatically rise without intervention on the part of macroeconomic policy. Some state intervention attempts came too late and were badly sequenced. For while the post-communist economy is not yet a market economy, it is no longer a planned economy either. It is a certain 'systemic void' in which the known fiscal and monetary policy instruments function somewhat differently than in a developed market economy. The problem is not only in using an appropriate set of policy instruments, but also in doing so at the right time. This has not been done. What we have is a general overshooting of the program, combined with wrong responses resulting from undue insistence on the automatic functioning of certain mechanisms—a kind of 'overliberalization' of the economy has taken place, perhaps in reaction to its past bureaucratization.

The above-mentioned overshooting is felt especially in the excessive scale of reduction in households' incomes (among other things, in real wages) as well as in the excessive limitation of the liquidity of enterprises resulting from the wrong sequencing of the monetary policy. As regards the former, the adoption of an indexation coefficient permitting wages to grow by only 0.2 of the price rise has led to a drastic drop in the households' demand and consequently to a decline in sales and productions. The desired stabilization effect could have been achieved through a much smaller (around 20 percent) reduction in real wages, while the real reduction in the first two months of the stabilization was twice as high.

What is more important, the mechanism for controlling the pace of nominal wage increases is constructed so as to permit 'carrying over' unutilized admissible wage rises.[4] This has been the case especially in the latter half of the year (Tables 9.3 and 9.4). This is a bad mechanism. In the initial period its effect was recessionary (through a reduction in effective demand and, consequently, in sales and production), whereas later its effect was inflationary, since an acceleration of wage increases does not automatically lead to output growth but, in the first place, to an acceleration of inflationary processes. This has been particularly visible since September 1990. Thus, the statistical indices of real wage changes cannot be averaged out, since the excessive drop at the beginning of the year is not offset by the excessive rise in the latter half.

As to the drastic rise in interest rates in January 1991 and their maintenance at a restrictive and pro-recessionary level until the end of February, it almost provoked a collapse in the manufacturing sector. It was mainly during these two months that the huge recession (a 30 percent decline in output) took place, and the economy has been in recession ever since. The so-called corrective inflation took place mainly in the first half of January 1991, when the high interest rate was already exerting a mainly recessionary rather than anti-inflationary influence, since the negative real rate on deposits did nothing to overcome the inflationary expectations of the household sector. The administrative regulation of interest rates in monthly cycles—which have little in common with real economic cycles—was not flexible enough. Appropriate modifications to the interest rate policy were made only in November. Interest rates on household deposits have been raised—although in some cases they are still negative in real terms. This raise affected mainly medium-term (three and six months) deposits, which, under stabilization conditions, are actually quite long terms. But the move was made too late; by now, inflation, interest rates and inflationary expectations are all growing. The increase in interest rates only confirms and supports the inflationary expectations of the public. In such a situation, raising the interest rate to positive levels can bring about a perverse effect in accelerating rather than stopping the inflation. If interest rates on deposits had been set at a really high level as early as the 7th or 8th week of stabili-

Table 9.3. Normative and Actual Rates of Wage Increases in Five Basic Sectors of the National Economy

	Corrective coefficient	Percentage rate of price increase		Actual rate of wage increase	Normative rate of wage increase	
		Projected	Actual		By projected price increase	By actual price increase
1990						
January	0.3	45.0	78.6	4.6	13.5	23.6
February	0.2	23.0	23.9	5.4	4.6	4.8
March	0.2	6.0	4.7	10.5	1.2	0.9
April	0.2	6.0	8.1	2.5	1.2	1.6
May	0.6	2.5	5.0	8.7	1.5	3.0
June	0.6	3.0	3.4	5.6	1.8	2.0
July	1.0	5.5	3.6	14.4	5.5	3.6
August	0.6	3.0	1.8	5.9	1.8	1.1
September	0.6	4.5	4.6	8.7	2.7	2.8
October	0.6	4.0	5.7	13.8	2.4	3.4
November	0.6	3.0	4.9	12.8	1.8	2.9
December	0.6	4.0	5.9	1.6	2.4	3.5

Source: Author's calculations based on GUS data.

Table 9.4. Normative and Actual Wages in Five Basic Sectors of the National Economy (thousands of zloties monthly per employee)

	Actual wages excluding profit payments	Normative wages (corrected by drop in employment) by actual price increase	Margin (normative *minus* actual wages) by actual price increase	Cumulative margin (normative *minus* actual wages) by actual price increase	Hypothetical wages after a single payment of cumulative margin (normative *minus* actual wages)
1990					
January	618.3	738.1	119.9	119.9	738.1
February	651.9	782.2	130.3	250.1	902.0
March	720.1	799.9	79.8	329.9	1,050.1
April	738.2	823.4	85.2	415.1	1,153.3
May	802.2	864.8	62.6	477.7	1,279.9
June	846.8	892.5	45.6	523.4	1,370.2
July	969.2	939.7	−29.5	493.9	1,463.1
August	1,026.3	965.3	−61.1	432.8	1,459.2
September	1,115.7	1,006.0	−109.7	323.2	1,438.8
October	1,269.1	1,054.1	−215.0	108.1	1,377.3
November	1,431.2	1,085.1	−346.1	−238.0	1,193.2
December	1,454.4	1,123.5	−330.9	−568.8	885.5

Source: Author's calculations based on GUS data.

zation, such a move could have overcome strong inflationary expectations. It was not too late even in the third, fourth or fifth month of the package implementation. But in November–December 1990 it was the right move at the wrong moment, and thus was ineffective.

The third basic aspect of overshooting is the scale of devaluation. The official exchange rate was simply brought down to the market level, thus anticipating the so-called corrective inflation. Indeed, this was what really happened, although inflation was much higher than expected. Nevertheless, the exchange rate has been maintained throughout the whole year (initially, only a three-month period was assumed). On the other hand, such a large devaluation—with simultaneous additional charges imposed on imports—was an additional impulse stimulating both the corrective inflation and the recession. In the latter case, the impulse consisted of a clear reduction in imports, leading to an even deeper drop in production.

A peculiar kind of overshooting also took place on the political plane. The fundamental political breakthrough in Poland in 1989, which brought Solidarity to power, also resulted in widespread popular support for the new government. This fact—as well as a fundamental change in the West's attitude towards Poland—permitted the government to undertake the extremely difficult and socially painful economic program, part of which was stabilization. However, this popular support, confirmed by all public opinion polls, convinced some politicians that the prospects of social resistance were very remote and that even an extreme measure such as a shock stabilization program was feasible. Whereas in previous periods stabilization measures did not go far enough, this time social confidence was clearly abused and the ensuing restrictive fiscal, monetary and income policies far overshot the limits of social acceptance. Worst of all, a similar political conjunction is not likely to occur again in the foreseeable future. The overshooting with respect to exploiting popular support was a fundamental political mistake, which rendered the contemplated stabilization effort unfeasible. This has been an irreversible loss.

'Cold Turkey' versus Gradualism

There are many arguments in favor of the cold-turkey type approach over gradualism. Dornbusch and Fischer (1990) stress that a shock therapy is the only one that can gain the necessary credibility. After the initial shock—by its very nature, extremely painful for the population—one can obtain spectacular short-term effects in the fight against inflation. Thus, the shock therapy can be effective if it is not followed too soon by relaxation of financial restrictions. In Yugoslavia, for example, the 64 percent inflation in December 1989, was reduced to zero in the second quarter of the following year. This was a spectacular effect that vindicated the cold-turkey approach

(Kolodko *et al.*, 1992). But soon afterwards a renewed acceleration of inflationary processes took place (up to about 10 percent monthly in the last months of 1990) which stripped the program of its credibility.

In Poland, the program failed to gain the necessary credibility to begin with, because the inflation rate did not fall—even temporarily—to the level set by the government. By December 1989, the inflation rate had been reduced from 55 percent in October to less than 18 percent, but it bounced back to 80 percent in January 1990, and to 23 percent in February. A degree of stabilization followed, with an inflation rate several times higher than that announced by the government and—as a result of these announcements—than that expected by the population. The right conclusions were not drawn from this fact and implementation of erroneous assumptions continued, based on the misconception that overcoming the inflation was,under the given institutional, structural and political conditions, merely a matter of time. The cold-turkey approach failed, but it does not follow that the gradualist approach is necessarily better. It must be clearly stated that given the enormity of disequilibrium and inflation in Poland in 1989, shock therapy was the only justified one. The fault lies not in its use as general method, but in the faulty implementation of the methodologically right shock approach. The unique chance has been wasted.

Another aspect of the cold-turkey versus gradualism dilemma is the need to distinguish the three planes on which economic processes in general, and in particular those bearing on a transition to market economy, take place. These planes are stabilization, transformation and restructuring. The shock approach applies only to stabilization; in cases of especially severe inflation it is frequently the most justified one. Such was Poland's case. Whereas with respect to institutional systemic change—although here too, there is need for rapid progress—the cold-turkey approach is not applicable, with one exception, however, of which I take no account here, namely the now defunct German Democratic Republic.

Hence, there has not been a Big Bang in the systemic sphere. The transformation in this area evidently accelerated as part of the general historic process of change spreading throughout the whole post-communist world, and was even feeding back into these changes. But what we have here is not a shock approach but gradualism, natural for such cases, although the transformation itself is revolutionary. Of key importance in this kind of institutional change is the proper sequencing of the measures taken (Nuti, 1990).

Moreover, shock policy is out of the question when it comes to structural change, since such a change, by its very nature, requires a longer time perspective. Against this background it must be concluded that the Polish Big Bang was exaggerated, since it can at most address stabilization—which was a failure—and not the broader institutional and structural market-oriented transformation of the economy. The latter is a long-lasting, gradually developing process, with extremely complex implications.

From Shortageflation to Stagflation

Peoples of the post-communist countries evolving toward a market economy believe—often prompted by politicians—they will soon have a Western-type market economy. Such illusions are also fostered by transplanting the patterns of mature market economies onto destabilized, crisis-ridden, post-communist economies, where the above patterns are not applicable. The underestimation of the perspective of the long, arduous road to the market also results from the lack of knowledge on the part of some Western experts of the realities and peculiarities of these economies and, in consequence, from the lack of sufficient imagination and responsibility in framing the goals and outlining the perspectives.

On the other hand, no such lack of imagination hampered Nuti, when he remarked many years ago (Nuti, 1982, p. 47):

> If Poland were a capitalist country in a similar crisis, painful but fairly automatic processes and policy response would be set in motion. There would be hyperinflation, currency devaluation, drastic public expenditure cuts and deflationary taxation measures, tight money, high interest rates, disinvestment, bankruptcies and plant closures, and a couple of million unemployed. Some external creditors would get very little, or nothing at all, following the financial collapse of their debtors; some of the remaining debt would be offset by the sale to foreigners of financial assets (shares, bonds), land, buildings and plants. Fresh external finance would be available to the more credible borrowers. Unemployment would keep the unions in check, restraining real wages and ensuring labor discipline. The drop in real wage trends and industrial streamlining would eventually promote exports and encourage new investment, attracting foreign capital; in ten years or so the economy would be getting out of crisis.

The above view was based on an observation of the 1980–1982 crisis, but it seems all the more appropriate to the larger-scale crisis of 1989–1992. In the latter case the Polish economy is already closer to being a capitalist economy than ever before. So it is understandable that it responds in a way similar to that outlined in Nuti's scenario of ten years ago, this time ever more resembling the market economies of Latin America rather than those of Western Europe (Kolodko, 1990). The dream of rapid stabilization cannot come true. Especially impossible are quick systemic transformation and rapid institutional and structural change (Kornai, 1990). Moreover, even the question of which transition path is preferable, important for many post-communist countries, remains unanswered. Poland's example shows the impossibility of direct transition from the sort of crisis typical of the state-controlled socialist economy where the main malaise is the shortageflation syndrome to a balanced, crisis-free capitalist economy. This path is much too long and tortuous, since it leads from shortageflation to a sound market economy only in the very distant future, first passing through stagflation and even slumpflation. It is not possible to take the road to radical transformation to a market economy under conditions of a relatively well functioning socialist economy. The situation must first deteriorate, i.e., destabilize to the point where the only way out is fundamental institutional transformation, because it is only then that both the population and the governing elite is ready for indispensable reforms.

Equally impossible is a direct transition from crisis[5] and shortageflation to an inflation-free and growing market economy. The hazard on this road is continued inflation, this time accompanied not by shortages but by recession and unemployment, whose proportions depend on many circumstances including the specific character of the systemic void created in the post-communist economy. Most of these symptoms are familiar from underdeveloped market economies.

Thus, as illustrated in Figure 9.2, the shortageflation curve moves to the 'other side of the mirror', i.e., to the other side of the Y axis. The inflation rate drops and some (not all) shortages are eliminated but at the same time unemployment appears.[6] If these processes are also accompanied by recession—or even a prolonged depression—the transition will be one from a pathology characteristic of a command-type economy (shortageflation) to a pathology typical of the market economy (stagflation). It is apparently impossible to avoid this arduous path in the transition to a market economy, but the acuteness of the symptoms met on this path depends on the stabilization policy adopted, systemic transformation and structural change. In the Polish case, the errors of this policy led to transition from a particularly intensive shortageflation to an exceptionally severe stagflation. As I have shown, this was not entirely unavoidable.

Perspectives

Talking about perspectives immediately raises the problem of time horizons. Over a longer period, estimated at many years, there is no reason why relatively optimistic forecasts and scenarios should not be framed. But over a short period, progress in economic stabilization cannot realistically be expected; both the point of departure and the results (in view of previously implemented policies) are very unfavorable. The shortageflation syndrome has been replaced by stagflation—and at very high rates of both inflation and recession.

The inflation–shortage tradeoff has been replaced by an inflation–recession tradeoff. Owing to the above-mentioned lag in the adjustment of employment to production, unemployment will continue to grow in the near future, even if the economy does regain its growth momentum.

Figure 9.2. The Shift from Shortageflation to Stagflation

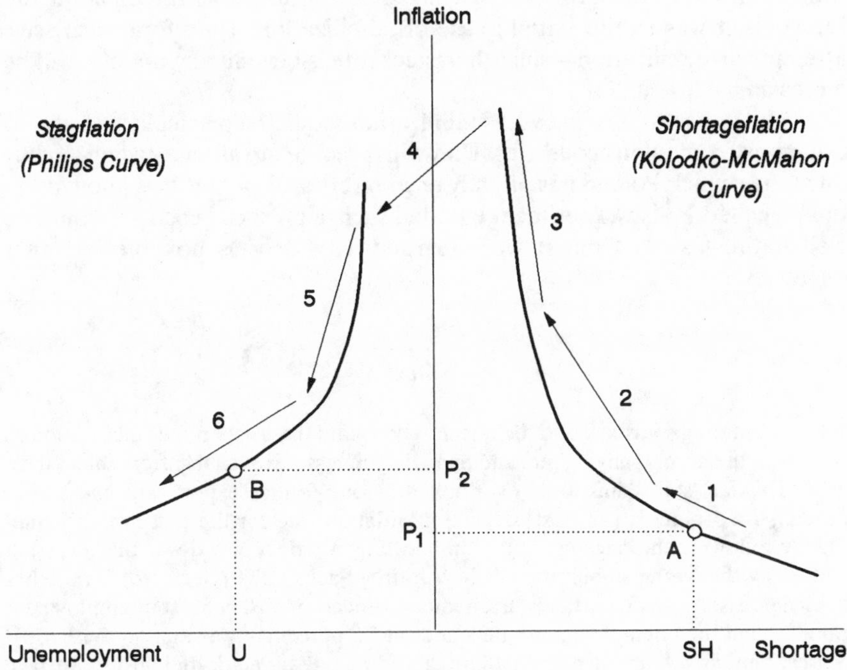

P_1 + SH = Rate of shortageflation (A).
P_2 + U = Rate of stagflation (B).

There is also evidence indicating that the acceleration of price inflation observed in the last quarter of 1990 and the beginning of 1991—and again in the first quarter of 1992—is not necessarily of a transient character, especially if a new, complex stabilization package is not initiated.

Moreover, the adverse impact of the external situation must not be overlooked: the price inflation induced by the change in payment arrangements between post-communist countries (beginning in 1991), and the rise in prices of energy carriers, in particular oil. The latter factor was already partly accommodated during the last months of 1990, but uncertainty still looms large, depending primarily on changes in international conditions. Some of these could—and should—have been foreseen (the transition from settlement in transfer roubles to settlement in US dollars with its inflationary and recessionary effects); others (the oil shock caused by the Gulf conflict) have complicated the situation in an unforeseeable way. But there also is a feedback link between the internal political situation and stabilization and transition. One can hardly expect this situation to be as favorable in the future as it was in the initial phase of stabilization. Therefore, successive attempts at stabilization—since their necessity is beyond any doubt—will be increasingly difficult.

The Polish experience with stabilization should be particularly useful to other post-communist countries. They will face—or are already facing—many dilemmas which Poland has already encountered. Now that it is known that the so-called Polish experiment entailed such high social costs, it would be well if the lessons from it were learned as widely as possible by other countries.

Notes

1. Additional statistical and technical background material on the stabilization as well as on the accompanying real and financial processes is available from the author.

2. This fact still seems to be overlooked by one foreign expert who had earlier predicted a 1 percent (at most) decline in inflation rate for the first month immediately following the package initiation and later tried to play down the recession caused by the wrong stabilization policy. Jeffrey Sachs (1990) declared: "There has been a persistent—and certainly erroneous—forecast of a 20 percent unemployment rate, though the unemployment rate stands at 5.5 percent, lower than in the United States. Similarly, fears of plummeting take-home pay abound, though the average industrial worker earned the equivalent of $131 in October, 1990, compared with $108 in October 1989." As noted above, government predictions of the unemployment rate were around 2 percent, not 20 percent. Besides, comparing open unemployment in Poland, which in one year grew from zero(!) to over 6 percent, with unemployment in the United States, cannot be taken seriously. Finally, suggesting a more than 20 percent wage rise by converting the wages into dollars, in a situation where they have really fallen by about 30 percent, is utter nonsense.

3. This index relates to the output of the socialized sector. In the private sector, whose share in total 1990 industrial production increased 13 percent, output has grown by about 8 percent (other estimates claim a much greater increase). For more on employment adjustment see Kolodko and Rutkowski (1991).

4. Firms exceeding this limit are liable to a fine of 200 to 500 percent.

5. I define this crisis as a general crisis of socialism, thus stressing its vulnerability in the absence of fundamental change (Kolodko, 1989b).

6. Therefore, in assessing the scale of stabilization effects in Poland, one should not compare the price inflation rate of the first half of 1989 (8.5 percent) with the inflation rate of the end of 1990 and the beginning of 1991 (about 6 percent), but the shortageflation rate (around 10–12 percent) with the stagflation rate (over 12 percent monthly), respectively. By spring 1992 such a rate was equal to about 17–18 percent.

References

Bruno, M., G. DiTella, R. Dornbusch and S. Fischer (eds.). 1988. *Inflation Stabilization. The Experience of Israel, Argentina, Brazil, Bolivia and Mexico.* Cambridge, Mass.: The MIT Press.

Coricelli, F., and R. Rocha. 1990. "Stabilization Programs in Eastern Europe: A Comparative Analysis of the Polish and the Yugoslav Programs of 1990." Paper presented at the World Bank Conference on Adjustment and Growth: Lessons for Eastern Europe, Pultusk (Poland), October 4–5.

Dornbusch, R. and S. Fischer. 1990. *Macroeconomics*. 5th edition. New York: McGraw-Hill.

Fischer, S. and A. Gelb. 1990. "Issues in Socialist Economy Reform." Paper presented at the OECD Conference on the Transition to a Market Economy in Central and Eastern Europe. Paris. November 28–30.

Frydman, R., S. Wellisz and G. W. Kolodko. 1991. "Stabilization Policies in Poland: A Progress Report." In: E. M. Classen (ed.), *Exchange Rate Policies in Developing and Post-Socialist Countries*. San Francisco: International Center for Economic Growth, Chapter 4, pp. 89–115.

Jorgensen, E. A., A. Gelb and I. Singh. 1990. "The Behavior of Polish Firms after the 'Big Bang': Findings from a Field Trip." Paper presented at the OECD Conference on the Transition to a Market Economy in Central and Eastern Europe. Paris. November 28–30.

Kolodko, G. W. 1988. "Crisis, Adjustment and Development in Socialist Economies: Case of Poland." Paper No. 1. Warsaw: National Bank of Poland, Banking and Money Research Institute.

——. 1989a. "Economic Reforms and Inflation in Socialism: Determinants, Mutual Relationships and Prospects," *Communist Economies*, 1 (No. 2): 167–181.

——. 1989b. "Reform, Stabilization Policies, and Economic Adjustment in Poland," *WIDER Working Paper*, 51. Helsinki: World Institute for Development Economics Research of the United Nations University.

——. 1990. "Un futuro giapponese o un destino argentino per la Polonia?" *L'Opinione*, October; 21–30.

——. 1991. "Polish Hyperinflation and Stabilization, 1989–1990," *Most. Economic Journal on Eastern Europe and the Soviet Union*, No. 1: 9–36.

—— and W. W. McMahon. 1987. "Stagflation and Shortageflation: A Comparative Approach," *Kyklos*, 40 (fasc. 2): 176–197. Reprinted in: M. Bornstein (ed.), *Comparative Economic Systems. Models and Cases*. Homewood, Ill.: Irwin 1989, Chapter 26, pp. 429–446.

—— and J. D. Sachs. 1989. "The Patient is Ready" (discussion), *The Warsaw Voice*, No. 52, December 24, p. 10.

—— and M. Rutkowski. 1991. "The Problem of Transition from a Socialist to a Free Market Economy: The Case of Poland," *The Journal of Social, Political and Economic Studies*, 16 (No. 2, Summer): 159–179.

——, D. Gotz-Kozierkiewicz and E. Skrzeszewska-Paczek. 1992. *Hyperinflation and Stabilization in Postsocialist Economies*. Boston-London-Dordrecht: Kluwer Academic Publishers.

Kornai, J. 1980. *Economics of Shortage*. Amsterdam: North-Holland.

——. 1990. *The Road to a Free Economy: Shifting from a Socialist System. The Example of Hungary,* New York and London: W. W. Norton.

Nuti, D. M. 1982. "The Polish Crisis: Economic Factors and Constraints." In: J. Drewnowski (ed.), *Crisis in East European Economy. The Spread of the Polish Disease*. London and Canberra: Croom Helm, New York: St. Martin's Press.

——. 1990. "Crisis, Reform and Stabilization in Central Eastern Europe: Prospects and Western Response." In: J. P. Fitoussi (ed.), *Eastern Europe: The Transition*. Paris.

Rosati, D. 1990. "The Sequencing of Reforms and Policy Measures in the Transition from Central Planning to Market: The Polish Experience". Paper presented at the OECD Conference on the Transition to a Market Economy in Central and Eastern Europe. Paris. November 28–30.

Sachs, J. D. 1990. "A Tremor, Not Necessarily a Quake, for Poland," *International Herald Tribune*, November 30, p. 8.

10

The Transition to a Market Economy: Lessons from the Experience of the CSFR

Miroslav Hrnčíř

The Czechoslovak economy, as well as some other former centrally planned ones in Central and Eastern Europe, is undergoing profound transition. In conjunction with the rejection of the communist one-party rule during the 'Velvet Revolution' of November 1989, the principles of the past economic system, i.e., state ownership and central planning and management of the entire economic activity, also have been fully discredited.[1]

The transition strategy adopted by the Czechoslovak government in the middle of 1990[2] opted for a market economy, i.e., an economy based on the predominance of private property under the institutional and political framework of a parliamentary democracy. The issue was thus a *substitution of the previous system*, and not a reformation.[3]

Initial Conditions in the CSFR in a Comparative Setting

While substantial political and economic changes have been taking place throughout Central and Eastern Europe since the collapse of communism in the course of the 1980s, Czechoslovakia joined Hungary and Poland in its firm commitment to a market-type economy and political democracy with a multi-party system. All three countries are well ahead on this track and have passed the point of no return. This development also found expression in the association agreements signed by these three countries and the EC in December 1991.

Unlike Hungary and Poland, Czechoslovakia maintained, in principle, the traditional institutional framework of a centrally planned economy until

1990. However half-hearted and partial the reform steps in Hungary and Poland might have been in the 1980s, they changed their initial legal and institutional conditions. In comparison to those countries, Czechoslovakia is a latecomer.

On the other hand, it is often claimed that as a result of its relatively stable domestic macroeconomic situation coupled with a low level of foreign debt and considering its industrial tradition and qualified labor, Czechoslovakia could enjoy a favorable opening position in the transition race.

Macroeconomic 'Stock' Conditions

Output. Throughout the postwar period the CSFR experienced a long-term deceleration of its growth rates (Table 10.1). That trend deepened significantly in the 1990s. The traditionally prudent monetary, credit, fiscal and wage policies are responsible for the fact that price levels increased only modestly since the 1950s.[4]

The official price indices reflect only part of the inflationary pressures that developed in the Czechoslovak economy. Under the previous regime, prices were subject to extensive state regulation. Consequently, in addition to the price increases identified by the official price indices, i.e., the rate of

Table 10.1. Growth Rates of Net Material Product, 1970–1989[a]

1970–75	1975–80	1980–85	1986	1987	1988	1989
5.7	3.6	1.8	2.8	2.1	2.3	1.3

[a] The concept of Net Material Product (NMP) was used in the official national accounting in the CSFR; only recently have unofficial estimates of the GDP consistent with the U.N. System of national accounts been constructed. The main difference between NMP and GDP is the omission from NMP of depreciation and much of the value added of the nonmaterial services sector, including personal transport and communications from NMP. On the other hand, however, nonmaterial costs in the material sector are not deducted. The difference between the two measures of output in the 1980s appears to be about 20 percent in the case of the CSFR (GDP higher than NMP); continual widening of the gap is due to the rising importance of depreciation costs.

Source: Compiled from data in the *Statistical Yearbooks* of Czechoslovakia.

open inflation, the effects of hidden and repressed inflation must be accounted for when assessing the total inflationary potential of the economy. Implications from the data in Table 10.2 tend to understate the true extent of inflation in the CSFR. Now the relevant, but rather controversial issue is: by how much?

The existence of excess demand ('shortages' in Kornai's terminology) due to suppressed prices, particularly consumer prices, is widely considered an inherent phenomenon of the framework of a centrally planned economy. Thus, this economic state is relevant for all the former socialist countries, including Czechoslovakia. On the financial side it is represented by a monetary 'overhang' or 'gap', i.e., the amount of money that remains unspent due to various constraints on the supply side. A number of studies have been undertaken to identify and evaluate the extent of monetary overhang.[5] However, in the case of Czechoslovakia, most foreign and domestic observers claim that, under the previous regime, the consumer market was fairly well balanced. That conclusion has only recently been disputed.[6]

In our estimation, the rate of hidden and repressed inflation for the whole economy increased in the 1980s, and particularly towards the end of the decade. Its annual average for the entire decade does not exceed 2–3 percent.[7] In any case, the degree of monetary overhang, although increasing, continued to be considerably lower than in other countries of Central and Eastern Europe. The extent of hidden inflation, even if comparatively smaller, requires that an important qualification be made to the official growth rates of output as indicated in Table 10.1. When corrected accordingly, they imply stagnating trends throughout the 1980s, i.e., a decade of virtually zero growth.[8]

Table 10.2. Developments in Wholesale and Consumer Prices (January 1977 = 100)

	1970	1980	1989
Wholesale prices			
Industry	95.2	102.3	126.1
Construction	101.9	100.0	120.9
Agriculture	91.9	109.8	162.2
Consumer prices			
Goods and services (total)	97.9	109.5	123.5
Foodstuffs	100.5	106.4	121.4
Manufactured goods	95.4	111.1	122.5
Public catering	98.2	106.5	138.1
Services	100.0	114.3	120.3

Source: *Statistical Yearbook of Czechoslovakia.*

Tables 10.1 and 10.2 also seem to suggest that the decline in economic growth in the 1980s was accompanied not by a loosening of inflationary pressure, but just the opposite. It reiterates the difference between the predominantly supply-constrained Czechoslovak economy and the demand-constrained market economies.

The external balance. Unlike Poland and Hungary, the CSFR has accumulated only a moderate foreign debt in convertible currencies, both in total volume and in per capita terms (Table 10.3). In per capita terms the gross debt amounted to US$444 per citizen. Even if the volume of the debt almost doubled between 1985 and 1989, it still does not imply a pressing foreign-exchange constraint. In fact, the resulting debt service was well below 20 percent of exports in convertible currencies.

Table 10.3. Foreign Indebtedness, Czechoslovakia and Selected Other Countries

	US$ (billions)	Percent of exports of goods and services for convertible currencies
Czechoslovakia	7.9	104
Bulgaria	9.2	227
Hungary	20.9	319
Poland	40.6	486
Yugoslavia	16.7	96

Source: *Statistical Yearbook of Czechoslovakia*; OECD statistics.

Microeconomic and Institutional Conditions: 'Flow' Constraints

Referring solely to macroeconomic dimensions, it is often claimed that in the case of the CSFR, the conditions under which transition was initiated were relatively favorable. Such a conclusion might be biased, even misleading, if not qualified by the assessment of other critical dimensions: microeconomic, institutional and legal. Unlike the reforming economies of Hungary and Poland, the institutional and socio-political framework in the CSFR corresponded closely to the traditional type of a centrally planned economy until 1989, despite partial reform steps taken during the previous communist regime. The private sector was negligible before 1990, including agriculture and services. In 1987 only about 0.6 percent of all employees were in the official private sector.[9]

The extent of shadow (or illegal) private activities was also marginal. Only in April 1990, when a new law on economic relations with the outside world was enacted, did the dismantling of the traditional state monopoly of foreign trade and foreign-exchange payments occur. Between 1948 and 1988 there was no legislation in Czechoslovakia on capital flows between the domestic economy and the outside world. A law on joint ventures in 1988 treated such ventures as an exception to the general framework of the domestic economy.

Furthermore, the traditional monobank system was restructured into a two-tier system of central bank and commercial banks only in 1989. The CSFR distinguished itself as a country with an unfavorable bias in the size of its enterprises: big units predominated, administratively created to facilitate vertical control from the center, while small units hardly existed at all. A comparative analysis reveals a much higher level of monopolization in the Czechoslovak economy than in other planned economies of Central and Eastern Europe.[10] A comparison of the size of state enterprises near the end of the centrally planned economy period shows that the average size in Czechoslovakia was over 2,000 workers, as against close to 1,200 in Poland.

As indicated in Table 10.4, the policy of dismantling the artificially

Table 10.4. Number and Size (Number of Employees) of State and Cooperative Organizations in the CSFR

	As of December 31, 1989		As of December 31, 1990	
	Number	Average size	Number	Average size
Total state and cooperative sector	8,856	872	10,890	684
Of which:				
1. State organizations	2,586	2,019	3,913	1,255
Industry	814	3,453	1,565	1,643
Construction	231	2,267	498	918
2. Cooperative organizations	2,581	445	2,979	355
Agriculture	1,861	385	1,918	331
3. Joint-venture enterprises	30	56	64	69

Source: Federal Statistical Office, *The Development of the CSFR Economy in 1990.*

big units and increased incentives for new entries, pursued since the beginning of 1990, contributed to the increased amount of registered enterprises and to a decline in their average size. Nonetheless, the share of smaller units in the industrial branches has continued to be rather limited.

The CSFR maintained a large proportion of industrial production, particularly in heavy industry, along with an inadequate share of services, both business and personal. The stock of productive capital was extensive, but most of it was obsolete.

One-sided trade with CMEA partners (the share of trade with CMEA was second highest after that of trade with Bulgaria) under the terms of 'secured' markets through government agreements, contributed to the petrification of the existing productive structure and diminished its capacity to adjust to the changing pattern of demand in world markets. As a result, the CSFR experienced a declining share of exports in the world market and an increase in the substitution of higher value-added exports to convertible-currency markets for lower value added ones, such as raw materials, intermediate products and standard consumer goods (Table 10.5). The CSFR was thus a case of 'regressive specialization'.

According to Kolanda and Kubišta (1990), exports of the Czechoslovak manufacturing sector to the West were rather uneven. In 342 of 866 enterprises (i.e., almost 40 percent) exports to the market economies did not exceed 1 percent of their total output. Hence, 4 out of every 10 enterprises had almost no contact with world markets and had no grasp of what real competition actually meant.

Table 10.5. Market Share of the CSFR and Neighboring CMEA Countries in OECD Imports (percent)

		CSFR	Hungary	Poland
Total imports by OECD	1975	0.28	0.21	0.54
	1985	0.19	0.19	0.28
	1989	0.18	0.19	0.29
Imports of machinery	1975	0.21	0.09	0.27
	1985	0.08	0.07	0.09
	1987	0.07	0.07	0.09

Source: OECD Trade Statistics.

The overwhelming orientation towards 'guaranteed' CMEA markets, particularly that of the Soviet Union, however nominally advantageous for exporters in the short run, proved highly detrimental and risky in the long run. First, the requirements of the autarkic CMEA markets fell short of international technological and quality standards. A long-term adjustment to such an environment calls for restructuring production and, particularly, a reorientation of the Czechoslovak foreign trade to world markets—a painful and highly controversial process. Secondly, the risks entailed in extreme dependence on a single trade area came to the fore, especially when the Soviet economy and CMEA institutions collapsed.

The above reasoning also explains the wide gap between domestic purchasing power parity and the market-type rate of exchange with respect to convertible currencies, as experienced in the CSFR at the onset of the transition process.[11]

The microeconomic, institutional and structural constraints identified above offer several important caveats to the widespread conclusion regarding the unambiguously favorable character of the initial macroeconomic conditions in the CSFR. The advantage of low foreign debt in convertible currencies appears less persuasive considering that it was achieved at the cost of a rather low (and diminishing) share of trade with market economies and by strict control of imports, particularly of consumer goods and machinery. Thus, the merits of the low foreign debt are outweighed by the resulting negative impact on the degree of competitive environment and on the technological standard of Czechoslovak producers, constraining future development potential, as well as on the standard of the domestic consumer goods markets.

In sum, the initial conditions for transition in the CSFR were mixed and controversial. Certainly, there was some comparative advantage thanks to a relatively stable macroeconomic situation and the absence of a pressing foreign-exchange bottleneck as in Hungary and Poland. But the CSFR lacked a gradual adjustment of both the institutional framework and the production and foreign trade structures. Unlike Hungary and Poland, a reorientation of foreign trade toward market economies did not materialize in the CSFR until 1990.

The microeconomic, institutional, structural and social rigidities described here impose a substantial constraint for the future, as they are likely to develop and disseminate disequilibrating tendencies in the course of the transition process itself.

Economic Trends in the Transition Period

As 1991 drew to an end, the transition process in the CSFR remained in its initial stage. However, two sub-periods can be distinguished since November

1989. (a) *An intermediary period*, extending into 1990, when several preparatory institutional, legal and economic steps were taken to secure the 'minimum' preconditions necessary to make transition feasible. (b) *The transition proper*, starting in Czechoslovakia in the beginning of 1991 with a package of liberalization and stabilization measures (domestic price liberalization, foreign-trade liberalization, introduction of internal currency convertibility on current account transactions) coupled with the initiation of the privatization process (Table 10.6).

Table 10.6. Basic Indicators of Macroeconomic Developments, 1990 and 1991[a]

	1990	1991
A. *Percent change from previous year*		
Net material product	−3.1	−19.5
Gross domestic product	−3.5	−15.9
Gross industrial production	−3.7	−21.3
Construction	−6.6	−24.4
Export	−0.5	−6.0
Import	+11.0	−22.0
Producer prices in industry[b]	+4.5	+54.8
Consumer prices[b]	+10.0	+45.3
Real wages	−5.6	−21.0
Living costs	+9.9	+49.5
B. *End-of-period figure*		
Unemployment ('000)	77	523.7
Unemployment rate (percent)	1	6.6
Current account balance in convertible currency (US$ bn)	−1.1	+0.3
Gross foreign debt (US$ bn)	−8.1	−9.4
State budgets (CSK bn)	+3.5	+18.6

[a] Output data include corrective estimates for contribution of small units and private enterprises as calculated by the Statistical Office.

[b] Annual average.

Source: Federal Statistical Office, *Statistical Bulletin.*

Table 10.7. Initial Forecasts and Outcomes of Economic Developments in 1991

	Authorities' forecast	Outcome at end of year
Net material product (percent)	−5	−19.5
Gross domestic product (percent)	—	−15.9
Consumer price index (percent)	+30	+53.6
Balance on current account in convertible currency (US$ bn)	−2.5	+0.3
Industrial production (percent)	—	−21.3
Unemployment rate (percent)	+5–6	+6.6
Real wages (percent)	−10–12	−21.0
Money supply (percent)	+5.9	+20.8

It is imperative that these two sub-periods be borne in mind when evaluating the results of the transition and the costs incurred thus far. From the very beginning there was no doubt that the move to a new economic, social and political setting, often described as 'the return of the CSFR to Europe', would inevitably be a painful, costly and lengthy process. The same lesson could be learned from the experience of all other countries in Central and Eastern Europe, which have also embarked on the path toward a market-type economy.

Nevertheless, in comparison with the initial expectations (identified in government documents), the implied costs appear to be considerably higher than expected, the time horizon for institutional and ownership changes longer, and the risks involved greater (Table 10.7). Were the expectations optimistically biased, or are the costs of transition unnecessarily high?

The Level of Economic Activity

After a prolonged deceleration in the economic growth of the CSFR, a significant drop in aggregate output occurred in 1990, leading to a deep recession in 1991. The economic decline is expected to continue in 1992, possibly at a much more moderate rate (of, say, −5 percent GDP growth), and some signs of revival are likely to appear only toward the end of that year.

The fall of Net Material Product by around 20 percent in 1991 (GDP fared better, thanks to the services sector) is far worse than the modest 5 percent drop predicted by the government before the beginning of the year and even worse than even the most pessimistic scenarios of independent researchers, who only predicted a 10 percent decline.

Two reservations are in place, however, with respect to the nominal statistical figures. First, owing to the institutional and ownership changes taking place, the available data understate the real recent performance of the economy. Even if there is some rationale behind the argument, the corrective deviation estimates by the Statistical Office (already included in the output figures for 1991) indicate that in the case of the CSFR the difference could be significant only in construction and in some (particularly local) services.

Secondly, a certain share of the output under the previous (centralized) framework was in fact of no use (because of planning mistakes, low quality standards, etc.), and was ultimately largely lost in unsalable stocks. Such an argument is certainly justified, and if the output lost recently is indeed of that character, the respective fall would be desirable and even therapeutic. The evidence tends to suggest, however, that the above might be true only to some extent, if at all.

The volume of stocks kept increasing in the first half of 1991, with plummeting production hitting particularly manufacturing branches (electrical goods—30.5 percent, clothing—33.22 percent, leather—26.3 percent as against the first half of 1990) while in heavy industry the drop was significantly lower. The fuel industry was the only area to increase its production (2.4 percent in the same period).

Employment

The number of registered unemployed (i.e., of those effectively seeking employment) as of December 31, 1991, reached 523.7 thousand, or 6.6 percent of the labor force. This is still a favorable ratio by international standards and it is certainly considerably lower than the decline in economic activity. At the same time we should note the following points:

1. Unemployment started rising from virtually zero in the second half of 1990 (not considering various forms of disguised unemployment); by the end of 1990 it stood at only about 1 percent of the labor force. As seen in Table 10.8, there was a steady increase in the unemployment rate in the course of 1991; at the end of October it was already five times higher than it had been at the beginning of the year.
2. Even if the total number of unemployed did not exceed 530 thousand by the end of 1991, the fall in employment might accelerate in 1992 as a result of real restructuring, rationalization of production and closing down inefficient units in the course of privatization.

Table 10.8. Unemployment in 1991 (percent of total labor force)

	January 31	June 30	December 31
CSFR	1.51	3.80	6.6
Czech Republic	1.10	2.60	4.1
Slovak Republic	2.37	6.32	11.8

Source: Federal Statistical Office, *Statistical Bulletin.*

3. The distribution of unemployment is unequal, both between the Czech and Slovak Republics and among the various regions within them. Table 10.8 reveals a much higher level of unemployment in Slovakia (in December 1991 it exceeded 11 percent). There is a considerable difference between conditions in Bratislava (less than 6 percent unemployed) and Western Slovakia (almost 12 percent), and—in the Czech Republic—between Prague (1.4 percent) and Northern Moravia (5.7 percent).

As a result, even with relatively modest average figures, the issue of unemployment has already become a sensitive social issue in particular regions and for specific social groups.

Prices, Wages and Living Costs

The anti-inflationary stance has dominated Czechoslovak economic policies since the onset of the transition. Unlike Poland and Yugoslavia, the issue was not how to cope with an already spiralling hyperinflation; rather, the goal was to avoid such a development altogether in the transition itself, particularly after domestic price liberalization.

When evaluating price developments in the relevant period, two different regimes must be distinguished: before and after the domestic price liberalization of January 1, 1991.

Under a strict price-regulation regime, the level of consumer prices remained stable until the second half of 1990 (see Table 10.9). A number of administrative price corrections followed (associated primarily with a substantial elimination of subsidies to foodstuffs) as preparatory steps for price liberalization.

Table 10.9. Consumer Price Developments, 1989 and 1990 (goods and services, percent change from corresponding quarter in preceding year)

	Quarter				Annual average
	I	II	III	IV	
1989	1.1	1.4	1.5	1.5	1.4
1990	3.3	3.9	14.1	18.4	10.1

Source: *Statistical Yearbook of Czechoslovakia.*

The development of consumer prices under the liberalized regime is described in Table 10.10. Compared with earlier trends, the consumer price index soared in January 1991. That jump was an anomaly—a once-and-for-all shift resulting from price liberalization rather than an inflationary process per se. Fortunately, the steep price increases gradually eased off and, in the third quarter, inflation was virtually zero.

Such a development could be considered a policy success and was hailed as such by the IMF. But at least two qualifications should be stressed. (a) Any claim that the inflationary aspect of the transition has been solved is premature. Lasting microeconomic and structural rigidities are likely to generate inflationary pressures again, particularly once economic activity revives. (b) A certain success in the anti-inflationary effort came at the expense of major losses in output.

Real wages decreased 5.6 percent in 1990 and by a further 21 percent in 1991. These figures differ substantially from the magnitudes set out in the Tripartite Agreement of 1991, whereby the upper limits for the decrease in real wages were 12 percent in the first quarter of 1991 and 10 percent over the rest of the year. Even if wage regulation had set strict guidelines for nominal wage increases, the resulting deviation from the Tripartite Agreement resulted from the fact that domestic recession was much deeper than originally envisaged. Consequently, many firms were unable to grant even those nominal wage increases permitted by such regulation.

The two consecutive years after the 'Velvet Revolution' of November 1989 is too short a period for any conclusive value judgments on the costs and benefits of the transition in the CSFR. However, some tentative suggestions might follow from the foregoing discussion.

Table 10.10. Consumer Price Developments in 1991 (monthly figures)

	Jan.	Feb.	Mar.	Apr.	May	June	July	Aug.	Sept.	Oct.	Nov.	Dec.	Year average
A. Percent change from December 1990													
Total goods and services	25.8	34.6	40.9	43.7	46.7	49.2	49.2	49.1	49.5	49.4	51.8	53.6	45.2
Foodstuffs	31.4	32.6	29.7	27.7	27.0	26.7	27.2	27.0	28.0	27.9	32.3	36.1	29.5
Manufactured goods	23.3	40.0	56.0	62.0	67.6	68.4	67.4	67.2	67.2	66.4	66.9	67.7	60.0
Catering	43.7	46.3	44.9	44.7	44.2	45.4	46.2	45.7	45.4	44.7	44.7	46.3	45.2
Services	8.6	12.4	13.8	19.2	24.1	40.0	40.9	41.8	42.5	46.1	51.3	52.2	32.7
B. Percent change from preceding month													
Goods and services	25.8	7.0	4.7	2.0	1.9	1.8	−0.1	0.0	0.3	−0.1	1.6	1.2	

Source: Federal Statistical Office, *Statistical Bulletin*.

Without doubt, the Czechoslovak economy has changed considerably in two years. Quite a few institutional, economic, socio-political and legal changes have been successfully implemented, or at least started, among them the initiation of privatization, stabilization measures, price- and foreign-trade liberalization and limited currency convertibility. On the other hand, one can hardly claim that a desirable change of regime on the micro level has been achieved. For this to happen, entrenched behavioral patterns and values will have to adapt, and this can only be done gradually.

In view of this state of affairs, the outcome of the transition is cast in doubt. In the real sphere, especially as far as the level of economic activity is concerned, the results tend to be much worse than initial expectations. On the other hand, most elements in the financial sphere (public budgets, balance of payments) were in better shape than expected.

Such a configuration is rather unstable and cannot be maintained for long, owing to both economic and social pressures. Any loosening of the restrictive policies and revival of economic activity will lead to financial deficits (as in Poland) if no substantial progress is achieved in the micro sphere—in restructuring, and in the level of competitiveness and efficiency of enterprises as a whole.

Explaining Recent Developments in the CSFR

The controversial consequences, delays and uncertainties described above are certainly not specific to the transition process in the CSFR. The lessons learned from developments in other, former centrally planned economies, suggest more-or-less the same experience: Transition involves more complex and long-term goals than reforms in many other parts of the world, and are therefore also more costly than initially expected. The widespread euphoria following the fall of the communist regimes in Czechoslovakia and elsewhere is gradually being replaced by dissatisfaction, declining confidence and pessimistic expectations.

According to the World Bank, Central and Eastern Europe will not recover its 1989 level of economic activity (aggregate output) before 1996. A comparison with the medium-term prospects of the OECD countries suggests that the existing substantial gap in economic levels between Western and Eastern Europe will not narrow in a mere five to six years; rather, the gap will probably widen. However, if no visible signs of economic revival in Central and Eastern Europe emerge, the widening gap between West and East will only exacerbate the already existing elements of instability and risk inherent in the restructuring of Central and Eastern European countries, including the threat of mass migrations, brain drain and social unrest. There is, however, also evidence of substantial differences in the development trends of individual reforming countries.

In addition to the impact of the different initial conditions, at least three categories of relevant factors are generated in the course of the transition and affect its outcome: (i) The type of the transition strategy chosen and the degree of its consistency with the country-specific conditions; (ii) the economic policies pursued to implement the strategy and their degree of proper calibration, timing and adjustment; and (iii) the impact of various exogenous factors.

The CSFR used to be considered a country with relatively favorable initial conditions. Our discussion stressed important qualifications of such an assessment: while the initial stock situation (monetary overhang) was certainly in better shape, there were important constraints on economic flows in the existing institutional and structural rigidity. It is apparently just these microeconomic, institutional and structural constraints that were not properly taken into account by the government policies and by most domestic and foreign observers. But if the initial conditions were relatively favorable then the question is: What went wrong in the course of the transition itself?

Exogenous Factors

Undoubtedly, a number of hazardous exogenous shocks coincided with the implementation of crucial steps in the transition process. Among these are the collapse of the CMEA institutions and of regional trade, along with the growing uncertainty as to the future development of the former main trading partner. Also important was the onset of economic recession in the West, the maintenance of trade barriers with respect to the CSFR by the EC, and the substantial cut in oil supplies from the USSR combined with the impact of the Gulf conflict.

The depressive impact of these external factors on the CSFR economy would have been substantial even if there were no transition costs.[12] According to Landesmann (1991) the CSFR may have been hardest hit of all the Central and East European countries by the trade shocks. In attempting to distinguish between transition costs and the costs of these exogenous shocks, some analysts attribute roughly the same percentage weight to both.

In addition to exogenous shocks, there are several factors that, although of domestic origin, are extraneous to the economic sphere: social coherence and integrity, social consensus and political support for the transition strategy. It is only natural that the various Czechoslovak political forces, once united in their opposition to the communist regime, turned into a disunited group of political parties (at present, there appear to be too many of them). Even more detrimental is a lack of political culture and the capacity to solve public issues in a democratic and efficient manner, combined with a lack of institutions, procedures and experience in running state and public matters consistently within a market economy framework.

In addition to the above-mentioned constraints, all of which were present to some degree in other reforming countries too, some issues were specific to the CSFR, and these worsened the prospects for a smooth and successful transition. First among these constraints is certainly the unresolved question of the state's form of organization—will a federative scheme be maintained? If so, what sort of division of functions between the federal and republic levels will be feasible and, at the same time, secure a workable federation?

The deliberations went on long after the formation of the new state and its parliamentary bodies (June 1990), without a conclusive outcome. A lack of consensus hampered several steps in the implementation of the transition scenario, unduly preoccupying the governments, and diverting the attention of the public from the main issues of transition. The perseverance of such institutional uncertainty harmed the international image of the CSFR as well as affecting the terms on which loans on financial markets could be obtained, leaving potential foreign investors at best increasingly cautious.

The sensitive nature of Czech-Slovak relations grew more acute because of the different social impacts of transition. For a variety of reasons, the Slovak republic is affected more adversely:[13] the existence of a substantial share of military industry slated for conversion, the lower level of efficiency, regional disparities, a less-homogeneous population with a number of minorities. The fact is used (or rather, politically misused) as an argument against radical transformation, against a common economic regime for all of Czechoslovakia's territory, and consequently against a federation scheme itself, in spite of a continuing massive reallocation of resources to the Slovak part of the state. Even if the constitutional crisis was evidently a crisis of politicians rather than a crisis of mutual relations between Czechs and Slovaks, it remains a potential threat to the success of the Czechoslovak transition.

The Czechoslovak Transition Strategy

The type of strategy adopted in the CSFR, its elements, timing and sequencing, resemble to a considerable degree the approaches previously followed elsewhere. Reference here is particularly to a number of reforming countries in Latin America in the 1980s. In the case of former centrally planned economies such a strategy was applied in a clear-cut form in Poland one year before it was in the CSFR.

The basic elements of the strategy and their sequencing can be summarized as follows:

- Macroeconomic stabilization through aggregate demand restriction is the key goal of the initial phase (first place the economy on a sound footing).
- Adoption of suitable anchors for the stabilization process (fixing the

nominal exchange rate and/or setting targets for nominal money supply, wages and incomes).
- Privatization and reduction of state involvement in economic activities.
- Promotion of the supply-side response: foreign trade liberalization and the elimination of trade barriers, currency convertibility, enhancing competitive environment.

The strategy described above was developed against the background of a certain conventional wisdom reflecting experience gained and lessons learned in several countries that were under pressure and faced similar challenges of reform implementation. That conventional wisdom was also expressed in the 'IMF conditionality'—the principles of the IMF policies and recommendations addressed to those member countries that found themselves in economic trouble. But the elaboration of these reform strategies and of their accompanying policy packages evolved under specific conditions. Their common basic features represented two dominant challenges: (i) The economies suffered from destabilized macroeconomic conditions, usually resulting in hyperinflation, and (ii) from the microeconomic and institutional points of view, those economies were market economies, with market institutions and market agents. Their trouble was that state intervention became too extensive and the public sector too costly, inhibiting market functions and distorting firms' behavior and hence their efficiency.

To a certain extent, the conditions inherited by the Czechoslovak economy resemble those indicated above, but there are also significant differences.[14] While the dominant target and success indicator in countries with hyperinflation was the rapid stabilization of the economy, the dominant challenge (and consequently also the dominant policy issue) in the CSFR was different. Here, the lack of markets, market institutions and market agents, and institutional and structural rigidities, were the critical features. Unlike Latin America, not only a quick reestablishment of macroeconomic stability, but changes in the microsphere, in behavior patterns, institutional and regime changes were of crucial importance and should have been the main success indicators.

Adopting the above conventional wisdom in the Czechoslovak case implies, at least to some extent, a mistaken diagnosis. Consequently, too much weight was attached to the macroeconomic dimension, too much attention was paid to the benign effects of macroeconomic restrictive policies. The implied consequences in the form of transition costs and delays experienced in the 'real' job of restructuring are readily apparent.

Controversial Issues and Biases of Economic Policies in 1990–1991

The economic policies pursued in the period under review developed under two discernible influences: the type of transition strategy chosen, consistent with the IMF approaches and conditionality, and the intellectual attractiveness of the neoclassical tradition and the monetarist approaches of the Chicago School.[15]

The key controversial issues related mainly to the following four policy dimensions: (a) macroeconomic stabilization, (b) privatization, (c) opening up of the economy and (d) the speed of transition.

Macroeconomic stabilization. Macroeconomic stabilization is, perforce, an integral part of any transition policy package in formerly centrally planned economies. The open issue is, however, the costs and the efficiency of the macroeconomic restrictive policies under given conditions. Some drawbacks of the policies recently pursued in the CSFR were due precisely to the fact that too much was expected of the macroeconomic restrictive policies themselves and much less attention was devoted to deliberate measures to overcome microeconomic constraints and rigidities. As a result, an inevitable asymmetry between the macro and micro dimensions of the transition tended to persist, if not deepen.

The experience gained in the Czechoslovak case confirms that if the underlying micro conditions are not satisfied, at least to some degree, i.e., if the responsiveness of economic agents to the policy instruments and price and wage adjustment in the short run is sluggish, then:

- The conventional transmission mechanism of the macro policy cannot operate satisfactorily.
- A significant restructuring of economic agents cannot be expected to follow automatically, however restrictive and tough the stabilization policies.
- Unless restructuring of economic agents occurs, the more effective the restrictive policies in the financial sphere of the economy, the higher will be the costs incurred in the real sphere.

Even if the restrictive policies do succeed in coping with the aggregate demand overhang, they can hardly be expected to cope with the structural factors of inflation. And it is precisely these institutional and structural causes that dominate in the CSFR. Consequently, restrictive policies alone cannot eliminate the inflationary threat and the risk that once the restrictions are relaxed inflationary pressures will reappear.

In the ongoing discussion on implemented macroeconomic stabilization policies it is often claimed, when confronted with a severe recession, that the restriction's aim must have overshot. Our arguments point out the one-sided reliance on demand restriction, which then had to be rather tough when the simultaneous adjustment of microeconomic conditions was lacking.

Privatization. Privatization is certainly the core of the transition, especially in Czechoslovakia, where economic activity was almost totally 'socialized'. It was clear that reliance solely on traditional, standard procedures and adopting a case-by-case approach would prolong the privatization process for decades. The government therefore allowed for a plurality of privatization procedures: it gave the enterprises themselves a choice as to the path privatization should take, by enabling them to submit privatization tenders; it also entertained offers by any other interested party. In an endeavor to speed up the progress, a controversial non-standard coupon method was given a significant though not dominant role. Nevertheless, experience shows that even under such conditions, privatization is a long-term process. Furthermore, one should allow for a lag between the formal act and the real impacts of privatization on firm efficiency. New coupon holders are certainly not assertive shareholders.

Government policy in the micro sphere seemed to be deliberately limited to the implementation of privatization. The implied assumption apparently was that only through privatization was it feasible to enhance the efficiency of firms and to regain the heritage of the past, including the enterprise indebtedness.

No matter how important privatization may be for the success of the entire transition, it should be recognized that privatization is a long-term process, where administrative delays and various time lags are unavoidable. The experience of the CSFR shows the delays in the preparation of the legal framework and in the ensuing administrative steps as well. In addition, privatization will not necessarily do away with the existing monopolistic structure and behavior. Privatized monopolies may simply replace state monopolies. Finally, there will still be a substantial public sector not only before the privatization wave, but also after it.

In spite of these arguments, the issues of control over and incentive schemes for state (or public) firms were apparently beyond the scope of government policy. Consequently, a certain management and control vacuum developed in the state sector, with a negative impact, referred to even by the cabinet ministers as 'agony'. To allow the evolution of such agony in the pre-privatization phase is a distinct policy flaw.

By the same token, there was no determination to cope with the state firms' past debts by declaring a general moratorium. On this issue, government policy relied almost solely on privatization, in spite of the ensuing delays in the potential recovery in the activities of enterprises.

It was only after a considerable delay that it was recognized that the entry of the new small and medium-size private firms should be supported to overcome their initial constraints, particularly with domestic demand contracting considerably.

Opening the economy and introduction of currency convertibility. Two alternative solutions were discussed with respect to the opening of the

Czechoslovak economy in the course of transition: (a) a simultaneous liberalization in the domestic and external spheres at the very beginning of transition (i.e., introduction of currency convertibility and foreign-trade liberalization along with domestic price liberalization); and (b) priority to be given to domestic liberalization. The loosening of administrative regulations in the external sphere should be spread over a few years.

The government opted for the first option, assuming that the benefits of such an early move to trade and foreign-exchange liberalization would outweigh the implied costs. These benefits included attracting foreign competition and setting up countervailing power to the monopoly of domestic producers and traders; 'importing' foreign price ratios; and initiating a reallocation of resources that would mirror the conditions of an open economy.

These are potentially powerful arguments, and considering the strategy adopted in the CSFR the choice made seems justified. At the same time, however, its sustainability was expected to rely on a heavy depreciation of the exchange rate,[16] while there was no set of consistent policies aimed at promoting exports and temporary protection, including tariff instruments, export credits and their insurance, improvement of commercial, banking and financial services. These elements appeared only in the second half of 1991; signs of a change in approach, in the direction of more pragmatic policies, is now beginning to be felt.

The speed of transition. The strategy adopted by the CSFR has often been called 'radical' by its designers, who claim that it would guarantee both the qualitative change (system substitution) and the swift progress of transition.

After the lessons learned from the failures of partial reform attempts, there was a broad consensus that a system replacement could not be achieved without a severe initial shock. Apart from that, Czechoslovakia, being a relative late-comer to the transition process, had to catch up in the transition race. However, under the rapidly changing domestic and international conditions, with considerable shifts in preferences and expectations of economic agents, the time factor became important.

The assertion that the Czechoslovak scenario focused on rapid transition is sometimes disputed by pointing to 1990, which is difficult to account for, given that the crucial measures (including privatization) were initiated only in the beginning of 1991. With reference to the state of affairs toward the end of 1989, which was entirely different from the Hungarian and Polish cases, a certain 'preparatory' period seems unavoidable in the CSFR case.

Our analysis points to an inadvertent asymmetry between the progress of macroeconomic stabilization and liberalization measures, on the one hand, and the microeconomic and institutional spheres on the other. The strategy and the policies pursued in the CSFR have so far not succeeded in balancing this asymmetry. Thus, because of unavoidable delays in real restructuring, the strategy adopted may not prove to be a faster one in reality.

Notes

1. The failure of the centrally planned economy is perhaps most apparent in the case of the CSFR, particularly in the western part of the CSFR, Bohemia and Moravia, which belonged to the most developed industrial countries before the World War II; its economic level is now relatively much lower. The present economic level of the CSFR is estimated at somewhere between one-half and two-thirds of that of Austria (with all the reservations about the comparability and consistency of the available data), while in 1937 Czechoslovakia was more or less at the same level and immediately after the war it appeared to be even slightly ahead of Austria.

2. "Scenario of Economic Reform," *Hospodářské noviny*, No. 75 (September 4, 1990).

3. That is the basic distinguishing feature of the contemporary efforts when compared with all the earlier reform attempts which started in Czechoslovakia as early as 1958. Those were oriented rather at an 'improvement' or 'perfection' of the traditional system of the centrally planned economy, allowing for the move from 'direct' to more indirect methods of management and trying to introduce some market elements leaving, however, the basic features and institutional framework of a centrally-planned economy intact.

4. That tradition dates back to the period after World War I. Immediately after the war the newly created Czechoslovak republic adopted conservative fiscal and monetary policies and, as a result, avoided the hyperinflation experienced by all its neighbors: Germany, Austria, Hungary and Poland. See Sargent (1986).

5. Especially important is the study by Portes and Winter (1980).

6. Cf. Charemza, (1991).

7. Such a range coincides with the calculations of other researchers. Klacek *et al.* (1990) estimate the hidden inflation in the period since 1960 at 2–2.5 percent annually. See also Vaňous (1990).

8. The phenomenon of hidden inflation is evidently one of the factors explaining the gap between the figures for the long-term average growth of the Czechoslovak economy. The official statistics report this amount at 5 percent while the implicit growth rate resulting from the international comparison of economic levels is, at most, half this figure.

9. The number of registered private entrepreneurs has been increasing since early 1990. Toward the end of 1990 it amounted to 488,000 and as of September 30, 1991, the figure was 1,130,000. Only about one-third of those, however, engage in private activity as their main occupation. The share of the private sector in GDP increased to 3 percent in 1990 and is expected to increase further, to 7 percent, in 1991.

10. Zemplinerová (1989).

11. The domestic purchasing power of the CSK was estimated at 6–7 per US$1 in 1990. *Plan Econ Report* calculations put the respective ratio at CSK6.26 per US$ for that period (1990). At the same time the exchange rate of the CSK, after three

devaluations in 1990, was established at CSK28/US$1, implying a deviation coefficient of 4, which signals a rather wide gap for a developed economy.

12. To support this argument, we might look at the analogous case of the Finnish economy. Even though far less dependent on Soviet trade than the CSFR, the collapse of the Soviet market was evidently the main factor behind the 5–7 percent fall in the Finnish GDP.

13. See also Table 10.8 on unemployment rates.

14. Compare the discussion in Section 2 of this paper. For a more elaborate analysis see Hrnčíř and Klacek (1991).

15. Note the observation by Lavigne (1990), that ". . . in the economic field, the advocated policies are much more conservative than in many Western governments. Central European economists are more committed to monetarism and to neoclassical concepts of economics than many of their Western colleagues."

16. There were three devaluations of the CSK with respect to convertible currencies in the course of 1990, amounting to almost 90 percent devaluation.

References

Charemza W. W. 1991. "Alternative Paths to Macroeconomic Stability in Czechoslovakia," In: *European Economy*, Special edition, No. 2.

Hrnčíř, M. and J. Klacek. 1991. "Stabilization Policies and Currency Convertibility in Czechoslovakia." In: *European Economy*, Special Edition No. 2.

Klacek, J. *et al.* 1990. *Macroeconomic Analysis 1990*. Prague: Institute of Economics.

——. 1991. *Economic Reform in Czechoslovakia*. Prague: Institute of Economics, pp. 24–25.

Kolanda, M. and Kubišta, V. 1990. "Costs, Performance and Behavior of the Czechoslovak Manufacturing Enterprises On the World Markets in the 1980s," Prague: The Institute for Forecasting.

Landesmann, M. 1991. "Industrial Restructuring and the Reorientation of Trade in Czechoslovakia." In: *European Economy*, Special Edition No. 2.

Lavigne, M. 1990. Economic Reforms in Eastern Europe, Prospects for the 90s," Conference paper, Tokyo, December.

Portes R. and Winter D. 1980. "Disequilibrium Estimates for Consumption Goods Markets in Centrally Planned Economies," *Review of Economic Studies*, 47 (No. 1): 137–59.

Sargent T. J. 1986. *Rational Expectations and Inflation*. Harper & Row.

"Scenario of Economic Reform," *Hospodářské noviny*, No. 75, September 4, 1990.

Vaňous, J. 1990. Czechoslovak Economic Performance during the First Half of the 1990s," *PlanEcon Report*, No. 36–37.

Zemplinerová, A. 1989. *Monopoly in a Centrally Planned Economy*. Prague: Institute of Economics.

11

The Currency Union and the Economic Road to German Unity

Maria Haendcke-Hoppe-Arndt, Michael Keren and Günter Nötzold

The political entity once called the GDR is no more. Such an unusual—even unique—historical event, of a country disappearing after existing for 45 years, calls for a brief review of the last days of the GDR as well as an analysis of its economic transition to the new regime. This we try to do in the present chapter. We start with an introductory section, which details the background to the collapse of the socialist economy on German soil and the path to the currency union of July, 1990—the actual end of the GDR. The next two sections analyze some of the economic policies of reunification: the former looks at the choice of the conversion rate from the GDR Mark (referred to as Mark) to the D-Mark (DM); the latter section questions some of the microeconomic policies of the unifying agencies. The fourth section looks briefly at the economic effects of the policies analyzed, and the last section concludes the chapter.

Background: The Last Decade of the GDR

Together with Czechoslovakia, the eastern part of Germany that became the GDR had for many decades been considered the most developed economy in the region. It continued to hold this position under the socialist regimes, and therefore maintained the highest standard of living among all socialist countries. Since its foundation in 1949 it was the most important supplier of investment goods in the CMEA, in terms of quantity and quality. About 80 percent of its exports of machinery and transport equipment were sent to the east. Next to Bulgaria, the GDR was the CMEA member with the highest degree of intra-bloc involvement. At first three-quarters and later two-thirds of its entire foreign trade turnover was with the east. The Soviet Union's share in this trade was 35–45 percent. This regional and commodity structure arose from the political division of Europe and Germany after World War II. The division also meant the separation of the East from the previously-integrated all-German economy. Separation caused greater disruption to East German production and trade flows than it did to the West German economy for the following reasons:

1. East Germany's highly specialized industry (consumer goods, chemicals) had a limited energy and raw-material base, and this fostered a much stronger dependence on external markets than the more widely based West German industry.
2. Its production and transportation potential was much more seriously weakened through Soviet dismantling and reparation payments than was the old Federal Republic. Although the western part of Germany suffered heavier damage from bombing, it was soon to profit from the Marshall plan.

For these reasons, and given the hallowed status of heavy industry and the autarkic tendencies of Soviet-type economies, the GDR had to construct parallel production facilities to those of the old Federal Republic—heavy industries in which the GDR had no comparative advantage, such as steel and rolling mills, and shipbuilding industries which did not exist before the split. The shift of foreign trade to economically less-developed partners, especially the Soviet Union, required new types of facilities to supply low-quality, mass-produced commodities. Traditional branches, such as highly specialized chemicals used in the manufacture of textiles, were neglected. Costly raw materials and energy had to be imported. Coal, for example, which used to come from the Rhine region, was replaced by Siberian coal. The radical structural change, the disregard for comparative advantage, is one of the obstacles to the reintegration of the GDR industry into an all-German economy.

The GDR was in a unique position because of its special relationship with the Federal Republic (Haendcke-Hoppe, 1990a, p. 133ff). The economic benefits it enjoyed—alone of all CMEA members—arose from the special status of inter-German trade. It is generally and erroneously believed that the GDR's greatest advantage arose from its status as a 'quasi associate member of EEC'. The GDR never had this status, since the customs barriers between EEC countries and the GDR per se remained intact. Only inter-German trade was exempt from these customs duties. Of greater economic importance were the politically induced annual cash transfers, which were the result of contracts following the Quadripartite Agreement of 1971. These included, *inter alia*, a lump-sum payment for the use of transit routes to Berlin, payments in lieu of visa fees, and revenues from the minimal exchange fees for Western visitors to the GDR and the earnings of hard currency shops. Official payments from the Federal Republic and ancillary receipts were estimated during the 1980s at an annual rate of DM2.5–3 billion. This hard-currency income was the greatest privilege the GDR had.

The Economic Slow-Down of the 1980s

The economic policy of the Honecker era can be divided into two different periods. The concept in the 1970s was growth financed by foreign credits. In other words, the aim was to modernize production potential by importing Western, technologically advanced machinery. As in Gierek's Poland, it was intended that an export offensive should follow, to enable the GDR to repay its debts. This strategy failed because the new capacity did not deliver the expected increased efficiency, and because soaring energy prices in the 1970s raised the GDR's requirements for foreign exchange. The GDR's leadership was very slow to react to this sharp increase in import prices: only the second oil price shock produced an energy saving program in 1980, which was quite insufficient for the task.

This deterioration in the terms of trade, at first with the West, and since 1975 also vis-à-vis the Soviet Union, led to an increase in indebtedness to both regions. Economic policy in the early 1980s was therefore dictated by an urgent need to consolidate the balance of payments. But all hopes for such a consolidation vanished abruptly at the end of 1981, when all Western credit sources to the GDR dried up in the wake of the crisis of confidence caused by Poland's and Romania's inability to pay their debts.

In the following years crisis management consisted of export at any cost. This included exporting large quantities of processed oil, i.e., the sale of oil, purchased under soft CMEA terms (at prices which were then still below world prices, and for TR, Transferable Rubles) from the Soviet Union, for hard currency. The export campaign, combined with a rigid cut in imports, resulted in a sharp decline in consumption and investments, which affected particularly the replacement of the obsolete capital stock. An internal economic collapse was probably averted only by a large increase in deliveries from the Federal Republic, made possible because the GDR's indebtedness to the Federal Republic was less severe than to its other Western trading partners. Two unlinked financial credits, totalling DM2 billion in 1983 and 1984, and guaranteed by the Federal Republic, not only helped to consolidate the balance of payments, they also facilitated the reopening to the GDR of the international credit markets.[1] These events in the first half of the 1980s contributed to the accelerated slowdown of the economy at the end of the decade (Haendcke-Hoppe, 1989, p. 58ff).

Paradoxically, the decline of the world price of oil in the beginning of 1986 triggered a new severe attack on the GDR economy. The GDR, traditionally a heavy energy importer, earned one-third of its hard currency by exporting processed oil (and even crude oil) between 1982 and 1985. The sharp decline in oil prices led to the reduction of the export proceeds from the West by about US$1.2 billion in 1986. Until its demise the GDR was unable to find competitive commodities to substitute for processed oil. The lack of investments[2] and the reduced imports of modern western machinery in the early 1980s dramatically increased the GDR's productivity gap and its inability to compete in the West.

Severe financial problems were created by the decision of the SED[3] leadership to keep its promise of fixed consumer prices, made in 1970. The maintenance of the extremely low prices of basic foods, services and rents resulted in subsidies which by 1988 were three times higher than in 1980, and their share in the annual budget increased to nearly one-fifth. Nonetheless, Erich Honecker and his colleagues continued to claim that the GDR had developed a well-functioning system of a socialist planned economy which proved efficient, dynamic and flexible. The GDR was, next to Romania, the most reform-resistant member of the CMEA.

Modrow's Market Socialist Experiment

The GDR economy, in spite of its poor condition, would not have broken down without a prior political collapse. The peaceful revolution that followed the flight of hundreds of thousands of GDR citizens after the opening of the Hungarian borders forced the elderly Stalinist politburo to resign. On November 9 the wall collapsed and on November 17–18 Hans Modrow, the first SED Secretary of the Dresden Bezirk, formed a coalition government with the bloc parties of the Volkskammer.

Modrow belonged to the small reformist wing of the SED, but his reform proposals were modeled in the style of the 1960s. The basic premise was that all economic systems are mixed, and that the choice is one between more or less planning or more or less market coordination. The transition from a centrally planned economy to a market economy was often conceived as one of deregulation. The reform program by which Modrow tried to stabilize the GDR economy was a socialist market experiment, an experiment with the so-called 'third way'. Modrow appointed as his deputy Christa Luft, Rector of the Hochschule für Ökonomie, to whom he entrusted the preparation of the reform program,[4] namely, the fundamental transformation of the economic system, without altering the social order.

The central idea was to keep a 'real' central kernel of socialist property intact. The economy was to evolve a mixture of socialist (both state-owned and cooperative) and private forms of ownership. As stated in the declaration of March 1, it was ". . . in the interest of GDR citizens that property relations formed after World War II should not be questioned." To administer the state property[5] (organized in people's enterprises) the Trust Institution (*Treuhandanstalt*) was founded in March 1990, as the trustee of 8,000 state enterprises. All state enterprises were to be converted into joint stock companies whose shares were to be held by the *Treuhandanstalt*. The principal measures of the economic reform policy were:

1. Abolition of the central setting of production targets.
2. Termination of material balancing.
3. Reorganization of the economic administration (three industrial ministries instead of ten).
4. The State Planning Commission was to become part of a newly-formed Economic Committee.
5. Founding joint ventures with foreign participation of up to 49 percent was to be permitted.
6. Freedom for GDR citizens (but not for foreigners) to engage in private business.
7. Restitution of 5,400 small enterprises, expropriated in 1972, to their previous private owners.
8. Reform of the centralized banking system.

Today all these measures appear half-hearted. Remember that time was much too short, reforms came overnight without a clear conception or a preparatory debate, and (disregarding the NES of the 1960s) with no previous decentralizing tradition or experience as, for instance, in Poland or Hungary. Since the Modrow interregnum lasted only four months, it is hard to say whether the above measures could have provided the necessary impetus for the economy had they survived. On the other hand, it should be remembered that in the highly explosive phase that followed the opening of the Berlin Wall, the Modrow government did succeed in avoiding chaos.

As it happened, the political atmosphere changed very rapidly. Since mid-December unification with West Germany became the central political theme. The slogan of the great demonstrations in Leipzig and Berlin switched from "we are the people" to "we are one people." The result of the first democratic elections (March 18, 1990) was an overwhelming 75 percent majority for the parties that espoused the following policies: (a) The DM as the future currency; (b) a market economy as in the Federal Republic, retaining only a few of the social aspects of the GDR system; and (c) German unity. These elections ended the dominance of the SED. A CDU government headed by Lothar de Maiziere took over from Modrow.

The Road to Currency Union

Fundamental changes started after the March elections. Their outcome, aided by the external political climate, created extreme pressure for German unity. The Federal Republic's offer of a currency and economic union came as early as February 15. According to this offer the DM was to be introduced as the sole means of payment in the GDR and was to become the foundation of economic stability there. This went counter to the advice of most West German economists, including participants in government advisory committees, who supported the creation of preconditions for the development of a competitive market:

1. Privatization of state property.
2. Freeing prices.
3. The foundation of a competitive market.
4. Creation of labor market institutions—free trade unions and employers' organizations.
5. The gradual integration of GDR foreign trade into the world economy.

These preconditions could not, however, be realized by de Maiziere's new government. This government could not exert any authority, and inexperienced ministers had to depend on the old SED cadres even after March 18 (which marked the complete collapse of the SED party and its regime). The independently elected members of the last Volkskammer worked under tremendously difficult conditions. The competitive economy did not arise on its own. Furthermore, most of the political energy was spent on uprooting the heritage of 40 years of Stasi-based dictatorship. The degree to which the Stasi had penetrated the daily life of the GDR people became visible only gradually. Local Stasi networks functioned until autumn 1990, i.e., until final political reunification.

The Federal Republic's plan for an economic and currency union was adopted after the election of the de Maiziere government. The first state contract for the construction of an economic currency and social union—the second sealed the political union—was signed within three months and came into force on July 1, 1990. With it the Federal Republic's model of a market economy was imposed on the GDR.

The first state contract was concluded under incredible time pressure. None of the negotiating partners, neither the new team of the GDR nor the Western negotiators who came from the political ranks of the civil service, had any inside knowledge of the GDR economy.[6] Many problems were therefore not foreseen, and some were simply ignored in the rush. However, the heart of currency union was the politically motivated choice of an exchange or conversion rate. The background to this choice (which was far from simple) and its consequences are discussed below.

The Currency Union: Background and Consequences

The currency union meant that since July 1 the only legal tender in the GDR was the DM. The following conversion rates were used:

1. Wages, salaries, pensions, rents and all current payments were converted at DM1 per GDR Mark.
2. Savings deposits were converted at two rates—1:1 for the first tranche and 1:2 for the residual. The size of the part that received

the preferential rate depended on age: Mark 4,000 for 15–59 year olds, Mark 6,000 for persons over 60 (to compensate for low pensions), and only Mark 2,000 for those under 14. Some 70 percent of all savings deposits were converted at the 1:1 rate.

3. All private and enterprise debts and other contractual obligations were to be settled at a rate of DM1 per Mark 2.

The success of the monetary conversion in terms of internal and external monetary stability, as well as its technical execution, was above reproach. This achievement should not be underrated: even the logistics of the operations were quite complex, with DM25 billion in cash which had to be shipped from West to East within a very brief time span. 600 tons of banknotes and 400 tons of coin had to be distributed to 16 newly founded branches of the *Bundesbank* and some 4,200 other banking institutions in the ex-GDR. All this was accomplished without a hitch, let alone a robbery.

From a purely technical monetary perspective the currency union was thus highly successful. With it the GDR had a far better opening position than any other CMEA member, particularly since the initial transfusion of DM25 billion was accompanied by the development of a wide range of financial institutions and the transfer of administrative, legal and economic know-how. But this should not conceal the unnecessary pains of transition, due in part to the choice of the conversion rate from Mark to DM. The architects of German reunification were constrained by politics, or claims for equity, as well as by an extreme shortage of time when they designed the monetary union, the cornerstone of the rebuilt capitalist economy in the East. These constraints, which were not faced by countries east of the GDR, led them to select values for the most critical parameter, the conversion rate from Mark to DM (which turned out to be disastrous for the economy) with the result that most of the industrial structure inherited from GDR days now lies in ruins. Thus in the ex-GDR a very high proportion of the labor force is unemployed while unemployment in Poland and Hungary is much lower. The amount of West German capital that will be required by the reunification path chosen is therefore higher than necessary, and the avoidable social costs are severe. Simple international trade models can help explain the difference between the paths of the ex-GDR and the other East European economies, and suggest that additional policy instruments could have been used to mitigate the damage. Suppose, for example, that instead of a currency union a customs union had been established.

The Customs Union

Suppose we merge two hitherto separate economies into a single trading area. We usually assume (a) that a market exchange rate is established between the currencies of the two countries, and (b) that only goods, not production factors, can flow between the two countries.

While adhering to the second assumption, let us drop the first one, and assume that the exchange rate is imposed arbitrarily, at a level that overvalues the currency of country A. The immediate result is an export surplus for country B, leading to increased pressure on its resources, coupled with a deficit and Keynesian unemployment for country A. Under normal circumstances, the deficit country would lose reserves and money, the latter leading to a further reduction in demand, which would eventually reduce the deficit (but not unemployment), directly or with the help of a price decline. This is reinforced by an opposite development in the surplus country B. However, when the monetary authorities of country B keep on returning the transferred monetary resources to country A, and when wages are downwardly rigid, this automatic stabilizing effect becomes inoperative and the combination of deficit/unemployment in country A can continue indefinitely.

Of the various exchange and conversion rates fixed in the currency union for many different types of assets and transactions (see above), the only one which need occupy us here is the conversion rate of 1 Mark/DM for wages, because this in effect fixed the ratio between current costs in the ex-GDR and the West. The selection of a suitable rate was no simple matter. Neither the quotations on the West Berlin currency exchanges nor the GDR black market (and certainly not the set of official GDR rates) could provide any clue as to the market-clearing rate between Mark and DM.

The Berlin-based DIW has been computing periodical purchasing power parities (PPP) between the Mark and the DM, the latest in 1985.[7] It estimated that the internal purchasing power of the Mark equalled DM1.24 for a wage-earner's family, or even 1.45 for a pensioner's household in mid-1985. Just before the currency union the DIW estimated that a 1:1 rate, given the expected induced change in buying habits, would leave wage-earners with a roughly equal real income, but would reduce the income of pensioners.[8] It should be remembered that the nominal income level in the ex-GDR was some 30–40 percent of the Federal Republic level. Some West German economists have nonetheless suggested a principal conversion rate between DM1:Mark 3 and 1:5. Each DM earned cost Mark 4.40 to produce in 1989.[9] This low valuation of the Mark in relation to the PPP would have taken care of the low productivity of the GDR economy—at most 50 percent of the Federal Republic's.[10] West German economists had an historical basis to their recommendation: the low rate of DM4.20 per US$ was an important engine of growth for the West German economy in its formative years.

To sum up: relative productivity would have dictated a rate of about 0.3–0.4 DM/Mark. If we examine the free market exchange rates established in other East European countries, which are always far below any conceivable computed productivity ratio, an even lower exchange rate might have been justified if full employment were the target. Maintenance of previous living standards would have supported the 1:1 rate actually chosen, but equity or equality with the West would have led to a rate closer to DM2/1 Mark or even DM3/1 Mark. The rate the politicians selected was indeed a compromise, but given the wage-levels of mid-1990[11] it seems to have overvalued the GDR currency by over 100 percent, and at such a degree of over-valuation we should not expect a significant part of the tradables sector of the ex-GDR to survive.

The results should not surprise us. East German industry was producing only 50 percent of the 1989 level in October 1990, at a time when there were still many export obligations to the East, for which a special payments arrangement was preserved until the end of the year. Once these specially subsidized exports ceased, at the end of 1990,[12] the level of output in the first months of 1991 recommenced its plunge. Unemployment in industry should reach similar proportions; it has been masked by *Kurzarbeit*, a path which is designed to cushion, not avert, the road to unemployment, and has been climbing until the summer of 1991.

A Higher Conversion Rate

Suppose we relax assumption 2—banning any flow of labor between the two parts of the trading union. Clearly, a free flow of labor would lead to the equalization of wage rates, which should mean that labor of similar productivity should earn similar wages in the whole of Germany. In the past, East Germans who settled in the West proved to be a desired labor force, i.e., their human capital, once freed from its previous environment, must have shed its distortions and adjusted to the new environment. This may take longer for those who stay in the East and do not resettle. Wages in the East may soon be expected to rise from about 35 percent of Western levels to at least 75 percent. In other words, the single labor market, and not only social and political considerations, imposes another constraint on the conversion rate, a constraint that does not permit too large a discrepancy between the real incomes of 'Ossies' and 'Wessies'. Therefore, even if a conversion rate of 0.4 (rather than 1) were fixed, this might have been of temporary help, and with time it may seem that all ex-GDR industry would have been wiped out.

In the long run the low level of wages and salaries in the ex-GDR surely cannot be maintained. East Germany has not been in the past and cannot be in the future a low-wage, low-productivity enclave. Wages and salaries will eventually rise to the West German level, possibly within a short time.[13] Does this mean that the entire present structure of industry in the ex-GDR will be wiped out? There is one important exception: if some of the enterprises find a way to rapidly change their production processes and their bill of goods, thus raising their productivity. Under which conditions this may happen is discussed below.

Was There an Alternative?

If there was no alternative to the 1:1 conversion rate, then there is nothing more to add here. That an alternative did exist at the time is suggested by the existence of the additional constraint. It suggests that a different wage should have been fixed for the employer to pay and for the worker to receive, i.e., there should have been a wage subsidy. Suppose a rate of DM0.5 per Mark were selected, accompanied by a wage subsidy of 100 percent for 1991, declining annually by 20 percent to zero by 1996.[14] Two questions arise: (a) would this have helped? and (b) how much would it have cost?

a. The cause of the productivity gap can be seen as a distorted structure of capital (cf. Keren in this volume, Chapter 15). Consider the analogy of distorted railway lines: first, picture a bombed-out railway connecting two important centers, and second, a perfectly good railway leading from nowhere to nowhere. A temporary wage subsidy would have helped if ex-GDR capital (physical as well as human) could, within a reasonably short period, be radically upgraded, i.e., if the first picture came closer to reality. Nothing could save the second type of distortion; e.g., neither the new lignite mining and fabrication operations nor the great majority of large computer manufacturing installations (whose products ranged from inefficiently produced chips to mainframe and desktop computers embodying obsolete technology), could have been saved by a lower conversion rate. A possible exception is the photographic industry (or at least large parts of it), which relied on local traditions. The hopeless firms would have had to close down in any case; those with a chance would have been able to soldier on and possibly survive. What is no less important, their profit-and-loss accounts would have given some meaningful information to the overseeing authorities.

b. The costs of such a subsidy need not have exceeded those of the unemployment insurance and *Kurzarbeit* at present borne by the government of the Federal Republic. If we take the extreme case of all ex-GDR employees remaining in their jobs with a subsidy, against a 50 percent unemployed labor force, then the wage subsidy is more costly only to the extent that there is a difference between the pay of a fully employed worker and the dole payment to the unemployed. The potential gain lies in that subsidies would have benefitted enterprises with a chance of survival and made them easier to sell, and in that it would have been easier for the *Treuhand* to distinguish between hopeless enterprises and those which might be salvaged (see the following section).

The remaining question is whether anything can be done now, after the damage has been done and many enterprises wound up. Unfortunately, we have no answer: it all depends on whether some of the potentially viable enterprises may still be struggling on, and whether others, which have already been disbanded, can be revived.

The *Treuhand* and Microeconomics Aspects of Privatization

In spite of what has been said above, the ex-GDR is in many respects (and reference is not only to the availability of resources) better off than its neighbors to the east. The implantation of institutions of capitalism has been more straightforward, more immediate. Laws on property, contracts, liability—the foundations of a private-ownership economy—were imported and imposed with a single stroke of the pen. The organizations that maintain the institutions of property could be imported bodily from the West: some of the personnel needed to run these institution (lawyers, judges and bureaucrats) were borrowed from the old Federal Republic. The missing human capital was therefore readily available. In fact, even the privatizing agency, the *Treuhandanstalt*, was founded by the last government of the previous regime. All these institutions must still be developed in the other ex-communist countries, working by themselves, and this will, in all probability, take a long time.

Even in this area some mistakes were made. Most experts are agreed on one of these: West German law decrees physical restitution of rather than compensation for expropriated property. A veritable flood of applications for restitution ensued, nearly paralyzing the administration, since the land registry documents are often hard to find. This brought the real-estate market to a near standstill. The few established private owners are in a near-monopolistic position. As a result, investors are held up in their effort to rebuild the new Länder. This has made it very difficult for any trade in assets to take place and hence for new businesses to be set up.

The most serious mistake may have been in the way the *Treuhandanstalt*—the organization charged with returning ex-GDR state property to private hands—is trying to perform its mission. Forty years of bureaucratic economics have created a structure of capital that does not fit the demands of competitive capitalism. Some of that capital will not be easy to privatize, while the organization of the remainder first needs to be restructured lest an industrial structure should develop that will hinder entry and competition.

After breaking up the *Kombinate*—the giant (mainly) vertically integrated combines—into their constituent enterprises, *Treuhand* seems to look at each enterprise and ask whether it has any chance of survival, whether it could be sold as-is (and, if possible, with an undertaking to retain its labor force or as large a part of it as practicable). There are two organizational characteristics of firms in Soviet-type economies that make the sale of existing enterprises a potential obstacle to entry, a potential local monopoly. One is their sheer size: enterprises were almost always organized as single producers—this was what the single planner favored. Hence the single insurance company, the two alternative retail chains (controlling about 80 percent of all consumer turnover), the single state bank. Therefore the sale of existing 'monolithic' organizations is liable to create production units whose size exceeds the optimum, as well as monopolies. Excess size need not trouble us, because market pressures will lead their new owners to split them up; not so the perpetuation of local monopolistic structures.

Furthermore, industrial units are also excessively vertically integrated. This means that they have control over real estate and other assets that are essential for new entrants. If these assets are not released by existing firms, new entrants will find it very difficult to establish themselves. Of course, once these enterprises are privatized, again, market pressure may compel them to sell off unneeded urban assets. The difficulties arise in the case of enterprises that the *Treuhand* fails to sell for many years, i.e., the least efficient part of the ex-GDR stock of capital which the *Treuhand* may find politically inexpedient to shut down, or enterprises of doubtful viability. We may find that these two categories, which may account for a substantial part of the ex-GDR's heavy industry, will be held by the privatizing agency for many years to come. And it is the frozen assets in the possession of these enterprises that will hinder the establishment of a new, locally based private sector. The so-called 'small' privatization on a very large scale is a necessary condition for a faster flow of new entries.

Financing the start-up of new private firms is almost as much of a problem in the ex-GDR as in other reforming countries. Almost, because a new private banking system has been put in place, but this system is a transplant from the Federal Republic, dominated by the two largest German banks. They are probably unfamiliar with local potential borrowers in the new Federal Länder. Add to this the lack of collateral of new loan applicants, who are unlikely to own any real estate or other marketable assets, and the slow awakening of a locally based small private sector can be better understood.

There may be nothing new in our last point of criticism: There is a cost to distortion, which arises whenever regional incentives are provided to a single production factor, usually capital. Between January and May 1990, the *Forschungsstelle*, together with the Institute for Automated Machine Tools and Production Technologies of the Technical University of Berlin, carried out a far-reaching modernization project in GDR plants. The report of this project (*Pilotbericht*, 1990), initiated by the *Forschungsstelle* as early as 1988, was the first to be published after the changeover. It showed that many of the enterprises analyzed were in need of low-capital-intensity rationalization strategies. Such low-capital strategies would be oriented toward the use of qualitative factors of growth, e.g., job-qualification of personnel, organizational flexibility, training in market-oriented management skills and strengthening motivational factors such as identification with the firm, work satisfaction and enterprise culture.

Instead, a policy of capital-intensive rationalization has at times been pursued that may, within a few years, lead to the growth of highly automated industries. At the same time most enterprises that could have been transformed may collapse, and billions of DM are being paid out in unproductive unemployment insurance while teams of skilled workers are broken up. In other words, it is investment in human capital that may yield the highest payoff, that may, so to say, repair the bombed-out rail line. But macroeconomic policy (the choice of the conversion rate), and microeconomic policy (subsidies to investment in physical capital) militate against taking this track.

The Aftermath

The most significant turning point in German reunification occurred on July 1, the day of the economic union, and not on October 3, 1990, the day of political union. The rules of the game accepted in the first State contract did not leave the last GDR government much room for maneuver. It is pathetic that almost the only provision that the GDR side could force into the second *Staatsvertrag*, the Union Treaty (*Einigungsvertrag*), was a limited continuation of legal abortions, and even this almost led to the breakdown of negotiations for German unity (Schäuble, 1991, pp. 229ff). On the other hand, essential elements, such as preparing the ground for effective local authorities or steps to help develop small-scale private businesses, were simply left out, either forgotten or ignored.

As already noted, the social market economy of the old Federal Republic was, in effect, imposed on the GDR on July 1. The creation of a stable monetary system was doubtless a necessary condition for a successful transition to the market economy, but it was in no way a sufficient condition, especially since it was not synchronized with the replacement of centralized state monopolies by private enterprises. The inhabitants of the GDR expected the introduction of the DM and the market to act as *deus ex machina*. They had no idea of the interrelations between economic institutions and the market and their effects on the operation of the system. What was worse, it was overlooked by most in the West that effective markets were neither anonymous nor automata, but required sellers to generate supply as well as buyers to shape demand. This required the participation of active human agents (Arndt, 1984, p. 90).

Soon after July 1 it became evident that the centralized economic monopolies were still intact, and that they hindered competition and seriously harmed the economy of the ex-GDR. Thus, for example, West German firms signed joint-venture contracts with the two sole GDR trading organizations, the HO (state owned) and the *Konsumgenossenschaften* (cooperative), which together controlled 80 percent of all retail trade and restaurant turnover, and in this way excluded ex-GDR-produced goods from the market. After July 1, the HO and the *Konsumgenossenschaften* fixed arbitrary prices in each location, whose level was higher the greater the distance from West Berlin or West Germany. Local GDR producers, especially in agriculture and the food industry, discovered overnight that they were unable to deliver their goods to their customary distributors—the trade organizations—even though shoppers were still interested in the cheaper local goods. Thus the initial endowment of DM flowed back to the West, either through direct purchases in the West, or through the purchase of almost exclusively Western goods in stores operated by the trading organizations in the East.

Specific problems arose through the conversion of debts and obligations at the ratio of 2:1. According to the Staatsbank der DDR, the state industry of the GDR was in debt to the tune of Mark 250 billion. These were pure system-related debts, caused by centrally determined investment projects, by the loss-making production of consumption goods in investment goods industries, and especially through subsidies (provided as credits) for export to the West at any price. Enterprises found it hard to accumulate assets because of the high levies on profits. On July 1 they were suddenly burdened with debts totaling DM 125 billion, as against assets of only DM 15 billion. At the same time, the previous exchange rate of Mark 4.67 per TR was halved—to DM2.34—which meant that although costs (wages and other current expenses) were converted at 1:1, revenues for over 60 percent of exports were halved. This clearly required additional transfers for wage payments from the West. The red balance sheets, where liabilities exceeded assets, were an additional factor, on top of the uncertainty regarding property titles, complicating the sale of state assets by the *Treuhandanstalt*.[15] On the other hand, for many private craftsmen, tradesmen and merchants the conversion of obligations of Mark 1.6 billion at the rate of DM0.5:1 Mark meant financial paralysis or ruin. Generous credits allocated to small businesses could not be taken up because potential borrowers, who rarely own land or buildings, did not possess the collateral that banks required. It is particularly shocking that several owners of small private enterprises, who had survived socialism, committed suicide shortly after July 1.

The effects of the currency union on the economy (and especially on employment) were felt by the end of July, the first month under the new regime. Gross industrial output sank by one third in comparison with June, and stood at 58 percent of its July 1989 level. The number of unemployed doubled in one month, rising to 272,000. To this we must add 656,000 (7.4 percent of the labor force) *Kurzarbeiter*, i.e., workers who continue to receive full wages for reduced (often zero) working hours. The number of jobless persons has been increasing rapidly. At the end of March 1991 some 808,000 people were officially registered as unemployed, an unemployment rate of 9.2 percent; nearly two million were on *Kurzarbeit* and most of these will end up being jobless. Add the previously employed pensioners who lost their jobs, and those nearing retirement age who have ceased looking for jobs because they have no chance of finding one. Add, too, all those who know that their place of work (e.g., in institutes or universities) will soon be closed down for political reasons, and if it ever reopens, it will be with a new program and probably with new employees. Both recorded and hidden unemployment rose in 1991 and in the first quarter of 1992. Officially recorded unemployment was between 14 percent in Saxony and nearly 18 percent in Mecklenburg-Vorpommern in March 1992 (*Leipziger Volkszeitung*, April 5, 1992). As before, the official figures conceal the true severity of the problem. Persons with temporary jobs and engaged in retraining are not counted as unemployed. The flow of qualified workers to the West and those going into early retirement is continuing.

In addition, the potential contribution of East Germans to the reunification process has remained largely untapped. Almost all important positions in the reconstruction apparatus are manned by West Germans who are not familiar with conditions in the East. Paradoxically, it is the widespread ignorance of East Germany's past accomplishments that has awakened in many East Germans the consciousness of a separate identity.

In spite of the existing problems it is clear than the upturn forecast for 1992 is beginning to take shape. The increase in unemployment is levelling off in several regions (especially in Saxony) and fields (e.g., in services). In Leipzig, for example, unemployment has even gone down since February 1992. Renewal and modernization projects have been launched in various areas, harbingers of a top-notch infrastructure in the future.

Conclusions

The steady decline of the East German economy, which accelerated with the total cessation of trade with the Eastern trading partners after January 1, 1991, doubtlessly has its roots in over 40 years of centrally planned economics. However, the external trigger which led to the abrupt collapse of what until very recently used to be an economically stable member of the CMEA was the shock therapy of the currency union. Being aware of the immense problems faced by the Soviet Union and the equally huge problems facing other former socialist countries, it is hard to comprehend why the transformation of East Germany, in spite of all the exceptional financial and other resources it is receiving, is so painful.

The social upheavals that accompany unemployment, the mood of hopelessness and a new rise in westward migration in its wake, have deepened the psychological rift between East and West, bred by over 40 years of separation. Three cardinal omissions on the West German side have led, to the present predicament, in spite of the good intentions and the sincere efforts of many.

First, acquaintance with the GDR economy was extremely limited. The number of experts and researchers who worked on GDR-related issues in the Federal Republic was remarkably small, as professional perspectives, especially in academia, were practically non-existent. Scholars, such as those at the *Forschungsstelle*, who did not accept all the optimistic claims of the GDR authorities and criticized their economic policies, were regarded as spoilsports, as relics of the Cold War, especially in the last decade. This rejection by the establishment has been in force since Honecker and his regime became acceptable among West German industrial magnates and politicians.

Next, the Federal Republic was totally unprepared for the reunification and the problems related to it. The Research Committee for Problems of Reunification (*Forschungsbeirat für Fragen der Wiedervereinigung Deutschlands*), set up by the government in 1952, was dissolved in 1975, and no alternative was created. This committee, in which most leading political and economic institutions were represented, and whose research arm was the *Forschungsstelle*, prepared contingency plans for reunification, many of which were still viable in 1990 (*Forschungsbeirat*, 1952, 1956, 1961, 1965, 1969). The Federal Republic should have realized, at least since Gorbachev came to power in 1985 or, at the latest, in 1987, that a strategy for reunification should have been prepared.

Finally, since the tremendous burden of the transformation problem was not properly diagnosed (Gutmann, 1991), serious psychological errors were committed by the Federal Republic. In particular, the reunification was regarded from the start as a financial problem. Purely financial costs of unity were thus allowed to eclipse this unique historical event (Thalheim, 1991).

One should not lose sight of prospects for a brighter future in the midst of the present gloom. Historically, what is today the eastern part of Germany had not always been Germany's least developed region. In fact, some parts of the region were the most developed areas in Germany before the partition. For generations a complex, developed economy had thrived there, and a highly experienced and qualified labor force grew up. This is true mainly for the highly industrialized southern part of East Germany, especially in Saxony and Thuringia, where industry was like a great carpet covering the whole area. It was mainly fabricating industry—heavy industry was virtually absent. Take engineering: The first German engineering enterprise was founded in Chemnitz (later Karl-Marx-Stadt) in Saxony. The well-known Audi automobile also comes from Saxony. Leipzig has been the site of one of the most important fairs in Europe since the middle ages. It was the center of the printing industry. Its dynamic economic development was the result of a very fruitful meeting of intellectual, mental, cultural and economic life. That was the reason for the city's successful development, for new ideas, creativity and innovation. All this supports the belief that in this part of Germany the former dynamism will soon come back.

The last 45 years did not destroy all human potential. Most of the material basis may be blighted with wear and tear. But people learned to work productively despite a permanent shortage of material and energy and despite the low quality of raw materials, old-fashioned technology, and uncertain supplies. They also learned to develop home-grown solutions in the isolated socialist world. It was the absence of competition that limited their use of their resources.

When we now look at the ex-GDR we find that about 300,000 entrepreneurs have set up new enterprises. Nearly one million moved into jobs in Western enterprises and another million now reside in West Germany. Most of them are successful, and the number of people who are managers in Western enterprises is increasing. It is the human potential which assures us of the final success of unification.

Notes

1. A legend recently circulated by the former 'top procurer' of hard currency of the GDR, the notorious Schalck-Golodkowski, alleged that without these credits, the first of which was initiated by Franz-Josef Strauss, the GDR would have collapsed much earlier. This is absurd, since in the pre-Gorbachev era the political environment would not have permitted a collapse.

2. One-third of the meager investment funds were allocated to the energy base, mainly brown coal (lignite, soft coal high in ash content), another third to electronics; after reunification both turned out to be a total waste (see Section 2). Little remained for the rest.

3. *Sozialistische Einheitspartei Deutschlands*, the German Socialist Unity Party, the name of the party created by the coerced fusion of the Eastern SPD into the KPD, the German Communist Party, in 1946.

4. See Luft (1991, pp. 85ff) and Buck (1991, pp. 11ff). Reform ideas had been under discussion at the Hochschule für Ökonomie since the end of 1988. These were criticized sharply by Günter Mittag in late summer of 1989, weeks before the collapse of the GDR.

5. I.e., practically the whole productive sector. Hardly any private industry remained, and agriculture was nearly fully collectivized. Some 120,000 tiny private enterprises were still in existence only in handicrafts and retail.

6. The few GDR experts in West Germany were not consulted before the negotiations, and on the GDR side, only the SED (renamed the PDS, Party of Democratic Socialism) had any economic experts.

7. See Melzer and Vortmann (1986). The sources of previous PPPs can be found in Keren (1987).

8. Cornelsen and Kirner (1990): provided rents stay unchanged at their highly subsidized level. What apparently is meant is that a post-union Paasche index would have shown that the post-union basket at pre-union prices would have just equaled pre-union monthly incomes of wage-earners, etc.

9. Up from 2.40 in 1980: Haendcke-Hoppe (1990b). Figures that demonstrated the

rapid deterioration of profitability of exports to the West were first published during the brief rule of the Modrow government. See also Collier (1991).

10. See Cornelsen and Kirner (1990), who present evidence from several studies, all of which put the ratio of output per worker in the GDR in the mid-1980s at between 48 and 54 percent of that of the Federal Republic. The spread for various industrial branches is given as 20 to 88 percent, which indicates an even larger spread for individual enterprises. The authors cite a study by Filip-Köhn and Ludwig, based on exports to the West, which puts the productivity ratio at 30 percent.

11. See the following section for a discussion of the likely trend in wages.

12. These led the Federal Republic to accumulate some TR 10 billion in frozen accounts by the end of 1990 in export receipts for deliveries to the East, mainly the Soviet Union. A significant proportion of these was diverted as payment for fictional exports to the East. 44 charges regarding the diversion of DM1.7 billion were pending in February 1992 (*Tagesspiegel*, February 11, 1992).

13. The pace of wage convergence is quite fast: wages in the new Länder have risen 35 percent in 1990 alone. And, in the metal industry, for instance, they are expected to rise gradually to West German levels by 1995 (Fels and Schnabel, 1991, pp. 26f).

14. Similar proposals have been made by Begg and Portes (1991), Collier (1991), and Akerloff *et al.* (1991).

15. Nonetheless, the *Treuhandanstalt* has been selling off ex-GDR's state property at an impressive rate. Of the 8,000 enterprises it inherited, some 3,000 industrial firms were sold by mid-1991, and the 'small' privatization, the sale of over 20,000 small shops, restaurants and hotels, was nearly complete by that time. By the beginning of 1992 6,200 firm had been sold, but 6,000 were still on the hands of the *Treuhand*. The cost was considerable: the agency expected to receive some DM17 billion for the enterprises it sold, but to spend DM13 billion for restructuring these enterprises (as well as DM6 billion on the workers who lose their jobs; *The Economist*, September 14, 1991). See also *The Economist*, March 21, 1992, which in addition reports that about one-third of all firms now in the *Treuhand*'s hands are not viable. The agency has managed to close down only 600 enterprises, which shows the magnitude of the remaining task. It is hard to come by reliable statistics on the total volume of privatization up to the time this book goes to print: GDR industry employed 4.1 million in mid-1990; the enterprises still under the control of the *Treuhand* were employing 1.7 million at the end of 1991. In January 1992 the unemployment rate was 17 percent, and it is still increasing.

References

Akerloff, George, Andrew K. Rose, Janet L. Yellen and Helga Hessenius. 1991. "East Germany in from the Cold: The Economic Aftermath of Currency Union," *Brookings Papers on Economic Activity*, 1: 1–87.

Arndt, Helmut. 1984. *Economic Theory vs Economic Reality*. East Lansing, MI: Michigan State University Press.

Begg, David and Richard Portes. 1991. "There's a Better Way to Help Germany's New Länder to Catch Up," *International Herald Tribune*, June 19, 1991.

Buck, Hannsjörg F. 1991. "Von der staatlichen Kommunalwirtschaft der DDR zur sozialen Marktwirtschaft der vereinten Deutschland—sozialistischen Hypotheken, Transformationsprobleme, Aufschwungchancen [From the State Socialist Economy of the GDR to the Social Market Economy of the United Germany—Socialist Mortgages, Problems of Transformation, and Chances of a Take-Off]." Düsseldorf: Schriftenreihe Hochschule für Wirtschaft.

Collier, Irwin L. 1991. "On the First Year of German Monetary, Economic and Social Union," *Journal of Economic Perspectives*, 5 (No. 4): 179–186.

Cornelsen, Doris and Wolfgang Kirner. 1990. "Zum Produktivitätsvergleich Bundesrepublik—DDR [A Productivity Comparison between the Federal Republic and the GDR]," *DIW Wochenbericht*, 14/90 (April).

Fels, Gerhard and Claus Schnabel. 1991. "The Economic Transformation of East Germany: Some Preliminary Lessons," *Occasional Papers*, No. 36, Washington, DC: Group of Thirty.

Forschungsbeirat. 1952. *Erster Tätigkeitsbericht des Forschungsbeirats für Fragen der Wiedervereinigung Deutschlands beim Bundesminister für gesamtdeutsche Fragen*. Bonn.

——. 1952. *Erster Tätigkeitsbericht des Forschungsbeirats für Fragen der Wiedervereinigung Deutschlands beim Bundesminister für gesamtdeutsche Fragen*. Bonn.

——. 1956. *Zweiter Tätigkeitsbericht des Forschungsbeirats für Fragen der Wiedervereinigung Deutschlands beim Bundesminister für gesamtdeutsche Fragen*. Bonn.

——. 1961. *Dritter Tätigkeitsbericht des Forschungsbeirats für Fragen der Wiedervereinigung Deutschlands beim Bundesminister für gesamtdeutsche Fragen*. Bonn.

——. 1965. *Vierter Tätigkeitsbericht des Forschungsbeirats für Fragen der Wiedervereinigung Deutschlands beim Bundesminister für gesamtdeutsche Fragen*. Bonn.

——. 1969. *Fünfter Tätigkeitsbericht des Forschungsbeirats für Fragen der Wiedervereinigung Deutschlands beim Bundesminister für gesamtdeutsche Fragen*. Bonn.

Gutmann, Gernot. 1991. "Zur theoretischen Grundlegung von Transformationen [On Laying the Theoretical Foundation for Transformations]," *Gesamtdeutsche Eröffnungsbilanz*, Part I, *FS-Analysen*, 2/1991: 29–45.

Haendcke-Hoppe, Maria. 1989. "Erfolge and Mißerfolge in der Außenwirtschaft [Successes and Failures in Foreign International Relations]." In: Die Wirtschaftspolitik der Ära Honecker—ökonomische and soziale Auswirkungen [The Economic Policy of the Honecker Era—Economic and Social Effects], *FS-Analysen*, 1: 51–67.

——. 1990a. "Die Wirtschaftsbeziehungen zwischen beiden deutschen Staaten [The Economic Relations between the Two German States]." In: M. Haendcke-Hoppe and E. Lieser-Triebnigg (eds.), *40 Jahre innerdeutsche Beziehungen*, Jahrbuch der Gesellschaft für Deutschlandforschung. Berlin, pp. 119–140.

——. 1990b. "Umbewertung der Außenhandelsstatistik [Revaluation of Foreign Trade Statistics]." In: *Ausgewählte Probleme der Systemtransformation*, DDR-Wirtschaft, *FS-Aktuell* (April): 7ff.

Keren, Michael. 1987. "Consumer Prices in the GDR since 1950: The Construction of Price Indices from Purchasing Power Parities," *Soviet Studies*, 39 (No. 2, April): 247–268.

Keynes, J. M. 1929. "The German Transfer Problem," *Economic Journal*, 39 (March): 1–7.

Klinger, Fred. 1991. "Soziale Triebkräfte and Hindernisse des wirtschaftlichen Integrationsprozesses [Driving Forces and Obstacles in the Economic Integration Process]." In: *Gesamtdeutsche Eröffnungsbilanz*, Part II, *FS-Analysen*, 5: 67–78.

Kurjo, Andreas. 1990. "Zur gegenwärtigen Entwicklung der Land- und Ernährungswirtschaft der DDR [On the Present Development of Agriculture and the Food Industry]." In: *FS-Aktuell*, September.

Luft, Christa. 1991. *Zwischen Wende und Ende* [Between Change and End]. Berlin: Aufbau Taschenbuch Verlag.

Melzer, Manfred and Heinz Vortmann. 1986. "Das Kaufkraftverhältnis zwischen D-Mark and Mark der DDR 1985 [The Purchasing Power Parity Between the D-Mark and the Mark of the GDR]," *DIW Wochenbericht*, 21/86 (May).

Metzler, Lloyd A. 1942. "The Transfer Problem Reconsidered," *Journal of Political Economy*, 50 (June): 397–414.

Murrell, Peter. 1990. "'Big Bang' Versus Evolution: East European Economic Reforms in the Light of Recent Economic History," *Plan Econ Report*, 6 (No. 26, June 29).

Ohlin, Bertil. 1929. "The German Reparation Problem: A Discussion," *Economic Journal*, 39 (June): 172–173.

Pilotbericht. 1990. "Gestaltung des modernen Fabrikbetriebes im Spannungsfeld neuer Fertigungstechnologien, ökonomischer Chancen and sozialen Wandels in der DDR [Formation of a Modern Industrial Plant in the Range of New Manufacturing Technologies, Economic Opportunities, and Social Change in the GDR]." Pilotbericht des gemeinsamen Forschungsprojektes des Institutes für Werkzeugmaschinen and Fertigungstechnik der TU Berlin and der Forschungsstelle für gesamtdeutsche wirtschaftliche and soziale Fragen, Berlin, May 30.

Propp, Peter-Dietrich. 1964. *Zur Transformation einer Zentralverwaltungswirtschaft sowjetischen Typs in eine Marktwirtschaft* [On the Transformation of a Centrally Administered Economy of the Soviet Type in a Market Economy]. Osteuropa-Institut Berlin 1964, Reprint Edition Deutschland Archiv, Köln 1990.

Schäuble, Wolfgang. 1991. *Wie ich über die deutsche Einheit verhandelte* [How I Negotiated the German Reunification]. Stuttgart.

Thalheim, Karl C. 1991. "Der Weg zur deutschen Einheit and die künftigen Aufgaben [The Road to German Unity and Future Tasks]." In: *Gesamtdeutsche Eröffnungsbilanz*, Part I, *FS-Analysen*, 2/1991: 7–28.

12

Privatization in Hungary

Domenico Mario Nuti

The Hungarian Private Sector

In spite of getting off to a very early start on the way to economic reform in 1968, and until the collapse of the one-party state in 1989, privatization of state assets was not an element of Hungarian economic strategy. The target model was still a mixed economy with a large state sector.[1] However, even before the beginning of privatization in 1990, Hungary already had a private sector—smaller than in Poland, but larger than in other Central and East European countries—in trade, services, construction, agriculture, leasing of state assets to state enterprise staff after working hours, cooperatives and (since the mid-1970s) joint ventures. Much housing and land remained in private hands. In the 1980s, thousands of new cooperatives were established and old ones expanded, following favorable new legislation. In 1990 the private sector provided a significant share (estimated at around 10 percent) of Hungarian national income.

'Spontaneous' Privatization

Privatization of state assets in Hungary began earlier than in other Central and East European countries, and ahead of declared policy, through a process of 'spontaneous' or 'wild' privatization. This is the illegal, but tolerated process of self-appropriation of assets by managers and *nomenklatura* through the disposal of assets and shares, subcontracting, leasings and enterprise liquidation.

This process followed the 1984–1985 enterprise law, which was intended to decentralize management, not to alter property relations. In practice, however, it restricted the center's powers vis-à-vis state enterprises so much as to justify—in the new political climate of 1989—the interpretation that property rights had been effectively transferred from the state to Enterprise Councils, half of whose members were appointed (and hence controlled) by management. In fact, the 1984–1985 legislation gave enterprises the power to alter the production profile, and to split and merge; it stipulated specifically that the assets of enterprises controlled by a Council or by an elected management could not be withdrawn or transferred to another enterprise by the 'founding organ'; nor could central organs wind up the enterprise (Vekas, 1989).

From 1985 to 1987 most Hungarian state enterprises were transformed into self-managed enterprises. The preamble to Act IV on Economic Associations (October 1988) states that "in such cases the overwhelming part of state's ownership rights are implemented [sic] by an Enterprise Council...." and that such enterprises need not turn into companies, but the possibility is granted of "spontaneous transformation of such enterprises, based on their own decision, into economic associations" (joint stock companies, limited liability companies and similar organizations). Such 'spontaneous' transformations have been the basis of the Hungarian 'spontaneous' privatization process. The prevailing thesis at that time, as stated, for example, by the Deputy Minister of Justice, was that "enterprises belong to themselves"—an aberration unknown in the West except in rare instances (some mutual societies). In reality, "top management became the real owner of the company" (Bokros, 1990).

'Spontaneous' privatization led to abuses and scandals, and to the enrichment of the old party *nomenklatura*.[2] Popular resentment against this kind of free and privileged private appropriation actually speeded up 'proper' privatization (i.e., at competitive prices) of state assets which, following debates on and criticisms of this 'spontaneous', but undesirable process, began in earnest in 1990.

Features of Hungarian Privatization

As in other Central and East European countries, privatization in Hungary was promoted in order to restore a system of economic incentives, to depoliticize economic management (see Bokros, 1990) and to put an end to the profit redistribution performed by the state budget (well documented by Kornai, 1986), to harden budget constraints through private commercial banking and to raise revenue. Hungarian privatization, however, has several distinctive features:

a. It was preceded by a considerable, though gradual legislative and institutional buildup.
b. It focused on the transfer and redeployment of capital goods as well as on the transfer of ownership of entire enterprises.
c. It undertook the competitive sale of state assets and never indulged in mass distribution of free ownership titles to the population (as in Poland, Czechoslovakia, Romania and Bulgaria, through investment vouchers), and was thus much closer to the German *Treuhandanstalt* mode of operation.
d. It relied more on the promotion of new private enterprises and joint ventures, than on the mere transfer of state assets.

Alternative modes of privatization, such as the transfer of state assets to enterprise employees, mutual funds, state holdings, non-profit institutions, insurance companies and pension funds, were also discussed and considered, but never took on a major role in the course of implementation. The coalition government's first document on privatization (August 1990) dismissed "romantic ideas of self-management" (Kiss, 1991).

Property Restitution

As in the other countries, Hungarian privatization introduced restitution to the former owners of property nationalized after the war (so-called 're-privatization'). Restitution was a major commitment of the Smallholders Party, which was implemented when the Party joined the government coalition. The Hungarian Democratic Forum—the leading coalition party—advocated a slower, revenue-raising mode of privatization, unlike the Free Democrats, who promoted rapid privatization even at lower prices than otherwise possible (see Crane, 1990, and Kiss, 1991).

A Compensation Law was passed in the summer of 1991, after long and heated debates. Property confiscated after June 8, 1949, will be compensated for with vouchers usable to buy back land, shares, and flats. For land, compensation is 100 percent of historical value up to Ft 1 million; for buildings and enterprises the rate is 38 percent. It is estimated that the law will involve an overall expenditure of Ft 100 billion in compensation. Re-privatization in kind of church property confiscated after January 1, 1948 (much of which has already been restored), is the subject of another bill still under consideration. Such re-privatization in kind entails a risk of upsetting the present pattern of peasant farming.

Preparations for Privatization: Legal and Institutional Build-Up

At the beginning of 1990 state-owned capital (excluding agriculture) was 90 percent of the total; the number of state enterprises slated for privatization is 2,197, with a total book value of Ft 2,000 billion (about $30 billion).[3] The exceptions to this are public utilities, financial institutions and enterprises with a market share of over 40 percent (Ministry of Foreign Affairs, 1991a).

Hungarian privatization was preceded by several important steps. A law on bankruptcy (1986) gave initiative to creditors, beside founding ministries, and greatly accelerated the proceedings.[4] The already-mentioned law on the transformation of enterprises (1988) allowed state enterprises to turn into limited liability and joint stock companies, as well as allowing for private joint stock companies on a parity basis.[5] An Enterprise Development Foundation was designed to encourage private enterprise. There was considerable liberalization of prices (from one half of all goods, in value terms in 1988 to 90 percent in 1990) and foreign trade (72 percent of imports in convertible currency in 1991, fully exposing 32 percent of industrial production to external competition, to rise to at least 80 percent in 1992). Trade restrictions have been generalized to include all imports and have changed from a positive list of freely importable goods to a negative list of licensed items (see IMF, 1991).

New financial institutions were developed: a market for bonds issued by the government and by state enterprises (1983); the transfer of commercial credit functions from the central bank to autonomous (private, state and joint-venture) commercial banks, also set up as joint stock companies (January 1, 1987); and the establishment of a stock exchange for shares issued by private and state enterprises to the general public (January 1, 1989). By mid-1990 the Stock Exchange had 43 members and 10 traded shares, and the numbers are growing.[6] Hungarian shares are also quoted in the Vienna Stock Exchange, at an implicit exchange rate that is very close to the official rate.

A generous Law on Investment by Foreigners (1988) gave joint and foreign enterprises parity with domestic enterprises, permission to own up to 100 percent of Hungarian enterprises, and repatriation of capital and profit under a favorable tax regime (retaining only some restrictions on the sale of land).[7] This attracted a great deal of foreign capital, relative to other Central and East European countries (see below), although less than was expected. In 1990 a law regarding security trading afforded investors protection from fraud, and set rules on capital adequacy and disclosure. New laws on accounting and banking are to come into force in 1992.

The prior establishment of appropriate legislation and financial institutions over a number of years is one of the distinguishing features of Hungarian large-scale privatization. In this, the Hungarian experience differs substantially from the rushed, but ultimately slower, processes in countries like Poland and Czechoslovakia, which sought to privatize before having an operational stock exchange.

The State Property Agency

Laws on Safeguarding State Assets and on State Assets Funds and the Administration and Utilization of its Assets were introduced in 1990, to prevent any risk of further privileged appropriation of state assets. A State Property Agency (March 1, 1990) was declared the owner of state assets and responsible for its good use and privatization. The Agency at once started an active privatization program for the larger enterprises. It is a powerful agency, initially answerable to Parliament, but now under the direct control of the government. Its management board and director are appointed by the Prime Minister.

Small-Scale Privatization ('Pre-Privatization')

In September 1990 the Hungarian Parliament approved a pre-privatization program[8] for the sale of smaller establishments in catering and retail trade (the so-called 'small' privatization). Under this program all catering establishments with less than 15 employees and shops with less than 10 employees —about 10,000 establishments in all—are to be offered for sale through auction, starting January 1991, unless already leased. Half were to be privatized in 1991; the rest in 1992. First the State Property Agency takes all these establishments under its control, audits them, and announces the sale. Former owners are given first option rights. The successful bidder needs permission from the local authorities and the SPA to change the profile of production in the first five years. Shop premises can only be leased, not purchased; this discourages many bidders and keeps prices low.[9]

Credit for the Privatization Process

Fearing a shortfall of private liquid assets with respect to the estimated value of enterprise assets (Ft 312 billion versus Ft 2,000 billion in 1989; see Crane, 1990), two special credit institutions were set up granting preferential credit to buyers. These are the Privatization Fund and (for real assets only) the Subsistence Fund, granting up to Ft 50 million per loan, subject to a substantial down-payment by the buyer, at three-quarters of the NBH refinancing rate *plus* bank margins of 4 and 5 percentage points, respectively, for the two Funds.[10] Every year the government issues Guidelines on Property Ownership. Government plans to privatize 8–10 percent of state enterprises' capital assets by 1991, 20–24 percent in 1992, and 34–40 percent by 1994 (according to "The Government's Strategy on Property and Privatization," March 1991; see Kiss, 1991, and IMF, 1991).[11]

SPA Programs, 1990–1991

The State Property Agency launched its first program in September 1990 (mostly hotels, catering, tourism, transport and some industrial establishments; see Grosfeld and Hare, 1991, for details). A second program was announced in December 1990 (involving 'shell state holdings' generated by the transformation of state-enterprise assets into shares). Each program involved about 20 companies, worth about Ft 32 billion in the first round.[12] The procedure for privatization involves the appointment of expert panels (representing management, creditors and government) specifying guidelines and fees for privatization managers selected by tender (in the first round these were mostly international banks and accounting firms; the Agency manages $6 million provided by the EC PHARE Program to finance foreign consultants giving technical assistance to privatization).

The first round was to be completed in 18 months, but is running behind schedule. The most successful endeavor in this group is the privatization of IBUSZ, a financial services and travel company, whose first share issue was over-subscribed by a factor of 23 (for the part reserved for foreign buyers). The issue attracted world-wide attention also because it coincided with the reopening of the Budapest Stock Exchange and was simultaneously traded in Vienna; its market price more than doubled in the first three days (see Bokros, 1990, and Apathy, 1991). IBUSZ privatization will be completed with the sale of SPA shares to the public, delayed by recent drastic falls in the IBUSZ share price, down to 40 percent of the original issue price.

In the second round of the program, delays were caused because half the selected firms needed prior financial restructuring and administrative reorganization. Subsequent programs have been announced every three or four months (real estate in Budapest, state farms and quality vineyards, the construction industry[13]). In all, about 100 enterprises were expected to be involved in SPA privatization in 1991. However, implementation is slow; it is also being delayed by missing legislation regarding the Treasury, the local authorities, and cooperatives, and the transformation of land ownership.

Other State Enterprise Sales

Meanwhile, sales of enterprises also take place at the initiative of the enterprises themselves (called 'self-privatization') or of potential buyers ('the third way'). These sales, now referred to as 'spontaneous' privatization, are not to be confused with the earlier spate of illegal appropriation, which also went by the same name. In these cases, SPA involvement is limited to a check on transparency and appropriate valuation of capital. In the twelve months since April 1990, the SPA received 232 proposals, examined 176 of them, and approved 84 percent of asset transfers and 54 percent of company-initiated transformations (see Financial Research Ltd., 1991; rejected deals involved primarily real-estate proposals). Thus, these sales have made even faster progress than direct privatization by the SPA.

Employee Ownership

Under the current Employee Share Ownership Program (ESOP), employees can purchase up to 25 percent of their enterprise shares when it is privatized, partly through a foundation organized within the company, but the purchase can be blocked by the SPA if outsiders offer better terms. A minimum down-payment of 2 percent is required, with the rest financed by credit at an interest rate that is three quarters of the NBH refinancing rate (Ministry of Foreign Affairs, 1991a). Direct workers' purchases of shares at a substantial discount, with loans subject to a ceiling of 6 months' pay, have been contemplated (Kiss, 1991).

Privatization Proceeds

Eighty-five percent of privatization proceeds are to be used to service the retirement of government debt (100 percent in case of privatizations financed through credit, including credit from the Privatization and Subsistence Funds), with any residual being allocated to covering privatization expenditures, including financial restructuring.

Foreign Capital

Foreign capital has played an important role in the privatization process. While in 1972–1988 foreign investment totaled about $200 million, in 1989–1990 it reached $800 million (Ministry of Foreign Trade, 1991a). By mid-1991 Hungary had attracted $1.6 billion, half of which came from the United States (according to Janos Martonyi, State Secretary in the Ministry of Foreign Relations; *International Herald Tribune*, November 14, 1991). By early 1991, 70 medium or large enterprises have been sold, partly or entirely, to foreign investors; a total of about 4,500 enterprises operated with foreign partners (IMF, 1991). Recent references in official documents to the need for 'national privatization' in official documents suggest that foreign capital is now regarded as a necessary evil (Kiss, 1991).

The inflow of foreign capital into Hungary accelerated in early November 1991. In one week, investment totaling more than a quarter of a billion dollars was announced by General Motors Corp. and Beacon Co. This may be attributed partly to good trade performance (heading for a healthy trade surplus instead of the expected $1 billion deficit), commitment to debt service, and a compliant trade union. Partly the inflow may represent the diversion to Hungary of funds no longer attracted by other Central and East European countries: Yugoslavia because of civil war, Czechoslovakia because of republican conflicts, Poland because of political uncertainties, Romania and Bulgaria because of the slower progress of economic reform, and the Soviet area because of republican disintegration and economic collapse—all features that have worsened considerably in recent months.

The Consequences of Privatization

There is anecdotal evidence of efficiency improvements in privatized firms (see, for example, Crane, 1990). Case studies quoted by Kiss (1991) suggest that there is no evidence of performance improvement after transformation, "though the very fact that they have managed to survive can be interpreted as an achievement both for the companies and for the state budget" (Mora, cited in Kiss, 1991); that although enterprise transformations did not create either a healthier property structure or stricter public control over big state enterprises, in most cases they led to a more rational internal allocation, accountability and growth flexibility (Csillig, cited in Kiss, 1991); that the latest round of 'spontaneous' privatization has mobilized private savings and entrepreneurial capacity (Miszei, cited in Kiss, 1991). At the same time, skepticism has been expressed about 'privatization magic' and the true extent of change in property relations: "Privatization is often just a pseudonym for market processes that have nothing to do with it or even jeopardize it" (Kiss, 1991[14]).

Predictably, there has been an adverse effect on tax revenues: until 1988 enterprise profits were syphoned off into the state budget and a 5 percent capital tax was levied; now, taxes on capital have been abolished and the profit tax has been reduced. The replacement of turnover tax by VAT (misleadingly called a 'generalized turnover tax') has not raised additional revenue. It is difficult to assess how much unemployment has been generated by privatization as such, rather than by price and trade liberalization and the necessary accompanying restructuring, out of a total of about 150,000 by the first quarter of 1991 or 3 percent of those actively employed (8 percent by the end of 1991). A safety net, consisting of welfare payments, unemployment insurance, retraining and job placement support, has been devised to alleviate this problem. A side effect of privatization has been the rapid growth of ownership litigation.

The Growth of the Private Sector

A positive aspect of Hungarian privatization, in the broader sense of development of the new private sector by any means (i.e., through entirely new enterprises as well as the transfer of state enterprise ownership) is the large number of new entrants. In 1990, 29,000 new firms were set up, 90 percent of them employing less than 50 employees, mostly in the private sector (new entrants include a minority of enterprises created through the dismantling of larger companies). At the end of 1990 there were 5,700 joint ventures in operation in Hungary, i.e., four times as many as there were a year earlier (Financial Research Ltd., 1991). Their capital stock was Ft 274 billion and average foreign participation was 37 percent; in 1990, 3,894 joint enterprises were set up (Kiss, 1991). Beside the acceleration of foreign capital inflow in the autumn of 1991, indicated above, it is believed that private capital accumulation is proceeding much faster than the privatization of the state economy. This year bank accounts in hard currency have nearly doubled to $1.5 billion, in spite of a 6–8 percent contraction in GNP.

The size of the private sector is now estimated at around 25 percent of national income (also because of the decline of the state sector); this is probably an underestimate in view of the faster growth of the 'hidden' economy. The National Association of Entrepreneurs today represents 30,000 private entrepreneurs. As in other countries, such as South Korea, the fall of the state sector share might be easier and faster to obtain through the growth of the private sector than through the divestiture of state ownership. If so, there is a very important lesson for the rest of the post-communist area.

Notes

1. On the early stages of Hungarian reform, see Marer (1986).

2. One notorious attempt at 'spontaneous' privatization was the leveraged buy-out of APISZ, the monopoly retailer of office supplies, which was to be funded by Citicorp's partly owned subsidiary in Budapest; "Popular outrage led to the collapse

of the deal" (Crane, 1990; see also Bokros, 1990). Another major scandal involved the cheap purchase of HungarHotels by a 'dummy' Swedish-based corporation through the intermediation of managers; the contract was declared void by the Hungarian Supreme Court. Other forms of appropriation of state capital were less detectable: the use of depreciation funds to cover wage increases under pressure from workers' councils, and the sale of enterprises by managers cheaply in exchange for higher salaries. For other instances of this process see Bokros (1990) and Grosfeld and Hare (1991). Stark (1990) characterizes this process as a switch, not from plan to market but "from plan to clan," a danger also implicit in centralized privatization managed by the State Property Agency established in March 1990 (see below).

3. Of these, 63 percent were established by different ministries. Of the total, 37 percent were state-administered and 56 percent were self-managed, while only the remainder had been transformed into joint stock companies on the eve of privatization (see Kazar, 1991).

4. This law, unlike similar ones in Central and East European countries, did not remain dead a letter; in the second half of 1990 alone, for example, bankruptcy proceedings were initiated against 37 enterprises employing 57,000 workers. In all, 542 liquidation actions were filed with the Budapest Court in the course of 1990, and more than 700 actions were in progress. A new Bankruptcy Law was enacted in 1991, making enterprises liable to bankruptcy proceedings after three months arrears in tax and social security payments.

5. By September 1989, there were 2,598 applications for the formation of limited liability companies; for example, a state enterprise, Medicor, split itself into ten separate joint stock companies and sold shares to raise capital for modernization (Crane, 1990).

6. In 1991 the Budapest Stock Exchange index rose 23 percent from the beginning of the year to early April, then fell gradually but steadily by 35 percent by early November.

7. Tax exemptions are granted, for example, if more than half the gross revenue comes from manufacturing activities. An amendment that came into effect on January 1, 1991, allows 100 percent foreign-owned enterprises to set up without special permission by Hungarian authorities (Ministry of Foreign Trade, 1991).

8. Law on the Privatization of State Enterprises in Retail, Catering and Consumer Service Sectors.

9. The exclusion of premises ownership has led to popular talk about "the program for the privatization of air" (Kiss, 1991).

10. Another fund with German government resources is to be established for setting up new small- and medium-sized enterprises.

11. "The state will maintain a share in 64–85 transformed companies, of which 64 will remain state owned up to 51 percent. These assets may be controlled by the new state owner organization [presumably SPA] on a long-term basis." These will include fine glass and ceramics, the National Oil Industrial Trust, the Hungarian Electricity Board, the Hungarian Aluminum Industrial Trust, the Precision Engineering Company, some research institutions and nitrochemical industrial plants. They will not include mining, metallurgy and other chemicals (Ministry of Industry, 1991).

12. Out of an initial list of 50 enterprises, 13 firms managed to withdraw, 17 were left out by the SPA because they were either too valuable or too close to bankruptcy.

Eight of the remaining companies did not attract any buyers. For the remaining ones, auditing and restructuring is underway; they will probably be sold in 1992 (Kiss, 1991).

13. "Within 3 to 5 years the state wishes to withdraw entirely from the construction industry and trade" (Ministry of Industry, 1991).

14. Kiss (1991) complains that the SPA withholds information from the public, is too favorable to powerful Western investors and too subject to government direct commands; that there is a conflict between speed on the one hand and, on the other hand, revenue-maximization, the probability of fraud, the monopoly role of SPA; there is also a conflict between the will to privatize and the desire to retain a large state sector, which is a power base for the government. There are incompatibilities between the Ministry of Finance (with a very radical and liberal approach) and the Ministry of Industry and Commerce (which is more gradualist and aims at retaining a larger state sector), between the SPA and the Privatization Committee (which criticizes it). This creates insecurity and questions the credibility of privatization programs.

References

Apathy, Ervin. 1991. "A Case Study of the IBUSZ Privatization." OECD Seminar on Privatization. Warsaw. September.

Bokros, Lajos. 1990. "Privatization in Hungary." IMF Institute Seminar on Centrally Planned Economies in Transition. Washington, DC, July.

Crane, Keith. 1990. "Privatization in Hungary." Washington, D.C. Mimeograph.

Financial Research Ltd. 1991. *Reports From the Tunnel: A Summary of the First Year of the Antall Government*. Budapest. June.

Grosfeld, Irena and Paul Hare. 1991. "Privatization in Hungary, Poland and Czechoslovakia," *European Economy*, Special Issue No. 2, pp. 131–46. Brussels.

IMF. 1991. *Hungary Staff Report*. Washington, DC. January 25.

Kazar, Peter. 1991. "Privatization for Top-Down Market Design—The Hungarian Case." Mimeograph. Budapest.

Kiss, Yudit. 1991. "Privatization in Hungary—Wishful Thinking or Economic Way Out?" Conference on International Privatization: Strategies and Practices. St. Andrews. September.

Kornai, Janos. 1986. "The Hungarian Reform Process: Visions, Hopes and Reality," *Journal of Economic Literature*, 24 (No. 4, December): 1687–1737.

Marer, Paul. 1986. "Economic Reform in Hungary: From Central Planning to Regulated Market." In: Joint Economic Committee of the US Congress, *East European Economies: Slow Growth in the 1980s*. Washington, DC, pp. 223–97.

Ministry of Foreign Affairs. 1991. *Investment by Foreigners in Hungary*. Budapest. 30 June.

Ministry of Industry. 1991. *Privatization in Hungary*. Budapest.

Stark, David. 1990. "Privatization in Hungary: From Plan to Market or from Plan to Clan?" Ithaca, N.Y.: Cornell University, *Working Papers on Transition from State Socialism*, Vol. 90.2.

Vekas, Lajos. 1989. "Changes in Ownership and in Ownership Theory," *The Hungarian Quarterly*. Spring.

13

Who Will Own the Factories and the Land?

Márton Tardos

Seventy years of socialist rule and forty-five years of one-party dictatorship have come to an end in Central and Eastern Europe. Most countries of the region are now convening parliaments and local governments that will meet the requirements of parliamentary democracy. All the economies, on the other hand, are still in bad shape, bearing the scars of the old system. Even though the slogans of the market economy ring out loud, business is still dominated by the large state-owned and cooperative firms that were established by the elimination of private property 40–45 years ago.

Paradoxically, Marxian dogma has been proven right in an unexpected context. The creation of socialism is a special task because, unlike earlier changes in social formations, the germs of the new classless society do not exist in a capitalist society, while capitalist trends of production were present in feudalism. Now that it has become clear that the socialist revolution—nationalization of capital assets and collectivization of agriculture—did not live up to its promise, namely, the complete and planned satisfaction of people's needs, the call can clearly be heard for a return to the markets and to capitalism. In order to overcome the deep economic crises caused by communism, to achieve efficiency, to expand the economy, the countries of Central and Eastern Europe have to turn back to a system of production resting on those institutions of private property which were almost completely eliminated in accordance with Marxism. The new situation requires unprecedented programs of mass privatization. We have to analyze the aim of mass privatization; whether society will accept it, or rather, how society will respond to the privatization program (particularly in its rapid form); whether it is possible to create demand at home and abroad for the accomplishments of the program; and finally, what are the best means of encouraging this demand and achieving its benefits.

The Aim of Privatization

The total stagnation in communist countries that resulted from socialist management, and the success of the developed market economies (and notwithstanding the more modest success of developing market economies) have convinced everyone of the relative advantage of an economy based on private property. This explains the unanimous effort in Central and East European countries to wind up the structure of property rights inherited from the socialist political systems: to privatize.

It must be said, however, that the reordering of property rights is not an end in itself. Privatization is a special form of a mass transfer of ownership. On the sellers' side we find the state, which must ensure that the new owners carry out economic reconstruction by organizational measures, by reinvesting profits, and by making new investments according to the requirements of efficiency, i.e., in ways which will lead to greater utilization of production factors and an increase in national income for the benefit of society as a whole, while maintaining efficient but high employment.

A further goal of this change is to dedicate the income from the sale of state assets to reducing state indebtedness. These complex goals must be carried out by involving wide strata of the population so as to avoid social unrest; this is so because privatization entails a rapid redistribution of wealth and income, influenced or managed by the state bureaucracy, which will in any case cause social conflicts.

It has to be understood that privatization always requires a compromise between the above-mentioned conflicting goals. The specific feature that distinguishes privatization from other takeovers is that its high price is not the sole requirement of the state as seller: privatization is not like a normal market transaction. The business is not over when the contract price is paid; the 'deal' must also ensure that the new owner will play an active role in the economy. And this means that the state is keenly interested in setting up a new structure of owners that will work hard to reform the Hungarian firms that lost their entrepreneurial spirit. Moreover, firms are facing increased competition from Western firms in the shrinking domestic markets and in the collapsed market of the former CMEA countries. This does not mean that the state should not seek the highest prices possible for the privatized assets. The high prices paid by foreign buyers reduces the paralyzing burden of foreign debt servicing. Equally important is the price paid by domestic purchasers of former state assets, since this reduces the high internal debt. Moreover, the withdrawal from circulation of the money thus raised neutralizes the inflationary effect of the export surplus created by servicing foreign debts.

The Difficulties of Privatization

A couple of years ago it was widely believed that the main (perhaps only) obstacle to the development of a full-fledged market system in Central and Eastern Europe, including Hungary, was communist rule and the Soviet dominance that sustained it. The collapse of the communist system has taught us that one of the most depressing legacies of communism is the abolition of the formerly leading structure of private property. Communism, in spite of the hope placed in it, not only had negative results, but resulted in a crisis that might be even more painful than the imposition of dictatorship. Markets and market institutions have to be set up rapidly and from scratch in a technically fairly well developed country whose citizens are used to low but secure wages and most of whom are quite unprepared for entrepreneurial activities or involvement in capital market transactions. The task of privatization can be compared in magnitude to the achievements of Prince Geza and King Stephen in the 10th and 11th Centuries, who settled the nomadic Hungarian tribes and replaced their freedom and equality with the efficient system of Western serfdom of that time.

Is the quick reestablishment of markets, based on private property, necessary? The answer, I believe, is a clear yes, even if the transformation is painful. Theoretically, a strong, enlightened centralized political system, which recognizes the failure of the socialist economy, could find a less painful way of transformation. It could pave the way for the evolutionary development of private property, for a gradual opening of the economy to world markets, and for a step-by-step transformation of state-owned and cooperative firms to meet the demands of the markets and the requirements of efficiency. In the Central and Eastern Europe of the 1960s and 1970s such a gradual program of reforms was possible because the government was strong enough to carry out such a change; but no real systematic transformation emerged because the leading political institutions were not ready for the change in all its complexity. Thus, in theory, the program could have succeeded, but in practice (as shown in East Germany, Czechoslovakia, the USSR, and even in Hungary and Yugoslavia), reforms brought only limited success.[1]

Under these circumstances, it is not unjustified to assess the endeavors of the communist reformers, among them the reformers in the Kadar era after the 1960s, in a positive light. The constraints under which the 'socialist' economic reforms were pursued can be seen from the history of the Hungarian New Economic Mechanism. The NEM was unable to complete the task of transformation because the leading political strata in Hungary was afraid that offering firms independent status would undermine its own power base; it therefore did not hesitate to accommodate pressures from the Soviet Union and from conservative elements in its own party. The failure of the Kadar reforms was no accident, nor even the result of internal and external pressures only. This half-success of the Hungarian NEM was the result of the inner logic of the system.

With the unexpected final collapse of the socialist system, new possibilities of systemic change arose. Under such conditions a need is often felt for a strong, enlightened central government, capable of implementing an evolutionary process of change that would lead these countries from a centrally planned economy to a full-fledged market economy with low transformation costs. But the conditions for such a strong government to emerge do not exist. The only remaining choice is between (i) avoiding the pains and failing to escape the deepening crisis that threatens to sweep us away for many years, if not forever, from the ranks of industrial countries, or (ii) seizing the opportunity for radical change that promises new horizons for development. The latter path would mean that instead of a gradual transformation of the system, we would quickly open the way for competition on the world market and encourage the economic activity of private entrepreneurs through rapid privatization.

But the main problem with radical change and rapid privatization is not opposition by those who stand to lose or fail to profit from privatization. They are (or can be) convinced of the need to privatize. The real problem arises during the stagnation and the unavoidable decline in living standards, when it is very difficult to convince the public at large to accept the rapid inequality in income and wealth that would accompany privatization. It is not easy to find a generally acceptable way to deal with the consequences of denationalization, that is, how to sell state property to domestic and foreign investors, how to compensate the large number of people who lost property decades ago without getting tied up in the inevitable ensuing social tensions. One of the awkward aspects of the socialist-economy heritage is that it would take 100 years for Hungarian citizens to accumulate sufficient private savings to 'buy back' the land and factories nationalized by the communists.

Finally, a word about one particular problem facing privatization: the uncertainty surrounding the valuation of assets. Economic theory states that real value of assets is the present value of future profits—quite different from the book value of capital (the calculated cost of acquiring and maintaining assets), or from the cost of reproducing the capital. The latter two can be estimated quite exactly. The real price of capital, however, is a subjective value that can only be rendered objectively where market bargaining exists between large numbers of buyers and sellers. It is also clear that even a healthy capital market cannot guarantee the price stability of assets. Recent experience in leading industrial countries shows that the price of capital is much more sensitive to random market forces than that of products, or even that of raw materials listed on the stock exchanges. Obviously, Central and Eastern Europe (including Hungary) will not enjoy the kind of effective, well-populated capital market that operates in the West. Such a market cannot be stimulated by any administrative or legal process. It should be remembered that the best legal system in the West only regulates the rules of bargaining, not the terms of the bargain, i.e., the division of the advantages and disadvantages among the partners. Thus, we cannot expect legislation to accomplish a just privatization, which, so to say, mimics the market. Therefore, even with the best organization, privatization deals will inevitably come under attack because the prices and other conditions agreed upon will not be considered fair. And these attacks will be exacerbated by the fact that only one state body (or its agent) will be representing the unclearly defined interests of the seller, i.e., all the citizens of the country against the buyer, i.e., the individual. Thus charges of corruption, whether fair or unfair, will be unavoidable.

Who Will Buy?

Only now can we come to the question of who should be allowed to buy the privatized property, and how the change of ownership should be effected. Theory offers two extreme solutions, from the extreme liberal and conservative market wings. One, proposed by Friedman and Klaus immediately after the political transformation of the region started, would divide the denationalized property in one step as vouchers that can be rapidly distributed throughout the population.[2] The other approach, associated with Janos Kornai, which represents his earlier view,[3] would confine sales to the amounts of existing private savings, and in the national interest, would not sell off loss-making companies to foreign buyers until they stand on their own feet.

While respecting the logic of both solutions, I nonetheless regard them as fundamentally mistaken. I would rule out the first as a general solution, since the speed it boasts of could only be achieved at a very high price. The first result would be rapid enrichment of some and relative impoverishment of others at a rate not experienced in developed market economies. This would not only occur because the players are relatively uninformed, but also as the result of random administrative decisions. A further danger is that this proposal will increase inflationary pressures: some strata of the population may prefer to increase consumption rather than acquire capital, thus increasing aggregate demand and weakening the effect of monetary policy. Another risk involved in pure voucher privatization is that the property owners created in this way would not be able to fulfil the role of principals in the companies.

The second extreme solution is problematic because it calls for a very long period of transition during which state management would continue to dominate the economy.

For these reasons I would say that both extreme suggestions must be rejected. Rapid privatization is only possible if, on the demand side, a pragmatic varied approach is developed.

It is clear that domestic and foreign investors must be offered the chance—indeed, encouraged—to seek new business opportunities in the Central and East European economy.

It is worth paying particular attention to what is often called 'small' privatization. This is useful both in terms of restructuring the overcentralized economy and in other respects. Experience shows that Hungarian families, for example, are more willing to use their savings to buy a store or a workshop in which they are better able to act as owners, than they are to invest in larger businesses.

Even in this form, privatization is not without its contradictions. It favors rich foreigners over the generally poorer local buyer; the wealthy homeowner over the poorer one, regardless of how the former acquired his or her wealth. Both factors could cause political tension.

The second method is compensation. It is usually impossible to return formerly owned property in kind. This property may have changed in form, or may not even be in the state's hands. Consequently, the best solution would be to give vouchers or coupons to those who incurred losses due to the nationalization. A more socially acceptable solution would be regressive—as opposed to proportional—compensation, i.e., a higher rate of compensation to people who lost relatively little than to the very rich who lost a great deal. However, preference could be given to dispossessed owners when the property they lost to nationalization—land for example—is privatized in an unchanged form. The system adopted by the Hungarian Parliament in 1991 accepts this main principle; thus we consider the law to be proper. The only problematic part is its extreme bias in favor of former landowners and against urban citizens.

It is undoubtedly expedient to ensure the goodwill of the workforce in companies that are privatized and the citizenry at large in the privatization process. The free transfer of state assets to citizens, using different channels, or selling them at a discount price, can be seen as one of the substantial channels of privatization. One way is to offer private citizens, workers and managers a share of the property being privatized—either free of charge or at a considerable discount. Moreover, the Friedman-Klaus method of voucher privatization can also be used. The practicality of this approach is that vouchers or coupons, rather than money, are given to potential buyers. The chances of success of that type of privatization would improve if private financial intermediaries were set up to compete in offering assistance to beneficiaries, as in Poland.[4] This would check both the threat of inflation and the flow of privatization-generated demand into the commodity markets. At the same time it would enable uninformed citizens to improve their information and to invest their capital in more than one business, thus reducing their risk. Moreover, it would allow investors to combine forces to play the role of the principal in supervising the use to which the capital is put and thus exercise a beneficial influence on the managers.

The fourth channel of privatization is to transfer capital from the state to insurance companies, pension funds, local authorities and nonprofit organizations. Once again, the voucher or coupon method seems to be appropriate for the transfer of property rights. The new owners can use the services of competing financial institutions when investing their certificates in the capital market and afterwards when they exercise their rights as principals in the management of the enterprise. There are two clear advantages to this form of privatization. First, new property owners would be created without the accompanying social tension. Secondly, it would grant independence to important institutions that had formerly been stripped of their property and put at the mercy of the state budget. One disadvantage is that these measures would create new and powerful institutions that might assert their own interests in the economy at the expense of the new owners, the people at large who own these fiduciary institutions. For this reason some form of state regulation of these institutions would have to be worked out.

The Extent of Preferential Privatization

The use of preferential privatization—through vouchers and coupons or preferential credit-launching, as already mentioned—has its pros and cons. On the pro side are the following arguments: first, there is no other way to generate sufficient demand for rapid privatization; second, this form of privatization is socially acceptable since the property goes to and serves the population and institutions that are controlled by the public and cater to it.

On the negative side, only individuals or institutions who have devoted their own savings to privatization can act unambiguously as responsible owners. Second, a country with a heavy national debt and facing the task of serving foreign loans needs the income generated by privatization.[5]

In view of these pros and cons we note that the internal debts can be covered by a healthy economy and that the foreign debt can be managed by soundly developing exports. Consequently, income from privatization need not be used exclusively, or even primarily, to reduce the national debt. One part of the domestic debt, which earlier governments used to finance through the state budget deficit, is offset by the money supply controlled by the central bank.[6] There is no need to pay off the entire debt if the economy is enjoying uninterrupted development and growth.

To improve the fiscal and monetary position of the country we need first of all to pass a State Budget bill (already tabled in Parliament) and regular supervision by the State Audit Office on behalf of the Parliament of the management of state finances. A rational and accountable-to-society fiscal policy can put an end to the state's present unsupervised manipulation of the money markets. In addition, bold political decision must be taken to simplify the chaotic situation that has developed in money circulation, in order to encourage rational behavior by economic agents, including state firms. Included here are the winding up of nonperforming bank credits and intra-firm lendings. It must be made clear that writing off some state credits can only be done once in this transition period; it has to be insured that in the future there will be economic and legal sanctions against any wasteful use of bank credits. Modest revenues from privatization may play a supplementary role in the improvement of the fiscal and monetary stance.

What has been said above does not permit us to draw any conclusions on how income from privatization should be used to reduce the state debt. Certainly almost all revenues from direct foreign investment should be used to reduce the foreign debt, and a part of the domestic revenues from privatization should be used to reduce the internal debt. Here attention should be paid to the consequences of inflationary pressure caused by serving the foreign debt. In the coming years Hungary will have to have a considerable export surplus with which to service its foreign debt. In order to reduce the inflationary effect of the export surplus, fiscal policy must absorb income from the economy. This cannot be done simply by cutting the money supply —since beyond a certain point restrictions in the money supply will only worsen the crisis. Thus, there are two options: to ensure an income surplus in the state budget and to bring in real income from privatization that can be withdrawn from circulation. With this in mind we can set the constraints of such privatization, which can be realized either preferentially or free of charge.

Who Should Do the Privatizing

After this analysis of the demand aspects of privatization, we should also mention how the supply side of privatization should be accomplished. At present, the task of privatization lies exclusively in the hands of the State Property Agency (SPA). It is now apparent that this small body is unable to cope with this massive task on its own. This, together with the fear of 'spontaneous privatization', is leading to increasing demands on the limited capacity of the Agency. However, the problem is not solved by setting up a large state organization like the *Treuhandanstalt* in Germany. The German style of privatization has already caused many social tensions and conflicts of interest that might be considered tolerable only where the massive inflow of money and the legitimacy endowed by the promise of the success of another West Germany stands behind the changes.[7] In my opinion, what is needed in other countries, and specifically in Hungary, is to privatize privatization. This means that the SPA should put the task of privatization out to tender, and that the companies, banks and financial institutions established for this purpose should compete for it. The company awarded the contract of privatizing a given state property would be empowered to execute the process under certain conditions. It would be part of the agreement with the SPA that if the privatizing company achieves better results than stipulated in the contract, the privatizing company would be entitled to share in that surplus.

The Present State of Privatization in Hungary

After discussing the theoretical options for a program of privatization let us return to the facts. Hungary is involved in a process of change focusing on the status of enterprises. From 1989 on, Hungarian state-owned enterprises started to commercialize themselves, and a rapid development of private firms has begun. The fundamental laws of business were changed step by step. The big state monopolies have been dismantled into smaller, limited liability companies and into joint stock companies. However, the property structure has not changed substantially. State property remains dominant. Only a small part of the value of assets was sold to foreign firms in the form of joint ventures or otherwise. An even smaller part was taken up by local private agents. The ownership rights of managers and employees has appeared, but remains an exception.

This change definitely had a positive effect: the reorganized enterprises are more sensitive to market signals, to profitability criteria. On the other hand, the changes have produced political opposition. The process called 'spontaneous privatization' (after the gradual collapse of the one-party system) was used by the old communist *nomenklatura* as a 'golden parachute' for establishing itself in the market system.

In 1991 the new State Property Agency started to control the transformation. Its activity in reorganizing state firms, small-scale privatization and the inflow of foreign investment accelerated developments.

The abstract scheme of the present Hungarian privatization is a two-step endeavor: first, SPA sets programmes for privatization—i.e., it designates the objects of privatization; next it tries to sell its assets for liquid money. The process is proceeding apace (see Table 13.1).

Clearly, a small central bureaucracy cannot remain involved in all privatization cases, but a big body would be too bureaucratic and inefficient to manage the changes.

In Hungary there has been a revolutionary change in the stand taken by the firms. The inflow of foreign capital to Hungary alone exceeds the inflow of capital to all other countries of the region. However, the privatization process is not satisfactory. Vital problems of the past few years remain

Table 13.1. Privatization—Commercialization of Enterprises (No. of enterprises)

	1988	1989	1990	1991
	End-of-year			End-of-year
Registered business agents	10,745	13,169	29,405	62,756
State enterprises	2,377	2,399	2,363	2,362[a]
Joint stock companies	116	307	646	1,672
Limited liability companies	451	4,485	18,317	41,206
Cooperation	7,414	7,546	7,641	7,738[a]

[a] End-July 1991.
Source: Central Statistical Office, 1991/7 *Monthly Bulletin.*

unsolved. State control over the sale of real estate and office buildings, which are not part of the balance sheets of the so-called socialist firms, has not been developed, although there is much more demand for these assets than for industrial firms.

Besides the old unsolved problems, new ones are cropping up. The second conflict is connected with the demand side of privatization. Domestic and foreign investors are opting only for the best part of the assets, looking for the plums in the pudding, so to speak, and the SPA either cannot or is likely to find it difficult to sell off many of state assets destined for privatizaton.

The third conflict arises because due to the present limited liquidity, demand on the privatization market cannot be brought into harmony with the large volume of desired privatization sales. Consequently, the price of the assets is decreasing and the prospects of it actually affecting trade are very vague. Because of this, the SPA is coming under some very heavy political fire.

Fourth, because the present liquid demand on the privatization market is not attuned to the volume of privatization sales envisaged, the price of the assets is decreasing and the prospects of trade turnover are very vague. The SPA is therefore the target of political criticism. An important group of leading political figures in the government, the so-called Monopoly Group (MDF), has tabled a bill in Parliament, that contradicts the whole government program of privatization. The importance of the conflict can be seen from the fact that a new bill on state property policy was tabled by the government but was not even slated for plenary discussion in Parliament. Thus the legal basis for the SPA's activity is lacking because the law requires effective regulations, and the old ones expired in September 1991.

An even more important conflict relates to the fact that firms—commercialized or not—held in state handshave remained much more interested in ongoing operation and in keeping employment high than in making a profit. Undisturbed, they are subsidizing themselves by eroding the value of assets. This means they are taking advantage of the changing regulations and the lack of functioning active principals. They sell real estate and office buildings—which by itself is not bad—but use the revenues not for development but to cover current expenditures. They do not use the low depreciation funds for replacement of assets, and they tolerate nonpayment of credits by their trading partners as long as the employment level is kept high even at the cost of incurring losses. All this shows that the Hungarian government has not taken an unambiguous stand in the most important questions of privatization, which bodes ill for the future.

To sum up, I believe that privatization is unavoidable and the different processes cannot be solved by evading anything that might result in social tensions. Hungarian society is capable of solving the problems entailed in the transition to privatization, but only if the policy adopted is able to mobilize the people for brave measures.

Notes

1. For details see Kornai (1986).
2. See Klaus (1991) and Triska (1991).
3. See Kornai (1990).
4. See Kornai (1990).
5. See Petschnig and Voszka (1991).
6. See Oblath (1990).
7. See Sinn (1991).

References

Fryman, R. and A. Rapczynski. 1991. "Evolution of Design in Eastern European Transition." Mimeograph.

Klaus, V. 1991. *A Road to Market Economy*. Prague: Top Agency.

Kornai, J. 1986. "The Hungarian Reform Process: Visions, Hopes and Reality," *Journal of Economic Literature*, 24 (No. 4, December): 1687–1737.

——. 1990. *The Road to a Free Economy: Shifting from a Socialist System: The Case of Hungary*. New York: Norton.

Lipton, D. and J. Sachs. 1990. "Privatization in Eastern Europe." Washington, D.C.: Brookings.

Oblath, G. 1990. Államodósság—külső—fizetési mérlag. Ki fizet a végén? Bita a magyar gazdaság pénzügyi helyzetéről 1991. [State debt—External balance of payments. In the end, who pays? Discussion about the financial situation of the Hungarian economy.] pp. 65. MTA KTI. Budapest.

Petschnig, M. and E. Voszka. 1991. "Lefekezi a tulajdonosi rendszervaltas az inflaciot?" [Does privatization break down inflation?]. Kozgazdasagi Szemle/10.

Sinn, H. W. 1991. "Privatization in East Germany." University of Munich Working Paper 8.

Triska, D. 1991. "Privatization in Post-Communist Czechoslovakia." Mimeograph.

14

Strategies for Privatization in the USSR

Joseph S. Berliner

Introduction

The legalization of limited private and cooperative enterprise was one of the early measures of economic restructuring in the USSR.[1] It was not until late 1989, however, that the privatization of state enterprises became part of the programs of all major policymaking groups (Hanson, 1990, p. 98). The subject finally reached the political agenda in the summer of 1990, when the '500 Day Plan' was presented to the government by a committee headed by Academician Shatalin (Shatalin *et al.*, 1990). The rejection of that plan by Gorbachev signaled the end of the momentum for privatization, and little was said of it during the subsequent period of Gorbachev's close association with the conservative wings of government and party.

The defeat of the August 1991 coup drastically changed the political alignment, and in October 1991 Russian President Yeltsin announced a bold, new program of reform for the Russian Republic. Among its provisions is the immediate privatization of half of all small- and medium-sized enterprises and the beginning of the privatization of large state-owned enterprises.[2]

Coming to the water's edge of privatization, the Soviets now have a large literature upon which they can draw for guidance on how to proceed. Part of the literature is theoretical, and part is empirical, drawing heavily on the experience of those East European countries that started the process some years earlier. That literature has much to contribute toward an understanding of how privatization might best be conducted under the special conditions faced by the former USSR, which is the subject of this chapter.[3]

The most prominent privatization programs in public discussion have a number of features in common. They all presume that centralized economic planning is to be rapidly replaced by markets for products, for labor and also for capital to the extent possible. They uniformly agree that macroeconomic stabilization is a necessary condition for both marketization and privatization to succeed. They recommend maximum encouragement for the expansion of what may be called the 'pure private sector', consisting of enterprises that were founded as private enterprises. They agree that investment funds must be made available to private enterprise on much the same terms as state enterprises. They all favor 'small privatization', that is, the sale to private persons of state assets of relatively low value, such as apartments, small shops, food establishments, trucks, industrial equipment, small buildings, and so forth. Finally, most programs recommend that, before privatization, the size structure of state enterprises be reviewed with an eye to breaking up the large ones into smaller units whenever this is deemed necessary by economic considerations. These conditions will be assumed in what follows.

A major point of difference in the various privatization programs is the disposition of enterprises in the state-owned (non-farm) sector of the economy. Two strategies have been presented, which I shall refer to as the 'incorporation' and the 'evolutionary' strategies. The principal difference is that the former seek to carry out wholesale privatization, while the latter are more inclined to a retail approach. The sketches of the two strategies presented here are composites of a variety of proposals currently under discussion.

Two Transition Strategies

The primary objective of the wholesalers is to denationalize (or 'de-statize') the state sector as rapidly as possible; that is, to put a quick and final end to the government's control over the activities of enterprises. The first step is to incorporate (or 'corporatize') all state enterprises by giving them the status of joint stock companies, all of whose shares are initially owned by the state. The state therefore still owns the enterprises, but now under the *de jure* form of stock ownership rather than under the *de facto* conditions of the past.

In the second step, a state agency undertakes to transfer all the ownership shares as rapidly as possible to new owners, four classes of which appear in the various scenarios. One class consists of governments—local, republic and union (Feige, 1990). A second consists of institutions that are charged to serve as fiduciary agents of the public, such as government-owned investment and commercial banks, finance companies, holding companies, pension funds, and other denationalized enterprises (Lipton and Sachs, 1990; Shatalin *et al.*, 1990). Third are privately owned (or recently privatized) companies such as commercial banks (Lipton and Sachs, 1990). Fourth are private persons or groups such as workers and managers of the enterprises, or outsiders who may be individual citizens, foreign investors or cooperatives formed for the purpose of buying blocs of shares. Public organizations normally receive their shares free of charge, but shares sold to others must be paid for at a nominal or market rate.

The programs envision different distributions of the shares among the final owners, with various mixes of governments, governmental and fiduciary institutions, and private persons or groups. Denationalization by incorporation is therefore not equivalent to 'privatization', if by that term one intends to exclude all government ownership, for the proportion of strictly private ownership may be relatively small, particularly in the initial distribution. I shall refer to these incorporated enterprises as 'mixed-ownership', since they share some of the properties of both private enterprises and 'public enterprises' found in capitalist countries.[4]

By that initial distribution of stock, the state surrenders its right of ownership of the enterprises, which passes on to the new holders of the stock. The stockholders appoint representatives to the boards of directors that set policy for the enterprises and supervise their management. Some programs provide that in the course of time an increasing proportion of the shares is to be sold into strictly private ownership, so that some of the incorporated enterprises would look increasingly like normal private enterprises in which the government merely owns a minority interest.

The process of incorporation is to be largely completed in a relatively short time—no more than a few years. After it has been completed, the economy consists of a relatively small, purely private sector, and a large sector of autonomous mixed enterprises with varying proportions of state, institutional and private ownership.

The retailers take a more cautious approach to the denationalization of state enterprises. Their program lays primary emphasis on the gradual expansion of a pure private sector rather than on the rapid denationalization of the state sector. The growth of private ownership is to be an 'organic' (Kornai, 1990) or 'evolutionary' (Murrell, 1990) process. The private sector is to be given maximum encouragement to expand, and, in the course of time, as the market economy matures, private persons or groups buy out an increasing proportion of the assets of state enterprises on a case-by-case basis. Privatization is carried out in a process of acquisition and merger that is normal in capitalist economies, and the speed of the process depends on the rate of private capital accumulation, supplemented by borrowed capital.

Reacting against the disappointing experience with 'market socialism', the evolutionists insist that the state continue to exercise control over state enterprises during the transition, rather than convert them into autonomous corporate units. The enterprises may remain under direct government ownership and control (Kornai, 1990) or may be managed (but not owned) by public bodies that are fiduciary agents of the state, like British public corporations (Murrell, 1990).[5] In its long-run steady state the economy consists predominantly of private enterprises, but with a residual sector of state enterprises whose size and composition is determined by public policy considerations of the kind that prevail in capitalist countries, i.e., natural monopolies and so forth.

The two strategies therefore differ in two principal respects. The incorporators are primarily concerned to divest the state from ownership and control as rapidly as possible, while the evolutionists would have that divestiture take place over a longer period of time. Second, in the long run, under the incorporation strategy the former state enterprises are owned by public and semi-public institutions, with strictly private owners having a relatively small share. In the evolutionary strategy private ownership in the long run will be of the conventional kind.

In this chapter I assess the merits of the two strategies in the light of five considerations that should enter into any such assessment. The conclusion is that the evolutionary strategy is the better approach under the conditions of the former USSR. It would not be at all surprising, however, if a similar analysis for East European countries would lead to a different conclusion. Since the five issues discussed here do not exhaust the considerations that should enter into a full assessment—macroeconomic issues, for example, are only indirectly addressed—this conclusion should be regarded as tentative.

Equity

In Eastern Europe there are people still alive who can lay claim to properties they or their families owned before they were confiscated by the state. The matter has also been raised in the Baltic countries, but for most of the USSR the confiscation occurred so long ago that private claims of that sort are likely to be negligible. The reproducible capital assets of the country have virtually all been produced since the Revolution. They are the product of the high rate of investment out of an output that may be considered the product of the land and labor of the entire population. If the ownership of that property is no longer to be vested in the state, equity demands that some recognition be given to the right of every citizen to share in it.

The 'voucher plan' has been advanced as a way of distributing the ownership of state enterprises equally among the citizens (Lipton and Sachs, 1990, pp. 81–82). Each citizen receives a voucher that may be converted into shares in any enterprise. The number of shares that a voucher can buy depends on the share prices that emerge as trading in shares develops. Both incorporationists and evolutionists acknowledge the equity of the voucher plan, but both generally reject it on the grounds of an alleged tradeoff between equity and efficiency.

The efficiency question revolves around the control over enterprise management. Efficiency requires that decision-making in the denationalized enterprises be made on the same basis as it would be made if the enterprises were privately owned; roughly speaking, with the purpose of maximizing the long-run value of the enterprise's assets. If the pursuit of equity resulted in an ownership distribution in which no citizen owned more than a few shares in any enterprise, ownership would be so diffused that control would be forfeited to management. For familiar reasons, management would then tend to make decisions that reflected their own interests, which may differ in various ways from the interests of the owners.

It is for that reason that incorporation strategists propose to distribute the ownership shares in large blocs to institutional stockholders. Since the institutions derive their income from the profits of their enterprises, they would have an interest in the profits earned and in the value of the assets. And since they hold sufficiently large blocs of shares to give them representation on the boards of directors, they would exert the kind of control over management that is found in large capitalist corporations. The evolutionary strategy accomplishes that same objective directly, for the state assets pass eventually into the ownership of private persons or groups who would not risk their wealth unless they were assured of sufficient control over management.

This view of the matter reflects a certain misunderstanding of the nature of property rights. A tradeoff between efficiency and equity exists only if one thinks of ownership as consisting solely of the right to control the use of an asset. In the more general framework of property rights theory, ownership is regarded as a bundle of different kinds of rights, not all of which are always present in any concrete form of ownership. One of those rights is the right to control the use of the asset; another is the right to the income from that asset; a third is the right to the proceeds when an asset is sold.

When these distinctions are made, the tradeoff problem disappears. I would think that the great mass of the Soviet people have very little interest in participating in the control of enterprise management, and would not feel cheated if that were left to competent professionals. What would violate the workers' sense of equity is to come to work one morning to find that their bosses now owned their factory; that the *nomenklatura* and the black-marketeers had tricked them out of the property that was built with their sweat. The outrage in Poland and Hungary over the 'spontaneous' privatizations with which those reforms began would be greatly multiplied in the USSR. If that particular outcome were avoided, the people would not feel violated by a transfer of control from a nebulous 'state' to an equally nebulous 'board of directors'. Their equity concern, in my judgment, is not invested in property as the right to control the use of an asset, but rather in property as the right to the proceeds from the sale of an asset. What would be intolerable is that a few people became rich from the denationalization of their property while the masses ended up with nothing at all.

If this psychopolitical judgment is correct, the equity concerns of the Soviet population could be satisfied by recognizing their claims to the proceeds of any sale of state-owned assets, unbundled from any claim to a right to control the use of the assets. That could be accomplished by distributing the proceeds from the denationalization of state enterprises in a way that would recognize the entire population's prior ownership.

The distribution could be carried out by the establishment of a National Property Bank, which would be the lawful recipient of the revenues formed by the denationalization process. Every citizen would be given an account in the Bank. From time to time the Bank would declare a dividend out of its revenues. The flow of dividends would constitute a tangible and equitable benefit that the citizens receive from the denationalization of what were formerly the entire people's assets.

The revenues of the Bank would consist of two types. One is the proceeds from the sale of state assets to private citizens. This would apply to both the direct sale of state enterprises or assets under the evolutionary strategy, and the sale of shares to private persons under the incorporation strategy. This portion of the dividend would constitute a capital distribution. The other source of revenue would be the profits (or a share of the profits) earned by the fiduciary institutions of the incorporation strategy.[6] This portion of the dividend would constitute a flow of current earnings.

There are a number of other advantages to the use of the proceeds-distribution method rather than the shares-distribution method of dealing with the equity issue:

1. The citizen can always use the funds deposited periodically in his bank account to purchase securities if he or she is disposed to become a shareholder. A deposit in a bank account is something that would be understood by all Soviet people. A share of ownership would be of dubious value to people most of whom had not yet had the experience of writing a personal check.
2. If there were a public purpose to be served by encouraging citizens to purchase shares of stock with their dividends, this could be done by offering say, a 20 percent bonus. That is, the recipient of a dividend of 100 rubles could either withdraw it in cash, or use to purchase 120 rubles worth of stock in a denationalized enterprise (or perhaps a state bond with a par value of 120 rubles.)
3. If the political authorities were motivated to encourage privatization the Bank could be authorized by its charter to lend some portion of the proceeds to the public for the purchase of state-owned assets. That would speed up the rate of purchase of state assets by the private sector. The interest earned on these mortgage transactions would constitute Bank revenues, available for distribution as dividends.

4. The Bank could serve as an instrument of macroeconomic stabilization by reducing the rate of dividend distribution under inflationary conditions and accelerating it in order to stimulate demand during periods of recession. The inflationary potential of dividend distribution could be diminished by distributing only the cash receipts from the sale of assets financed in part by mortgage loans. The dividend would then represent only an exchange of assets among the population and not an increase in privately held cash balances; investors exchange their money for real assets and the rest of the population exchange their real assets for money. Payments made periodically toward the reduction of mortgage-loan principal could then be treated as Bank revenues.[7]

   Even the exchange of assets generates an inflationary potential, however, for cash balances are likely to flow from high savers to low savers.[8] To dampen the resulting increase in aggregate demand for consumer goods, the Bank would have to reduce further the rate of dividends distribution.
5. The distribution of dividends would offset some of the public hostility to the sale of state assets to persons who had obtained their wealth during the pre-reform period. The initial distribution of wealth is highly unequal, and there is a widely held public perception that those who had gotten rich under the preexisting socialist system must have done so illegally. That popular view is no doubt valid to a great extent. While some of the wealth created since 1985 is derived from genuinely productive activity, a very large proportion of it, and virtually all the wealth accumulated before 1985, was derived by capitalizing on the extensive disequilibria in the planned economy. Economists can make the sophisticated argument that society benefits from the risk-taking activity of the black market operator who manages to buy goods at low state prices and sell them to people who are willing to pay higher prices for them. In the political economy of privatization, however, it would be wise to reckon with the unsophisticated popular view that such wealth was ill-gained. Since the first wave of purchases of state property, such as the 'small' privatizations, will be financed out of that kind of wealth, there is bound to be a widespread sentiment that the black market operators and the *nomenklatura* whom they bribed have finally run off with the property of all the people. That sentiment would be offset to some extent by the dividend distributions. Many people will still feel that the speculators and crooks got away with murder, but at least the ordinary people got a reasonable share in the form of the proceeds from those sales.

The treatment of equity as the property right to the proceeds of the sale of an asset rather than the property right to control its use is consistent with both strategies of privatization. The proceeds of the sale of state assets to private owners under evolutionary privatization go directly to the people. Under incorporation, the people benefit because the dividends declared by the fiduciary institutions are deposited in the National Property Bank and subsequently distributed to the depositors. The relative merits of the two strategies can then be assessed on grounds of efficiency alone, equity considerations having been satisfactorily handled by the distribution of the proceeds of denationalization.

Efficiency

Efficiency requires that the managers of the denationalized enterprises strive to maximize the present value of the stream of future profits. A test of their efficiency is whether they make those decisions that would be made by a corresponding enterprise in a conventional capitalist economy. That is a weak test, for it is a matter of long-standing dispute whether the professional managers of capitalist corporations, who are not the principal owners, do in fact maximize the profit that accrues to the stockholder-owners. It would nevertheless be regarded as highly satisfactory if the denationalized enterprises performed as well, in this respect, as the typical capitalist corporation.

The source of the efficiency problem is similar to that in the capitalist corporation: managers of denationalized enterprises may make decisions on a basis other than the interests of the principal owners unless they are controlled by an authoritative external entity. They might serve their personal interests, for example, by channelling business in directions from which they personally benefit, or they might serve local political interests by keeping large numbers of political hangers-on on their payrolls. The two strategies offer different solutions to the problem of controlling management in the interest of efficiency.

The incorporation strategy proposes the device of a joint stock company to provide such an outside authority. If the distribution of shares is carried out in a way that some blocs of shares are sufficiently large—say 20 percent or more of the total number of shares—then the holders of those blocs can appoint members of the board of directors to exercise control over management. The holders of those blocs might be governments, holding companies, pension funds and so forth. Eventually they may include private investors who have bought blocs of shares large enough to qualify for membership on the board of directors (Lipton and Sachs, 1990).

The evolutionists doubt that institutional owners of mixed-ownership corporations can perform the function of control over management as well as private owners do in the case of capitalist corporations.[9] They cite the experience of countries that have employed a form of 'market socialism,' like

Hungary, to argue that unless the enterprises are owned under genuine conditions of private property, they will fall under the patronage of the state and will not operate independently. The evolutionists propose that during the transition period the enterprises should not be incorporated but should continue to be supervised by governmental ministries or similar supervisory bodies. The transition period would then be one in which a growing, purely private sector coexists with a declining state sector that continues to be administered much as in the past.

Neither solution is fully satisfactory. The institutional owners of mixed-ownership enterprises will indeed not be fully empowered principals but will themselves be agents. If a unit of government is a major stockholder (Feige, 1990) it will have an interest in matters other than the long-run profitability of the enterprise. The fact that a portion of the government's revenues is derived from the profits of the enterprises whose shares it holds is unlikely to deter political officials from pursuing other purposes. At the very least they will be concerned to press their enterprises to maintain employment, and it is impossible to imagine that the near-universal practice of political patronage will not strongly influence the appointment of directors and of managerial and other personnel.

There may be ways of insulating the enterprises from the direct influence of government shareholders. The government shares may be non-voting, or they may be turned over to mutual funds as in the Polish government plan. But neither the mutual funds nor the other fiduciary institutions are principals in the same sense that private stockholders are principals; they are agents of the population, and as agents they have personal interests of their own. The directors they appoint to the enterprise boards are therefore agents of agents, and the management appointed by the directors are agents thrice removed. Monitoring management in this multi-level principal/agent environment will be exceedingly difficult to carry out.

The likely result is that enterprises organized as mixed-ownership corporations will be largely controlled by management, and run in the interest of management, and to some degree of the workers. It will be difficult to prevent management from appropriating the profit of the enterprise in the form of their own salaries and wages.[10] The interests of political and governmental officials will also find expression in managerial decisions, but the public's interest in the economically efficient use of the resources is unlikely to occupy the most prominent place.

The evolutionist solution poses problems of a different sort. The central planning mechanism will presumably have been abandoned, so that state enterprises will be functioning in a market system. Since they are still state owned, the state must find some organizational device for supervising them. If they are still supervised by the ministries, it is unimaginable that their decisions will not be heavily influenced by government, rather than by an orientation toward profits earned in the market. As described by Kornai in the case of Hungary, direct bureaucratic regulation will be replaced by indirect bureaucratic regulation (Kornai, 1990, p. 59). As in the case of mixed-ownership corporations, local political considerations, patronage, employment maintenance and other such considerations will intrude heavily upon decision making.

On the basis of these general considerations, it is difficult to choose between the two strategies for denationalization. The issues can be somewhat clarified if the problems of the long run are distinguished from those of the transition.

The long-run objective of evolutionary strategy is quite clear; it foresees an economy in which productive assets are predominantly privately owned. The incorporation strategy, however, permits of a range of views of the long run. At one extreme, the mixed-ownership enterprises may be regarded as the permanent organizational form of the former state enterprises. In the long run, then, the economy consists of a relatively small private sector and a large sector of mixed-ownership corporations whose shares are predominantly owned by fiduciary institutions.

At the other extreme, incorporation may be viewed as a transitional phase in which the shares are gradually sold off to private owners and most of the mixed-ownership enterprises are transformed into corporations similar to those in capitalist countries. In the long run, then, the economy is dominated by the private sector, much like the evolutionary scenario. Intermediate positions may also be imagined, but I shall concentrate on an assessment of the two extremes.

The Long Run

If the mixed-ownership corporation is regarded as the permanent disposition of former state enterprises, then the evolutionary strategy has the stronger case, in my opinion. For the general reasons adduced above, an economy dominated by former state enterprises now organized as mixed-ownership corporations is unlikely to perform as efficiently, by market criteria of profitability, as an economy dominated by private enterprises.

The evidence of the performance of public enterprises in capitalist economies is mixed, but in any case that experience should not be taken as a basis of inference on how an economy would perform if it were dominated by public enterprises. In capitalist economies private enterprise sets the pace of competition, and well-run public enterprises like Renault can find a niche, although even Renault requires a public subsidy. But an economy consisting predominantly of Renaults is unlikely to perform as well.

The principal disadvantage of an economy dominated by mixed-ownership enterprises is not primarily in its performance with respect to allocative efficiency. Nor will the problem of control over management be insurmountable, for the principal/agent problem will not differ greatly from that in large private corporations. The directors of mixed-ownership corporations can design management compensation packages similar to those in private enterprise, with reasonably similar results.

The major disadvantage is likely to be found in the innovational performance of the economy. As former proponents of market socialism have now concluded, it is in entrepreneurial activity that the weakness of non-private enterprise is most evident (Brus and Laski, 1989, p. 140). Of the many reasons for that judgment, perhaps the most fundamental is the matter of incentives.

The effect of a successful innovation is to increase the expected earnings of the enterprise. The market value of the enterprise rises to the level of the present value of the stream of future earnings. It is that prospect of a large increase in private wealth that energizes the innovational activity of capitalism. The fiduciary directors of mixed-ownership enterprises can provide strong income incentives for the managers, which would elicit a certain degree of innovative effort, but they cannot lawfully give the managers a property right in the wealth created by innovation. A predominantly mixed-ownership market economy is therefore unlikely to match the innovative performance of a private enterprise economy. For this reason the evolutionary strategy promises a stronger economy in the long run than one dominated by mixed-ownership enterprises.

The Transition

If the long-run objective is a predominantly private- enterprise economy, former state enterprises should be organized during the transition in a way that would best facilitate their eventual transfer to private ownership. It would be helpful, for example, if they were to operate under market conditions for a sufficient period of time to enable both the state and potential buyers to assess their profitability. That would require that they follow the profit-and-loss accounting practices commonly used in market economies, and that they publish standardized and audited annual reports, income statements and balance sheets.

Incorporation as mixed-ownership enterprises would be one way of satisfying these requirements. Viewed as a transitional form of organization, however, incorporation involves the creation of a vast apparatus of new fiduciary institutions that have to learn how to exercise control over their enterprises for a limited period of time; when the enterprises are eventually sold to a private investment group, these institutions would lose their control function. Moreover, since they have fiduciary obligations and are not principal owners, legal arrangements have to be made to ensure that they honor these obligations; someone has to control the controllers. It is somewhat alarming to think of 47,000 former state enterprises run by hundreds of new institutions that are agents of the public rather than principals, with no other public body bearing the responsibility for assessing their performance. Moreover, since the government has surrendered all right of ownership in the enterprises, there would be no agency with the power to continue promoting the process of privatization. The stockholding institutions and the management of their enterprises could very likely work out mutually beneficial arrangements that would leave them quite content to continue their relationship indefinitely.

The alternative is a Lange-like form of 'market socialism', with the important difference that it is an avowedly transitional arrangement, rather than the permanent form of socialism Lange envisioned. It may be called an 'autonomous state enterprise' arrangement. The purpose is to keep the government involved in the supervision over enterprises during the transition. Instead of surrendering all rights of ownership under incorporation, the government would continue to serve as *de facto* owner. The enterprises could be removed from direct ministry supervision and placed under the supervision of state holding companies, which, in turn, would appoint boards of directors to monitor management.[11] The enterprises would be autonomous, however, in the sense that they make their own production decisions under market conditions, unlike their status when they were supervised by ministries. In the course of time enterprises that cannot operate at a profit will be dissolved by the holding companies, and most of the others will eventually be sold to private owners, as wholes or in parts.

Both organizational forms serve to prepare the way for eventual privatization. Under both arrangements the enterprises will produce a public record of their profitability and will publish annual reports and other audited financial information that potential private purchasers need for purposes of valuation. Unless one believes that the fiduciary institutions will act like fully private owners in their supervision of management, neither form seems to be decisively superior to the other in dealing with the principal/agent problem.

The autonomous state enterprise arrangement, however, seems to me to best serve the purpose of promoting the transition to a predominantly private economy. If the government is committed to privatization, it will still possess the right of ownership and can promote that objective over the resistance of management. With incorporation, on the contrary, the government gives up that right. The autonomous enterprise arrangement also preserves some portion of the preexisting ministerial system, to represent the interests of the state as the owner of the enterprises. But the ministries are confined to the appointing and monitoring the boards of directors, and may not intervene in the management of the enterprises in ways that would compromise their autonomy. If it turns out to be impossible to insulate the enterprises from political pressures emanating from the government, the case for incorporation would be that much stronger.

A final advantage of the autonomy arrangement is that prospective private purchasers will place a higher value on an enterprise that can be bought free and clear from the government than on one that is encumbered by a large volume of outstanding shares. Mixed-ownership enterprises, once established, might therefore remain the dominant form of organization indefinitely, arresting the transition to the private enterprise economy at some midway point.

Macro-Privatization

The term 'privatization' was originally applied to the sale of public enterprises to private owners in capitalist countries. It is unfortunate that the same term has now come to be used in reference to the socialist countries, for it creates the illusion that it is really the same process, except that it is more widely applied. Properly viewed, however, the privatization of a few dozen public enterprises in Mrs. Thatcher's Great Britain has only the remotest similarity to the privatization of 95 percent of the productive assets of the USSR. The two processes might better be referred to as 'micro-privatization' and 'macro-privatization'.

There is a great deal of experience in the world with the privatization of individual enterprises. There is no experience in the world with the privatization of an entire economy. It is truly a "leap in the dark" (Murrell, 1990). To apply the lessons of individual privatization to the privatization of an entire economy is to commit the classic fallacy of composition.

Under normal conditions, production enterprises are embedded in an economy containing a wide range of complementary institutions; a partial list includes banks, commodity and security exchanges, financial intermediaries of various kinds, insurance companies, accounting firms, law firms and courts of law. The scope of each of these activities is determined to some extent by the size of the others. For example, an increase in the number of production enterprises increases the demand for bookkeeping, accounting and auditing services, which stimulates an increase in the number of schools of accounting, accountants and accounting firms. This institutional infrastructure of the economy may be thought to tend toward a rough sort of equilibrium with respect to the volume and kinds of economic activity.

As in any system of general interdependence, small disturbances are easily accommodated; an increase in the demand for one product involves simple adjustments, which is why partial equilibrium analysis is of value under appropriate conditions. As the number of simultaneous disturbances increases, however, the capacity of the system to adjust diminishes, as does the possibility of predicting the outcome. At some point the disturbances may be so great that the adjustment process simply breaks down.

Consider the legal system alone. First, an orderly market economy is unthinkable without a legal mechanism for enforcing contracts. Few people would risk their own wealth without some assurance that commitments made by others would not be ignored the moment a more profitable opportunity came along. A doubling of the number of legal actions for breach of contract in a short time would place a great strain on the legal resources and increase the time required for a legal judgement. People on the margin of deciding whether to honor an inconvenient commitment would find it increasingly profitable to breach the contract. Second, in the absence of conflict-of-interest protection under law, every manager is tempted by the endless opportunities to benefit personally at the expense of the organization. It takes a long time to write and police such laws in ways that are specific to the culture and the economy. Third, it has taken centuries to fashion a body of bankruptcy law that protects creditors from having property looted by the management of an insolvent company (Hetzel, 1990, p. 16). More generally, any change in the organization of ownership or control weakens the pre-existing system of security over the enterprise's resources. The weaker the system of legal sanctions, the greater the frequency with which some people will seize control or ownership of the assets of enterprises.

The same story can be told of all the other parts of the institutional infrastructure; if their resources are strained beyond their capacity to supply the normal level of service, the efficiency of the production system will suffer. It follows that the larger the scope of the denationalization process, the stronger the case for an evolutionary strategy. The time rate of privatization can be accommodated to the size of the initial administrative resources capable of doing it right. The first large privatizations will generate certain demands upon the other institutions of the newly functioning market system. Cases of breach of contract, fraud, and so forth will begin to tax the resources and experience of the courts of law; society will require time to respond by training new lawyers and judges and expanding the capacity of the legal system; similarly for accounting services, insurance companies and the rest. In that way, the gradual increase in the size of the private sector, through internal expansion and through privatization will produce 'backward linkages' generating the required increases in the supply of the services of other organizations.

The proponents of the incorporation strategy are, of course, aware of the need for these infrastructural services. They seem to have in mind attending to that need by creating a network of new institutions simultaneously with the rapid incorporation of the state production enterprises. In the language of the former centrally planned economies, that would be regarded as the use of 'administrative methods'. But founding a banking system is not like founding a bank only more so. Either the newly incorporated enterprises will have to forgo some of the services normally employed by a private enterprise, or the services will be provided by a set of 'instant' bankers, lawyers, accountants, insurance agents and others with little experience in their business.

All this does not argue that it is impossible to privatize a whole country in a short time. The danger, in fact, is that it is entirely possible and may therefore actually be tried. The main concern is that a rapidly privatized economy will not perform like the private enterprise economy it is intended to be like. There is a reason why literary stylists recoil from the suffix 'ize'. Just as a 'tranquilized' person is different from a 'tranquil' person, so a 'privatized' economy is different from a 'private' enterprise economy.

Incorporationists argue that the "potential costs of overly rapid privatization must be traded off against the high costs of maintaining the present system" (Lipton and Sachs, 1990, p. 63). Except for the state budgetary indiscipline in the USSR in recent years and its disastrous consequences, the preexisting system was a going concern that put food on the table, and the costs, though high, were well known. The potential costs of sudden macroprivatization are completely unknown, however, and there is good reason to fear that they may be incalculably large.

The greatest of these potential costs is that the combination of economic dislocation, unemployment and the fraudulent looting of public property will so discredit the processes of privatization and marketization that the popular demand for a return to the stable (if inefficient) centralized system would find a victorious political expression. That would set the cause of the reform back by a generation.

More to the point, however, for the purpose of the present argument, it is not the costs of the present system that must be compared with the costs of overly rapid privatization. It is the costs of gradual, evolutionary privatization that are at issue in this paper, and there is good reason to believe that these costs would be substantially lower than those of overly rapid privatization.

Valuation

Privatization of single enterprises is relatively easy when it occurs in a country with a long established market, because both owners and prospective buyers can estimate their value with reasonable confidence. The absence of a market in the socialist countries greatly complicates the task of valuation. A prospective buyer may guess at the value of an asset, but until the newly established market settles down to some sort of stable relationship among prices, any valuation must be made with great uncertainty.

The discussion of valuation is often couched in such terms that it appears that there is such a thing as *the* value of an asset, and the problem is to discover what that value is. In fact there is no unique value to any asset. A more appropriate conception is to associate an enterprise with two sets of values. One set is a schedule of different values, representing the assessments of all prospective purchasers. The marginal prospective purchaser is a liquidation company, which would evaluate the enterprise on the basis of the resale and scrap value of the physical assets. Another prospective purchaser would place a high value on some part of the enterprise's assets that can profitably be incorporated into his or her own production operations, but the remainder of the assets would be sold off. A third purchaser would value the enterprise as an ongoing productive operation, including not only its physical assets but also its goodwill; by trimming the labor force, introducing its own management, and changing the product line to fit the parent company's marketing profile, it can be a highly profitable purchase. A fourth valuation would be based on the trading value of its shares. In general, the value of the enterprise to each prospective purchaser will depend on the purchaser's own objectives and organizational characteristics.

The second set consists of the values to the state of employing the assets in different uses. One value, again, would be the price of the assets if the enterprise were liquidated. Another would be the standard capitalization value; that is, the present value of the discounted stream of expected future net earnings if the enterprise were maintained in operation. The state's reservation price would be the larger of those values. If the enterprise is thought to serve some social purpose in additional to its direct production uses, the reservation price should be increased by an amount approximating the value of that purpose to the society. The state needs to know its reservation price in order to determine whether to sell the enterprise, scrap it or maintain it in its best use. If the state's reservation price is higher than the valuation by the highest prospective purchaser, the enterprise should not be privatized but maintained in operation as a state-owned enterprise.

Hence the range of valuations of a given asset may be very wide, even in a long established market economy. For example, in the negotiations over its bid on a proposed merger with National Cash Register, AT&T initially offered a price that was equivalent to $90 a share. At the time NCR shares were trading at $48. The company management, however, seeking to prevent a takeover that might remove them from office, insisted that the value of the company was $120 a share (*Economist,* January 26, 1991, p. 16). An army of analysts is at work in investment houses estimating the values of the companies in which their clients might seek to invest.

From this perspective, the evolutionary strategy has the advantage of offering a firmer basis of asset valuation. The first few years after the introduction of market relationships will be years of great turbulence. Price relationships will take a long time to stabilize, costs will change correspondingly, profitable lines of production will turn into losses and, perhaps, losses into profits. During this period, of unpredictable duration, uncertainty will be so great that neither the state nor the prospective buyers will be able to make reasonable assessments of the assets' long-term value. Moreover, the private sector will still be so small that the market for privatization will be very thin.

As the private sector grows organically over time, however, both the state and prospective purchasers have a more secure basis for valuing the assets. Private capital accumulates and business experience grows, the number of prospective purchasers increases and the market for privatization 'thickens'. Price and cost structures stabilize, and financial markets expand and become more efficient. Both the state and the purchasers can have more confidence in their forecasts of future costs and prices. Product demand can be forecast more accurately, so that reasonable present-value estimates can be made. The state has a firmer basis for estimating its own reservation price, and is less vulnerable to selling off the assets for far less than they are worth. The gradual assimilation of state enterprises into the private sector would therefore occur under conditions that should minimize ex-post regrets about having made hasty and ill-advised decisions.

Under the incorporation strategy most of the shares will be transferred without charge to public bodies like local governments or public holding companies. Since there is no charge, there is no need to establish an initial value, which is a point in favor of that strategy. When the market eventually stabilizes, however, it will turn out that some of the public holding companies had become owners of highly profitable enterprises, and others owners of basket cases. The ex-post inequity of the initial distribution could have severe political repercussions.

Some of the shares, however, are to be offered for sale directly to private purchasers, including foreign purchasers under certain limitations. Since the state cannot set its own reservation price with any confidence, there is a distinct possibility that it may be giving the assets away at a bargain-basement price.[12] The greater the pressure to privatize rapidly, the greater the likelihood that the assets will be sold at excessively low prices.[13]

Unemployment

British Coal is the next large public enterprise that the British government plans to privatize. In preparation for that action it had earlier closed 102 of its 170 collieries. The government's estimate of the size of an efficient British coal industry implies that only 20 of the remaining 68 collieries will survive, which would reduce the workforce by an additional 50,000 jobs (*Economist*, February 9, 1991, p. 55).

The closing of the mines was preceded by a bitter strike, but the government ultimately prevailed. In the long run, the British economy will clearly benefit by closing down inefficient production operations, but the burden on the miners and their communities has been enormous. The ability of the British polity to accomplish that wrenching reorganization is the mark of a stable society.

Capitalist economies are very good at clearing out the debris of inefficient production. In the United States, in any ten-year period, 50 percent of all manufacturing plants close down, and their capital and labor are reallocated to more productive uses. Every year 2 percent of the labor force takes up employment in new plants (Murrell, 1990, p. 7). A remarkable characteristic of socialist societies is that they have managed to avoid that gross way of dealing with inefficient enterprises—they have changed management, reorganized production, and reequipped them with more modern machinery, but they have rarely (if ever) closed them down. In the end they have subsidized them year after year. One can only speculate on how much more productive those economies would have been, even under central economic planning, had they developed a more reasonable way of coming to terms with the natural process of obsolescence of production activities.

Soviet authorities estimate that about 20 percent of all enterprises are subsidized. One cannot judge what proportion of all enterprises would be insolvent if prices were free to reflect real scarcities, but there is no doubt that there would be a very large number. With marketization of the economy and the freeing of prices, none of these enterprises could survive without subsidies. The incorporation strategy, however, would thrust all Soviet enterprises into a market environment in the course of a few years. As prices gradually escalated to their market-clearing levels, many enterprises would become insolvent. The government would then have to choose between letting them go bankrupt and close down, or continuing to subsidize them.

No one can forecast with confidence the level of unemployment that would accompany rapid incorporation. No Soviet (nor, perhaps, any) government could survive a rapid rise in unemployment to perhaps 20 percent of the labor force. Nor would the policy of marketization that brought that result about be long accepted by the population. An unemployment rate of that magnitude would generate an irresistible demand for the rejection of the marketization reforms and a return to the system of central planning, which, for all its defects, did accept a certain responsibility to provide jobs for the workers. The government will therefore have to continue subsidizing a large number of inefficient enterprises. Assuming that to be the case, the question is: which of the privatization strategies would be best under that circumstance.

The purpose of the incorporation strategy is to get the government out of the business of running enterprises as quickly as possible. The government will therefore find itself paying out subsidies to enterprises it no longer owns or controls. It might seek to introduce sufficient restrictions so that it could refuse to subsidize activities that the government auditors regard as uneconomic. But it would be difficult first to set up such an efficient national auditing inspectorate very rapidly, and then to second-guess the managerial decisions of thousands of autonomous mixed-ownership enterprises.

The evolutionary strategy offers a much better prospect for coping with unemployment, which may prove to be the critical problem in the transition. In particular, since there is no insistence on immediate denationalization, the government can, like British Coal, begin the process of 'desubsidization', that is, the closing down of inefficient enterprises in advance of privatization. Initially, when prices have not yet found their equilibrium levels and costs are still in flux, desubsidization should be applied only in those extreme cases where it is clear that an enterprise would be unprofitable under any prospective set of prices. As the price level stabilizes, insolvency becomes an economically more meaningful guide to inefficiency, and desubsidization could accelerate, to an annual rate judged to be politically viable.

While that process is going on, the private sector is expanding and can therefore absorb a certain proportion of the labor force left unemployed by the closing down of state production facilities. The availability of that labor force will also serve to hold real wages down and to facilitate the expansion of the private sector. The absorption of some of the unemployed by the private sector will also reduce the burden on the state of providing income support for the unemployed. The physical assets of the enterprises closed down can be scrapped, reallocated to other state enterprises or sold off to the private sector.

This scenario places the burden of eliminating the mass of inefficient enterprises on the state. In a moral sense that is where it belongs, because it was the state that was responsible for permitting the problem to mount to such proportions. In practical terms, however, if economic reform is to be acceptable to the population, it had better be done by the state, for the alternative is that it be done by the workings of the market. In that case, popular reaction may be so strong that the government may be forced from office and the transition to the market derailed.

Summary and Conclusions

In the short run the incorporation strategy would dismantle the structure of centralized state ownership much more rapidly than the evolutionary strategy. Insofar as some of the shares would be privately held, the proportion of all assets in private ownership would initially be larger. The economy would not function as efficiently under the incorporation strategy, however. Control over management would be weaker and the production enterprises would lack many of the services that complementary institutions provide in a market economy that has evolved organically. As the price system stabilizes, the initial distribution of the assets will prove to have been quite inequitable and arbitrary in many cases; some of the new owners will end up with highly profitable enterprises and some with insolvent enterprises. Some of the inequity, however, could be offset if the proceeds of the sale of the former state assets to the private sector were returned to the citizens in the form of equal capital distributions.

The greater danger lies in the legacy of inefficient enterprises, many of which will quickly prove to be insolvent. Political considerations will require the state to continue subsidizing many of those newly incorporated enterprises, in which case their independence from the state will be difficult to maintain. The attempt to transform the organizational structure of an entire economy in a short time could create such dislocations and unemployment as to discredit the market and provide popular support for a restoration of state ownership and control.

The evolutionary strategy offers the greater opportunity to avoid these pitfalls. In the short run it involves less of a shock to the economy and is likely to maintain output at a higher level. The production enterprises and the complementary economic institutions grow in an organic relationship to each other. In the long run it will be a stable market economy, with the proportion of assets in private ownership determined by the political process, in the manner of democratic societies.

The discussion has dealt primarily with the economics of the two strategies. When the choice between them is made, however, it is more likely to reflect political considerations than economic ones. Before the August 1991 coup, the strategy of rapid incorporation may have had the stronger case from a political perspective.

Dr. Shatalin and his colleagues no doubt understood that the program they presented could not in fact be implemented in 500 days, and that any attempt to do so would have been very costly. They must have had some purpose in mind other than economic transformation itself. My guess is that they simply did not trust the *nomenklatura* and the ministries to actually introduce any serious program of transformation. They foresaw the likelihood of endless temporizing and delay.

The introduction of a precise and legally mandated set of dates for implementation of the program was their device for forcing the government to go ahead with the recommended changes. That, indeed, was precisely what the government feared, for the program they finally adopted was similar to the Shatalin plan in many ways,[14] but pointedly omitted a time schedule. The government could thus appear to be in favor of radical reform—but not now.

The defeat of the coup, however, dramatically changed the constellation of political forces. Power has shifted decisively to the republics, and republic leaders like Boris Yeltsin are on record as strongly supporting privatization. Promoters of privatization need no longer favor whichever strategy would best force the hand of a resistant government bureaucracy. The choice between the two privatization strategies can now be made primarily on grounds of their relative economic merit. By that standard, the evolutionary strategy is to be preferred.

Notes

1. The Law on Individual Labor Activity was published in *Izvestiia* on November 20, 1986.

2. The *New York Times*, October 29, 1991.

3. With the October 1991 speech of Boris Yeltsin as president of the Russian Republic, that Republic appears to have taken charge of the privatization of all state enterprises on its territory. It is very likely that as a general matter the privatization process will be carried out by the republics rather than by the enfeebled union government. I continue to use the term USSR in this chapter, however, for there has not yet appeared a compelling alternative way of referring to the region that formerly went by that name.

4. Parris *et al.* (1987, p. 23) describe three types of public enterprise: 'state enterprises', 'state-sponsored enterprises', and 'state-owned enterprises'. The latter have the same legal status as private enterprises, but their shares are owned wholly or partly by the state, e.g., British Leyland. That description comes closest to fitting many of the denationalized enterprises envisioned in the incorporation strategy. I use the term 'mixed-ownership enterprise' because the term 'state-owned enterprise' would convey the wrong meaning when applied to a former socialist country.

5. The transition period may be thought of as Lange-type market socialism, except that it is intended as a transitory state, not as the permanent state envisioned by Lange. It also differs from Lange in the presence of a growing private sector and in price-determination by markets rather than by a Price Board.

6. Under the incorporation strategy the stock-holding institutions—public holding companies, state commercial banks and the like—would presumably not be the residual claimants of the after-tax profits of the denationalized enterprises. Since they are not themselves private enterprises but fiduciary agents of the public, the public should be the residual claimant of their profits, which includes the dividends received from the denationalized enterprises whose stock they own. These after-tax profits might be turned over to a government body, but since the point of the whole exercise is to divest government of ownership of the enterprises, the government should not be brought back into the act as the residual claimant of the profits of the fiduciaries. The most reasonable course is for the National Property Bank to serve as residual claimant of the fiduciaries' profits.

The Bank might also be charged with appointing the boards of directors of the fiduciaries and with supervising their activities. Unless there is some public accountability by the fiduciaries, there is no doubt that they will metamorphose from agents into principals. That would be a scandal of much greater proportions than 'spontaneous privatizations'.

7. A concern for macroeconomic stability would advocate the use of the proceeds by the government to reduce the monetary overhang and the state budget deficit. There is merit in that policy in cases of extreme short-run instability, and the current situation in the former USSR may qualify as such a case. Keynes' reminder that "in the long run we are dead" has too often been used to justify irresponsibility, however. To cope with the problems of macroeconomic disequilibrium by the use of funds that could otherwise be directed toward meeting the popular demand for equity could be laying the groundwork for more serious political problems in the future. Moreover,

it is always bad policy to finance current deficits by the sale of assets rather than by the review of revenue and expenditures policies, and the government is likely to delay indefinitely the task of creating a modern system of tax collection as long as it can sell off state properties instead.

8. The problem would occur even under the voucher plan. The citizens receive their vouchers free of charge or at a nominal price. Those with low income and low savings are likely to wish to sell their vouchers to others with high income and high savings. Cash balances would thus flow from high savers to low savers, stimulating an increase in aggregate demand. I am grateful to an anonymous referee for pointing out this problem.

9. Evolutionists agree that if a private investment group can be found to purchase a bloc of shares large enough to serve as a dominant shareholder, that would provide adequate ownership control over management (Kornai, 1990, pp. 91–92). Their concern is that institutional investors, who do not have a direct personal stake in the profit of the enterprise, would not be motivated to exert adequate control.

10. The Polish government had to introduce wage controls in 1990 to prevent enterprises from appropriating their own profit (Lipton and Sachs, 1990).

11. This is the method recommended by the IMF, except that in their proposal the enterprises would be converted to joint stock companies before their ownership passed to the holding companies (IMF, 1990, p. 28). The proposal in the text does not require the joint-stock form, on the ground that privatization would be more readily accomplished if the prospective private owner were free to decide for himself what the best legal form would be for the assets he proposes to purchase.

12. The reservation price might also be set too high, causing the state to lose a potentially beneficial sale. The pressure for privatization, however, is more likely to lead to undervaluation than to overvaluation.

13. The sale of state assets far below their value is one of the causes of public outrage against rapid privatization. A typical case is the Polish firm Igloopol. The firm's managers "have been accused of putting too low a value on company assets and then acquiring those assets" (*New York Times*, December 12, 1990, p. D1). In this case the difficulty of valuing assets is combined with the absence of legal protection against conflict of interest—both manifestations of an effort at macro-privatization before the economic infrastructure has matured.

14. The other major difference between the Shatalin plan and the plan later adopted by the government is the division of authority between the central government and the republics. The Shatalin plan gave the republics much more authority than Gorbachev was willing to accept.

References

Brus, Wlodzimierz and Kazimierz Laski. 1989. *From Marx to Markets: Socialism in Search of An Economic System*. Oxford: Clarendon Press.

Feige, Edgar L. 1990. "Perestroika and Socialist Privatization: What Is To Be Done? And How?" *Comparative Economic Studies*, Fall 1990, 1–54.

Hanson, Philip. 1990. "Property Rights in the New Phase of Reforms," *Soviet Economy*, April-June, 95–124.

Hetzel, Robert L. 1990. "Free Enterprise and Central Banking in Formerly Communist Countries," *Economic Review,* Federal Reserve Bank of Richmond, May/June.

International Monetary Fund, The World Bank, Organization for Economic Cooperation and Development, and European Bank for Reconstruction and Development. 1990. *The Economy of the USSR: Summary and Recommendations,* Washington, DC: The World Bank.

Kornai, Janos. 1990. *The Road to a Free Economy: Shifting from a Socialist System: The Case of Hungary.* New York: Norton.

Lipton, David and Jeffrey Sachs. 1990. "Privatization in Eastern Europe: The Case of Poland," *Brookings Economic Papers,* Vol. 2, 293–339.

Murrell, Peter. 1990. "Big Bang Versus Evolution: Eastern European Reforms in the Light of Recent Economic History," *Plan Econ Report,* June 29.

Parris, Henry, Pierre Pestieau and Peter Saynor. 1987. *Public Enterprise in Western Europe.* London: Croom Helm.

Shatalin, Stanislaw *et al.* 1990. *Transition to the Market.* Part I. Moscow: Arkhangelskoe, August.

15

The Socialist Firm, the Value of Capital and Transition to Capitalism

Michael Keren

Privatization is usually understood to mean the transfer of ownership of existing state enterprises to the private sector. As it may take place in Eastern Europe, this transfer, I claim, is very difficult, unprofitable and time-consuming, and may permanently damage those economies. It is difficult because the existing enterprises are of little value, their capital stock may be ill-adjusted to the task of generating profits and their capital value is highly uncertain.[1] All these will make it difficult to negotiate their sale, and any fair and reasonable transfer method will be long drawn out. The damage incurred by the sale of such enterprises as working units derives from their structure, size and tendency to tie down assets needed for founding new private firms. If sold as is, without prior reorganization, they are liable to hinder the growth of a new private sector, which is the only hope for the reconstruction of these sick economies. An examination of the meaning of investment processes in bureaucratic socialist economies leads to the conclusion that state-owned enterprises tend to be machines that destroy rather than create value; they are liable to degrade good resources into low-value capital; and they will probably continue to do so even under private ownership unless market conditions force them to change.

The state of the capital stock in Eastern Europe is an initial piece of evidence supporting this allegation. The statistics of investment in Eastern Europe do not prepare one for the shortage of capital discovered there: East European countries have been investing more, not less, than Western countries—significantly more as a proportion of GNP (Table 15.1).[2] They are nevertheless visibly starved of capital, and their stock of machinery and structures is antiquated. Their incremental capital-output ratio has also been very high, higher (on average) than in Western Europe. Add this to the high rate of investment in GNP, and any simple model would indicate that all

Table 15.1. The Share of Investment, Selected Countries

		GNP/Capita ($ US)	Investment/GNP 1980s (%)	ICOR 1980s
A.	*Eastern Europe*			
	Bulgaria	5,633	26.5	57.3
	Czechoslovakia	7,603	21.1	10.0
	East Germany	7,361	20.8	5.2
	Hungary	6,491	28.1	18.0
	Poland	5,453	27.7	12.7
	Romania	4,117	32.8	7.4
	Yugoslavia	4,898	39.3	55.7
	Eastern Europe, average	5,946	28.0	11.6
B.	*Western Europe*			
	Benelux	8,379	18.5	12.6
	France	9,451	20.2	10.4
	West Germany	10,014	20.4	11.7
	Italy	7,386	21.3	9.5
	Southern EEC	2,519	20.9	6.9
	Scandinavia	11,655	21.1	8.3
	UK	7,902	16.8	5.8
	Other EFTA	9,941	23.4	12.0
	Western Europe, average	7,260	20.1	9.1

Sources:
Eastern Europe—Jefferson and Petri (1990), p. 5. Western Europe—OECD (1990). Panel B: Per capita GNP—average of country's GDP, 1980–1988 at 1985 prices converted at the 1985 exchange rate, *divided by* population average of 1980 and 1988. Investment/GNP ratio—Ratio between total 1980–1988 Gross Fixed Capital Formation and GDP. ICOR—1988 GDP *minus* 1980 GDP, *divided by* sum of investment, 1980–1987.

the capital actually in use for the production of present-day output must be new. The ratio between capital and GNP should be at least as high as the equivalent ratio in Western Europe, or the ratio of the stock of capital in countries East and West should be at least equal to the ratio of their GNPs. One should find plenty of capital there, not too little. It is true that considerable old capital has accumulated (because the depreciation and scrapping of aged facilities has been extremely slow). If this were all that were wrong, all that would need to be done would be to scrap a large number of decrepit machines. But this apparently is not the remedy: it is *new* capital that is missing. The explanation seems to be that something was basically wrong with the investment mechanism in Eastern Europe and that this mechanism led to a great deal of investment that failed to produce new capital.

The investment mechanism consisted of enterprises and the central authorities. Both lower and upper tiers in the hierarchy were involved in planning and executing investment projects, and both seem to have been particularly poorly equipped for their task. I shall argue that they are also unlikely to perform much better in the future; here the Nelson–Winter paradigm is handy: in a competitive economy it does not matter whether one considers firms as satisficers, because a firm with a poor decision rule is driven out by its competitors whose policies are closer to firm-value maximization. This is not the case in an environment where enterprises simply cannot die and can be reorganized only with great difficulty. Such an environment preserves the existing mode of behavior of the firm, which is strongly embedded in the specific human capital of its employees.

But if this is the case, the argument put forward by Peter Murrell (1990) is surely convincing: there is little to hope for from the existing firms in Eastern Europe. They cannot be relied upon to raise their efficiency substantially—to become 'sanitized', as the Germans put it—unless they are first privatized. In fact, they should, as far as possible, be deprived of any investment funds, because it is most likely that they will throw good new money after wasted old money. Instead, priority must be given to building a new private sector in the interstices of the existing state sector. Privatization is surely needed, but the so-called 'small' privatization, i.e., selling off shops and small plots of land, is much more urgent than 'big' privatization, i.e., selling off existing enterprises.

The meaning of the 'value of the stock of capital' in East European economies, in light of the investment process and the investor's incentives, is examined in the first section. The second section shows that all types of capital—human and physical alike—are flawed; this theme is continued in the third section, which examines the enterprise as a badly structured network of specific human capital. Policy conclusions are drawn in the concluding section.

The Investment Process

Crucial, strategic investment decisions are made in the Eastern bloc by central authorities, planning boards, the industrial ministries, sometimes even by the highest political echelons of what used to be the Soviet Union and its satellites. These bodies are responsible for major blunders that created visible white elephants in the East European landscape. The details of the investment projects (their machinery and structures) are determined by lower rungs in the hierarchy, among which the enterprises play a very important role. I shall concentrate first on the enterprises and their responsibility for the particular profile of the stocks of capital accumulated in the countries under discussion. First, however, a brief note on investment statistics.

The value of new capital is usually defined as the sum of past net investments (the cost of new capital equipment product *minus* the depreciation of old capital). This procedure is totally inappropriate for the socialist economies. The value of capital is the present value of its expected marginal product, or, in a competitive economy, the expected value of the profits (or net cash flow) it creates. In a capitalist economy a profit-maximizing firm will invest in each project until the cost of the marginal invested unit equals the marginal expected present value of profits. It is this equality which allows us to use the cost of investments as the yardstick by which to measure additions to capital. This is not the case in the Soviet bloc: in what follows it is argued that the value of capital is usually well below its production cost.

When examining an enterprise in a socialist country we cannot assume, even as a working hypothesis, that it maximizes profits. Its aims are quite different: it is part of a bureaucratic hierarchy, it receives production targets from its superiors and its aim is to satisfy these upper echelons. When the issue is investment decisions it therefore seeks to expand its production capacity; it is much less concerned with production costs, since cost-minimization is only a secondary consideration. High profits or low costs may be rewarded, but only if the assigned physical targets assigned are fulfilled. Furthermore, when the costs of an enterprise are considered, present costs in each enterprise are compared to its own past level, not to those of other enterprises. This is the origin of the insatiability of enterprises for new capital, an insatiability which can be controlled only by the central allocator of investment funds and physical inputs. This also explains why enterprises are loath to scrap old capital (it may be of use some time in the future); true, this may require high maintenance expenditures, but these merely increase costs—which are of secondary importance.

The introduction of cost-saving new technology and equipment that embodies such technology is also accorded low priority. A case in point is the slow conversion to the oxygen process of steel production (Amann *et al.*,

1986, Tables 1.1 and 1.2, pp. 12–13). The introduction of the more modern, cost-saving process occurred at roughly the same time in the Soviet Union and in the Western industrial countries, but the share of steel produced by older methods did not decline at the same pace. Some 25 years later, over 70 percent of all Soviet steel was still being produced by the old methods, while in the Western countries in the tables the proportion was between 20–40 percent. In other words, in the Soviet Union some of the new capacity installed incorporated the old, obsolete production methods. The same is true for continual casting of steel, numerically controlled machine tools, and synthetics (fibers and plastics). Amann *et al.* (1986, p. 12) cite ". . . the failure of new technologies to drive out or 'extinguish' obsolete ones. Whatever the principal reason. . . , whether it is conservatism pure and simple or a conscious desire to retain old facilities as a buffer."[3] It is clear that if all new facilities built after the introduction of oxygen steel in 1956 had used the new process, by 1980 the share of oxygen steel would have exceeded 30 percent. If not, then clearly not only was old plant not scrapped, but new equipment incorporating the old techniques was still being produced and installed.

This can be seen in Table 15.2: columns (5) and (6) of this table show that in the USSR a great deal of new capacity incorporating old technology has been installed since the 1950s: this was at least twice total output in 1956, the year commercial production of oxygen steel started in the USSR, and over 50 percent of additional capacity installed since then. In Japan, too, output of non-oxygen steel produced in 1982 was more than double the 1956 output, but this was only one-sixth of all new capacity installed (possibly new plants in the pipeline at the time the new process started to spread). In the Soviet Union, it seems, producers of steel-producing equipment embodying the older processes did not switch over to the more efficient process and continued to supply obsolete plants.

No capitalist producer would accept an inferior process if an economically and technically superior one were available. Soviet producers apparently did not consider the old processes inferior: the equipment was readily available, and it could produce a given amount of output using a well-tried technology. These producers were not concerned with quality and costs; their superiors, who had approved the investment, were not strict about the former and were willing to provide the necessary inputs. Thus, capital that, in a different environment, would be slated for scrapping, was being newly turned out in the Soviet Union, possibly because there was no pressure on the producer of the capital goods to change over to the modern technology, to improve the quality of output.

In other words, the capital equipment manufactured and installed in Eastern Europe can be expected to require more inputs, and hence be more expensive to operate, than capital installed in a capitalist economy. This is one reason why the fuel and raw-material intensity of production is much

Table 15.2. Steel Output, Selected Countries, 1956, 1982

	Total steel output (tons)		Oxygen steel (percent)	Non-oxygen steel		
				Tons[a]	Percent[b]	New capacity (percent)[c]
	1956	1982	1982	1982	1982/1956	
	(1)	(2)	(3)	(4)	(5)	(6)
USSR	48.7	147.2	29.6	103.6	212.8	55.8
USA	104.5	67.7	62.1	25.7	24.6	n.a.
Japan	11.1	99.5	73.4	26.5	238.4	17.4
West Germany	26.6	35.9	80.9	6.9	25.8	n.a.
UK	21.0	13.7	66.1	4.6	22.1	n.a.

n.a.—not applicable.
[a] (1)×(3).
[b] (4)/(1).
[c] [(4)−(1)]/[(2)−(1)].

Sources: Steel output, 1956, 1982—*United Nations Statistical Yearbook*, various years. Oxygen steel, percent of output—Amann *et al.*, Table 1.2, p. 13. "n.a."—not applicable.

higher in the East than in the West. But this also means that the true social value of capital (its marginal product) and its private value in a capitalist environment (its capacity to produce a stream of profits) is usually lower than the cost of its own production. In fact, the value added, at international prices, of certain outputs may sometimes be negative.[4] If we hear that an aluminum plant in Romania consumes as much electricity as all the consumers in the country (Montias, 1990, p. 5), it is quite likely that this cost exceeds the value added generated by aluminum production.

The tendency of economic units to hedge against suppliers' unreliability by producing their own inputs leads to production units whose scale is far below the efficient level and whose inefficient capital equipment is underutilized. Much of the major overhaul work being carried out (often recorded as investment) may, in fact, help keep in operation machinery that should have been discarded. The organization responsible for much of this is the enterprise; it has learned to function in a bureaucratic environment that has created a giant rift between public costs, as an economist would measure them, and private costs to the bureaucratic decision maker.

As for strategic investment decisions, these were made at the top of the hierarchy. The structural development decision to invest in heavy industry, with complete disregard for comparative advantage, environmental factors, and often locational economics, was taken by the political leadership. The blame for the decision to opt for hydraulic oil-drilling technology and to exclude the alternative rotary-drill technology used in the West (Campbell, 1968)[5] cannot be placed on any enterprise. These decisions, too, burdened the economies with a great deal of capital that is of little use. The decisions to go for large enterprises and to concentrate production in few centers was also taken at the center. It was a decision that may have made sense at the time, given the need to economize on decision making, but it created an enterprise structure that may make it almost impossible to develop a competitive economy and may therefore be incompatible with privatization.

The Types of Capital Stocks Affected

The previous section presented a few examples of capital projects in which the capital produced was of low—possibly negative—value. These examples point first and foremost to poorly structured physical capital, and the quality of physical capital in many East European enterprises is, indeed, very poor. But it is also important to note that investment in other types of capital was also defective.

The damage investment has inflicted on the *environment* is well known. The reason for this can also be formulated in terms of the divergence between private and social costs. In capitalist market economies, where the dividing line between the private and the public domains is relatively clear, special agencies were formed and entrusted with prevention of social costs to the environment. These agencies made the prevention of social environmental costs their private concern, and achieved a certain amount of success. In socialist economies, where externalities were presumably abolished by the inclusion of the entire economy in a gigantic monofirm, every individual unit was nevertheless judged according to its contribution to its specific sphere, which clearly did not include the environment. If an agency is created whose specific sphere is the environment, then its standing in the bureaucracy is usually so low that it has a very little chance of influencing the stronger protagonists, those whose activities have a sharper and more direct effect on the well-being of the community or the individual in his daily life. Therefore, negative investment in the environment is very difficult to halt, and the cumulative damage to the environmental capital cannot be remedied in any brief period of time.

Investment in technology, research and development is another factor whose productive contribution was over-valued. The low economic contribution of new technology has been well known ever since Berliner's *Innovation Decision in Soviet Industry* (1976), and little needs to be added here.[6] The value of R&D lies in the development of new processes that, once they are adopted by producing units, increase the social value of the producer. The producer must be interested in adopting potentially profitable new techniques that may either save costs or strengthen the firm's market position. Neither is of any concern to the bureaucratized socialist firm. There is a gap here between private and social benefits to innovation: the private manager does not benefit from the social benefits of lower costs. He does, however, bear the associated public costs of risk, as well as the private costs of greater short-term instability imposed by the artificial periodicity of the planning cycle. Since the incentives to put into production the fruits of research (or even copy well-tried new technologies) are so low, the value of marginal research results is also lower than the cost of research. This is why the technological level of industry can be low in spite of the resources spent on research being quite substantial, even when compared to the West.

The *design of goods* produced by the enterprises is also defective. The considerations underlying the development of these designs may seem quite bizarre to a Westerner. Zielinski (1973), for instance, has argued that the so-called *Tonnenideologie* often led to the design of goods that are intensive in costly inputs, because this would lead to a higher price, higher plan fulfillment, and higher profits. Consumer needs or the quality of output were rarely the most important considerations in the design of new goods. To survive in a competitive environment, East European enterprises will have to redesign a substantial part of the lines of goods they produce, surely not an insignificant task.

Finally, and perhaps most important, human capital is also deformed. Both formal and specific investment in human capital create skills that are unsuited to a market environment. Certain categories of skill that are essential to running a decentralized economy are missing: all skills related to the capital market, the legal skills needed for business-oriented counselling and adjudication, and modern commercial skills, to cite only a few examples. East European engineers have no regard for costs; many economists are bookkeepers—essential in a large bureaucracy—who do not comprehend the relations between the rules of the economic game and human behavior. All firms have large planning and procurement divisions, but not enough people in marketing (and those who are in marketing have little experience in competitive conditions).

A particularly important type of human capital distortion is the enterprise itself, and the implications of this fact are taken up in the following section. It should first be noted, however, that the distorted structure of capital did not pop up in overnight; it took decades to deform the structure of capital and it will, perforce, take a long time to correct it. And this is of relevance to the transition problem.

The Specific Capital of the Firm

In economic theory the firm is assumed to be a profit maximizer. In the case of a bureaucratic environment, this assumption is unwarranted. In fact, the assumption that a bureaucratic firm maximizes *any* objective cannot be made without further support. Nelson and Winter (1982 and elsewhere) have attacked this assumption as regards the competitive firm, too, but they have, in effect, shown that Darwinian competition keeps surviving firms from straying too far from profit-maximization. In the absence of such competition it has to be accepted that firms adapt to their environment, in our case—a bureaucratic environment. However, when the environment changes they cannot easily change with it. The firm (or enterprise) is a human network. Its mode of operation is established by its founders and is picked up by the incumbent labor force in the process of its operation (Nelson and Winter, 1982). It may change over time, but its evolution is slow, especially when there are no strong forces that press for change. Once the firm has established certain procedures of arriving at needed decisions, and these lead to given patterns of outcomes, neither procedures nor normal outcomes can be freely altered without expending a serious amount of effort and real resources.

Consider first investment decisions. Suppose a decision has been made to embark on a given project. A team of engineers is instructed to prepare a detailed set of blueprints in accordance with an accepted set of rules; once these are approved—again, in a manner that follows a routine that may involve the superiors—purchasing agents are instructed to buy the selected capital goods. Each of these actors follows a set of rules that was acquired in a learning-by-doing process; their decisions and the questions they ask are all part and parcel of these rules of thumb. Suppose we now tell the enterprise that it should henceforth follow the rules of profit maximization. To be effective, this change will have to permeate throughout all rungs of the hierarchy and supplant all the existing rules. Would this work if the new rules were only announced? Clearly not. First of all, the new rules have to be formulated and made operational. Each of the actors has his human capital, his own routines, which he will not easily give up, because learning new rules requires investment of time and energy on his part. If the firm were to be privatized, it would be a different story, since then the new owners would be the ones to press for the adjustment of old routines to a new environment.[7] If the old hierarchical bureaucracy were to take upon itself the task of changing the mode of operation of existing firms the effect would be close to nil.

Support for these assertions can be found in the experience of enterprises in reform regimes such as labor-managed Yugoslavia or Hungary's NEM. The general impression is that enterprises did not change their behavior pattern radically with reforms. For Hungary we have Granick's evidence, three years after the inception of NEM, and in its heyday: examining key behavioral patterns—the holding of inventories, the choice of the mix of output or of investment projects—Granick concludes that most firms did not change their basic mode of operation. They did not become profit maximizers, but continued to adjust to an environment in which, as before, they knew they were responsible for their 'past trade', for supplying the usual demands of their regular buyers, regardless of whether this policy enhanced or reduced their profitability (Granick, 1975, Ch. 10). The formal change of the firms' objectives under NEM apparently did not affect their behavior, certainly not that of larger firms. In particular, most of them did not display greater readiness to innovate. And this is what counts, since large firms still produce the greater part of output in both countries.

Indeed, the process of amalgamation continued in Yugoslavia and was not reversed in Hungary, in spite of the presumed change in the allocation mechanism which should have favored small enterprises. This does not mean, of course, that *none* of the enterprises reacted to the change in the announced incentive system; only that those that mattered did not. Therefore a change in the rules of the game—namely, realizing that the continued existence and well-being of the firm depends on its profitability, and that profitability depends on the organization's unending struggle for a good product range and efficient production—may affect the behavior of some (perhaps many) firms, particularly the smaller and nimbler ones. But it is not likely to affect the behavior of large, top-heavy firms, which are likely to feel fairly secure in their continued existence and at the same time be hard to privatize. These cumbersome firms may therefore remain in the hands of the state for many years to come.[8]

Product design may be the weakest link in many firms. Products were designed to please the planner, not the market, and the first steps a firm will have to take if it is to survive in the new competitive environment is to redesign its product line. Suppose a firm that has just been freed from the shackles of the plan discovers that its output is poorly adjusted to the competitive market. The pressure to change its product mix in a market-oriented firm would come from sales personnel. In East European firms the sales department carries little weight; even if it were to propose a new line of goods—hardly likely for a group of people used to having an insatiable demand for everything it sells—it would not have much effect on the organization. Traditionally, the production people rule supreme, and it is doubtful whether they would let lowly sales people gain the ascendancy. Furthermore, redesigning the product range is both costly and time-consuming, and its success for any given firm is in no way assured.

Paradoxically, if this analysis is correct, the task of the privatizing agency becomes both much more difficult and much simpler. Simpler, because there is little hope that they will improve the operation of the enterprises it oversees prior to their actual sale or transfer to private owners. After all, the agency itself is also a bureaucracy, albeit one with different terms of reference and easier constraints, since if the economy is opened the agency is to a large extent freed from the need to balance the economy. The task becomes more complex because one cannot privatize existing firms as they stand, and because the agency has to see to it that as few as possible resources (such as investment, much of which is bound to be misguided), are wasted by the firms before that event.

Other changes that the privatizing authority can make may be more promising. The very structure of industry suffers from the gigantomania of the past and is too top-heavy. An important task is to unravel these colossi, to decide how to convert the existing enterprises into potentially competitive firms. This is mainly a problem of vertical and horizontal disintegration. Some of the aggregation was done by the planners, who had to simplify their all-but-impossible task by reducing the number of enterprises under their direct command. They therefore set up horizontally integrated associations or trusts, or vertical *Kombinate*. These organizations would not permit the growth of any competition in the new markets. Furthermore, each enterprise was interested in controlling its own material inputs by producing the most important ones itself. These often primitive facilities can be discarded, now that the problem of obtaining inputs is one of cost rather than administrative availability. Many of these facilities are likely to be of such low capital value that scrapping them would be best; others might survive until they are absorbed by new, non-state owners into bigger units. Some of these facilities tie down assets such as stores, urban real estate, and means of transport that are essential for any new sector of private firms.

Why not entrust this task to the privatized firms? In many cases this can be done. These firms are likely to find out by themselves which operations they may find cheaper to perform through the market once supplies become assured. They will also find ways of splitting up when the scale of operations is too large. In two cases, however, these firms cannot be left to their own devices: the first is when enterprises form local monopolies. Take two ex-GDR examples: the single ex-GDR insurer was sold to the largest insurance company in the Federal Republic and all branches of the ex-GDR state bank were divided between the two leading West German commercial banks. In both cases, regional competition in the area was, at least for several years, lessened. The second case relates to all those assets tied up in firms that are likely to remain state-owned for many years to come, mostly because they are neither easy to privatize nor sure candidates for winding up. The latter firms often have no incentive to divest themselves of unprofitable assets; they may even be legally proscribed from doing so. In either case they may keep assets off the market that are urgently needed to help form new private firms and small enterprises.

Clearly, all this will take a long time to accomplish. These firms cannot be valuated by using old balance sheets, since the discrepancy between the value of the capital and its original cost does not follow any simple formula. Each firm has to be evaluated separately by experts in the field, a time-consuming, stochastic operation. And finally, the outcome is bound to be very disappointing as far as the value of the existing capital stock is concerned.[9]

Conclusions: What to Do?

The conclusions to be drawn from the foregoing analysis are quite simple, and closely follow the suggestions of Murrell (1990). The bureaucratic managing hierarchy is the bane of the socialist economies, whose productive sectors must be freed from its yoke as fast as possible. This does not mean that the present structure of state industry should form the basis for a better functioning economy: what little capital value the existing firms have is costly and difficult to ascertain. It is dangerous to privatize them in their present organizational shape because of their monopolistic standing and inefficient scale. They need to be stripped of many assets in a process of 'small' privatization. However, their dismemberment and reorganization may take quite some time.

This may sound discouraging, but it does point to a promising way out: the establishment of new, non-state, private or cooperative firms, not necessarily in the fields of operation occupied by existing enterprises. Many of the latter have to be replaced for the reasons given above, though differently named in the literature: the weight of industry in the employment and production structure is far too high; the weight of services is far too low. Industries with no comparative advantage may be the easiest to scrap; they are often major energy and raw-material guzzlers—hence also the greatest poisoners of the environment—and their capital value may well be negative. The service industries that have to be put up will often exhibit no economies of scale and will function well as small, independent firms. Those that prove successful can grow and develop into the big firms of tomorrow. They are the suppliers of the 'thousand little things' which the planner found so difficult to supply in the past, as well as those producer and commercial services which are essential bulwarks and lubricators of a market system.

Such private small firms will need some aid to develop, and this should be the first priority of the central government. They need a place locate: their need for land may be limited, but the privatization of some urban land and stores for rent or sale (the so-called 'small' privatization) is perhaps the most urgent task of all. The firms may be helped by the availability of some loan capital. Hence the establishment of some small investment banks may be beneficial (they should be small, since large banks may find it too transaction-costly to pay attention to such small fry); they should be freed from all the old regime's legal restraints, e.g., on type of business and number of employees; and they need some protection for private capital—a clear definition of ownership rights, courts of law, a judicial system. Most of all, the new private sector must be protected from the populace at large that equates any profit-making with reprehensible 'speculation'. This is no small order of desiderata, but it pales into insignificance compared with the needs of the 'large' privatization of the existing state industry.

The state is thus not relegated to a less important role. Its role is changing and it has to provide those services that only it can supply, many of which were neglected during the period when it sought to perform tasks for which it was ill-equipped. The state has to look after the infrastructure, physical as well as human (e.g., education), and provide the basic institutions of the market economy (see Tardos in this volume, Chapter 13), especially the legal framework.

The latter is an especially difficult priority area. The basic framework in which a private entrepreneur can work is missing in most East European countries: the regulation and definition of property are usually unclear, the existing contract law in most countries is not suitable for the adjudication of disputes between private firms and a commercial liability law may be non-existent. Even more serious may be the sorry state of those who will be charged with providing the missing legislation: the judges, tainted by their subservience to the *ancien regime*, may be unable to function independently. Even if they were able to do so, they might not be perceived as such. The entire legal profession used to be the hand-maiden of the authorities. Its members are also very few in number. They are unable either to formulate laws that could stand up in a courtroom litigation, or to advise or represent a client, as they would have to do in a private economy. The East Germans were lucky: the legal system of the Federal Republic could be imposed on them, and the missing judges and attorneys could be borrowed from the West. In all other countries of the Eastern Bloc this would be much more difficult.

The human capital problem might be alleviated by the repatriation of trained emigres, who may try to step up the pace by copying from the West. It will nevertheless be a protracted affair. Even here, a legal framework sufficient for the working of a new private economy composed mainly of small firms may be simpler to develop than the more complex needs of large, monopolized industry, slated for privatization. The privatization process itself may be the most complex economic, political and legal problem faced by the regime. This is another reason why 'large privatization' will take time, which should not be wasted on idle waiting.

All this implies that the existing state sector may remain in limbo for a fairly long period. During that time existing industrial enterprises may have to be kept on a very short leash until they are finally let out of state ownership. In particular, their budget constraints must be hardened and they must not be allowed to squander resources either through investment (see the previous section) or through raising employment or wages. Clearly, if the privatizing agency were given the discretion to oversee all these firms and rule on each of their requests individually, it could not possibly fulfill its task. As a result, the budget constraint of the as-yet unprivatized firms will be extremely soft, and the resources consumed by this sector could be quite substantial. These firms should therefore be subjected to strict rules, with no discretion left to the agency.

There are also obvious implications for the sequencing of privatization. Enterprises that do not threaten to impede competition, need no basic restructuring and generate profits should be privatized first. Hindering their investments and working conditions places them in danger of stagnation and further deterioration as long as they are not set free. Their staff is likely to support early privatization because only this will allow them both to improve their present lot and secure their future. Once the privatizing agency has fewer enterprises to handle, it may be able to pay closer attention to its remaining flock. It may then be possible to determine which are the hopeless enterprises, and which, with some reorganization and luck, may be salvageable. But this topic is beyond the scope of this chapter.

Notes

1. See Berliner in this volume (Chapter 14) for a discussion of problems of evaluation.

2. It is not yet easy to come by comparable data on the ex-CMEA and Western economies. I therefore had to use data from different sources in the two panels of the table, and they are not necessarily comparable. This is particularly true regarding the level of per capita GNP.

3. The authors refer to a "buffer against the scarcity of commodities." The scarcity that old machinery 'buffers against' is scarcity of production capacity in times of need. It provides spare capacity in case of increased targets, breakdowns and the like.

4. Compare "The Value-Subtractors of Eastern Europe," *The Economist*, January 5, 1991, p. 55.

5. As Campbell shows, it was the main research institute of the oil industry, with party backing, that made and enforced this strategic decision, by essentially blocking the development of alternative techniques. Campbell agrees that hydraulic drills may have raise the efficiency of Soviet drilling as long as drilling depths were not too great, but it became a liability in the late 1960s and 1970s. In spite of a decision to shift to other drilling techniques, the share of the hydraulic drill declined very little, from 85 percent at its peak to about 75 percent in the 1970s, where it seems to stay toward the end of the reported period (Campbell, 1968, pp. 103–120; 1976, p. 22).

6. See also Levine (1982).

7. For evidence of how expensive this can be, see report on losses made by West German banks and insurers during their first year of operation in the GDR, in "Finance in East Germany: Fingers Burnt," *The Economist*, March 16, 1991, p. 90.

8. More on these points in Keren (1991).

9. See also Berliner in this volume (Chapter 14).

References

Amann, Ronald and Julian Cooper. 1986. *Technical Progress and Soviet Economic Development*. Oxford: Basil Blackwell.

Berliner, Joseph S. 1976. *The Innovation Decision in Soviet Industry*. Cambridge: The MIT Press.

Campbell, Robert W. 1968. *The Economics of Soviet Oil and Gas*. Baltimore, MD: The Johns Hopkins University Press.

——. 1976. *Trends in the Soviet Oil and Gas Industry*. Baltimore, MD: The Johns Hopkins University Press.

Jefferson, Gary H. and Peter A. Petri. 1990. "From Marx to Markets," *Challenge* (September/October): 5.

Granick, David. 1975. *Enterprise Guidance in Eastern Europe*. Princeton: Princeton University Press.

Keren, Michael. 1991. "On the (Im)Possibility of the Socialist Market." Paper presented at the Conference of the Jerome Levy Economics Institute, *Moving to a Market Economy: Economic Reform in Eastern Europe and the Soviet Union*, October 25–26.

Kornai, Janos. 1986. "The Hungarian Reform Process: Visions, Hopes, and Reality," *Journal of Economic Literature*, 24 (December): 1687–1737.

Levine, Herbert S. 1982. "On the Nature and Location of Entrepreneurial Activity in a Centrally Planned Economy: the Soviet Case." In: Joshua Ronen (ed.), *Entrepreneurship*. Lexington, MA: Lexington Books, pp. 235–267.

Montias, J. M. 1990. "The Romanian Economy: A Survey of Current Problems." Mimeograph. Berlin.

Murrell, Peter. 1990. "'Big Bang' Versus Evolution: East European Economic Reforms in the Light of Recent Economic History," *Planecon Report*, 6 (No. 26, 29 June).

Nelson, Richard R. and Sidney G. Winter. 1982. *An Evolutionary Theory of Economic Change*. Cambridge, MA: Harvard University Press.

Nuti, D. M. 1990. "Market Socialism: The Model that Never Was." Paper presented at the 4th World Congress for Soviet and East European Studies, ICSEES, Harrowgate, 21–26 July.

OECD. 1990. *National Accounts*, Vol. I: "Main Aggregates, 1976–88." Paris: OECD.

Zielinski, Janusz G. 1973. *Economic Reforms in Polish Industry*. London: Oxford University Press.

16

Is There a Future for Regional Economic Cooperation in Eastern Europe?

Sándor Richter

This chapter focuses on an analysis of short-run prospects for mutual trade between the former European COMECON[1] countries and on the emerging concepts for institutionalized economic cooperation of the region's economies. Before discussing these issues in detail, a short review of the traditional COMECON cooperation, its consequences and an evaluation of the experiences of 1990 is provided.

The Old System

The now dated practice of economic cooperation among COMECON countries was based on four tenets: bilateral clearing and its accounting unit; the 'transferable ruble'; the peculiar price formation system; the decisive role of government institutions in all respects of trade; and the predominance of political considerations over economic issues in decision making (see Rácz and Richter, 1989, p. 25; Richter, 1989, p. 49).

Price formation of individual commodities in bilateral trade relations was subject, at least theoretically, to the so-called Bucharest price principle. This, in its last version, stipulated the application of a moving average of the previous five years' world market prices. In reality, these stipulations were followed more or less consistently only with respect to raw materials and energy. For many manufactured products, application of 'world market' prices was simply impossible, since some of these commodities had never been marketed outside the COMECON. Regarding several other manufactured goods, the quality of the products exported to Western markets differed so radically from those marketed in COMECON that price comparison was simply irrelevant. Moreover, the prices of manufactured goods were influenced by the negotiation tactics of the government officials concerned.

For this and for several other reasons the rules of price formation bred a practice whereby actual relative prices for the same commodities were different in Western and Eastern markets, and in individual bilateral relations within the CMEA. Nor did they have any connection with production costs and demand for the commodities concerned. In short, prices could not fulfil the role they play in market economies or in international exchange between market-economy enterprises.

Another prerequisite of COMECON cooperation was the transferable ruble (TR). This accounting unit—the means of settling payments in the bilateral economic relations within the COMECON—was neither convertible nor transferable among COMECON members. Even its function as a means of payment in individual bilateral relations was rather limited, since the flow of payments was only the reflection of intra-governmental agreements on mutual deliveries, determined primarily in physical terms. It was extremely difficult to use a TR earned in a given bilateral relation to buy any commodities in the bilateral partner country, that had not already been allocated for exchange in the inter-governmental agreements. This is the main reason why all partners tried so diligently to avoid a trade surplus in bilateral relations.

Bilateral clearing, this anachronistic form of settlement, could survive in the past because it was the optimal framework for international exchange of goods in the classical version of central planning. The bilaterally bound utilization of the TR made the rigidities inherent in all versions of clearing even more explicit. Switch deals, generally used to solve clearing problems where this form of payments prevailed, could not be applied.

Perhaps the most important tenet relates to the role of the government. Trade within the COMECON was based on government-level negotiations preceding actual deliveries. In the earliest stage of negotiations, mutual deliveries to be made in the upcoming five-year plan were coordinated; then, after a separate set of negotiations, an agreement was signed on deliveries in the five years after that. Representatives of the Ministries of Foreign Trade met again at the end of every year to finalize the quantities and, possibly, the prices of the commodities traded; the agreement signed on this occasion obliged the governments to guarantee the deliveries agreed upon. Although actual deliveries were preceded by enterprise-level negotiations and contracts, enterprises played only a subordinate role in the process. Advantages of trade were hardly identifiable at enterprise level. Under the peculiar circumstances of intra-COMECON transactions, the real value of commodities traded was expressed in two categories: 'soft' goods and 'hard' goods, referring to the scarcity of the commodity concerned in the trading countries and to its sales prospects outside the COMECON. Only the negotiating government officials had an overview of the interrelated mutual deliveries, and only they could perceive (if anyone could) the global, macroeconomic advantages provided by trade with COMECON partners.

The Consequences

As (until recently) the COMECON countries conducted most of their foreign trade with one another, it is no wonder that the very special system described above had serious consequences. Enterprises in COMECON countries that had specialized in regional markets could not become competitive outside that region. The generally low level of technology in the region's industry, low quality requirements, and the absence of motivation to increase efficiency spoiled the enterprises. The confusing signals transmitted by the peculiar price-formation system delayed adjustment to the changing environment in the world economy. At the macroeconomic level, duality emerged in the trade patterns: while sophisticated manufactured products played a major role in trade within the region, their share in the exports of the COMECON countries to the OECD region was low.

The extent of technological backwardness of the COMECON countries is clearly illustrated by the following statistics: in 1988, South Korea, Singapore and Hong Kong together exported machinery and transport equipment to the OECD area in the value of US$ 32 billion, while respective exports of the Central and East European economies[2] (henceforth: CEE economies) and the Soviet Union amounted to only US$ 3.5 billion (Table 16.1).[3]

Table 16.1. The Share of Machinery and Transport Equipment in Exports of CEE Countries and the Soviet Union According to Destination in 1989 (percent)

Czechoslovakia[a]		Romania[b]	
Comecon	60.7	Ruble-accounting area	56.7
OECD	11.8	Dollar-accounting area	8.6
Hungary[a]		Bulgaria[b]	
Comecon	48.6	Total export	59.8
OECD	14.2	Soviet Union[b]	
Poland[a]		Socialist countries	20.9
Comecon	56.4	Non-socialist countries	9.2
OECD	15.5		

[a] According to the SITC classification of the UN (SITC 7).
[b] According to the CTN classification of the COMECON (CTN 1).

Source: WIIW Data Bank.

When the diagnosis is so clear, the cure may seem simple: introduction of free bargaining on prices, hard currency settlement payments and the elimination of the state's role in trade will bring about an environment in which the enterprises of the region have no choice but to adjust to the requirements of the world economy. Although it is obvious that in the long run the shift to the new system of cooperation will have beneficial effects and, moreover, that this step is unavoidable, the question is whether the COMECON countries will survive the shock of this shift without their economies collapsing with all its frightening social and political consequences.

The Consequences of Introducing Hard-Currency Payments in Trade

After the shift to the new system, categories of 'hardness' and 'softness' become a question of prices (see Richter, 1990). The price of what were formerly 'hard' goods (mostly raw materials, primary energy supplies and semi-processed goods) immediately approaches actual world market prices. Not so in the case of 'soft' goods (mostly manufactures). For energy and raw materials, prices had been different inside and outside the COMECON, though the commodities themselves were the same; for manufactured products, however, not only were prices different in the two major markets, but the quality of the product differed as well. After the shift to hard currency payments, the limited ability to compete with Western products is reflected in lower prices; taking into consideration the direct comparison with prices of imports from the West, no previously 'soft' goods can stay on the market if its price does not correspond to its quality.

Poorer quality notwithstanding, manufactures mutually traded within the COMECON constituted a substantial part of the intermediates and the consumption of the population in the countries concerned. In most cases, imports from the defunct COMECON cannot be replaced from domestic sources, whereas a large volume of imports of better quality (and much costlier) from the West is out of the question, because of the shortage of hard currency. Thus if low prices are demanded by a former COMECON supplier, and if the cost of substitution is high, this may create a situation in which former soft goods can be sold even after the change-over to hard currency. (At an identical expenditure, 10,000 pairs of medium-quality shoes may be preferred to 5,000 pairs of high-quality shoes.) The other side of this problem is more controversial. Where there is also demand for 'soft' goods, and the shortage of hard currency notwithstanding, (which compensates for the weaker performance compared with competing Western imports) the price level will most probably not cover the cost of production. Solvent demand may emerge in the case of prices reflecting the discrepancy in 'quality' of commodities imported from the former COMECON area as compared with the West. The question, however, is whether the required exports can be produced profitably.[4]

Warning Signs in 1990

1990 could have been the last peaceful year before the transition to hard currency payment, but it was not. Trade within the COMECON contracted sharply. This sharp decline reflects, on the one hand, the contraction of CEE-Soviet trade as a consequence of the cut in crude oil deliveries by the Soviet Union. Actual deliveries were 30 percent below the quantity contracted for (see Balabanov and Havlik, 1991). The drop in Soviet imports from the CEE region can be explained by the limited willingness and ability of the CEE economies to maintain the 1989 level of exports. The Soviet Union also refrained from importing a part of its traditional purchases from the CEE economies (Tables 16.2 and 16.3).

Table 16.2. Development of Non-Convertible Currency Trade of the Central and East European Economies and the Soviet Union, 1988–1990 (preceding year = 100)

		1988	1989	1990 (estimate)
Bulgaria[a]	Export	106.5	119.3	74.7
	Import	94.7	111.2	82.6
Czechoslovakia[a]	Export	98.7	91.5	79.5
	Import	94.3	97.0	91.1
Hungary	Export	101.2	96.2	73.6
	Import	100.1	91.9	79.3
Poland	Export	109.0	102.3	88.8
	Import	89.9	93.4	60.0
Romania	Export	n.a.	92.7	58.2
	Import	n.a.	106.8	86.6
Soviet Union[b]	Export	96.0	97.2	78.3
	Import	102.5	101.9	91.9

[a] Trade with socialist countries in national currencies converted to TRs at the official exchange rate.
[b] Trade with CMEA countries.

Source: Calculations based on data from the WIIW Data bank.

Table 16.3. Soviet Oil Exports to Central and East European Economies, 1988–1991 (million t)

	1988	1989	1990	1991	
				Plan[a]	Estimate[b]
Bulgaria	12.7	12.6	7.8	6.5	11.0
Czechoslovakia	16.8	16.9	13.0	7.3	13.0
Hungary	8.4	7.8	4.8	4.5	6.5
Poland	15.8	15.2	9.7	7.0	13.0
Romania	4.0	3.9	3.4	2.5	16.0

[a] Optimal import of individual CEE countries from the Soviet Union via all channels (inventory list, trade with Republics, etc.)
[b] Total estimated crude oil import demand in 1991.

Source: 1988, 1989: WIIW Data bases; 1990 and 1991: estimate.

According to WIIW estimates exports traded with the Soviet Union dropped by 15-20 percent in the case of Czechoslovakia and Hungary, at current prices and in national currencies, and the respective imports sank by 19 percent and 11 percent. Romania's exports fell by some 10 percent, and its imports by about 17 percent. Bulgaria's exports to the Soviet Union declined by 24 percent, its imports by 15 percent.

Nevertheless, according to WIIW estimates the decline in mutual trade between the CEE economies was even more dramatic. In some individual bilateral relations—although data from the national statistical sources are often controversial—a quarter, one third (in extreme cases even one-half) of the turnover simple vanished. While it is not easy to explain this phenomenon, it might be mentioned that in Poland and Hungary, and to some extent in Czechoslovakia, an export boom to the West took place which diverted part of the former intra-COMECON trade. The economies of Bulgaria and Romania were nearly crippled by the uncertainties of the political transition. Finally, perhaps there was no room left for the traditional exchange of 'soft' goods; the mere fact that in mutual trade of 'soft' goods the disadvantages deriving from poor quality are balanced out did not provide a motivation strong enough to maintain the traditional level of trade.

What to Expect from 1991?

In 1991 CEE trade with the Soviet Union was the focus of attention. The actual development of CEE-Soviet trade was determined by various (often interrelated) issues. An overview of selected issues follows.

1. Internal Soviet problems
   a. The economic situation in the Soviet Union
   b. Internal regulation of foreign trade
2. The framework of CEE-Soviet economic relations
   a. Agreements on technical terms of trade in hard currency.
   b. Agreements on unsettled problems of the TR era.
3. External factors
   a. Oil prices
   b. Western assistance.

The *economic situation* of the Soviet Union deteriorated in 1990 and there is no reason to expect a recovery in 1991.[5] The ongoing political and economic disintegration creates uncertainty, first of all regarding the ability of the Soviet Union to extract the quantities of crude oil and other primary sources of energy needed for the energy deliveries to the CEE economies undertaken for 1991.[6] Political disintegration casts doubt on the reliability of intergovernmental, Republic and regional level agreements, and of contracts drawn up between enterprises. The political and economic crisis threatens to decrease the level of overall Soviet imports, among them imports from the CEE economies.

Soviet *foreign trade regulation* has undergone several changes since decentralization began in 1986. From Spring 1991, exporting enterprises could retain part of their foreign currency income after transferring 40 percent of their export revenues to the Vneshekonombank.[7] Having foreign currency facilitates (theoretically) autonomous enterprise-level imports. Although barter deals were forbidden in early 1991, 'small border trade' and exchange of goods among cooperating enterprises were still being transacted. Barter is regarded by the Soviet authorities as a diversion of commodities from regular exports, which diminishes central foreign-currency income. The ban on barter dealt a serious blow to CEE-Soviet trade, since the easiest solution to the shortage of hard currency trade problem could not be applied.[8] Certainly there is no guarantee that the above mentioned allocation of export incomes will not be modified in the course of the year, either in light of the actual foreign trade performance or as an outcome of the political struggle between central and republic-level authorities. There most probably will be attempts to reallocate both exportable commodities and foreign-currency incomes.

Agreements on the technical terms of trade in hard currency between individual CEE economies and the Soviet Union contain standard provisions. There is an inter-government inventory listed in all bilateral agreements,[9] which contain, on the one hand, energy, raw materials and other commodities whose export is to be licensed by the Soviet central authorities, and, on the other hand, commodities whose import by Soviet enterprises is to be facilitated via allocation of the necessary hard currency from the all-union currency fund. This list is not a state-level obligation to delivery. Such obligations are part of enterprise-to-enterprise contracts. In Bulgarian-Soviet, Czechoslovak-Soviet and Polish-Soviet trade, the list provides the basis for a peculiar settlement of payments called 'quasi-clearing', whereby mutual deliveries of commodities are registered in the accounts of designated banks. This solution may streamline the bureaucratic process of 'normal' trade and maintain a higher level of exports to the Soviet Union, but in view of the present instability, a surplus in trade with the Soviet Union in this quasi-clearing may prove rather risky. Nevertheless, there are voices in the Soviet Union which criticize these lists on the grounds that they serve as a tool for continued subsidization of CEE economies through further imports of 'soft' goods. Another Soviet opinion believes that quasi-clearing makes Soviet enterprises uninterested in exports to the countries concerned.

Some trade in commodities that are not included in the list will be conducted on the Soviet side, at the republic or regional level. Part of the revenues will flow to republic and regional level foreign-currency funds, where the authorities may allocate these sources to enterprises in the region.

A third channel of trade will be direct enterprise-to-enterprise transactions. Potential importers of CEE commodities are those Soviet enterprises which either possess foreign currency (retained from export incomes) or which are designated importers of commodities registered on the bilateral indicative lists. The unclear conditions of barter make the import from the CEE by other enterprises extremely difficult.

Several unsettled problems remain, that were inherited from the transferable-ruble accounting era. It is not clear how the accumulated TR trade surplus of the CEE economies will be compensated for by the Soviet Union. Deliveries calculated in TR terms continued in the first half of 1991 (deliveries based on contracts signed in 1990), no data are available as yet on final TR balances. According to estimates made, Czechoslovakia has accumulated a surplus of around TR 2.8 billion vis-à-vis the Soviet Union; the Hungarian surplus for the past two years amounts to TR 2 billion; the accumulated Polish surplus is estimated at TR 7.6 billion; the surpluses of Romania and Bulgaria are smaller: TR 400 million and 500 million, respectively.[10] The TR conversion coefficient was 0.92:1 for Hungary and 1:1 for the Czechoslovakia in 1990. No information is available about the rates for other countries. Some details of vital importance are still unclear: how long will the repayment last? What will the interest rate be?

Will repayment be made in cash or in kind? Will there be linkage between accumulated trade surpluses and other unsettled problems in CEE-Soviet relations? Although some of these issues have already been resolved in bilateral CEE-Soviet agreements, in none of them have all these issues been finally settled. Thus it is completely unclear to the CEE economies to what extent they can rely on Soviet compensation in the coming critical years.

The problem of trade surpluses carried over from the former trade regime is only one of many unsettled questions. It is not clear how former credits provided in TR are to be repaid. This is a major problem in Poland, which owes the Soviet Union TR 4.7 billion (plus US$ 1.8 billion).[11] Although an agreement has been reached about linking the junction of the Polish trade surplus with the Polish TR debt, Poland insists on mutual exchange of goods while the Soviets prefer a financial arrangement. The future of joint investment projects in the Soviet Union is also uncertain. The re-calculation of CEE contributions in dollar terms and compensation for them by Soviet deliveries is still unsolved. The same problem emerges with the two CMEA banks and other CMEA institutions. There has been a major Soviet military presence in Hungary and Czechoslovakia since 1945 and 1968, respectively. Soviet troops left both countries in the Summer of 1991, but there is no agreement in sight on the extent of compensation the two countries should pay for military and non-military projects built by the Soviet army that can be utilized after the Soviet troops leave. To complicate the problem even further, Hungarians and Czechoslovaks demand compensation for all the environmental damage caused by the Soviet army.

Future *oil prices* will exert a decisive influence on CEE-Soviet relations. Relatively low oil prices after the Gulf war helped the CEE economies to cover their energy bills in 1991. Nevertheless, these low oil prices did not help CEE-Soviet trade, as the Soviet Union has relatively less income from overall energy exports. Severe problems in oil extraction mean that smaller quantities will be exported. Less foreign currency income translates into less imports, also from the CEE economies, and into a (tougher) negotiation policy dealing with unsettled issues.

Western assistance can influence CEE-Soviet relations directly if the idea of an East European Payments Union is realized, with the participation of the Soviet Union and with massive Western financial support. This seems unlikely in the immediate future. Western support for individual CEE economies and the Soviet Union (by providing easier access to Western markets) will narrow the basis for mutual trade as it intensifies economic relations with countries outside the region. Western humanitarian aid for the Soviet Union (free deliveries of food and medicine) may involve some deliveries from the CEE economies, financed by the West, but individual Western governments may prefer deliveries by their own domestic producers.

It is extremely difficult to evaluate the first experiences of the hard currency trade regime in the mutual trade of former COMECON countries.

One reason for this is that the old trade system partly survived because deliveries on contracts signed in 1990 were denominated in TRs up to the summer months, with varying deadlines in individual bilateral relations. Another reason is that it is still impossible to separate the decline caused by technical difficulties of transition to the new regime (which may lead to a temporary drop in the turnover) from the decrease in trade caused by lasting effects. Nevertheless, in 1991 Soviet exports to CEE economies dropped by 57 percent, Soviet imports from the CEE economies fell by 62 percent.[12] No reliable information is available on mutual trade between the CEE economies.

The Future of Regional Economic Cooperation

The introduction of hard currency payments on January 1, 1991, broke the backbone of the East European economic integration. The failed attempts to revive any kind of institutionalized economic cooperation led to the dissolution of the COMECON without being replaced by an alternative body. This development clearly indicated the lack of consensus in the countries concerned about future economic cooperation in the region.

Why is it so difficult to find consensus? Any attempt to find the proper answer should take into consideration the diverging interests of the former COMECON countries. The Soviet Union would like to preserve at least some of its former influence in the region, while minimizing the losses which could, under certain circumstances, derive from preferential treatment of former allies. Czechoslovakia, Hungary and Poland wish to be full members of the European Community and, till then, to promote closer cooperation with one another. The political instability that accompanied the transformation process in Bulgaria and Romania hindered the formulation of these two countries' approach to regional economic cooperation. The less-developed COMECON members (Cuba, Mongolia and Vietnam) wanted to preserve some of their privileges and the economic assistance they enjoyed earlier. Reconciliation of these interests proved to be impossible.

In early 1991 two versions of economic cooperation in the region were seriously discussed: trilateral cooperation within the Czechoslovak-Hungarian-Polish triangle, and the idea of a Central European payments union.[13]

Toward an East European Free Trade Association?

In 1990 the EC initiated negotiations on association agreements with Czechoslovakia, Hungary and Poland. Agreements have already been concluded in 1991.[14] These association agreements will make it possible for the three countries concerned to gradually achieve the present status of the European Free Trade Area (EFTA) countries. Tariffs and remaining quotas will no longer be applied for industrial products. Free trade will be implemented asymmetrically. Elimination of trade barriers will come quicker on the EC side, thus competition imposed by EC suppliers on the still fragile East European markets will emerge with a certain time lag.

However positive these changes may be for the countries concerned, Poland, Hungary and Czechoslovakia will have to heed the 'message', namely, that their hope for full membership within a relatively short time is not realistic. Before membership is seriously considered, these countries will have to go through a stage of association. Moreover, like it or not, associate membership does not provide any guarantee of full membership later.

Taking into consideration the enormous efforts required for completion of the EC's aims for 1992, and the negotiations about the possible entry of Austria, Sweden (and perhaps other Scandinavian states) open questions of coexistence with the EFTA, and the impatience of Turkey, still sitting in the 'ante-chamber' of the EC, there is little room for optimism in Czechoslovakia, Hungary and Poland. While all the advantages of the association agreements, soon to be concluded, will certainly have to be exploited, the trade policy of these countries should seriously analyze the conclusion of trade agreements with other groups of countries or single countries. These agreements cannot make up for the full membership in the EC, but they could complement the association agreement.

The most obvious such step could be the establishment of a free-trade association of radically reforming Czechoslovakia, Hungary and Poland. This could somewhat restrain the present and expected steep decline in the mutual trade of the economies concerned and could, in time, create trade as well. However, the Visegrad summit in February 1991 did not fulfill the expectation that the three countries would announce the establishment of a free-trade association. It is not clear what happened; 'intra-triangle' economic and political considerations may have played a role, and the politicians of the three countries may not have wanted to provoke the Soviet Union by the establishment of a new bloc before an arrangement to phase out the COMECON was achieved. However, it must be pointed out that besides the often mentioned readiness for cooperation with each other, these countries are not necessarily eager to be lumped together; each can argue for quicker entry in to the EC than the other two countries. Thus, rivalry in the region is a factor to be reckoned with.[15]

The Planned Central European Payments Union

As the burdens of a transition to hard currency settlement became obvious to a wider circle of Western experts, the idea of creating a regional payments union was raised.[16] This institution, professionally known as the Central European Payments Union (CEPU), would be a multilateral clearing system, similar to the European Payments Union (EPU) that was organized after World War II. The EPU had been supported financially by the United States as part of the Marshall Plan. The CEPU is also designed to generate external financing by the industrialized countries of the world. The basic idea is to forestall a dramatic decline in mutual trade among the members of the dying COMECON and to give impetus to trade creation within the region wherever possible. The center of the multiclearing system, most probably to be located somewhere in Western Europe, would try to smooth away trade imbalances, thus creating the presumed preconditions for a higher level of intra-regional trade.

Which countries would join the multiclearing system? The smallest circle would comprise the radically reforming countries: Hungary, Czechoslovakia and Poland. A wider version would include Romania and Bulgaria. In its broadest version the CEPU would include the five countries mentioned and the Soviet Union. The composition of the CEPU is the critical point of its construction. The CEPU with the Soviet Union would be a completely different organization from one without it.

The share of the CEE countries in each other's foreign trade is relatively low and declining. The lesson of 1990, when intra-CEE trade declined sharply despite the prevailing clearing payments, might be that 'soft' goods are no longer marketable in the region regardless of the form of payment. If nothing remains but hard goods, it is questionable whether a new clearing system is still necessary.

After the introduction of hard-currency payments, Soviet trade surpluses are expected to persist in Soviet-CEE trade. Thus the CEPU with Soviet Union membership would help the CEE economies to maintain their imports from the Soviet Union. However, multilateral clearing cannot cope with long-lasting one-sided imbalances, where deficits and surpluses persist over time. When the initial fund is used up, the system will cease to function. The crucial question is whether the Soviet Union, which recently abolished clearing agreements with Yugoslavia and Finland, and has an interest in emphasizing the losses which it suffered as a consequence of clearing with the COMECON countries, will be ready to join the CEPU.

The other side of this problem is whether it would be expedient to support the CEE countries so that they can carry on exporting to the Soviet Union (as long as the reserves of the clearing center last)? The answer is a qualified yes. Lower level of unemployment and less underutilized capacities will be the result. On the other hand, most of the enterprises in Eastern Europe that specialized in the Soviet market are big, inefficient, noncompetitive, state-owned enterprises. The danger is that the least competitive economic agents of the region might be encouraged by Western financial assistance to avoid adjustment by preserving their comfortable market.

Probably the financing of the CEPU is not the most effective way of utilizing Western support. The *economies* of Eastern Europe should survive the coming critical years—but not the less efficient segment of their state-owned industry. A more efficient mode of Western support could be debt service relief, setting up special funds to help privatization or to promote the export ability of medium and small enterprises.

While discussion has been going on about the pros and cons of the CEPU it should be pointed out that up to now no enthusiasm for this idea can be observed in the official circles of the COMECON countries.

Conclusions

It seems that the prospects of both simple trade relations and institutionalized economic cooperation are rather poor in the former COMECON region, at least for the immediate future. A decline in intra-regional trade seems to be unavoidable in the short run. Technical difficulties related to the new payments system, mutual distrust and the general aversion of the enterprises and of the population to products from within the region will probably eliminate not only trade in really obsolete products, but a substantial part of trade in manufactures of acceptable or good quality as well. Most probably neither a payments union nor a free-trade association will be able to prevent a temporary decline. The relevant question now is not how to avoid this decline, but the following one: once the nadir is reached, probably in 1991 or at the latest in 1992, what means could be applied to encourage the revival of intra-regional trade?

A minimalist target could be for the countries concerned to avoid a situation in which conditions for a free-trade association are created for trade between the individual East European economies and partners in the EC and the EFTA, while with respect to trade among former COMECON members, the Most Favored Nation treatment is to be applied. This situation may emerge if the agreements on associated membership between the two West European blocs and individual former COMECON members come in force while the former COMECON countries cannot come to terms on new conditions of mutual trade. If this happens, CEE countries will in effect discriminate against one another in favor of trade with Western Europe.

Although it is really a minimalist program, the creation of a free trade association of former COMECON economies seems to be feasible in a relatively short time, while more ambitious targets, as mentioned earlier in this article, are not feasible under the present conditions. Nevertheless a simple removal of trade barriers and placing trade with Western Europe on an equal footing with mutual trade may in itself be enough for the revival of mutual trade in Eastern Europe in the longer run. Revitalized mutual trade will differ substantially from trade settled in TRs terms, both as concerns the economic agents participating and with respect to the commodities traded. Traditional participants (a small number of big, inefficient, state-owned, specialized foreign-trade companies with monopolistic rights to conduct trade in selected groups of commodities) will be replaced by thousands of competing firms: big and small, domestic and partly or fully foreign owned, private and state-owned. Commodity composition will change substantially as well. The obsolete manufactured products dominating under the old TR trade regime, will be driven out. With regard to the mutual distrust and the prevailing bad image of products of East European origin, most probably the only commodities with any future in the emerging new intra-regional trade will be those that have excellent references from Western markets. Thus the shortest way to the neighbors may lead via the Western markets, at least in the immediate future.

Notes

1. The COMECON ceased to exist at the end of June 1991.

2. CEE economies include Bulgaria, Czechoslovakia, Hungary, Poland and Romania.

3. UN Databank.

4. For further contemplations on the effects of the shift to hard-currency payment see András Köves (1991).

5. For a detailed analysis of the economic situation of the Soviet Union see Havlik (1991).

6. For a detailed analysis see Balabanov and Havlik (1991).

7. *Ekonomika i zhizn*, No. 1, January 9, 1991.

8. The ban on barter was lifted in July 1991, but information on the effects of this measure is not yet available.

9. Such inventories have already been agreed upon by some Soviet Republics and some CEE countries.

10. *Lidové Noviny*, February 6, 1991; *Rzeczpospolita*, March 1, 1991; *Magyar Hirlap*, March 9, 1991; *Világgazdaság*, January 25, 1991.

11. *Rzeczpospolita*, March 1, 1991.

12. Estimate based on data from supplement to *Ekonomika i zhizn*, No. 30, 1991.

13. In this chapter the author could not take into consideration the acceleration of political and economic disintegration of the Soviet Union after the unsuccessful military coup in August 1991.

14. Similar agreements are under negotiation with the EFTA.

15. The second 'triangle' summit in Cracow (October 1991) did not bring about a breakthrough either.

16. UN Economic Commission for Europe (1990), pp. 5–26, 140–150; Jozef van Brabant (1990).

References

Balabanov, T. and P. Havlik. 1991. "Soviet Energy and Petrochemical Industries Face Crisis," Manuscript, Vienna 1991.

Brabant, Jozef van. 1991. "On Reforming the Trade and Payments Regimes in the CMEA," *Jahrbuch der Wirtschaft Osteuropas*, Band 14/2 1990, pp. 7-30.

Havlik, P. 1991. "Soviet Union: Economy Heading for Collapse," Manuscript, Vienna.

Köves, A. 1991. "Transforming Commercial Relations within the CMEA: The case of Hungary," In: *Foreign Economic Liberalization*, edited by András Köves and Paul Marer, Boulder, San Francisco and Oxford, Westview Press, pp. 171–183.

Rácz, M. and S. Richter. 1989. "Some Aspects of the Hungarian-Soviet Economic Relations in 1971-1985," *WIIW-Forschungsberichte*, No. 153. Vienna. February.

Richter, Sándor. 1989. "The Economic Relations of Austria, Finland, Yugoslavia and Hungary with the Soviet Union," *WIIW Forschungsberichte*, No. 161, Vienna. October.

——. 1990. "Hard Currency Settlement of Payments or Bilateralism and Clearing: How Long will the Dilemma Remain?" In Michael Marrese and Sándor Richter (eds.), *The Challenge of Simultaneous Economic Relations with East and West*, London: Macmillan.

UN Economic Commission for Europe. 1990. *Economic Survey of Europe in 1989–1990*. New York.

17

The Transition from the CMEA System of International Trade

Arye L. Hillman

The transition from socialism entails many changes in the organization of economic activity and the role of government. This chapter focuses on the transition in the conduct of international trade. Trade policy is interlinked with domestic transformation, and issues arise regarding the relationship between domestic and foreign trade liberalization. I begin with the framework of the Council for Mutual Economic Assistance (CMEA) within which socialist international trade was conducted.

Protectionism via the CMEA System

The CMEA system of international trade and payments, which was formally abandoned in January 1991, provided the institutional framework for the organization of international trade among the planned socialist economies.[1] The commodity composition of CMEA trade was part of each country's broader national plan; the international trade of the planned economy was also planned. Unplanned international trade would disrupt the national plan, and might wreak havoc with the domestic economy. Also, an appropriate non-market negotiating framework was required to facilitate international trade, since in a centrally planned economy both the output of the enterprises and raw materials and intermediate inputs are preallocated. The centrally planned economy did not rely on the market for domestic allocation and was therefore inconsistent with direct market transactions between domestic agents and foreigners. If enterprises had no discretion in domestic transactions, they could not be expected to be permitted to transact independently with foreigners. The CMEA system allowed the centrally planned economies to trade among themselves by facilitating government-to-government negotiation of international trade, in a manner consistent with domestic planning in each country.

Trade was, in principle, to be balanced. There was therefore no need for the settlement of imbalances in the value of goods traded, the balances denominated in transferable rubles could not automatically be carried over from one year to another, nor transferred from one country to another to balance a trade surplus in one country against a deficit in another. No international capital market transactions were made to accommodate trade imbalance, indeed they were inconsistent with a domestic economic system that had no internal capital market.[2] Precedent was important in the determination of the composition of international trade, both for purposes of stability and for the manageability of trade negotiations.

Since the economies' domestic prices of different goods differed and exchange rates were not rationalized,[3] there were potential gains from arbitrage between domestic and international transactions. Potential arbitrage gains were eliminated via a price-equalization mechanism that was, in effect, a system of trade taxes and subsidies which ensured that domestic prices and prices of internationally traded goods were equalized.[4] In a market economy, such a price-equalization mechanism is a protectionist device. For example, the variable levies of the European Community are precisely such a 'price-equalization mechanism' which ensures that prices of imports are no less than internal European prices, i.e., a protective tariff or an anti-dumping or countervailing duty in the West likewise equalizes the price of a domestic good and an import that is a close substitute. In a market economy, such equalization takes place via market adjustment (if the law of one price holds), as market supply and demand accommodate to the extra cost imposed on importers by the protective duties.

One can also view the price-equalization mechanism of the CMEA system as a protectionist device, although protection was not really necessary in the sense of the Western market economy. The international trade negotiators committed their respective countries to deliver prenegotiated quantities of goods. The execution of the exchange of goods was conducted by a Foreign Trade Organization (FTO) which had sole responsibility for international trade in particular products. This concentration of international trade in every product assured domestic 'stability'. The domestic enterprises did not confront competitive imports in the Western sense. Protection also encompassed exports, in that the CMEA protocols ensured export sales (if the protocols were adhered to). Interpreted in a market context, the FTO ensured stability by being the monopolistic supplier of imports, and the monopsonistic purchaser of goods for sale abroad. The application of market concepts to describe the FTO as a monopoly would however be inappropriate, since the FTO was (like everything else) a government agency—it followed orders rather than exercising independent discretion in transactions with foreigners. The price-equalization mechanism assured that the FTO made neither profits nor losses in its international transactions; surpluses or losses were absorbed, directly or indirectly, by the government budget.

The protective, non-competitive nature of CMEA trade led to the creation of a category of 'soft' goods; these goods, because of quality deficiencies, might not be marketable in a decentralized exchange conducted by individual enterprises. 'Soft' goods could be exchanged in bilateral trade, each country's negotiators agreeing to take the other's; or (a characteristic feature of trade between Eastern Europe and the Soviet Union), East European 'soft' goods could be exchanged for Soviet 'hard' goods.[5]

The soft/hard good distinction was a basis for comparative advantage in CMEA international trade;[6] although not a satisfactory one from the Soviet Union's point of view. Not only did the Soviet Union supply 'hard' goods in exchange for 'soft' goods, but also—owing to the terms of trade for such exchange—the Soviet Union provided East European economies with sizable resource transfers.[7]

The Soviet Union thus lost on two counts from CMEA trade: imports were inferior to Western substitutes in both quality and technological level, and exports of 'hard' goods (oil, raw materials, etc.) were supplied at prices that were, in relative terms, lower than Western market prices. This does not mean that there were no gains for the Soviet Union from CMEA trade. Rather, the Soviet Union would have gained more from its international trade, had it been conducting trade at prevailing world prices and had it chosen (or been free to choose) sources of imports without regard for the obligation to maintain the special relationships of the CMEA system.

Conversely, the CMEA terms of trade were advantageous to the East European economies; it has been proposed that this was intended to be so, to maintain the loyalty of these countries to the Soviet Union.[8] The Soviet Union was paying the price of the 'cost of the empire'. Once the Soviet leadership ceased to see the 'need' for an empire, this might be expected to lead to the demise of the CMEA system of international trade—as did indeed occur in January 1991, when the CMEA transferable ruble (TR) clearing system was replaced by trade payable in convertible currency at world prices. The disappearance of East Germany made the change more abrupt. Enterprises in Eastern Europe lost the protection of the CMEA system that had been provided by assured planned-in-advance sales of 'soft' goods.

The CMEA system of international trade came to an end regardless of whether the East European economies were ready for it or not. The enterprises could not readily adjust from CMEA-negotiated sales to Western markets, since their capital stock, technology, and approach to 'marketing' were not suited to Western market transactions.[9] If the end of the CMEA system of trade and payments also meant an end to the prior special trading relationships, and the imposition of a requirement of orientation towards Western markets, substantial adjustment would be required of domestic industry. Moreover, whereas in Western economies, the need for adjustment due to trade-related changes might affect one industry at a time, or perhaps several industries at once (as, for example, in the case of across-the-board liberalization following GATT negotiations), in Eastern Europe the need for adjustment affected the entire domestic industry.[10]

This cost of adjustment had kept the enterprises oriented toward their CMEA sales, even if the government might have wished otherwise. The resistance to a reorientation towards Western markets is demonstrated most explicitly by the failure of Polish enterprises in the early to mid-1970s to absorb and utilize the vast quantities of Western capital that the Polish government acquired and allocated to the enterprises.[11] It has been proposed that the Polish restructuring endeavor failed because of inadequacies of central planning.[12] But whatever these inadequacies, the enterprises had no incentive to leave the cozy, protected system of CMEA trade for the competitive environment of the world market. When the departure came, it was instigated by the Soviet Union—although not necessarily equally resisted by all East European countries.

Hungary, in particular, despite some ambivalence regarding the terms-of-trade loss and concerns about sustaining past CMEA exports to the Soviet Union, was prepared to quit the CMEA system, given its protracted difficulties with imbalances under the CMEA clearing system. However, in Hungary, where central planning was officially abolished in 1968, CMEA trade nevertheless also offered favorable conditions to domestic enterprises relative to Western market exchange. There was little reason for the enterprise to expose itself to competition in the West when government negotiators could ensure sales that were guaranteed in advance in the CMEA. Exports to the West would require both price and quality competition. Price competition, in turn, would encounter the anti-dumping codes and other protectionism devices of the Western economies.[13] A few enterprises could, and were prepared to confront Western competition for some ranges of their output, and Hungary was successful in increasing exports to the West in the 1980s,[14] but quality was often poor by Western standards (the soft–good phenomenon).

Since CMEA sales were negotiated by the state and specified via state protocols, and because forint payment for CMEA sales was immediate and CMEA quality demands were not stringent, it was in the interest of the enterprise to remain within the CMEA system as far as exports were concerned. Under the clearing system, this could result in a conflict of interests between the enterprises and the state. For example, Hungarian enterprises persisted in exporting to the Soviet Union in 1989, when, under the conditions of the clearing system, there were at the margin no goods forthcoming as offsetting imports from the Soviet Union, and the TR balances accumulated were of dubious value.[15] The state was therefore obliged to intervene, to impose administrative restrictions on exports.

Such intervention to limit exports in response to the appearance of a trade surplus is characteristic of bilateral clearing systems, and forms the basis of the case for replacing bilateral clearing systems of trade management (such as the CMEA system) with the multilateralism of a convertible currency regime of international trade.

The Soviet Union 'liberated' the East European economies from the CMEA clearing system in 1991, but also imposed trade at world prices. 'Liberation' came at a price.

Even in the post-CMEA regime, domestic enterprises had good reason to prefer a continuation of traditional Soviet sales rather than confront exposure to Western market competition. In anticipation of the 1991 changes, many prominent Hungarian enterprises in 1990 envisaged maintaining (even expanding) Soviet sales under the post-CMEA regime, (Hillman, 1992). However, under the new payments scheme, Soviet customers needed hard currency to purchase East European goods. Finding the hard currency became the issue; and even if it were found, the traditional Soviet customers were no longer bound by the state-negotiated trade protocols—they could just as well buy alternative Western goods. If the hard currency were not found, again, exports to the Soviet Union would decrease, as was the case when the CMEA regime ended in 1991.

Thus, in the post-CMEA regime, in Hungary and other East European countries, the protection provided by the CMEA system was no longer present—unless other bilateral clearing arrangements were negotiated.[16]

Paternalism, Protectionism and 'Socialist' Markets

Trade policy under the CMEA system did not have the same connotation as in a Western market economy since, as we have seen, CMEA trade was in itself inherently protectionist for domestic enterprises. Trade with the West could prove problematic, especially if the government professed to have moved from central planning to the market and sought to substantiate this claim by joining the General Agreement on Tariffs and Trade (GATT), or where conditionality obligations are accepted for World Bank loans, as in the case of Hungary. Since the Hungarian economy could not accommodate competitive Western imports without disadvantaging domestic enterprises and destabilizing domestic employment, trade liberalization obligations could only be a political liability for a government that still claimed to be 'socialist'. Trade policy towards the West could only be conducted surreptitiously, concealed by protectionist barriers that were never officially acknowledged.[17]

GATT membership was part of the facade of the markets that were contained in the 'market-socialist' system.[18] It is ironic that when in 1990, the Hungarian government sought to replace the quantitative restrictions (that had never officially existed) with tariffs that would allow accommodation to a more liberal trade policy, the problem encountered was that officially there were no quantitative restrictions to remove. Increased tariffs could therefore not be presented as part of a process of liberalization, but could officially only reflect increased protectionism, until the non-tariff barriers that had protected domestic enterprises from Western competitive imports in the past were formally acknowledged.

The experience of Hungarian 'market-socialism' takes on broader applicability because abolishing central planning without privatizing socialist industry yields precisely the institutional structure of the 'market-socialist' system. I have suggested elsewhere (Hillman, 1991) a model of endogenous international trade policy appropriate for this system.[19] The motivating puzzle in an evaluation of the determinants of international trade policy is that, in a capitalist economy, asymmetry in factor ownership underlies the gains from protectionist policies: that is, unequal ownership of capital gives some individuals an interest in maximizing the returns to capital ownership rather than maximizing national income, and therefore an interest in protection rather than in free trade.[20] In a socialist economy, these ownership asymmetries are moderated by the collective ownership of industry, and ostensibly (unlike in capitalist economies) free-trade tendencies should dominate—if ownership asymmetry were, as claimed by the neoclassical models of international trade, the fundamental determinant of individual interest in the outcome of trade policy. Of course, the neoclassical trade models *assume* sustained full employment, which contradicts the experience of the capitalist market economies; the assumption is justified in the literature by the long-run perspective of the models, and by the focus on long-run comparative advantage and efficient resource allocation rather than on stabilization concerns (which are left to macroeconomic theory). The sustained job security of workers is, of course, a prime consideration in an economy that professes to be socialist (Yugoslav experience aside here);[21] in such an economy hidden unemployment is politically (or ideologically) preferable to explicit unemployment and improved efficiency. If the planners have been dismissed and the market introduced in their place,[22] the government faces the problem that the market can be the source of employment and income instability for workers. This is in particular the case with respect to competition emanating from world markets. Without protectionist trade policies, competitive imports may compromise the objective of sustained full employment.

Potential labor unemployment due to import competition can also influence the conduct of trade policy in Western market economies, where governments can likewise be concerned with protecting 'jobs' against foreign competition.[23] Relative sensitivity to unemployment is a matter of degree reflected in the tradeoff between employment and other policy objectives. In the 'market-socialist' system, the (socialist) government was sufficiently sensitive to unemployment to make job security the prime policy objective.[24] To contain the potential instability of exposure to markets, an implicit social contract can be posited between the enterprise and the state, whereby the enterprise paternalistically undertakes to protect its workers, and the state paternalistically undertakes to protect the enterprise from competition. The justification offered by the firm for the 'need' for protection is that the firm should not be made to compete with producers (located abroad or at home) who do not have the same social obligations towards their workers. For in protecting the job security of workers from the consequences of market fluctuations in demand for its output, the firm incurrs costs that are avoided by a less socially conscious enterprise and, in particular, will not be incurred by Western producers who are the sources of competitive imports.[25]

In this 'market-socialist' system, the protection extended to the domestic enterprise is not only against imports; it is quite general, and there are administrative barriers to domestic entry as well. The legal 'responsibility to supply' of the enterprise under the planned economic system persists de facto, but becomes the 'right to supply' particular goods in the domestic market. Domestic stability is thereby sustained in the presence of 'markets', by means of a highly protectionist system. This system is inconsistent with liberalization of international trade. Trade liberalization breaks the implicit contract and denies the established rights of incumbent enterprises to their domestic markets, leading to liberalization dilemmas because of the government's commitment to protect domestic, socially conscious enterprises from import competition.

I am being overly abstract here, in the sense that 'socialist' markets in the CMEA were peculiar to post-1968 Hungary.[26] However, where Hungary has been, others will follow, as market allocative mechanisms replace planners, but privatization of state (or socialist) industry does not proceed at a pace that can lay the foundations on which a private enterprise economy can be established.[27] The analogy is complete if, in pursuit of objectives of domestic stability and employment security, the existing enterprises remain protected against foreign competition. Short-term stability objectives can then be met, while the government and policymakers ponder how to facilitate the transition from socialism with the least disruption to domestic economic life. If the battle against price instability had been lost, as in Poland, the government can attempt drastic change, as in the Big Bang of January 1990. However, although the Big Bang compromised the job security of many workers, hidden unemployment was not eliminated.[28] The Big Bang did not entail massive privatization, so that employment decisions were not being made by managers responsible to private residual claimants. Moreover, although the Big Bang introduced substantial uncertainty and instability, there is evidence[29] that the conception of anticipated paternalistic government policy response persisted; that is, managers believed that the government would not let enterprises fail. Given the political base of Solidarity, the Big Bang of January 1990 did not herald an end to the priority of government preoccupation with workers' job security. Financial discipline imposed on the state enterprises by the state could have compelled adjustment by imposing hard enterprise liquidity constraints.[30]

Privatization and Trade Liberalization

In the West the chain of paternalism—from the state to the enterprise, and from the enterprise to the job security of its workers—is broken by private ownership of firms and by the profit motive. This suggests that privatization is an essential prerequisite for a liberal international trade policy. The privatized enterprise would presumably seek to minimize production costs and would not be encumbered by 'responsibilities' towards its workers that provide the basis (or justification) for paternalistic protectionist policies.

Of course, privatization alone cannot ensure a liberal trade policy. It is, however, a precondition in the countries in transition from socialism, given the protectionism based on the tradition of paternalism. That privatization does not suffice to ensure a liberal international trade policy is evident enough from the protectionist policies pursued in Western market economies and elsewhere.[31]

Once enterprises are privatized, interests in the conduct of international trade policy associated with private ownership come into play. These interests are expressed in the specific-factors (or Ricardo-Viner) model of international trade, where residual claimants to capital in the domestic import-competing sector are shown to have an unambiguous interest in protection, while residual claimants in a sector in which the economy has a comparative advantage lose from protection. The position of intersectorally mobile factors with regard to trade policy depends on consumption preferences; they lose or gain from protection as consumption is biased towards goods in which the economy has a comparative disadvantage or advantage, respectively.

This specific-factors analytical framework for identifying gainers from protection is based on a short-run perspective, in the sense that the short run is defined such that capital is intersectorally immobile, or capital is committed to the production of a particular good. In a longer-term perspective where capital is intersectorally mobile and there are no sector-specific interests, the Stolper-Samuelson Theorem of the Heckscher-Ohlin model identifies gainers and losers from protection; an economy's relatively scarce factors gain from protection: the relatively abundant factors lose.

In each case, these are competitive models; monopoly rents are not the source of gain or loss from protection. However, the models indicate that even in a perfectly competitive private-property-rights economy, individual self-interest will not generally lie in the pursuit of a liberal international trade policy—precisely because of the private property rights that underlie asymmetric ownership. In these neoclassical models, a scheme of equal sharing of the returns to the economy's factors of production among the populace would dissipate all protectionist pressures, since a liberal trade policy facilitates efficient resource allocation and trade in accord with comparative advantage, thereby maximizing aggregate national income and hence average national income.

In a theory of endogenous protection, we look for the reasons for protectionist policies by considering the self-interests of the gainers and losers from protection. In making the transition from socialism via privatization, one set of endogenous determinants of protection is replaced by another; but the rules of the game also change. Job security is no longer sacrosanct in the private-ownership market economy and unemployment appears. Excess supply of labor replaces the employment security of the shortage economy. Unemployment is central here: as I have observed, the theoretical frameworks provided by the models used to portray international trade of the Western market economy *assume* full employment which the socialist shortage economy *assured*.

Thus privatization replaces one set of pressures for protectionism with another, and there is no assurance of emergence of a liberal international trade policy. But certainly, in the Western market economy, a countervailing influence on policy is present in the form of the gainers from a liberal international trade policy, while the socialist economy's overriding concern with employment stability is inconsistent with competitive unanticipated (or unplanned) imports.

It is not only workers who, via unemployment and job security, stand to lose from liberalization of international trade in economies in transition from socialism. Managers of the enterprises are also potential losers from liberalization, since their economic interests are tied to the continued viability of the enterprise. In a transitionary period, management can be expected to express concern lest restructuring or policy change result in displacement of employees, and, while seeking Western labor-saving technology, managers may nevertheless assume responsibility for finding alternative employment within the enterprise for 'their' workers. This responsibility is, on the one hand, an expression of the paternalistic aspects of the socialist enterprise; but also there is an element of managers' self-interest in the 'insurance' role of the workers. Managers can exploit the issue of workers' security, since political support of the government is adversely affected by policies that result in workers losing their jobs, that is, by exposing the enterprise to import competition.

The political constraints imply that restructuring will be most rapid where the political cost of unemployment is smallest. Thus, in East Germany, the pace of restructuring was rapid, in the sense of exposure of enterprises to liberal 'international' trade policies that were no longer international. East German adjustment became a regional rather than an international problem. The realization of the cost of adjustment (unemployment, and the rehabilitation or closure of nonviable former socialist enterprises) was a reflection of the ongoing process of restructuring. Had East Germany begun the transition from socialism as an independent state rather than via unification, the pace of restructuring would have been slower, and levels of unemployment lower. Confirmation is provided by comparing events in East Germany after unification with the pace of change and the protracted political deliberations on how and when to privatize and adjust in other former CMEA economies.

The losers in East Germany were the workers who lost their job security; in addition, the credentials of past management of socialist enterprises are of no value in a free-enterprise market economy.

Transplanted to other economies, where adjustment has a national rather than a regional focus, these experiences expose the origins of the resistance to trade liberalization and privatization. When a socialist enterprise is privatized, it is no longer the state's capital that is being protected by the state's protectionist policies; with the end of political party monopoly, the link between tenure in managerial positions in state enterprises and political connections lose significance, and in particular, managers exercise less political influence via the Party on the state's conduct of international trade policy. The paternalism of the state towards the workers is also correspondingly diminished when the enterprise is privately owned than when the state professes to be the guardian of the workers' collective claim to factors of production.

One step toward facilitating trade liberalization is thus putting an end to the ideology whereby the state is obliged to provide workers with employment security via protection against import competition (and against competition in general). Elements of this position are present in a private-property-rights market economy. The key question is whether ending or subduing this ideological influence on the conduct of international trade policy necessarily implies a need for privatization. The past traditions of state paternalism, expressed in the protection of the socialist industry, point to a positive answer, that is, to a need to privatize in order to abolish the notion of the state as the guarantor of the enterprise's right to operate without competition.

Transitionary Trade Policies

I shall now set aside the privatization issue to focus on international trade policy when domestic industries lag technologically behind Western competitors. The question I now wish to address concerns the pace of trade liberalization in the transition from socialism: is there a case for protection in the period of transition, or should trade liberalization be immediate? This is, of course, a normative question about what a government's decision *ought* to be, not what it *will* be. The question suggests the framework of the classical infant-industry argument, with the distinction that not an industry but the entire industrial sector of the economy needs to be restructured.

Related to the infant-industry argument is the concept of industrial policy, or targeting by the government, which identifies 'winners' and 'losers' and provides special assistance via tariff protection, quantitative restrictions or subsidies to prospective winners. The infant-industry argument explicitly assumes that protection or assistance is to be temporary, until the industry matures. The industrial-policy (or targeting) version of this argument does not bear this explicit temporal connotation.

The objective could not be to protect every enterprise that needs restructuring in the course of transition, since then every enterprise in the industrial sector becomes a candidate for protection. So 'targeting' appears to be an essential element of the infant industry argument as applied to restructuring in transition from socialism.

The graduated aspect of adjustment associated with the infant-industry argument—the idea that it takes time to adjust to new circumstances, to find one's niche, and to become competitive in international markets—fits in well with the more conservative policies that emphasize stability in the course of transition. But even a Big Bang approach is still consistent with targeting: blanket liberalization can be accompanied by special assistance for enterprises chosen by the government as the prospective winners.

There are well-known difficulties with the infant-industry argument for protection.[32] Temporary protection is nonetheless protection, and entails a cost. The offsetting social benefits could, it is argued, be the gains from facilitating the transition from the CMEA-oriented soft-goods economy to a level of technology and quality consistent with Western market competition. Are there legitimate positive 'externalities' associated with protection? Adaptation takes time, and it perhaps would be facile to suppose that domestic enterprises could survive import competition by superior Western products while at the same time seeking to restructure themselves.[33] The graduated proposal is to bar foreign competition for a while, to let the domestic enterprise 'prepare' for the more competitive environment and then to expose the enterprise to import competition.

The difficulty with such recommendations is that in the absence of foreign competition the domestic enterprise may have no incentive to restructure, certainly if the profit motive associated with privatization is absent. But even for a privatized enterprise, why restructure when the consequence of successful restructuring is exposure to foreign competition? The infant-industry argument applied here neglects the central role of incentives and moral hazard in influencing the restructuring process. Economies in transition from socialism cannot be exposed to the discipline of competition via the competitiveness of the domestic market, since high industry concentration and traditions of cooperation among enterprises preclude this. The sources of potential competitive pressures in the short to medium run can only be foreign competition.

However, protectionist policies rule out foreign competition. There is a solution to this dilemma, if the government is able to make a credible commitment that protection from foreign competition will be for a specified period of time. Such credible commitments are difficult, even impossible, if based on domestic conditions. Today's government is not tomorrow's government. Such a commitment advantages today's politician by imposing costs on tomorrow's politician—without a contractual arrangement that compels the latter to act in other than his own short-term interests as the date of liberalization approaches. The domestic political framework therefore cannot guarantee the requisite credible commitment that protection will be temporary. Realizing this, the enterprise, in accordance with its own incentives, will not be 'ready' to confront foreign competition at the time of the intended liberalization, and the outcome will be continued protection.

A credible commitment can be made if implementation is beyond the control of the national government, as via commitments bound by international obligations. A commitment to trade liberalization contained in a free-trade agreement, or by setting a date for access to the European Community, can counter enterprises' incentives to delay or indefinitely defer meeting the standards of foreign competitors.

Should the government in the course of the transition engage in an industrial policy of targeting particular enterprises? A benevolent government whose targeting is guided by considerations of comparative advantage in international trade may make mistakes; and the cost of such an error to a government official may not be all that great—especially if there is collective responsibility (or 'collective irresponsibility'). But it may be inappropriate to assume that the government is benevolent, i.e., that it is driven by an uncompromising quest for the greater social good. The choice may well be politicized, since there are benefits to be reaped from an enterprise's convincing politicians that it is a deserving candidate for special assistance. Politization of government decision making certainly occurs in Western economies, too. Economies that are abandoning the socialist system are seeking to distance themselves from the most politicized of economic decision-making structures. Enterprise targeting reestablishes the role of government in these economies as the central decision-making body with regard to investment allocation, which is a regressive rather than progressive move in the transition from socialist economic organization.

There are, however, natural pressures for targeting associated with the very fact of an enterprise's prior existence. The circumstances differ from those of an infant-industry argument applied to a new enterprise. Given that the enterprise already exists, the issue is whether it should be saved when confronted with bankruptcy. This leads to a further question, namely, will the comparative advantage exhibited by an enterprise under the CMEA system of trade be sustainable in the post-CMEA regime of trade and payments?

These are the types of questions that a government seeking to see a country through the transition will face. International trade theory would be helpful if it could assist in identifying comparative advantage. The simple answer that theory offers is that a competitive market will guide an economy towards its long-run comparative advantage. But this is of no avail to a government beset by short-run political problems, that is sensitive to unemployment, that seeks to secure a financial return from privatization of its enterprises (which may not have a comparative advantage) and where the domestic market structure is anything but perfectly competitive.

It is important to note that unqualified, traditional Heckscher-Ohlin type predictions do not provide a useful basis for identifying comparative advantage. Whether an economy in Eastern Europe is relatively capital-intensive is not a relevant question for ascertaining comparative advantage, without first considering what this capital is composed of. The capital that was specific to CMEA transactions may be of little relevance to international trade. If the CMEA-specific capital is written off, these economies become highly labor-abundant, in relative terms. But is the comparative advantage of the Central and East European economies the same as that of China?

Identification of comparative advantage by the government for the purpose of targeting, even if decision making were efficiency guided and non-politicized, is therefore problematical. Ultimately, we can only fall back on the market. In some enterprises, investors will find it worthwhile to upgrade and replace the capital stock, but not in others. The best judges are those people prepared to lay out the money—although there are also no guarantees that they will not make mistakes in particular instances. But this is what entrepreneurship and the rewards for risk taking are all about.

The government's problem is that in the course of restructuring by private investors (implying privatization and, in general, joint foreign ventures), the hidden unemployment sustained by the outgoing protectionist system will become explicit—thus evoking protectionist pressures.

Regional Preferential Trading Arrangements

Although the CMEA ceased to function at the beginning of 1991, the end of this system of trade and payments does not necessarily mean the end of demand for CMEA-quality goods. Goods of different qualities are traded in international markets. Income elasticities matter. While the conditions of trade with the prominent trading partner for the East European economies —the (former) Soviet Union—have changed, the prospective market remains. Due to internal economic conditions and political change, Soviet participation in international trade declined in 1990 and 1991. In particular, there were substantial decreases in Soviet oil exports. However, because of geographic proximity, the European republics of the former Soviet Union and the East European economies remain natural trading partners.

The links among the East European economies have led to proposals that these economies form a post-CMEA East European Payments Union (EEPU) similar to the European Payments Union (EPU) of the early 1950s.[34] Circumstances appear similar. The EPU was intended to facilitate international trade among the European economies by alleviating the difficulties associated with the need for dollars to undertake international transactions. An EEPU could overcome the liquidity constraints imposed by the need for hard currency payments in the East European economies' mutual trade. Like the EPU, the EEPU would facilitate multilateralism in exchange among members. Countries would not have to be concerned with their bilateral balances with one another, only with their aggregate trade balance vis-à-vis all trading partners within the Union. Since under post-CMEA arrangements the Central and East European economies need convertible currency for trade, the EEPU would allow gains from sharing hard-currency reserves, via intertemporal allocation that permits the surplus of one member to finance the deficit of another.

The disadvantages of an EEPU are prospective trade diversion and inward orientation of member countries.[35] The EEPU would be a preferential trading arrangement that would make it easier for enterprises in member countries to trade with one another rather than with outsiders. The concern is that such a preferential trading arrangement would give rise to a pattern of international trade inconsistent with the evolution of the East European economies towards integration in the wider international market. Also, credit would be allocated by an EEPU on the basis of a country's intra-union imbalances rather than aggregate imbalances, thereby distorting credit allocations. Basically, given the benefits and disadvantages, the desirability of an EEPU depends upon the alternative, specifically, on whether such an alternative is a multilateral arrangement or bilateralism that mimics the previous CMEA system.[36]

Conclusion

Geographically proximate countries are natural trading partners. For the countries of Central and Eastern Europe the issue is not one of evaluating the prospective consequences of opening trade between neighboring countries where previously there was none. The CMEA integrated these countries' international transactions. There is an issue, however, regarding how relevant post-'socialist' comparative advantage is to a future pattern of trade that is based on comparative advantage reflected in world market prices.

How, in a post-CMEA regime of trade and payments, the Central and East European economies were to trade with one another, and how they were to trade with the republics of the former Soviet Union, were fundamental policy questions. Transition would be required from the past dual structure of international trade with East and West. Convertible-currency requirements for trade among former CMEA members had upset traditional trading patterns by imposing cash-in-advance constraints; these constraints, because of the need for liquidity, inhibited mutually beneficial exchange. A clearing system avoids these constraints but introduces other problems. In particular, clearing systems require a monitoring role for government, when the aim is to eliminate the role of the state in monitoring international trade, and to facilitate enterprise-to-enterprise transactions in international trade.

Trade with the republics that had constituted the Soviet Union was subject to uncertainties regarding the nature and pace of change in the internal economic systems of these republics and effects on supply capabilities. The switch to convertible currency payment as of January 1991 meant that trade need no longer, in principle, be balanced, since deficits were to be made up in hard currency. However, the hard currency to facilitate trade was not available, nor were the institutions yet present that would permit enterprises in the republics of the former Soviet Union to conduct trade in the manner required by the new conditions. Under the circumstances, flexibility in adapting to the requirements of Western trade was the critical requisite, and some countries were, in this respect, more successful than others.[37]

With respect to Western orientation, economies with private property rights have been less protectionist than socialist economies. The considerations raised in this chapter suggest that trade liberalization is linked to the progress of privatization, as is the case with other objectives—efficient resource allocation, technological advance and effective stabilization policy—sought in the transition from socialism.

Notes

1. For a detailed exposition of the CMEA system, see Martin Schrenk (1992). A review of literature on international trade in the planned socialist economic system is provided by Thomas Wolf (1988).

2. If the state is the monopoly owner of all capital, there is no need for a market to facilitate trade in claims to capital.

3. For examples of types of distortions, drawn from the experience of Poland, see Tarr (1990a,b).

4. Schrenk (1992) describes the price-equalization mechanism. The Hungarian version is described by Abel, Hillman and Tarr (1992).

5. That is, goods that could in principle be sold in world markets for convertible foreign currency at prices that would cover costs of production—if such costs were known.

6. For an elaboration on the socialist concept of comparative advantage in CMEA trade, see Hillman and Schnytzer (1992).

7. Initial estimates of the transfer from the Soviet Union to the East European economies via the CMEA terms of trade were provided by Marrese and Vanous (1983). Further studies confirmed the transfers. See, e.g., Oblath and Tarr (1992) on the consequences for Hungary's terms of trade at the end of the CMEA era.

8. See Marrese and Vanous (1983).

9. The capital stock of the enterprises was to a large degree specific to CMEA transactions. On transaction-specifity of capital in East European enterprises, see Hillman and Schnytzer (1992).

10. See Hillman (1992) on the consequences of the magnitude of adjustment, with particular reference to Hungary.

11. Terrell (1992) reports, among other empirical results, a lack of adaptation of Polish industry to the availability of Western capital; the marginal product of CMEA capital in use by the Polish enterprises remained invariably positive, whereas overall the marginal product of Western capital in Polish industry was zero or negative.

12. See Terrell (1992) for a discussion of the reasons for this failure.

13. On the protectionist policies confronted by Hungary in access to the European Community, see Tovias and Laird (1991). Schuknecht (1991) documents the European Community's use of anti-dumping codes against imports from the East European economies.

14. For data on CMEA trade in the 1980s, see Schrenk (1992).

15. The Soviet Union subsequently agreed to convert the Hungarian TR surplus to dollars at a favorable exchange rate, ostensibly to facilitate the transition to trade at world prices in 1991 by providing Hungary with a means of adjusting to the terms-of-trade loss. However, ambiguities followed regarding access to and use of these funds.

16. As, for example, negotiated between Russia and Czechoslovakia in March 1991.

17. See Oblath (1989) and Gacs (1989).

18. On the nature of 'socialist' markets, see Hillman (1991) and Hinds (1991).

19. A theory of endogenous international trade policy seeks to explain why protectionist policies are adopted in face of the presumption of the Pareto-efficiency of free-trade policies, and also why protection takes different forms in different circumstances. Central to the theory of endogenous protection is the optimizing behavior of the policymaker. The theory of endogenous protection is to be contrasted with an approach to international trade policy that focuses on the effects of different protectionist policies, without reference to the motives and reasons underlying policy choice. The literature on endogenous protection is reviewed in Hillman (1989).

20. See Mayer (1984) for a model where the roles of factor-ownership are explicit in establishing international trade policy. Mayer shows how, in a system of direct democracy, where individuals vote on the single issue of the height of a protective tariff, the individual relative factor endowments of the median voter underlie deviations from Pareto-efficient free trade.

21. There is a substantial body of literature on the failure of the Yugoslav variant of market socialism. On the Yugoslav system in a comparative perspective, see Milanovic (1989).

22. Or there never was a central planner in the first place.

23. See Baldwin (1985) on the United States, and Schuknecht (1991) on the European Community.

24. On sustained full employment under Hungarian 'market socialism', see Hillman (1990).

25. For an elaboration on this model of endogenous protection, see Hillman (1991).

26. Yugoslavia was an associate member of the CMEA.

27. For a statement of the obstacles to privatization, with a focus on Hungary, see Tardos (1991). Milanovic (1992) provides a far-ranging analysis of privatization issues in the context of Eastern Europe.

28. I make this statement with a time horizon of a year after the Big Bang, which appears sufficient given the connotation of immediacy associated with this set of policies.

29. Gelb, Jorgensen and Singh (1992).

30. One year after the Big Bang, the objective of price stability had not been achieved. Moreover, owing to the links between the enterprise budget constraint and the fiscal discipline of the government, this had implications with respect to the financial discipline of the enterprises. See Hinds (1992).

31. In Western market economies, the conception of property rights to domestic markets by domestic producers—or the right to supply—is present, and is reflected in the nature of international trade negotiations where countries exchange market access for each others' producers. The absence of a necessary relationship between private ownership and liberal trade policies is also evidenced by the protectionist policies pursued by the less developed and developing countries of Asia, Africa and South and Central America. Havrylyshyn and Tarr (1991) provide a comparison between the roles of trade liberalization in the latter countries and the socialist economies in transition.

32. See, for example, Baldwin (1969).

33. The East German experience provides evidence.

34. Ethier (1992) describes in detail how such a union would function.

35. See Michalopoulos and Tarr (1992).

36. Ethier (1992) emphasizes that the judgment regarding an EEPU depends on what the 'default' is.

37. See Condon and Dervis (1992) on the success of Hungary.

References

Abel, Istvan, Arye L. Hillman and David Tarr. 1992. "The Government Budgetary Consequences of Reform of the CMEA System of International Trade: The Case of Hungary." In A. L. Hillman and B. Milanovic (eds.), *The Transition from Socialism in Eastern Europe: Domestic Restructuring and Foreign Trade.* Washington, DC: The World Bank.

Baldwin, Robert. 1969. "The Case Against Infant-Industry Tariff Protection," *Journal of Political Economy*, 77: 295–305.

——. 1985. *The Political Economy of U.S. Import Policy*, Cambridge, Mass.: MIT Press.

Condon, Timothy and Kemal Dervis. 1992. "Hungary: An Emerging Gradualist Success Story." Washington, DC: The World Bank.

Ethier, Wilfred J. 1992. "International Trade and Payments Mechanisms: Options and Possibilities, Another View." In A. L. Hillman and B. Milanovic (eds.), *The Transition from Socialism in Eastern Europe: Domestic Restructuring and Foreign Trade*, Washington, DC: The World Bank.

Gacs, Janos. 1989. "The Progress of Liberalization of Foreign Trade in Hungary," presented at *Conference on Attempts at Liberalization*. Budapest, November.

Gelb, Alan, Erika Jorgensen and Inderjit Singh. 1992. "Life After the Polish Big Bang: Episodes of Enterprise Behavior." In A. L. Hillman and B. Milanovic (eds.), *The Transition from Socialism in Eastern Europe: Domestic Restructuring and Foreign Trade*, Washington, DC: The World Bank.

Havrylyshyn, Oleh and David Tarr. 1991. "The Role of Trade Liberalization in the Transition to a Market Economy." In P. Marer and S. Zecchini (eds.), *The Transition to a Market Economy in Central and Eastern Europe*. Paris: OECD.

Hillman, Arye L. 1989. *The Political Economy of Protection*. London and New York: Harwood Academic Publishers.

——. 1990. "Macroeconomic Policy in Hungary and its Microeconomic Implications," *European Economy: Economic Transformation in Hungary and Poland.* Brussels: Commission of the European Community.

——. 1991. "Liberalization Dilemmas." In A. L. Hillman (ed.), *Markets and Politicians*. Boston and Dordrecht: Kluwer Academic Publishers.

——. 1992. "Enterprise Restructuring in the Transition from Hungarian Market Socialism." In: A. L. Hillman and B. Milanovic (eds.) *The Transition from Socialism in Eastern Europe: Domestic Restructuring and Foreign Trade.* Washington, DC: The World Bank.

—— and Adi Schnytzer. 1992. "Creating the Reform-Resistant Trade-Dependent Economy: Socialist Comparative Advantage, Enterprise Incentives, and the CMEA." In A. L. Hillman and B. Milanovic (eds.), *The Transition from Socialism in Eastern Europe: Domestic Restructuring and Foreign Trade.* Washington, DC: The World Bank.

Hinds, Manuel. 1991. "Incentives and Ownership in Socialist Countries in Transition." In A. L. Hillman (ed.), *Markets and Politicians*, Boston and Dordrecht: Kluwer Academic Publishers.

——. 1992. "Policy Effectiveness in Reforming Socialist Economies." In A. L. Hillman and B. Milanovic (eds.), *The Transition from Socialism in Eastern Europe: Domestic Restructuring and Foreign Trade*. Washington, DC: The World Bank.

Marrese, Michael and Jan Vanous. 1983. *Soviet Subsidization of Trade with the Soviet Union*. Berkeley: University of California Press.

Mayer, Wolfgang. 1984. "Endogenous Tariff Formation," *American Economic Review*, 74: 970–985.

Michalopoulos, Constantine and David Tarr. 1992. "Proposals for Post-CMEA Trade and Payments Arrangements." In A. L. Hillman and B. Milanovic (eds.), *The Transition from Socialism in Eastern Europe: Domestic Restructuring and Foreign Trade*. Washington, DC: The World Bank.

Milanovic, Branko. 1989. *Liberalization and Entrepreneurship: Dynamics of Reform in Socialism and Capitalism*. New York and London: M.E. Sharpe.

——. 1992. "Privatization Options and Procedures." In A. L. Hillman and B.

Milanovic (eds.), *The Transition from Socialism in Eastern Europe: Domestic Restructuring and Foreign Trade*. Washington, DC: The World Bank.

Oblath, Gabor. 1989. "Opening up in Hungary: The Relevance of International Experiences and Some Peculiarities." Presented at *Conference on Attempts at Liberalization*. Budapest. November.

—— and David Tarr. 1992. "The Terms of Trade Effect of the Switchover to Hard Currency in Hungarian-Soviet Trade," *Journal of Comparative Economics*.

Schrenk, Martin. 1992. "The CMEA System of Trade and Payments: Initial Conditions for Institutional Change." In A. L. Hillman and B. Milanovic (eds.), *The Transition from Socialism in Eastern Europe: Domestic Restructuring and Foreign Trade*. Washington, DC: The World Bank.

Schuknecht, Ludger. 1991. *The Political Economy of EC Trade Policy*. Ph.D dissertation, University of Konstanz.

Tardos, Marton. 1991. "Restoring Property Rights." In A. L. Hillman (ed.), *Markets and Politicians*. Boston and Dordrecht: Kluwer Academic Publishers.

Tarr, David. 1990a. "Quantifying Second-Best Effects in Grossly Distorted Economies: The Case of the Butter Market in Poland," *Journal of Comparative Economics*, 14: 105–119.

——. 1990b. "Second-Best Foreign Exchange Policy in the Presence of Domestic Price Controls and Export Subsidies," *World Bank Economic Review*, 4: 105–119.

Terrell, Katherine. 1992. "International Technology Transfer and Efficiency in Socialist Enterprises: The Polish Failure of the 1970s." In A. L. Hillman and B. Milanovic (eds.), *The Transition from Socialism in Eastern Europe: Domestic Restructuring and Foreign Trade*. Washington, DC: The World Bank.

Tovias, Alfred and Sam Laird. 1991. "Whither Hungary and the European Communities?" *The World Bank*, International Economics Department, International Trade, PRE Working Paper, No. 584.

Wolf, Thomas. 1988. *Foreign Trade in a Centrally Planned Economy*. London and New York: Harwood Academic Publishers.

About the Contributors

Shlomo Avineri is Herbert Samuel Professor of Political Science at the Hebrew University of Jerusalem and a former Director General of Israel's Ministry of Foreign Affairs. A graduate of the Hebrew University and the London School of Economics, he also taught at Yale, Cornell, the Australian National University, and Oxford. His publications include: *The Social and Political Thought of Karl Marx* (1969), *The Making of Modern Zionism* (1979) and *Communitarianism and Individualism* (1992). He was a member of an international team of observers at the first post-communist elections in Hungary and Czechoslovakia in 1990.

Joseph S. Berliner is a Fellow of the Harvard Russian Research Center and Professor of Economics Emeritus at Brandeis University. His main field of research is the economics of socialism, with a focus on planning, management and technological change. He has served as President of the American Association for the Advancement of Slavic Studies and of the Association for Comparative Economic Studies. His publications include: *Factory and Manager in the USSR* (1958), and *The Innovation Decision in Soviet Industry*, (1976).

Mario I. Blejer is currently Senior Adviser, Europe and Central Asia Region, The World Bank. He holds a Ph.D. from the University of Chicago and has taught at the Hebrew University of Jerusalem, Boston University and New York University.

Oleg T. Bogomolov is Director of the Russian Academy of Sciences, Institute of International Economic and Political Studies, Member of the Presidential Consultative Council of Russian President Boris Yeltsin and his key economic advisor. He graduated from the USSR. Ministry of Foreign Trade Institute in 1949, receiving his doctorate in Economics in 1967 and his professorship in 1969. He was elected Corresponding Member of the USSR Academy of Sciences in 1972 and a Member in 1981. Professor Bogomolov has written and edited over 300 published works analyzing economic, political, and ideological developments in Eastern Europe and the USSR, including its relations with Western and developing countries.

Silviu Brucan is professor of international relations at the Bucharest University. From 1956 to 1959 he was Romania's ambassador to Washington, and from 1959 to 1962 its ambassador to the UN. Over the past twenty years he has lectured and taught at universities in the United States and Europe. Prof. Brucan has published five books in English: *The Dissolution of Power: Sociology of International Relations* (1971), *The Dialectic of World Politics* (1978), *The Post-Brezhnev Era* (1983), *World Socialism at the Crossroads* (1987), and *Pluralism and Social Conflict* (1990). He has just completed his memoirs under the title *The Wasted Generation—A Personal Experience of Two Revolutions: From Capitalism to Socialism and Back.*

Carlo Cottarelli is a Senior Economist in the Fiscal Operations Division I of the Fiscal Affairs Department, The International Monetary Fund. He is a graduate of the London School of Economics and Political Science.

Theodore H. Friedgut is Associate Professor of Russian and Slavic Studies at the Hebrew University of Jerusalem. He has served as Director of the Hebrew University's Centre for Soviet and East European Research and as Chairman of the Department of Russian and Slavic Studies. His major publications include *Political Participation in the USSR* (1979), *Iuzovka and Revolution*, Vol. 1, *Life and Work in Russia's Donbass, 1869–1924* (1989), and Vol. II, *Politics and Revolution in Russia's Donbass, 1869–1924* (forthcoming, 1993) and, with Lewis H. Siegelbaum, *The Soviet Miners' Strike, July 1989: Perestroika from Below* (1990).

Stanislaw Gomulka is Reader in Economics at the London School of Economics, where he has been since 1970. He is Program Director of the Post-Communist Reform Group at the LSE's Centre for Economic Performance. Since September 1989 he has also been Economic Advisor of the Polish Government. In Autumn 1991 and Winter 1991/92 he was adviser to the Russian Government. Educated at the University of Warsaw, he has also taught at the University of Pennsylvania (1984/5), and held Fellowships at the Netherlands Institute for Advanced Study, Stanford, the University of Columbia (1986) and Harvard University (1989). His most recent books are: *Growth, Innovation and Reform in Eastern Europe (1986/7), The Theory of Technological Change and Economic Growth* (1990) and, as editor and contributor, *Economic Reforms in the Socialist World* (1981) and *Polish Paradoxes* (1990).

Maria Haendcke-Hoppe-Arndt is economist, senior researcher and administration director of the Research Institute of German Economic and Social Issues in Berlin. This Institute was the research arm of the Committee for Problems of Reunification (1952–1975). Her publications include *GDR—Foreign Economic Relations* (1980), *The Private Economy in GDR* (1982),

Foreign Trade Reforms in the GDR (1988), *Inner German Economic Relations* (1990) and, in collaboration with Alexander Fischer, *On the Way to Realization of German Unity* (1992).

Arye L. Hillman is the William Gittes Professor of International Economics and Managing Director of the Economics Research Institute at Bar-Ilan University in Israel. He has been a visiting professor of economics at UCLA and Princeton University and a visiting research fellow at the World Bank. He has a Ph.D. in economics from the University of Pennsylvania. He is the author of *The Political Economy of Protection* (1989), editor of *Markets and Politicians* (1991) and joint editor of *The Transition from Socialism in Eastern Europe: Domestic Restructuring and Foreign Trade* (1992). He has also published widely in professional journals on issues relating to international economic policy and the conduct and role of government.

Miroslav Hrnčíř is Senior Research Fellow at the Institute of Economics, Prague, and adviser to the Governor of the State Bank of Czechoslovakia. He specializes in international and monetary economics. Recently he as written widely on issues of Czechoslovak transition to a market economy and participated on a number of international projects. His publications include *Foreign Trade in Czechoslovakia* (1987) and *Macroeconomic Stabilization and Currency Convertibility* (1991).

Michael Keren is Professor of Economics at the Hebrew University of Jerusalem. He studied at Keele University (UK), at the Center for Development Economics at Williams College, and at Yale University. He has worked on the economy of the ex-GDR, on problems of planning and incentives in Soviet-type economies, and is currently engaged in research on the economics of hierarchies and bureaucracies.

Grzegorz W. Kolodko is Professor of Economics and Economic Policy at the Warsaw School of Economics, and Director of the Research Institute of Finance, Warsaw, a leading Polish think tank dealing with economics of transition to a market economy. He graduated from the Warsaw School of Economics where he was appointed the youngest professor in Poland. He attended the Round Table negotiations in Poland in 1989 and served as a member of Economic Council to the Polish Government in 1989–91.

Professor Kolodko has written widely on crises of communist economies, transition to a market economy, inflation and stabilization policies. His latest (jointly with Gotz-Kozierkiewicz and Skrzeszewska-Paczek) book in English is on *Hyperinflation and Stabilization in Postsocialist Economies* (1992). Recently he has worked on issues dealing with fiscal reforms and adjustment, as well as recession and conditions for sustainable growth in post-communist economies.

Günter Nötzold is Professor of World Economy and Director of the Center for International Economic Relations at the University of Leipzig, Germany. He studied in Leipzig (1947–1951), where he served as *assistent* and lecturer before being appointed to the Chair of World Economy (1971). In 1984 he founded the International Seminar in World Economy on East-West economic relations. His publications include *The Arab Countries* (1973) and *Contributions to Economic Integration and Transformation in East Germany*.

D. Mario Nuti is Professor of Comparative Economic Systems at the University of Rome "La Sapienza" and Adviser to the Commission of European Communities on Central-East Europe at the Directorate General for Economic and Financial Affairs, Brussels. He graduated in Law (Rome) and received his Ph.D. in Economics from Cambridge University, England. He has published extensively on capital theory, on comparative economic systems and in particular on the reform of centrally planned economies and their transition to capitalism.

Gur Ofer received his Ph.D. in Economics at Harvard in 1969 under Abram Bergson and Simon Kuznets. Since 1969 he has been a professor at the Departments of Economics and of Russian Studies at the Hebrew University in Jerusalem. He has been visiting professor at Harvard, The Rand Corporation, UCLA, The Kennan Institute, the Brookings Institution, and the Harriman Center at Columbia. He publishes extensively on many aspects of the Soviet and socialist economies, including *The Service Sector in Soviet Economic Growth* (1973), *The Soviet Household Under the Old Regime* (with Aaron Vinokur, 1992), and "Soviet Economic Growth: 1928–1985," *Journal of Economic Literature* (1987).

Sándor Richter studied economics in Budapest. Between 1979 and 1990 he worked as a researcher of the Economic Information Unit at the Hungarian Academy of Sciences. In 1986–1990 he was Managing Director of ECHO, a consulting firm. Since 1990 he has been on the research staff of WIIW. His fields of specialization are: the economy of Hungary, regional cooperation in Eastern Europe, and East-West economic relations.

Márton Tardos is Professor of Economics at the University of Budapest, member of the Hungarian Parliament and faction leader of the Alliance of Free Democrats. From 1960 to 1989 he was engaged in research on socialist economies. During the political transformation in Hungary his field of research is related to the introduction of a full-fledged market system based on private property and strong monetary institutions.

Name Index

Subject Index